THE LIFE AND LETTERS OF

SIR EDMUND GOSSE

By the same Author

AFFAIRS OF SCOTLAND, 1744-46

WILLIAM AUGUSTUS, DUKE OF CUMBERLAND,
EARLY LIFE AND TIME

WILLIAM AUGUSTUS, DUKE OF CUMBERLAND,
AND THE SEVEN YEARS' WAR

JOHN SARGENT

EDMUND GOSSE

THE LIFE AND LETTERS OF SIR EDMUND GOSSE

by

THE HON. EVAN CHARTERIS, K.C.

NEW YORK AND LONDON
HARPER & BROTHERS PUBLISHERS
1931

First Edition

F-F

TO

TESSA, SYLVIA, AND PHILIP GOSSE

IN MEMORY OF THEIR FATHER

ILLUSTRATIONS

My thanks are due to Sir Edmund Gosse's correspondents who have kindly lent the letters which appear in the pages which follow, also to Mr. Edward Marsh, who has read the proofs and given me much information connected with the subject of the Memoir. Also to Mr. Leslie E. Bliss, Librarian of the Henry E. Huntingdon Library, California, for his kindness in providing photostatic copies of many valuable letters to Robert Browning and others; and to Mr. William Bellows for photographs taken by him.

E. CHARTERIS

1931

THE LIFE AND LETTERS OF
SIR EDMUND GOSSE

The Life and Letters of

SIR EDMUND GOSSE

CHAPTER ONE

In a diary kept by Philip Henry Gosse, the distinguished naturalist, there is the following entry dated September 21st, 1849: "E delivered of a son. Received green swallow from Jamaica." The son was Edmund William Gosse, the subject of the pages which follow. The "Green Swallow from Jamaica" is still to be seen in the Natural History Museum. Philip Henry Gosse was the son of Thomas Gosse (1765—1844), a miniature painter, and his wife Hannah Best, the daughter of a Worcestershire yeoman. There is no need to look further into the Gosse genealogy for traditions of industry and bookishness. Thomas Gosse, a painter by profession, was an indefatigable writer, and though never contriving to publish a single line, was unwearying in the variety and multiplicity of his literary efforts. Dialogues, tales, epic poems, philosophical treatises and allegories raced from his pen. His wife, recognising that these activities brought no money to the pool, classed them under a general indictment as "that cursed writin'." But her disapproval did nothing to stay the output, merely driving it into secretive methods of production. The literary tradition was there, and it was too strong to be repressed.

Philip Henry Gosse, born in 1810, was the second son of this marriage. At an early age he was sent as a clerk to a counting-house in Newfoundland. Carrying with him the atmosphere of Puritanism in which he had been brought up, he held aloof from the frivolities with which the Colonists beguiled their leisure, and went his own way, developing his natural aptitude for zoology and botany, and acquiring the spirit of religious fervour which was to dominate his future years. At the age of twenty-nine he returned to

England to spread a knowledge of the truth in religion as well as in science. Poor and obscure, but with a resolute purpose in his heart, he drifted from place to place, finally coming to anchor as schoolmaster and preacher in the suburb of Hackney. Thence after a few years he once again crossed the Atlantic at the instance of the authorities of the British Museum, as insect collector in the West Indies. He returned in 1846 and once more settled in Hackney. Here in the course of his ministrations he made the acquaintance of and in 1848 married Emily Bowes, a member of the Plymouth Brotherhood frequenting the common meeting-place of the sect in Hackney. Emily Bowes was the daughter of William and Hannah Bowes of Boston, Massachusetts, both of New England ancestry. It was only in 1888, after his father's death, that Edmund Gosse unravelled his New England pedigree, discovering that through his mother Emily Bowes he was descended from Lucy Hancock, daughter of the seventeenth-century Minister of Lexington and aunt of the General who signed the Declaration of Independence. This he recorded with evident satisfaction, declaring to a correspondent that his love for America, entertained "without a suspicion of this relationship and without any exterior encouragement whatever," might be regarded as "a case of atavism." However that may be, Edmund Gosse on his mother's side was purely American in origin.

Emily Bowes was of a devout and pious turn of mind, a successful writer of tracts and a lifelong practitioner of good works. She was ethereal in appearance, with a skin of dazzling whiteness, and auburn hair touched with tinctures of gold. Under a marked gentleness of manner, she had a will of steel, by the help of which the whole energies of her mind were dedicated to the practice of her religious faith. At the time of her marriage she was forty-two and Philip Gosse thirty-eight. It was therefore to parents mature in years that Edmund Gosse was born in their Hackney home in 1849.

The material circumstances of the Gosse family, though not actually straitened, were far from well-to-do. Philip Gosse's scientific writings, though earning for him fame among the learned, brought little in the way of income, while the failure of a principal investment still further contracted their means. To the parents devoted and sufficing for each other, the one immersed in scientific pursuits and both in the practice of their evangelical faith, it mattered little in the early days of their son's childhood that there should be no variation in routine, and no intrusion of recreation or amusement. It was otherwise for the child. He was cut off from companions of his age. The home was full of taboos. The ordinary literature of infancy was denied him. At an age when fairy tales and stories enliven the imagination, and religious instruction is being absorbed in its simplest form, his mind was directed to books of travel and geography, to "queer varieties of natural history"—and as soon as he was capable of reading, to the reading aloud of Jukes on *Prophecy* and Newton on *The Apocalypse*. In the whole range of literature there is probably no narrative of childhood so vivid and so complete as Gosse's volume, *Father and Son*. Published in 1907, it is described in the opening lines as "the record of a struggle between two temperaments, two consciences and almost two epochs." And here in its pages the psychologist can judge as he has rarely before been able to judge from any literary document how far "the child is father to the man," how far the traces of early environment can be divined in later developments of mind and character, and how far in the case of Edmund Gosse childhood tended to kindle revolt or establish the grip of the tradition in which he was brought up.

It was certainly no normal inheritance to which he was born. Here were none of the toys and trifles of early years, none of the indulgences of childhood. Dedicated in his fifth year to the Lord's service and destined in the fond fancy of his mother to figure in manhood as a missionary and even as a martyr, every influence in his "uniform and cloistered infancy" was directed to moulding him as a vessel worthy to contain the saving graces. At the age of seven, delicate and impressionable, precociously observant and intelligent, he was taken with his mother, then stricken with mortal illness, to a dismal lodging in Pimlico where she might be nearer to a prescribed course of medical treatment. Six weeks later she died, and it was left to the father alone to continue the task of directing the footsteps of the child towards the throne of Grace.

In 1858 Philip Gosse and his son moved to Marychurch in Devonshire to a house where Philip Gosse was to reside for the next thirty years.

The change from Hackney to Devonshire was an event of romantic excitement for the child. Under the wide skies, in sound of the sea, and at the foot of the moorlands, the everlasting fires of the Day of Judgment and the dogmas by which an evangelical faith had been imposed upon him gave place before the first flush of this new-found world. Here there were mitigations to modify the close and studied uniformity of his upbringing. The literary inhibitions it is true continued. Indeed till his ninth year his sole knowledge of fiction had been derived from a magic occasion when rummaging in the garret of the London house he came "with indescribable rapture upon a skin trunk the lid of which was lined with the sheets of a sensational novel." But even in Hackney there had been compensations. Instruction had not been confined to religion. The boy had been taught to observe. He had been led to interest himself in the colours and habits of birds and fishes and the smaller mammals. He had learnt to use the microscope. In natural history he had found a substitute for Robin Hood and Jack the Giant Killer, and in the antics of protozoa he had been given an alternative for the pastimes and inventions of infancy. And here at Marychurch and by the sea, there was no more waiting on grey days with a face pressed against the window for the coming of Punch and Judy, the postman on his rounds, the cry of the milkman, and the to-and-fro of passers-by. The change to the sea was complete, organic and satisfying, richer and stranger than mind could imagine. In *Father and Son* he writes of it thus: "But on that earliest morning, how my heart remembers! we hastened—Miss Marks, the maid, and I between them—along a couple of high-walled lanes, when suddenly, far below us, in an immense arc of light, there stretched an enormous plain of waters. We had but to cross a step or two of downs, when the hollow sides of the great limestone cove yawned at our feet, descending like a broken cup, down, down to the moon of snow-white shingle and the expanse of blue-green sea." It was the first conscious impact with nature, the "here" and "now" of a memorable contact from which the boy returned with a flame in his heart that was to burn to the last of his days.

While the forbidden areas of literature remained just as extensive and to the boy himself not the least less alluring, there was at the same time no slackening in the pressure of doctrinal teaching. The system of instruction which the father had adopted lost none of its austerity; on the contrary the idea which to his own satisfaction he cultivated that his child was "a being to whom the mysteries of salvation had been divinely revealed and by whom they had been accepted" was insisted on with an even greater measure of prayer and exhortation on every possible occasion. At the same time in the letters of this date between Philip Gosse and his son the outline of the system becomes a trifle less uncompromising, an unlooked-for warmth of colour spreading through the strange struggle of the two temperaments. The letters are rich in affection, and serve to illustrate and indeed to supplement the narrative of *Father and Son*. The first is dated shortly after the death of Mrs. Gosse, and is written when Philip Gosse was lecturing in Edinburgh.

Edinburgh,
Tuesday,
Feb. 24, 1857.

My own sweet Boy,—

I cannot tell you how much I love you. I seem to love you better than ever, now that I have to be separated from you. And now that beloved Mamma is gone to be with Jesus you are all that is left to me.

I pray much for you, that the Lord will make you a real believer. Your sins can be washed away, only by the precious blood of Jesus; and you can only get that, by believing in Him with your heart—by giving your heart to Him. O remember all the words of dearest Mamma, how she read to you, and taught you and prayed for you.

I trust you will be obedient to dear Cousin, who is so kind to you; and also obliging and kind to all your young Cousins. Do not think of self, but try to make others happy, and then you're sure to be happy.

Do not forget prayer, and do not forget to remind the Lord of his promise. Pray for me too.

Your most affectionate
Papa,
P. H. Gosse.

Much of the boy's time was given to watching and recording the behaviour of the tiny seaside creatures collected by his father and penned in a salt-water tank; the following letters show his absorption in this work, and in the other activities which came to relieve the rigour of his spiritual training.

April 2nd, 1858.

My dearest Papa,—

The Idotea is dead in the large tank and we think 1 astrina gibbeossa to. My catterpiller has changed its skin, it looks beautiful, it has changed the colour of its toes from black to pink, it is now sitting on the edge of the top of a primula leaf which I find it eats as well as dandelion, and I hope it will soon begin to eat. I am preserving its skin to pin if you think it is worth, before it changed its skin, its body was black, now it is light red, its hairs are very long and Susan says it is like a porcupine, its hairs are quite long enough—all the seeds which you sowed my side of the garden are up, Convolvolus minor looks best, Convolvolus major is coming up in my salt-cellar in-doors. I have put away 259 of my shells, 22 of which I wish to question you about as I do not know what they are—the Catterpiller has gone to sleep and the second plant in the Greenhouse Miss Andrews says is open. She says it is very beautiful. I have not seen it, for since it opened there has been very bad weather. The Peony is beautiful. I forgot to tell you that Miss Hannaford gave me several roots of a tall blue Anemone, a tall Anemone is coming into flower, the bud is scarlet, the violets are beautiful, one of the hoop petticotes has been blown down.

I remain,
Your afec. Son,
E. W. Gosse.

My very precious dear Papa,—

I hope that you will not much longer have bad headaches, and also be quite well.

I went to —— this morning and showed him my Porter of Licorish.

My book has got as far as Thyatira Batia.

Primroses, Cowslips, Laurestinus, Periwinkle, etc., are splendid, especially Primroses are really magnificent!

We are now going for a walk.

Violets, Peonys, Daffodils, Orchices, Frisias, Narcissus's, Gladioluses, Habrothamnus, Periwinkles, Oxlips, Primroses, Snowdrops, Laurestinus, Rhubarb etc. are flowering or sprouting. We have had a nice walk to Oddicombe coming home we called at Mrs. Guy's—W. Guy is such a young Turk, I wonder if Helena Guy will be one too? When This reaches you in 3 days you will go to London, you are on the borders of Yorkshire now.

The Ierianthus Lyodii is very well.

I remain your
loving son
E. Wm. Gosse.

Many of the letters are illustrated with water-colour drawings of the creatures to which he refers and whose Latin names he cites with complete assurance. Here and there occurs a mention of a lapse from grace and a determination to amend—occasionally the name of the "Brother" who reads at the Meeting House is given, and the numbers of the hymns which were sung. They are homely letters, precocious in knowledge, childish in sentiment, but all overflowing with affection, as when he writes:

June 3, 1858.

My extremely precious Papa,—

I am quite longing for the month to end (but still it is shorter than I thought it would be) and it is so lonely sometimes without you—Bolcera egis auratus has fatally burst. This morning a Ierianthus Lyodii came (oh! such a monster) but I fear it is dead. I enjoyed myself very much at Miss Willses yesterday among the young ladies we played at Lotto, and Bell & Hammer and solitaire and I saw the gymtastics and held them too. We have not had such a brilliant day for a couple of months—how is it with you?

I remain your

afectionat Son

E. Wm. Gosse.

When he was ten years old, there occurred the episode of his public baptism which he describes as the central event of his whole childhood. "Everything," he adds, "since the earliest dawn of consciousness, seemed to have been leading up to it. Everything, afterwards, seemed to have been leading down and away from it." The literary skill with which the event has been described in *Father and Son* will ensure it a high place in descriptive prose-writing. But to the boy himself it was less a religious or even solemn experience than "inexpressibly exciting" and "an initiation into every kind of publicity and glory."

It must have indeed been dazzling to one so temperamentally inclined, so wakefully aware of what was taking place, so already conscious of the outward significance of social phenomena, to find himself at ten years of age the centre, the very heart and occasion of an assembly of devout brethren and curious visitors, drawn as they were not merely from the locality but from places distant as Exeter, Dartmouth and Totnes. We may indeed wonder whether such an inflation of momentary importance at such an age was not bound to lead to some lasting distortion of outlook, and some narrowing in the scale of relative values. However that may be, to the father it was a moment of deepest consecration—but he had from the first failed to recognise that he was dealing with a boy entirely unfitted by nature to absorb or greatly profit by the religious ministration to which he was subjected. Zeal had blinded Philip Gosse. He had never comprehended that here was no vessel to contain the Holy Spirit but, to use the son's own words, an "adroit little pitcher," a child utterly detached and analytical, repressed where he should have been allowed to grow, and driven along lines which could only lead in his case to doubt and bewilderment.

But if the son failed to see this central event eye to eye with his father, he was quite capable of appreciating the change which had been effected in his status as a member of the community of Brethren. Thenceforward he could stand in the high places, he could exercise his bright spirit for mischief from the seat of the scornful. Indeed, concluding his account of the ceremony, he says: "I would fain close this remarkable episode on a key of solemnity, but alas! if I am to be loyal to the truth, I must record that some of the other little boys presently complained to Mary Grace that I put out my tongue at them in mockery, during the service in the Room, to remind them that I now broke bread as one of the Saints and they did not." On a less clear and spirited nature there might now have descended a veil of studied hypocrisy. The boy earnestly desired to follow where his father led, he had perforce to submit to an intellectual surrender, but there was a discrepancy between the forces essential to conformity and "the hard nut of individuality deep down in his childish nature." That discrepancy grew. He had been overtrained on uncongenial lines. Emotionally he was unscathed.

Writing in 1895, he notes in his *Life of Coventry Patmore* that the poet in a fragment of autobiography had said that he was an Agnostic until his eleventh year, when on reading a devotional book it struck him "what an exceedingly fine thing it would be if there really was a God." Religion had been so placed before Edmund Gosse in these early years, God had been so depicted to his childish imagination, that it may be doubted if he could have subscribed to such a view with any enthusiasm. He had been crammed, injudiciously crammed, on stern and narrow lines. Specialised beliefs had been forced into a mould which it was believed had been prepared for their reception. None other would do; no modification could be admitted. But the mould was wanting. The public baptism was a turning-point. After that the rift between the two temperaments slowly widened. Every day the boy grew more conscious of another world, but it was not the world to which his father was directing him. Shakespeare, Coleridge, Ben Jonson and Christopher Marlowe, surreptitiously acquired and furtively read, were opening new vistas and turning his thoughts to the domain which later he was to tread with such distinction. Religious exercises continued, were even intensified; but there was a difference. Faith in the imposed forms was evaporating. There is a sense of unreality when on the occasion of the father announcing his second marriage the boy then eleven years of age asked, "But Papa, is she one of the Lord's children? Has she taken up her cross in baptism?" and then shaking a finger, "Papa, don't tell me she's a pedobaptist?" There were, it is true, recurrences of pietistic aspiration. Even at sixteen he describes himself as "still but a bird fluttering in the network of my father's will, and incapable of the smallest independent action." "I was," he continues, "at one moment devoutly pious, at the next haunted by visions of material beauty and longing for sensuous impressions. In my hot and silly brain, Jesus and Pan held sway together, as in a wayside chapel discordantly and impishly consecrated to Pagan and to Christian rites." But the new wine was too strong. He was approaching the period of complete emancipation of spirit. In his seventeenth year we find him settled in London lodgings. The Throne of Grace so fondly and insistently figuring in the ministrations of his father had become a shadowy kingdom. For the moment at any rate Pan had gained the upper hand. The boy had floated out from a cavern darkened by religious inhibitions to an azure sea. He was caught in the wonder and rapture of the poets.

CHAPTER TWO

When Gosse came to London at the age of seventeen, his friends would have hesitated to foretell a literary career for him. Up till then his general education had been neglected. One side of his mind was surfeited, the other was starved. He was familiar to the point of weariness with the language, the facts and the doctrines of the Bible: indeed he was so saturated with its literary beauties that the complete absence of its influence in his writings becomes remarkable. Four years of school had given him some knowledge of Shakespeare and a few of the English poets. Of fiction he knew nothing except a few volumes of Walter Scott and *Uncle Tom's Cabin*. His acquaintance with English or foreign literature hardly went beyond that; but he had a good working knowledge of Italian, French, German, and in a less degree of Latin and Greek, and during his last year at school had been working on his own account at Swedish.

His efforts at writing had so far been no more than juvenile records of his observations in natural history and by no means precocious attempts at essays and verse, but in 1865 he had started a much more ambitious literary project, and composed in ten days in the intervals of school work *Jonathan: a lyric drama in 3 Acts*, the idea of which was suggested by his father. This must be the tragedy "in pale imitation of Shakespeare" to which he refers in *Father and Son*. The "paleness" is apparent in the opening lines:

Abinadab. Thrice has the sun slow dipped his golden rim
Into the western waters, thrice again
Uprose above the far Piræan hills.

The tragedy runs to 1600 lines, and shows great verbal facility, and a power of characterisation justly praised by his father. His Muse was spreading her wings in preparation for flight. Verse is now found scattered in diaries, on the back of accounts, and on the fly-leaves of books.

But the moment had come for choosing a profession. With that high-minded sincerity which distinguished Philip Gosse's every thought, heavenly assistance was invited with prayer and supplication. The answer vouchsafed was, to Philip Gosse at any rate, free from ambiguity. A favourable commercial offer from Mr. Thomas Brightwen, the brother of his second wife, was rejected with emphasis. "If," he said, "there were offered to his beloved child what is called 'an opening' that would lead to an income of £10,000 a year and that would divert his thoughts and interests from the Lord's work, he would reject it on his child's behalf." In 1862, when his son had been one term at school, he had said much the same thing in writing to the master.

"There is one thing," he wrote, "which I greatly desire for Willy" (his father invariably called him this) "which is wanting at Mt. Veden. A converted child himself, he needs spiritual companionship and this he does not meet with. He does not find one boy who is of the slightest help to him spiritually. You may say, he ought to stand out for Christ and give the tone to the School. Perhaps he ought: but he does not. He lacks the courage; his spirits are high: he loves play as much as any boy, and he is carried away by the general tone, which without being morally evil is earthly. With his youth and his subordinate position in the school, I do not see well how it could be otherwise. But we think we discern the result in the deterioration—or at least the dulling of his spiritual life.

"Now I had rather see him a warm devoted man of God than the brightest scholar or the most successful business man in the world. And this I must seek for him whatever sacrifice it may involve."

He was to say it often again. His fanaticism leapt forth like a sword drawn from its scabbard, at the thought of worldliness. His mind blazed up at the least sign of relaxation in the service of the Lord. Without further discussion Mammon was laid on one side. Through the influence of Charles Kingsley an "opening" was found for Edmund Gosse in the cataloguing section of the British Museum at a salary of £90 a year, rising by increases of £5 annually to

£150. A home was secured for him in Tottenham at the house of two elderly ladies, Miss Buckham and Miss Baker, both members of the Plymouth Brotherhood. Their influence, it was hoped, would keep him within the fold and counteract the temptations to wander which were inherent in the new life in London. Gosse always spoke of these two ladies in after years with affection. He visited them often. Miss Buckham was the spiritual leader. She addressed her correspondents, "My dear Brother in the Lord." She was expert in doctrine. Even in her eighty-ninth year (1884) she could repeat "the whole of the Gospel of St. John, the Epistles to the Hebrews and First of St. Peter almost perfectly, besides many of the Psalms and other portions of the Scripture." Hymns were trifles light as air in her memory. Miss Baker remained in Gosse's mind as a kindly maiden lady with dark ringlets and piercing black eyes, who broke into occasional ventures of gaiety, and was even known to murmur as she went about her household tasks a refrain that ran:

The best of all ways
To lengthen your days,
Is to snatch a few hours
From the night, my dear.

Among the workers at the British Museum there was at this time an active literary tradition. Gosse applied to it the Johnsonian phrase "a nest of singing birds." Coventry Patmore had recently (1865) relinquished his job of cataloguing the folios of the Fathers. But Richard Garnett was there "inditing idylls and epigrams," and Théophile Marzials, poet and composer and author of one of the most popular songs of the day, *Creole Love Song*, with the refrain:

But oh that my heart had wings,
I'd fly like the blue bird far
Away and away to the end of the day
Where the cool and the palm trees are.

and set to music by Mrs. Moncrieff, equally well-known perhaps for the music which she wrote for Swinburne's lyric "Ask nothing more of me, Sweet." Marzials edited a popular collection of old English songs called *Pan Pipes*, illustrated by Walter Crane. When the Museum authorities learnt that while in receipt of £90 a year for cataloguing he was making £1000 a year by his songs outside, they suggested that he should make way for a more needy worker. Another poet in Museum employment was Arthur O'Shaughnessy (1844-1881).

O'Shaughnessy worked in the Natural History Department, in which he had been appointed an assistant, to the annoyance of professional zoologists and in face of a protest from the Zoological Society. The protest at the time was not without justification. Gosse used to relate that O'Shaughnessy soon after his appointment sought to repair an accident in the department by uniting the head of one fish with the skeleton of another, thus creating a new species and puzzling the savants. In the end his ability confuted his objectors and he became an adequate master of his subject. In 1870 his *Epic of Women and other Poems* appeared. Gosse writes that a great many army officers bought it, "deceived, it was said, by the apparent gallantry of the title." But the volume had a deserved reputation with readers of poetry, containing as it did lyrics of a delicate and melancholy charm, not charged with any high passion, but melodious and expressing a simple and poignant emotion never "far from the edge of the fountain of tears."

Yet another "singing bird" was John Payne, steeped in what Tennyson condemned as "the poisonous honey brought from France," a compound which the Victorian seers were anathematising both in literature and in the visual arts.

By the end of 1867 Gosse himself was proposing to publish a volume of poetry, and wrote to his father asking him to finance the venture. The reply was earnest but discouraging: "But you have not yet submitted a single word of your Poems to my examination. . . . There is one test indeed . . . you praised in strong terms a Poem (*St. Paul*. F. W. Myers, 1867) which since you have sent for Mamma's perusal. We value the love which prompted your sending it; but was it also sent to indicate to us the standard of poetic excellence to which you aspire? I hope not indeed! . . . but

I will ask you: How can you be captivated with this turgid rant? When the brass band in front of a puppet-show in a village fair plays up, the open-mouthed bumpkins have all their attention given to the negro fellow that clangs together the two cymbals or brass plates, the more noise, the more music. Myers' clangor reminds me of this. Where are the *thoughts* amidst all this clash of words? They are like Falstaff's ha'p'orth of bread in the endless pints of sacks. . . . My object is to show that the noblest in Poetry is ever the simplest; that our best poets know nothing of this craving after the uncouth, the intense, the obscure, the mystical. You will perhaps impatiently say that you know all this. I reply, I thought you *did* know it; now I doubt. How else could you admire such a style as Myers'? Would Gray or Cowper or Shelley ever have thrown together such words as these

Thence the wide eyes upon a hushed dominion
  Looked in a fierce astonishment of prayer

or

Bright in a light and eminent in amber
  Caught the serene surprises of the sun.

. . . The poor ass! He thinks he is very grand and he is only very muddy: he makes a terrible flapping of feathers and mistakes it for lofty soaring. You speak of an impatience of shams: do you not see that this style of writing is an utter sham? I have said nothing about the doctrine, tho' the Paul of Myers has no resemblance to the Paul of the N.T.; nor is his rant about Christ anything more than profane human interest.

"And here again I am afraid for you, I am afraid lest you lose the things that you have learnt in the School of God. I am afraid lest you take up with this hollow, sickly, fashionable tone of mere human sentiment and mistake it for godliness. A lost sinner saved from deserved Hell by the atoning blood of Jesus—this is the very sum and substance, the foundation and topstone of Paul, as of every true believer. . . . But I would feel stricken down by a terrible calamity in my hoar hairs, if my only son took his place in the ranks of the frothy, sentimental spouters of the day, avoiding the blessed name which is above every name, or touching it only to pollute it. Spare me this agony my darling child."

And so through twenty close-written pages the exhortation goes on, transparently sincere, and with love for his son in every line. All idea of publication was put aside. At an earlier date *Good Words* had been asked to include a poem on *Hope*: writing on February 5th, 1867, Philip Gosse said:

"When I got your pretty little poem on Hope, in January, I forwarded it immediately to Dr. Norman Macleod asking him to put it in *Good Words*. I saw it not in the January number but thought it might have been possibly too late, now another number is out, and it does not appear so that I conclude he declines it. I had asked the Lord much that if it were according to His will it might be inserted, but it is plainly not His Mind and we must submit."

It must not be assumed that Edmund Gosse acquiesced with alacrity or without misgiving in the spiritual divergence from his father, of which he was daily becoming more aware. As yet it is true the difference between them was mainly one of form rather than of substance. Edmund recoiled from what was bleak and puritanical in his father's creed, he still clung to the core of Christian belief which glowed within it. And in London he maintained many of the religious habits and traditions he had acquired in his Devonshire home. He attended worship at a Meeting House with the two devout ladies of Tottenham on Sundays and Wednesdays. And his interest in doctrine remained so alert that we find him writing to his father: "There are some really good devoted people in the East End who say that they have got into a state of sinless sanctification. How startling this is! But surely it is unscriptural. Let me tell you more of their extraordinary and fascinating dogmas. They believe that Christians once saved (or justified) may fall away and be for ever lost! I cannot find that they can bring sufficient proof of this terrible and distressing doctrine. . . . Mr. Booth is the eloquent exponent of this theory. . . . The accounts given me of the almost hysterical frenzy of religious devotion produced by the gestures, the voice of Mr. Booth resemble the accounts I have read of the personal fascination of Irving."

In the evenings Gosse joined the two ladies in Bible-reading. He taught in a Sunday school—and his occasional lament that it was "very hard indeed to walk with Christ" was welcomed by his father as a sign that he was on the side of the Lord. There was nothing so romantic as fighting wild beasts at Ephesus, but he was now, as he remained through his life, punctilious to a fault, and suffered grievously at the idea of falling from Grace—less on account of the Grace than of the pain to his father. It was uphill work, and no love could make it otherwise. When he writes that he is "captivated by the beauty of the liturgy of the Church of England," instantly comes the retort: "Does worship depend on soft cadences?" "Is a contrite heart an affair of well-selected phrases?" "Oh my darling, read the Ep to the Ephe and then re-read the Liturgy and say whether both can truly give the status of the same body. You profess to love the truth and I believe you do. What is beauty of phrase devoid of truth? Is the liturgy true? . . . Could you go to God with it?" And when he expresses his admiration for works of art the answer comes: "Remember that idolatry (the putting Mary in the place of Christ) pervades, *saturates* Italian and Spanish art and therefore look at it all with your conscience wide awake somewhat as we may suppose Paul, with his fine taste and cultivated mind, would look at the art treasures in Athens and Corinth. You may admire what is beautiful, so long as you do not become indifferent to what is wrong." Such things were perplexing. To write with the enthusiasm evoked by his first sight of the Elgin marbles and the paintings of Botticelli, and to be told he must study them with the eye of a St. Paul, was disheartening. But none of these things affected his loyalty and devotion. He was beginning to see things from another angle; that was all. The focus had changed from Mary-church, with its settled habits and austere inhibitions, to London. The contrast was incalculable and bewildering.

From Keats he had learnt that "the imagination of a boy is healthy and the mature imagination of a man is healthy." It needed no effort to recognise that he was now "in the space between, when the soul is in a ferment, the character undecided, the way of life uncertain." Indeed, in writing to his father at this time he dwelt on the immaturity of his age "when all is yeasty and unstable and the bitter fruits of which are mawkishness and vain vague longing."

He was like a ship whose human freight, long battened down in a tempest, has been allowed for the first time on deck. In the sudden release aspirations and desires, curiosities and natural inclinations came trooping in vague disorder to the surface clamorous for air, for experience and expression. But after seventeen years he was still "heavy under the word"—"the word" was about his path in and out of season.

In *Father and Son* he has described the "torment of the postal inquisition" to which he was subjected. "To me," he writes, "the almost daily letter of exhortation with its string of questions about conduct, its series of warnings, grew to be a burden which could hardly be borne, particularly because it involved a reply as punctual and if possible as full as itself.

"The solitary letter, in its threatening whiteness, with its exquisitely penned address—there it would lie awaiting me, destroying the taste of the bacon, reducing the flavour of the tea to insipidity. I might fatuously dally with it, I might pretend not to observe it, but there it lay. Before the morning's exercise began, I knew that it had to be read, and what was worse, that it had to be answered. Like all its precursors, like all its followers, it would insist, with every variety of appeal, on a reiterated declaration that I still fully intended as in the days of my earliest childhood 'to be on the side of the Lord in everything.'"

Though, as the correspondence will show, they blazed up with great intensity in 1873, yet, as years went by, the terms of this postal inquisition were relaxed, and in the stress of authorship and scientific pursuits the voice of the parent grew less importunate. It was only when Edmund Gosse visited Marychurch that doctrinal pressure was revived with the old intensity.

Living in Tottenham and working at the Museum meant a three-mile walk twice daily to and from Wood Green station. Fifteen of the cataloguing staff gathered punctually at nine every morning in a chilly chamber "scented with rotten morocco, and an indescribable odour familiar in foreign barracks," and searched by every draught. Work finished at four, but the midday interval was long enough to give a certain time for reading and learning foreign languages; it was used to the full: Gosse worked hard at Danish and Swedish. In winter and rough weather the routine was exacting. But the novelty, the emancipation, the sudden flinging-open of the whole field of literature to such an eager pilgrim, made the rough places smooth. He sang as he went. His colleagues seem to have been a little puzzled by him. The lightness of his wit, the severity of his religious training, the patchiness of his culture and at the same time his frenzied desire to read and learn, tended to differentiate him from the general run. It was a full year before he made friends with Marzials and Cyril Davenport. The head of the Department was Mr. E. A. Warren. The immediate superintendent was the Rev. Frederick Laughlin. Laughlin ruled with an iron hand and an uncontrollable temper. Gosse, with his lively spirits and vivacious wit, with possibly now and then a touch of Sir Vinegar Sponge, soon became one of his selected targets. In the end Laughlin's mental equilibrium became disturbed, and a threat to use a revolver against a colleague led to his dismissal from the cataloguing staff. The juniors were much afraid of him. Gosse used to relate that on one occasion Laughlin went out to fetch a book. Discipline was at once relaxed. Some began to talk, others to sing. Suddenly he returned. Decorum was immediately restored. In the meantime Théophile Marzials had climbed to an upper gallery, also in search of a book; having found it, he leant over a bar looking with his wide aureole of golden hair like the Blessed Damozel, and smiled. There was no response. Dead silence save for the driving quills. Leaning still further out he boomed down on the workers below, "Am I or am I *not* the Department's darling?" Laughlin turned his head slowly and looked upwards—one look. Marzials fled, and the sound of his footsteps was heard echoing up the metal stairways till they seemed to fade away into infinity.

It was while working in the Museum that Gosse on July 10th, 1868, first set eyes on Swinburne. He had already in 1867 submitted some of his verses to Swinburne's judgment, which inevitably drew from his father the reproof, "How *could* you as a Christian seek Swinburne's acquaintance?"

The following entry in a journal which Gosse kept at the time records this episode at the Museum; "Friday, July 10 (1868). This afternoon about 2 o'clock I was walking through the Reading Room when I saw a crowd of people in the passage by which readers enter. I heard someone had had a fit, and on coming near recognised from the published portraits, the poet A. C. Swinburne. His great forehead, though bandaged, was bubbling with blood, and all his hair matted and gory. It was a great shock to me because unexpected and also happening to one whose works I knew well and from whom I have had a letter. It seems that the poet was working in the Reading Room, when he suddenly with a shriek of pain fell in a strong convulsive epileptic fit. He was obliged to be held awhile, but before he could be helped he had struck his forehead so violently against the staple of an iron ring as to make a gash 1½ inches long and penetrating to the bone. This distressing event made an immense sensation in the Museum and has acted on my nerves so as to agitate them painfully."*

But it was not till 1871† that the two men met in the studio of Ford Madox Brown under circumstances more favourable to the beginning of their friendship.

Gosse, as we have seen, described the struggle depicted in *Father and Son* as one between "almost two epochs." If this was true of the religious outlook in the 'fifties, he had only passed through that struggle to find himself, in the 'sixties, witness of another and equally disturbing manifestation in literature. Just as the *Origin of Species* had let loose a storm of controversy in the world of theology and science in 1859, so in 1866 Swinburne's volume *Poems and Ballads* had fallen like a bombshell on the reading world. Propriety was enjoying its most palmy days. The public was determined to brick up away from all sight whatever held a taint of sensuousness or could summon a blush to the most sensitive cheek. Swinburne was dubbed by responsible reviewers as, amongst other opprobrious things, "an unclean fiery imp from the pit" and "the libidinous

* *Cf.* Gosse's account of this in his *Life of Swinburne*, p. 178.

† Post page, 33.

laureate of a pack of satyrs." Society was shocked, and professed to be even more shocked than it was. "The excessive stainlessness of the Victorian angels" was outraged. Talk of prosecution was in the air. In London the book was temporarily withdrawn. In America, after producing five editions in as many days, the publisher capitulated and the circulation of *Poems and Ballads* was stopped. The defenders of Puritanism swarmed to the ramparts at the sound of this unequivocal music of the passions. The Press was made lively with protests. It was all very exciting to a youth of seventeen schooled in the restraint of evangelical teaching and flushed with his new-found intellectual freedom. The exhortation from Marychurch began to pale before *Poems and Ballads.* It required a greater effort now to give answers to such questions as "Does the candle of the Lord shine on you brightly?" "Do you get any spiritual companionship with young men?" "Do you find the ministry of the Word pleasant and above all profitable?" Gosse was immersed in his literary studies, reading here there and everywhere with an insatiable appetite, an exceptional memory, and an inborn discriminating taste. In the prolonged reaction from Jukes on *Prophecy* in prose, and Blair's *Grave, The Last Day* of Dr. Young, and *Death* by Bishop Porteous in verse, he seems to have flown to the dramatists in preference to all other reading. They were his first love in literature, and later on formed the basis of the library which he built up with enlightened enjoyment.

In 1868 he started philanthropic work in the East End under Dr. Barnardo. In this he carried on the tradition of his mother, one of the pioneers of this form of philanthropy. But he was "intimidated by the people, which was fatal." This liability to intimidation seems to foreshadow that special form of agitation to which he was subject in later life when projected into a company of strangers. On such occasions it was difficult for him to be at ease and "settle down" till he was sure of his bearings. He was at all times acutely sensitive to social climate. "Apprehensions came in crowds." He would require to know not only the names of individuals, but their vocations and almost their genealogies, even asking at times in tones of embarrassing audibility the maiden name of a married guest. These were the inevitable preliminaries to his conversational eminence, and had to be got out of the way, like the scraping of violins before the overture.

He has told us enough of his schooldays in *Father and Son* to prevent any surprise that he should have felt ill at ease before a throng of East End boys. Who were they, and what did they know of him? What possible advantage could they derive from his company? Anyone less constituted to be a recruit in the ranks of Dr. Barnardo's assistants can hardly be imagined. It is not known that he ever attempted anything of the kind again.

CHAPTER THREE

From Philip Gosse's letters it is clear that by 1869, three years after his arrival in London, Edmund Gosse was seeking wider social horizons, and that his evenings were no longer limited to the decorous restrictions of Tottenham. The change was noted at Marychurch. Statements complaining that he was "poorly from excess of recreation," and suffering from "nights invaded by exciting conversation," led to a retort from his father on the topic of dining with "an infidel." In acknowledging the journal which his son sent every week to Marychurch, Philip Gosse wrote: "All this I say gave us unalloyed pleasure to read. We could follow our beloved boy through such scenes and such companionships with true fellowship and with heartfelt thankfulness. But when the scene changed and we had to have him spending the blessed Lord's day in the house of a known and professed infidel, we could only grieve. Your heart responded to the sweetness of the name of Jesus, in the hymn at church; but did it appear to you that you were glorifying that name, in spending all the rest of that day as the guest of one who tramples it under foot? You tell us how congenial you found the talk around the dinner table. I do not know how to reconcile these two things: the sweetness of the name of Jesus in your ear and yet the congeniality of the talk at the table of an infidel. Let me tell you a little story of what happened to myself. In the spring of 1857 I was engaged to deliver a series of lectures at Birmingham. After the first, one of the committee asked me if I would, when I came again, dine with him. I assented with pleasure. But before the time came I discovered that he was an Unitarian. Recollecting 2 John 10 and perceiving how it bore upon accepting as well as dispensing hospitality, I sought the Lord earnestly as to what I should do. My path seemed clear, I immediately wrote the gentleman a courteous note, gratefully acknowledging his kindness to myself but humbly declining to be an honoured guest where the Divinity of my Lord was denied; that as I ventured to hope for a confession of my unworthy name by Him before His Father and before His holy angels, so I wished above all other considerations to honour His worthy name here. . . . Many passages of my life will not bear retrospect without a measure of sorrow and shame: but oh my dear Willy I have never been ashamed of the line I took then: nor do I think the Lord will disapprove it in that day."

To this voice from what already wore the semblance of another epoch Gosse made some astute replies—calling attention to the fact that there were certain weaknesses in his father's armour. Four days later his father writes again:

"Now with regard to my conduct at Birmingham, you looked at its influence on the Socinian, my 'showing' to him so and so, so too my 'convincing' him that etc. etc. You say the edification arising from my heroism would be confined to the few Christians who would read the obnoxious paragraph" (on "bigotry and science" in a Birmingham paper): "that the people themselves would not be impressed by it with any more love and respect for orthodoxy etc. And you add 'Our duty in this world is, it seems to me, to soften men's hearts and not to harden them.'

"Now my very first duty is to be true to Christ. My main thought must be not, How will man be affected by me? What will man think of me? But what will Christ think of me? He has distinctly told me that I cannot have the friendship of the world and *His* friendship too." . . .

It was useless to look for concession in matters spiritual. Gosse knew that no argument would affect the fortress from which these resounding monitions boomed, but he was not prepared to acknowledge defeat. He was rejoicing in life, only asking for it more abundantly. The friendship of the world was assuming an entirely new importance, and he felt it must be capable of being combined with an inward and spiritual life.

His social ramifications were extending very quickly. William Bell Scott (1811-1890), the painter and poet, states in his *Autobiographical Notes** that in March 1870, on the publication of his *Life and Works of Albert Dürer*, he received a note relating to the

* *Autobiographical Notes of the Life of W. B. Scott.* W. Minto, 1892, ii, p. 193.

Patinirs in the National Gallery and other artistic matters. The note came from Tottenham and was signed "E. W. Gosse." It had "all the aplomb of an amateur of long standing intimate with obscure early masters." Scott invited the writer to call and talk over old German art. This was the beginning of a friendship between Gosse and the Scott family. Friendship with Scott led inevitably to association with the Pre-Raphaelites, with Dante Gabriel Rossetti (1828-1882), Ford Madox Brown (1821-1893), and ultimately Swinburne. Bellevue House, Chelsea, the residence of Scott, was a meeting-place of the artistic world, then notably more exclusive and self-contained than later. Rossetti was living at Tudor House, now called Queen's House, Chelsea. It was the year of *Dante's Dream* and the publication of the "Poems," the MS of which had been recovered from his wife's grave in the previous year. Ford Madox Brown was living at 37, Fitzroy Square, and his weekly evening parties were probably responsible for some at any rate of "the nights invaded by exciting conversation." Gosse's youth and animation, his engaging eagerness to learn, and his natural deference to the prophets, ensured him a recognised place in the circle of the fraternity. He was helped by his boyish appearance; vivacity and dancing intelligence shone through his attractive candour.

He was above the ordinary height; he held himself erect; his figure, slight and active, was well adapted for the exercises of swimming and walking in which he delighted. His movements were quick, and he trod lightly, with his weight on the forward part of his feet. This resulted in a gait curiously suggestive at once of eagerness and caution. In later life the characteristic became more marked. He had nervous expressive hands, which stirred and fluttered in moments of excitement. His eyes of a luminous blue were set far apart, below a broad and finely-shaped forehead. They were restless eyes, not those of a dreamer, but on the *qui vive*, as if fearful lest anything should elude their range. A thick crest of fair hair parted in the middle ran back in turbulent abundance from his brow, and to his dying day retained its form and colour scarcely flecked with grey. His mouth was sensitive and rarely "set"—irony and humour would play in his expression—laughter and repartee hover on his lips—to give way now and then to a sarcasm or reproof snapped out with a mischievous sting. His manners were exceedingly complaisant except when he was alarmed or annoyed. His voice was admirably flexible, ranging easily from impressive fulness to a note of the lightest banter. In his youth he dressed with elegance and care; his frock coat was the very note of fashion—his ties and shoes were the last word in correctness. In spite of his slender means he contrived to defray the charges of a fashionable tailor in Savile Row. He did not underrate the conciliating influence of dress "in the first accostings of society and familiarity."

1870 was an eventful year for him. In September he started for "the misty Hebrides," an expedition which was to introduce him to R. L. Stevenson, and in December he published, with John Blaikie as joint author, his first volume of poems. The Scottish journey in September was made in the company of Mansell Dames, a former schoolfellow. The outbreak of the Franco-Prussian war had put an end to an intended expedition to France. The Western Isles seemed to promise the change and uncertainty that contribute to the perfection of a holiday, and so, with the blessing of his father and some help in the way of money accompanied by many exhortations to meditate on spiritual things and bring back Dames a convert to the fold, he set off by sea from London to Leith.

Edmund Gosse kept a journal covering some hundred pages of MS, the sheets of which were sent by instalments to his father. The journal is written with a remarkably fluent pen; the tone is that of a dutiful son fulfilling to his father a promise to record all that he saw. Little is taken in jest. The whole affair might have been an exercise in mental deportment designed to maintain a species of spiritual poise. In Edinburgh the Scott monument excited a decorous appreciation. "From the bedroom they gave us, we had an excellent view of the town: exactly opposite, towering above us, was the exquisite Scott monument, on whose lovely arches and pinnacles I was never tired of gazing." Of Holyrood he writes: "No place in Scotland interested me less or caused a greater feeling of disappointment. We saw all through the rooms redolent of that unpleasant personage Mary Queen of Scots; we viewed with weary eyes beds that had been slept in by veritable sovereigns, and tapes-

EDMUND GOSSE ÆTAT 13

EDMUND GOSSE ÆTAT 19

tries that had decked the rooms of several monarchs celebrated for their inanities or vices." In the dig at the Scarlet Woman we recognise echoes from Marychurch, echoes which never quite died away in his ears. Iona again reminds him of Rome, "the wild lonely rock where such mighty deeds were done not with man's arm, but by the spirit of God, the island that was true to the Apostolic simplicity of worship when all Europe else bowed at the feet of Rome." But did not Dr. Johnson say, "That man is little to be envied whose piety would not grow warmer among the ruins of Iona"?

A feature of the journal is the profusion of names. Every headland, cape, bay, every hill, stream and loch is carefully designated. In his cradle he had lisped in lepidoptera; names of every kind, species and categories, had been the familiar accompaniment of his childhood: here his training was of value. He had none of the mechanical acquiescence and immediate forgetfulness of the traveller who is told by a too explanatory native or a fellow-voyager the names of natural features. On the contrary, he stored these things with scrupulous fidelity in his mind and could produce them at will.

The meeting with Stevenson occurred on the vessel which was conveying Gosse and his companion homeward from Portree. It is not mentioned in the journal, and it was only when the two men met again in 1876 that they remembered having stood, two strangers, their names unknown to one another, side by side on the *Clansman* and talked the casual talk of wayfarers thrown together. But as friendship grew, every detail of that first encounter was recalled and became invested with a romantic value; later it figures in the opening lines of Gosse's exquisitely sensitive dedicatory poem to Stevenson, *Tusitala* (1894), and after the death of Stevenson in 1896 it supplies a descriptive paragraph in *Literary Kit-Kats* (1896):

> Clearest voice in Britain's chorus,
>   Tusitala!
> Years ago, years four and twenty,
> Grey the cloudland drifted o'er us,
> When these ears first heard you talking,
> When these eyes first saw you smiling.

Years of famine, years of plenty,
Years of beckoning and beguiling,
Years of yielding, shifting, baulking—
When the good ship *Clansman* bore us
Round the spits of Tobermory
Glens of Voulin like a vision,
Crags of Knoidart huge and hoary—
He had laughed in light derision,
Had they told us, told the daring
Tusitala,
What the years' pale hands were bearing—
Years in stately, dim division.

In *Literary Kit-Kats* he wrote: "At the tail of this chatty, jesting, little crowd of invaders" (they had joined the vessel at Portree) "came a youth of about my own age, whose appearance, for some mysterious reason, instantly attracted me. He was tall, preternaturally lean, with longish hair, and as restless and questing as a spaniel. The party from Portree fairly took possession of us: at meals they crowded round the captain, and we common tourists sat silent, below the salt. The stories of Blackie and Sam Bough were resonant. Meanwhile, I knew not why, I watched the plain, pale lad who took the lowest place in this privileged company. . . . We stayed on deck till the latest moment possible, and I occasionally watched the lean youth, busy and serviceable, with some of the little tricks with which we were later on to grow familiar—the advance with hand on hip, the sidewise bending of the head to listen. Meanwhile darkness overtook us, a wonderful halo of moonlight swam up over Glenelg, the indigo of the peaks of the Cuchullins faded into the general blue night. I went below, but was presently aware of some change of course, and then of an unexpected stoppage. I tore on deck, and found that we had left our track among the islands, and had steamed up a narrow and unvisited fiord of the mainland—I think Loch Nevis. The sight was curious and bewildering. We lay in a gorge of blackness, with only a strip of the blue moonlit sky overhead; in the dark a few lanterns jumped about the shore, carried by agitated but unseen and soundless persons. As I leaned over the bulwarks, Stevenson was at my side, and he explained to me that we had come up this loch to take away to Glasgow a large party of emigrants driven from their homes in the interests of a deer-forest. As he spoke, a black mass became visible entering the vessel. Then as we slipped off shore, the fact of their hopeless exile came home to these poor fugitives, and suddenly, through the absolute silence, there rose from them a wild keening and wailing, reverberated by the cliffs of the loch, and at that strange place and hour infinitely poignant. When I came on deck next morning, my unnamed friend was gone."

These picturesque memories are not afterthoughts. The journal contained not the things that appealed to the writer so much as those which would interest his father. By its very omissions it betrays what a distance Gosse had travelled away from the old epoch —and how unshakable he knew his father to be in his antagonism to the world and the ordinary stuff of life. Intellectually they were strangers, but still they would stand and parley within the gates. Blackie, Sam Bough, Stevenson, could have no interest for his father. On the contrary, the mere mention of their names might start an explosive mine which would go on muttering and hurling projectiles for indefinite periods of time. Gosse was wise and considerate in his discretion. These storms were so easily provoked. He never knew whether in the parlour at Marychurch his father was poring over his microscope and recording the changes in his stock of anemones and salt-water fauna—or getting ready to prepare some thunderous exhortation to beware of a new spiritual pitfall. The tact which excluded from the journal any possible topic of controversy could admit of no question.

Gosse returned to London from his Scottish expedition in a fever of expectation. His volume of poems was to be published in the autumn; the prospect filled him with anxiety. His father had written to him when in Scotland, "Refuse, of set purpose and determinately, to think of the poems, every time memory brings them up say, 'I've nothing to say to you: my business is with Scottish Islands!'" The advice was sound so long as Scottish Islands lasted. But back in London Gosse fell a prey to more than the ordinary apprehensions of an author. He felt that this first flying of his poetic kite was going finally to establish or disprove his own belief in a vocation. It was his wont to exaggerate the significance of passing events. He was incapable of thinking that a set-back, slight or otherwise, might after all not really count in the sum of things. What was the use of trying to look beyond it? When the theatre was burning it was absurd to stand and discuss what play you would go and see next day. This concentration on the immediate moment, this habit of taking passionately short views, was characteristic of him all his life. It made him ardently interested in every detail that concerned his own career or those of his friends. But it had its counterpoise in strain and worry. Moreover in the case of this first venture the moment was not altogether propitious for authorship, or at any rate poetic authorship. Gosse had been without any of "the grand essential leisure for writing poetry," and he was as it were in a middle state, hovering between two periods, impelled by contrary currents, and in doubt which star to steer by. He had ranged over a wide area of literature, but his knowledge was an undergrowth to which selection and pruning had still to be applied and from which the trees had still to emerge.

His verses showed the influence of Tennyson and Wordsworth —but there was a vein of poetry in them which as time went on he was to develop and make more indisputably his own. They show promise of that mastery of form which distinguishes his subsequent verse, as well as his delight in varying metrical schemes. He had already in his first years at the British Museum acquired "an extraordinary knowledge of old forms of versification." The poems themselves expressed moods of serenity. The writer looks on life, and his calmness is not disturbed; nature and the seasons are good to behold; "the long fields sloping to the ridg'd sea sand," "the shy ouzel's nest," "the waving grain," "the wine-dark pools," with these he is at home and rejoices; but with philosophy and with deeper meanings he has at present no concern. We do not hear the forest shaken by the tempest. This unintelligible world neither weighs on him nor wearies him; he sings the streams and meadows, hills and brakes, the roses of the spring and "the summer's velvet buds"; and his voice is melodious and clear.

The book had little sale: it was scarcely noticed in the press.

From Marychurch had come a word of warning. "I hope you have already prayed *earnestly* and *importunately*, that if this book should meet with praise and fame, this may not be a snare to your soul. It is a great danger and Satan will subtilely make use of it. The tendency will certainly be to make you more than ever in love with this evil world and to draw away your affection from Jesus as your chief joy. 'Forewarned is forearmed,' the adage says. May it be so with you and John. I have personally warned him of the danger and I have prayed for you both." It was a danger which Gosse and his co-author John Blaikie were very willing to incur, but the opportunity was denied them. The machinations of Satan were foiled by the reviewers. On December 8th Philip Gosse wrote in terms more congenial to the literary aspirations of his son. "The Tomb" to which he refers in the letter is the most ambitious of the poems in the volume, and deals with the burial of Christ.*

"Last evening's post brought us a copy of your Poems, sent by Longmans; arriving thus by the 4th post after your letter of 5th announcing it. We think it is a very pretty book, nicely put out of hand; the back very neat and simply elegant; and when opened the appearance of the pages attractive. On the poems I have already given my judgment in detail, as they passed under my eye and hand in correcting for Press, and that judgment I see no reason to alter. I think your poems will do you no discredit, considered artistically; fertility of imagination, richness and facility of description, intense perception of, and love to, the beautiful in nature, and (in general) a free and melodious versification, belong to both of you; while simplicity of phrase commends your own poems specially to my taste. As to harmony with the Truth of God—a matter of vast importance, there is (I speak of *your self* specially) nothing to complain of, except what I may call nature-worship; while here and there occur recognitions of God. In *The Tomb*, however,

* "It has the first cardinal merit of being definitely interesting as a story. It is written if not with great distinction, with unfailing sureness of touch and in some passages there is a beauty that seems to me to have survived quietly for fifty-five years." *The Poetry of Edmund Gosse*, by John Drinkwater, published in the *Bookman*, Vol. LXIII, No. 5, July, 1926.

which I think, *in every respect,* the very centre and gem of the book, you have sought to make the blessed *Son of God* the object of your readers' admiration and adoration, as well as of your own. And for this effort to exalt the Beloved Saviour with your poetic talent, I doubt not that He will bless and exalt *you.*"

Whatever Gosse thought of the public reception of the book, he had the reward of being recognised in the circles he frequented as definitely belonging to the company of poets. It strengthened his friendship with the world. Miss Baker, watching with the observant eye of a brooding hen, noted the change with distress.

"The great excitement of the last few months has been too much for him. The fortnightly meetings at the houses of these celebrities greatly exhausted him. Naturally, he was delighted, and it was most flattering to have such men as Dante Rossetti and others patting him on the shoulders and introducing him to one and another as 'Our youngest Poet'—invitations to visit them are frequent, but hitherto he has not accepted them, and those for *Sunday* he has had the courage not only to decline but to add, that he never visited on *that* day. Association with such characters may be valuable to him in a literary sense, but alas! it sadly lowers the spiritual tone, which is a great grief to us—and when we speak to him on the subject, he admits the force of it, but says it is *needful*; that he gains instruction by intercourse with them. How true it is, that 'a gift blinds the eyes.' Our only hope is, that God will keep him from falling—for this we anxiously 'watch and pray'—the Lord alone must deal with him. We are glad to think there will be no more of these meetings—until next winter—the Lord in His grace may teach him many lessons before that time. I ought to add for your comfort that he always reads the scriptures with us of an evg (when at home) using his Greek Testament and often he very nicely enters into the subjects of the portion read. The night before he left us—it was very late when all was packed and ready and the dear boy full of excitement—I said go to bed at once and quiet down—he said Oh! No! What, won't you both commend me to

God before I go to rest? Of course we did. I have again given you a peep behind the scenes that you may know how to pray for him."

This letter was written in the summer of 1871. Earlier in the year Gosse had met Swinburne, with whom he had at once made friends.* He has given an account of this meeting in one of those vividly descriptive passages in which he excelled.

"On this occasion I had the privilege of meeting for the first time several persons now celebrated. Mrs. William Morris, in her ripest beauty, and dressed in a long unfashionable gown of ivory velvet, occupied the painting-throne, and Dante Gabriel Rossetti, who, though still almost young, was yet too stout for elegance, squatted—for some part of the evening at least—on a hassock at her feet. The 'marvellous boy, that perished in his prime,' Oliver Madox Brown, carrying on his arms and shoulders tame white rats, shattered the nerves of the ladies. Spontaneity of behaviour in society was at that time encouraged by the Pre-Raphaelites. But among so much that was wonderful, I continued riveted to the aspect of Swinburne, who indulged me with quite a long conversation. His kindness, at once, became like the kindness of an elder brother. In some ways he fulfilled, and more than fulfilled, the promise of my hero-worship.

"At the same time, I have to confess that there was something in his appearance and his gestures which I found disconcerting, and which I have a difficulty in defining without a suspicion of caricature. He was not quite like a human being. Moreover, the dead pallor of his face and his floating balloon of red hair, had already, although he was but in his thirty-third year, a faded look. As he talked to me, he stood, perfectly rigid, with his arms shivering at his sides, and his little feet tight against each other, close to a low settee in the middle of the studio. Every now and then, without breaking off talking or bending his body, he hopped on to this sofa, and presently hopped down again, so that I was reminded of some orange-crested bird—a hoopoe, perhaps—hopping from perch

* See ante page 20.

to perch in a cage. The contrast between these sudden movements and the enthusiasm of his rich and flute-like voice was very strange. In course of a little time, Swinburne's oddities ceased to affect me in the slightest degree, but on this first occasion my impression of them was rather startling than pleasant."

CHAPTER FOUR

In the summer of 1871 Gosse went abroad. This was the first of those excursions which were to make him familiar with Scandinavian countries, and intimate with so many of the loveliest regions and byways of France. Like Burton he held that "the most pleasant of all outward pastimes is to make a petty progress."

Nearly every year with the same enthusiasm he used to contemplate and plan a scheme of summer travel. Everything connected with it was a delight in anticipation, and everything as it came true was lit with a glowing excitement. There were few villages in certain broad areas of France about which he could not give legend and verse, details and directions. He was an inveterate sightseer, a tourist *in excelsis*, punctual to the minute, inexhaustible in his researches, and leaving no stone unseen which could be credited with a literary or artistic association. Guidebook in hand, and embarrassingly unaware of the presence of strangers or the sanctity of his surroundings, he would read in full sonorous tones for the benefit of his fellow-travellers about the monument or building to which his curiosity had brought them. To the listless he might at times appear pedantic, to the independent dictatorial —but Zeal, the determination to mark, learn and inwardly digest, carried him beyond such considerations. He was there to enjoy in his own way, and enjoy he did.

In 1871 he chose as his objective the Lofoden Islands. His experience formed the subject of his first published article: and *Fraser's Magazine* for November introduced him to the public as a writer of prose. Like Landor he made his bow as an accomplished man of letters. Felicity of phrase, perfect lucidity, the ease and blandness of his address, and the balance and the cadence of his sentences, are fully apparent. Experience was to add weight to the content, and maturity was to sharpen the wit and deepen the humour of his prose, but he was already an expert writer. In anticipation of the appearance of the article on the Lofoden Islands he wrote to his father:

British Museum,
Oct. 24th, 1871.

My darling Father,—

On the very morning that your last kind and welcome letter arrived, I found a large packet lying beside it which proved to be the returned MS and the proofs of my Lofoden article. You may imagine how delighted I was, all the more so because I had begun to despair. I had even been consulting with Miss Ingelow what should be done with the MS *when I got it back*. It is very nicely printed (*i.e.* very few errata) and had been carefully "read," as a few little inelegancies of expression had been indicated and clever queries made. My name is given in full in the line under the heading. No intimation of acceptance was inclosed, but a slip of paper asking me to return the proofs with the least possible delay, which I did. So I suppose that it will be published in the November number.

Nor is this all that I have heard, for dining on Thursday last with the Scotts, Allingham the poet was there also, and it appears that he is sub-editor of *Fraser*. So Mr. Scott asked him in an offhand way if he had seen anything of an article on the Lofoden. "Oh! yes," said Mr. Allingham, "it's going in; it is interesting. Do you know anything of the man?" which created a good deal of fun of course, and pleased me very much. I was charmed with Allingham, and still more with another new acquaintance made on Thursday at the Scotts', *i.e.* Mr. Appleton, Editor of the *Academy*. We quite took to one another, I think; I rarely like any one so much on first sight; we went home most of the way together, and I am going to see him soon. The same night I met Dr. Hueffer, also, who is a prominent man of letters. It was very kind of Mr. Scott, I think, to ask me to a little party of people who were all sure to be useful to me; the only other people were Miss and Mr. Rossetti. I enjoyed the evening very much.

Yesterday I was at the Madox Browns', and Mr. Brown said he thought Morris would like to know me, so I am to go there some evening when he is visiting the Browns and see him by himself. Morris, the greatest gun of all! I tell you these little particulars because you told me you liked to know them, because they were all significant as steps gained in my profession.

I am afraid this letter will be an incomplete answer to your last because I have left the latter at home in another coat, and am writing at the B.M. My evenings have been so broken up lately with Bible-reading meetings and parties that I write at the Museum to-day. I have nearly finished translating one of Sars' pamphlets.

The ferns are sprouting beautifully in the light; it is quite a delight to me to watch their visible daily progress.

Little Arnold* was poorly on Sunday, though at the School. This wet cold weather is very trying to his chest.

You are very kind to offer the money for poor Miss Andrews. It will be more than Miss Buckham will know what to do with for her, together with my share. Shall Miss B. keep the remainder for her other charities? I need not say she has not suggested this.

We had the unexpected pleasure of seeing Mr. Hudson Taylor, of the China Inland Mission, with us at the Room on Sunday last. His health is entirely restored. He spoke in a very forcible and beautiful manner. On Sunday evening last we had our annual Thanksgiving service for the harvest, and the chapel was thronged.

Was it not amusing that Mamma's old friend, Aunt Lucy's companion at Saffron-Walden, should call on me? She appears to have retained an affectionate remembrance of me. She is now a Darbyite,† I am grieved to say.

With fondest love to both my dear parents,

I am,

Your devoted child,

EDMUND W. GOSSE.

The year gave occasion among the conscientious for some stock-taking in ideas. A sharp issue was momentarily raised between cul-

* One of Edmund Gosse's Sunday school pupils.

† A follower of John Nelson Darby (1800-1882), one of the earliest members of the Plymouth Brotherhood, who started a sect known as the Darbyites in 1845. He was a voluminous writer on religious subjects. Only one deeply versed in the doctrines of the Brotherhood could now appreciate his divergence from the orthodoxy of the main body.

ture and Puritanism. Whatever view of the question might be taken at Marychurch, there was no doubt as to the side on which Gosse himself would be found.

The controversy had little literary significance. But a contest between two leaders of literature on the subject of sensuality in poetry appealed to the popular taste. And when in October 1871 the Puritan die-hards, with Robert Buchanan as protagonist, launched an attack in the *Contemporary Review*, under the title of "*The Fleshly School in Poetry*," against the poetry of Rossetti, the public at once took sides. Swinburne sprang into the arena shaking his flying locks, with a spear of flame in his hand, and in a pamphlet entitled *Under the Microscope* (1872), which was largely bought by scientific authorities in Germany, mustered his most dithyrambic resources of irony and invective. The pamphlet discouraged further controversy. The die-hards organised a public dinner for their champion, Buchanan. The evening was varied by music and singing. By a strange fatality a song of Rossetti, "Between the lips, between the eyes, Within the heart of Love-Lily," figured on the programme and was sung by Malcolm Lawson. On this Gosse wrote the following lines:

Triolet

"Who wrote that song?" Buchanan said.
They answered with one voice, "Rossetti."
Embarrassed, shuffling, pale and red,
"Who wrote that song?" Buchanan said.
They laughed till they were nearly dead,
This affectation seemed so petty.
"Who wrote that song?" Buchanan said.
They answered with one voice, "Rossetti."

The hubbub died down quickly, and beyond a few feathers ruffled and a few left scattered in the arena, slight traces of the storm remained; except in the breast of Rossetti, in whom it confirmed a disastrous tendency to suspicious mania. Early in 1872 Gosse was introduced to William Morris.

"On Saturday," he writes to his father, "I was invited to Mr.

Madox Brown's to meet Mr. Morris by himself. The great poet, who is the biggest lion I have been introduced to yet, was very benign, and was good enough to say 'he had heard all about me.' He brought his journal of a tour he made last year in Iceland, hearing, he said, 'that I was interested in Northern matters.' As this journal, in spite of the statements which have appeared in the papers, is not to be published, it was a great privilege to listen to it. It was very vivid and amusing. The Icelanders pride themselves on being up in English Literature, and he found that his books had preceded him. He was announced in the one paper at Reykjavik as William Morris, *Scald*. Was it not funny to see the word in that modern connection? He is one of the most unassuming, homely people I have ever met. It seems to me very beautiful when great and sudden fame leaves the recipients of it modest and natural. Do not you think so?"

Gosse's knowledge of Swedish and Danish had given him a taste for modern Scandinavian literature. He told Mr. H. A. L. Fisher that before he started for the Lofoden Islands, Hutton, editor of the *Spectator*, had said to him: "The reason why you get articles refused is because you write about the great familiar English classics. Choose something out of the way, Scandinavian literature for instance, and you will get a hearing." At Trondhjem he went into a bookshop, and asked whether in Norway they had any poets and dramatists. The bookseller replied: "We have the greatest playwright in the world. His name is Ibsen and here is his last work just published."* Gosse with the help of a dictionary began at once to read the works of Ibsen—and through this accidental contact with the dramatist's writings became the first to introduce him to English readers.

Scandinavian literature was a comparatively unknown field, with robust and varied products, needing only a competent introducer to secure recognition. Gosse's right to be regarded as a pioneer in this direction can hardly be contested. No man was so qualified for the mission. He knew the writers themselves, he knew the languages in which they wrote; intimacy with the aspect and associations, the history and the literature of the countries was steeping

* See post letter to William Archer P. 221.

him in local colour. He took up the rôle with courage and success, and in doing so laid the foundation of his literary life.

As luck would have it, early in 1872 there appeared in London a distinguished Danish divine, Dr. Fog. Gosse, with his knowledge of Danish, and his association with one of the austerer religious sects of the country, came to be chosen as companion for the Doctor. An invitation to Denmark followed, and in August he started for Copenhagen.

He was now twenty-three years of age. His progress had been remarkable. He had come to London knowing no one, and lived for five years in an obscure lodging in Tottenham, working as a clerk in the British Museum; yet he had managed to make friends with many of the literary leaders of the day. By his own writings he had acquired a certain recognition, and he was now being invited to Denmark in a semiofficial capacity, to act as a literary liaison between the two countries. His open manner, his anxiety to please, his winning enthusiasms, his deference to which sincerity lent charm, and possibly a certain Scandinavian fairness of appearance, made him everywhere welcome.

At Copenhagen, under the guidance of Dr. Fog, who seems to have been completely fascinated by his young acolyte, Gosse found himself hobnobbing with the most distinguished figures of the Danish world. He heard Grundtvig preach his last sermon at the age of ninety, three months before his death. Hans Christian Andersen read aloud to him from the manuscript his penultimate fairly tale *The Cripple*, which he had just completed. With Hans Lassen Martensen, the Primate of Denmark, and generally regarded as the greatest Lutheran divine of the nineteenth century, he discussed English poetry, the question of England's neutrality in the Danish war, and the attitude of the Church in refusing burial in Westminster Abbey to the remains of Lord Byron. The Primate, reputed to be austere and formidable in his bearing, melted before the ardour of the young pilgrim's approaches, and parted with him on terms of firm friendship. But the culminating triumph was the storming of the defences of the poet, Paludan-Müller, who had been living in retirement for several years inaccessible to visitors. Here Dr. Fog played the part of the Trojan Horse—Gosse was introduced into the poet's garden and presence, ambushed behind the skirts of the Dean. At a given moment Dr. Fog stepped aside and Gosse stood revealed; thereupon the poet, burying his face in his hands, turned to go back into the house. "I was more shocked and confounded," Gosse writes, "than I can express, but before Dr. Fog could say a word, I had stepped two paces forward, and—I know not by what desperate deity inspired—had managed to say in high-piping Danish that I was a young English author, who adored Paludan-Müller's poems, and that in leaving England my greatest hope had been that I might see him whom I revered so greatly. . . . Paludan-Müller wavered and turned back: he fixed his azure eyes on me—then slowly took both my hands in both of his. Slowly he murmured 'You flatter me too much, but thank you.'" The most stubborn of all the citadels had capitulated. Before the interview ended Paludan-Müller declared his intention of going to London "and visiting his young friend," and in parting announced that he would once more take up the role of poet. It was very much as if the Archbishop of Canterbury of the day had introduced into the presence of Tennyson a Danish youth of no outstanding eminence and with an imperfect knowledge of English, and as though the seer of Farringford, after the rays of adulation had adequately penetrated his being, had declared that in spite of three years of silence he would again resume his pen. The technique of approaching whatever gods there be, to-day is different; but such as it was in 1872, Gosse, with the help of his enthusiasm, had become its master. And he had excited more than a passing warmth of interest. These Danish friends continued to write to him when he was back in England, and on his second visit to Denmark in 1874, received him as a cherished celebrity.

His literary activities were extending fast. In 1873 he became a contributor to the *Spectator*, then under the editorship of R. H. Hutton, and articles on Scandinavian subjects about that time can safely be attributed to him. He was writing regularly for *Fraser's Magazine*, then still in the hands of Froude, who was shortly to be succeeded by William Allingham. He also began to write for the *Academy*. In the same year he published his first independent volume of verse, *On Viol and Flute,* which he dedicated to W. B.

Scott. The critics gave it a much better reception. A second edition was called for within a few months, and a letter of praise from Browning himself set a seal on Gosse's claim to be regarded as a poet.

The literary controversies around him had not been without effect. He writes with more freedom; he has broken away from the shackles of his upbringing. His fancy is enlisted on the side of "love and sunshine," and he is even credited by the critics with "most of the virtues and few of the vices of the fleshly school"; indeed the amorousness of the verse was later condemned by Cardinal Newman.* He deals with more defined and visual images, but the flame he kindles flickers and has little warmth. Elegance of style and language is inadequate to carry the scantiness of a passion which is there to eke out rather than to be expressed by the verse. But the poems show Gosse's usual felicity in the choice of adjectives, and here and there sound a graver note of almost philosophic resignation.

The year marked a further stage in Gosse's spiritual alienation from his father. This alienation was progressive, but now and again it would acquire an impetus from a phrase, a letter, a review, or even a minor departure from habit. Those who take the view that *Father and Son* disregards reticence and respect will see from the letters which follow what forbearance Gosse exercised and how much he has toned down in that book. He could hit back with tartness and asperity; he could argue with firmness and force; but assertion of his intellectual sincerity and his right to think for himself left his devotion to his father undiminished. Few men have kept the fifth commandment so closely.

Vexed he might be and harassed to the point of exasperation, but both affection and respect for the nobility of his father's character outlived disagreement. The exact observance of every obligation, so definite a motive throughout Gosse's life, helped to tide over such difficulties. As time went by they both tended to lay aside religious differences, but 1873 was ushered in with storm and cloud: the spiritual volcano in Devonshire was in a state of final and unparalleled activity. The two temperaments clashed with a

* See post page 91.

shock that threatened their relation. The immediate cause seems to have been an article by Gosse on Ibsen, which unfortunately coincided with a sudden conviction in his father that the coming of the Lord was at hand. To that unbending spirit the calls of God allowed of no compromise. Everything was to be subordinated to preparation for the coming event. The "world" literary ambitions, the ordinary aspirations of youth, the companionship of friends and all liberality of culture, were to be regulated by an inflexible interpretation of isolated passages of Scripture. The authority was infallible; to question it was trifling with salvation. Thus it was that Marychurch rolled its thunders and tortured (the word is no figure of speech) the sensibilities of the son. Of all the letters received by Gosse from his father none can have caused him greater perplexity, or thrown him into deeper agitation, than one in the course of which Philip Gosse wrote as follows:

"Now I come to a matter more important, I think, than any that has ever formed the subject of my written communication to you: more important than has ever occupied your thought, with one single exception, your personal salvation.

"For some time past, being fully persuaded, as you know I have been—that the coming of the Lord is nigh, even at the door —I have been earnestly and prayerfully occupied in re-examining the grounds of my expectation: searching, step by step, *ab initio,* the testimony of Prophecy; particularly under the light of recent developments. One result has been—together with the confirmation of my previous conclusions that the historical interpretation of the Apocalypse is according to God—the suspicion (I can scarcely call it, as yet, a *persuasion*) that the Futurist scheme may also have a place. Or rather: that, as soon as the saints are caught up to the Lord in the air, a brief period of unexampled horrors—tyranny, persecution, blasphemy, diabolism—will begin, ever towering to greater height, till the King of kings descend with His saintly hosts, as in Rev. xix.

"All this, however, is preliminary to the momentous theme I allude to. It is, however, necessary, to make you *au courant* of my thoughts.

"Of late years, many devout students of Prophecy have thought they discovered, in the Word, intimations, that *not all* of the saints found living at the Lord's descent—*not all* who are real believers —will go up to Him *then*; but only those who are watchful, and practically ready; only those who are, in habitual affection, in separation from the world, in circumcision of the heart—wholly His. The Wise Virgins, in fact: the Foolish ones representing not, as ordinarily taught, and as hitherto believed by me, hollow professors, but unwatchful, unready, half-hearted, tho' at bottom *real*, believers. That these latter are the 'left,' when the former are 'taken': left, to be purified by the fiery trial under the personal infidel Antichrist. There are difficulties attending the reception of this view; texts which seem to militate against it; such as the words 'together with them in the clouds' in 1 Thess. iv. 17, and 'we shall *all* be changed, in a moment . . .' in 1 Cor. xv. 51, 52.

"On the other side, the view is strongly countenanced by the Lord's exhortation in Luke xxi. 36; which would seem to have no force, if the unworthy were not to endure what the worthy escape. And by the promise to the faithful but feeble church of Philadelphia (Rev. iii. 10) of preservation from the hour of trial, which shall be universal for the earth-dwellers. The very circumstance that there is, at the very last, *after* Philadelphia, a Laodicea, a *real* Church, loved by Christ, yet so lukewarm as to be spued out of His mouth; to be rebuked and chastened, and left for repentance, this fact, I say, is solemnly suggestive.

"These thoughts have been much exercising our minds of late, and have led me much to the Word of God. I cannot say *I am quite sure* the affirmative of this view is true; a good deal is to be said on the negative side; but I judge the weight and number of texts preponderate for the former. But, supposing they were evenly balanced; nay, supposing there were only an inferior measure of probability for the former, would it not be the highest wisdom to leave nothing to chance in so terrible an alternative?

"We have thought, with yearning hearts, of *you*, my only child. That you are the Lord's own: that the root of the matter is in you, I have strong reasons for believing. But, do you 'love His appearing'? Are you habitually *watching* for it? Is the world behind your back? Are you giving your heart to Him who gave His blood for you? O think seriously of this! I must, in faithful love, warn you. It is not enough to say, 'Perhaps it is not true!' Perhaps, I admit, it is not: but, perhaps it is! And oh! to be left behind to endure that terrible tribulation, which assuredly is coming soon; when, if the thoughts of many deeply taught are correct, the only choice possible will be, either open apostasy and demon-worship, or—the axe of the executioner!"

There had been a moment in the past when such views in the "Father" would have seemed less fantastic and repugnant to the "Son." But it was one thing to await the coming of the Lord at Marychurch, or even in Tottenham; it was another and a deeply different thing to be threatened with levitation from the world of Chelsea and at the beginning of an already enviable career. Such extravagances could only be thought of with patience, as an expression of his father's harassed and anxious faith. Gosse himself was much more disturbed by his father's intolerance than by the thought of the wrath to come. In March, battered and distracted by insistence and after much further correspondence, he was moved to define his whole attitude to religion in a long and reasoned statement, here given at length as it provides a key to much in the relation of the two men.

Tottenham,
March 4th, 1873.

MY DEAREST FATHER,—

In a correspondence of such an important and critical nature as this is, it is manifest that I, with my very limited leisure, constant interruptions, and enforced divided attention, am at a great disadvantage in competition with you. You will therefore, I hope, be patient with me, if my exhaustive reply to your letter, or series of letters, be rather tardy in its coming. You will also bear in mind, kindly, that the subject requires, what a busy man cannot always command, deep and continued thought and meditation.

Our conversation—for so I may term it—has reached a specially interesting point. I am glad that you took my last letter in so loving and fatherly a spirit. Your gentleness had removed what threatened to be a difficulty in the way of discussion, your own attitude of censor rather than of counsellor. With a censor it is obviously impossible to discuss, since the only position possible is acquiescence; but if you state your view of a certain line of life, and ask me for my view of the same, a platform is at once erected on which we can hold comfortable discussion.

At once, then, let me say that I will plainly and without concealment state my views and convictions; the attitude in which I receive your exhortations, and my judgments concerning them, laying down, for once, unflinchingly, the differences that I perceive to exist between your view of the Will of God towards us, and mine, not forgetting, what is to me the most welcome subject, that which we indubitably hold in common. And having so persistently, so irresistibly insisted on having a clear exegesis of my convictions, I hope that you will feel it a duty to respect them, and to bear with patience what may be unwelcome to them, remembering that I have not offensively thrust them upon you, but out of honour and respect to you sought to keep them in the background, and forborne to offend your conscience in any way. And I may also say, that I will not cumber my apology with any words of self-depreciation, because it is well-known between us that I am young and ignorant, and you learned with the accumulation of years.

1. Towards the middle of your last letter you express great anxiety to know whether I "accept the plenary inspiration of the whole Holy Scripture." I judge the word "plenary" to imply that not only the tenour of the sense, the accuracy of the facts, but even the wording of conversations was dictated with scientific accuracy by the Holy Spirit. That when it is recorded that Jezebel said "Had Zimri peace, who slew his master?" we are to believe that she actually made use of the very words of which these are a translation. This question is of deep interest, and more than a year ago I went through the New Testament to study it for myself. If any words might be supposed to be of paramount interest to us, they would be those spoken by our Lord Himself in the ordinance of His Supper. Yet these, given four times, are nowhere the same.

St. Mark xiv. 24. "This is my blood of the New Testament which is shed for *many*."

St. Luke xxii. 20. "*This cup* is the new testament *in* my blood, which is shed for *you*."

It is quite beyond denial that if the Lord Jesus spoke the Syriac words translated in the first quotation, He did not speak the words in the second. This finally settled my belief on this point. It is obvious to me that the inspiration of the Scriptures is one of tenour and matter, not of word. I hope this answer is plain, for you accuse me of "affecting indignation" at being asked this question, and purposely leaving it vague.

2. You promise me sympathy, yet you warn me not to render sympathy impossible. You urge and insist on plain dealing, yet you imply that plain dealing will be insupportable to you. I am obliged to say that you are very little acquainted with the condition and growth of my spirit. You speak of yourself as a surgeon, probing into a wound. Throughout, you speak of a great crisis in my life. I must plainly tell you that I perceive no crisis. You take for granted that you have to deal with a blunt and sleepy conscience, an ignorant mind in spiritual things, a dull soul that needs stabbing into painful and sudden wakefulness. You ground your idea possibly on the expressions I have used of refreshment and illumination; I have spoken of increased pleasure in spiritual matters and hence, apparently, you judge that my soul is unconsciously drifting towards a crisis. But it is not so. It is true that I have of late enjoyed a fuller sense of divine pleasures, of the value of prayer, and the assurance of God's gracious favour, but my intellectual perception of truth has been ahead of my emotional appreciation, and I have not been drifting helmless and pilotless. I have read no religious books; I respect them and acknowledge their value for others, but they do not appeal to me. I have read and reread the word of God alone. No book has been so much in my hands during the last year as the Bible. Especially have I read with deep thought the books of the New Testament, not chapter by chapter, but treatise by treatise, seeking to discover the large drift and purpose of each, and its bearing on the Christian life. And in doing so I have striven to put away from me all that I have merely gained by tradition, and sought to arrive at the real drift myself. And minute criticisms and obscure passages have had no importance for me. My desire

has been to grasp in some measure the meaning of the great scheme of Salvation, to perceive its development in the past and its character in the future.

I must here make a brief disgression. You will, I am sure, acknowledge that in the study of science, work is done by two totally distinct orders of minds. There is the collective and the comparative. One observer notes down microscopic details and laboriously stores up what seems chaotic material; another, incapable of microscopic work, seems called to compare one large body of facts with another, and form wide theories. Among naturalists, there are men like yourself, and there are men like Darwin and Huxley. The same inherent difference of mental direction is to be found, perhaps, in all branches of thought. If I am permitted to class my own mind at all, it is certainly with the latter that I find place, while the same minute industry that marked your investigations among rotifers and zoophytes marks your theologic study; I shall not easily forget the hours spent in oscillating between two microscopic interpretations of a passage in Peter* in one of your Tuesday morning lectures. For me, I frankly confess, such nice investigation has been never profitable; while the wide questions of the relation of Christianity to the whole world, to modern history, to life in its everyday circumstances, how far its precepts are flexible, how far rigid, what measure of growth (since all that is living grows) it has attained in these nineteen centuries, all these questions have an interest for me most enthralling and most intense.

3. Among these questions none has occupied me more than this: What is the proper mutual attitude of the Church and the World in our own times? And, indeed, as I have meditated during these past weeks over your criticisms and exhortations, it is increasingly plain to me that in these few words lies the core of all our argument. And I must draw your attention to a statement in your last letter which, surely, is a confusion of thought. "It is not so much a question of theology as of religion." In other words "of law as of practice." But practice is merely the fulfilment or exposition of law. Every "I do" has a "Why do I do?" behind it. And though a certain order of conscience may believe itself convinced that *a* is God's

* This must have been either 1 Pet. i., 17, 18 (July 27) or i., 19, 20 (Aug. 10, 1869).

will, and yet lazily drift into *b*; yet, among minds of any growth or fibre, it may be laid down that the only sure way to influence practice is to convince theory. Hence I venture to deny your remark and say, "This is not so much a question of religion as of theology." If it is proper to adopt a line of conduct, its propriety must lie in a theological law.

4. Then comes this matter of "separation." I am sorry that in your letters (I have just read them through for this purpose), I do not find what I may call the dogmatic side of your belief set down in any broad way. I rather find a series of side-arguments bearing entirely upon behaviour. Still, I think that I am right when I state your view briefly thus. "Even as, in the first century, Christians were called upon to separate themselves from the practices and even intimate conversations of their heathen connections, and to make their one object the proclamation of Christ, the crucified slave and incarnate universal God, so, in this age and country, are we called to separate ourselves from all that is not decidedly and evangelically spiritual in the life around us, and make the proclamation of the Gospel our single aim. Not neglecting business, but comparatively uninterested in affairs around us; less citizens of Great Britain than Jews in Rome were Roman citizens; even in useful matters, acting rather as travellers than residents." I think I have not overstated your thesis; it strikes me that yourself might perhaps put it more strongly. Well, this belief (which for a long time, in obedience to the authority of those whose age and study entitled them to my deep respect, I held, even to the continual vexing of my conscience, self-wounded with divers imaginary offences), I do not longer hold. And since you give me a caveat against the supposition, that a thing must be wrong because it is agreeable, I will give you another against thinking all things undesirable necessarily right. As a matter of fact, a human being who has a conscience is generally most happy when obeying it. St. Simeon Stylites, I take it, was extremely happy at the top of his tower, even while his self-righteous soul was most contrasting his own abstinence with the indulgence of the folks below. The recently published life of Lacordaire furnished me with some curious instances, which indeed all Popish history is full of, of mere arbitrary self-denial being a

positive pleasure, even while it was most real and excessive. Of course, especially to a person of my temperament, the idea of separation from the pursuits and desires of my fellows is very distasteful; and (so strong is the feeling in us that what is pleasant must be wrong), the very consciousness that my heart naturally went out in genial sympathy to all sorts of people, merely for themselves, without any impulse to teach them, for a long time staggered me; still I determined that I would not be biassed by preconceived impressions in my study of the Word, and it gradually grew into a conviction with me that this separation was a wholly uncalled-for, scarcely even desirable state, in a Protestant land like ours. When we think of what Greece, Italy, Asia were in the beginning of the Christian era and contrast the life then and there with life now and here, the difference is not one of degree but of character. The earliest Christians were knots of elect men and women left comparatively alone among a highly-civilized and developed heathendom. It was not that the Greeks and Romans worshipped nothing, or that they ignorantly adored a vague creative spirit in Nature. They actively worshipped a variety of sharply-defined deities, whose worship entered very closely into their everyday life. The pioneers of Christ had to destroy, and to build up again, in the conscience of every man and woman. It has been vigorously said that, at some of the shrines of the ancients, "a sin was a prayer"; and nothing is more striking to me than the difference of tone used in the books of the New Testament according to whether Jews or Gentiles were addressed. Our Blessed Lord in his marvellous Sermon on the Mount startles us, almost, with the high and spiritual morality of his teaching, while Paul, writing to Corinthian Christians, has to warn them at great length against incest, and squabblings at the Lord's Supper. One would say that the first audience must have been, though unconverted, immensely above the second in moral perception; but the difficulty vanishes when we remember that the Jews were a people worshipping the true God with pure rites; while all the nations around them had arrived at a condition in which their very religion was abominable; and morality, in its larger sense, desired only by a few uninfluential philosophers. It will not do to quote Scripture in violation of context; still less will it do to ignore history and philosophy in support of a doctrine. The Mohammedan conception of divine truth is, I am told, that God gave the Koran once, and every word of the Koran retains its inflexible significance to the end of time. The Mohammedan creed is the strangest parody on our own. Are we not apt sometimes to think that what was said to Corinth 1850 years ago is said exactly to England to-day? On this ground, the Southern planters triumphantly pointed to δουλοι in the New Testament as a clear proof that slavery was divinely sanctioned. We smile now at the hermits who strove to separate themselves from all earthly passion by entire isolation, but how is our conduct more logical than theirs if we take a warning to a Corinthian (accustomed to comedies to which Aristophanes was delicate) against foolish jesting as a prohibition of such innocent mirth as you had with me as a child ("the unseemly levity that was possibly a hindrance to you in your childhood," 10 Feb. 1870, p. 8)? We are not without analogies in this matter. Two examples help us to form our judgment. I have referred to the state of Palestine as contrasted with the rest of the world in the first century. The tone of morality (I always use *morality* in its broadest sense) was, perhaps, about as high there, actually, as in Portugal now. The Portugal of to-day, transported bodily into the heart of the Roman Empire, would have been a prodigy of moral and spiritual light. How much more England, where the glorious Gospel has, down all the ages, formed the very marrow of the best thought of the nation, where society conforms to Christian morality, where laws and edicts are steeped in the spirit and phraseology of the Bible, where not a book nor a newspaper is printed but shows either in light or in shadow the presence of the Light of Life amongst us—with what pretence of consistency can we urge the same exclusive conduct as in earliest ages was necessary to preserve the daily walk from pollution? Not that I dream that the heart of man is changed or that the prevailing tone of society is anything but a veneer, but the great crying evils no longer stare at us on every hand. Take an image. If one crosses a muddy road, one must step daintily and lift one's robes high out of the mire, but when the grass is reached, such caution is needless and affected. Yet under the decent grass lies the same dirty earth. Where the injunctions to separation do really, I believe, hold as much as ever, is in heathen countries. Missionaries are bound to feel that they are a set of men watched and criticised, and, besides this, men whose whole life is in antagonism to the heathen life around them. It is not for them to indulge artistic curiosity with the examination of the interior of temples, or spend long hours in studying ancient classics. These innocent and instructive pursuits are among the comforts they have voluntarily deprived themselves of, by leaving their own Christian country, and nobly taking the laborious work of pioneers. Pioneers must work in the dust and discomfort of newness; but all are not pioneers; and to create a fictitious discomfort is to indulge, it seems to me, not a tender, but a morbid conscience. This of missionaries is the second of the analogies I referred to.

4*b*. You will now understand why I was able to acquiesce with humility in your strictures on certain expressions used in my essays, while I left the matter of those essays untouched on. Your words in this connection are exceedingly painful to me. "Studies so essentially and incurably worldly," you term my critical investigations, because, as I gather from your own expressions, poetry and not "history or archæology or metaphysics" has been the object of them. For my own part, I am unable to see what intrinsic spirituality is connected with archæology; equally strange to me is the notion that poetry is "frivolous and prophane." Many books of the Bible are written entirely in poetry; some branches of oriental archæology are open to a much harder epithet than "frivolous." These things are a matter of taste. The study of poetry seems to me a loftier one than that of microscopic zoology; it does not seem so to you. There are some things in which we really must bear with one another. I must be allowed to mention that I have been in the habit of sending my articles to you, quite aware that they possessed no special importance for you, further than they were mine, and that I liked to feel that you followed me. If you had still been at work on the invertebrate animals, I should have, in the same sense, delighted in reading whatever you produced on the subject. I think you are the most difficult Father to satisfy in all the wide world.

5. I have put in the last passage parenthetically, as I do not allow that it has any theological bearing at all. Literature is my business as much as carpentering is a carpenter's business, and as long as we are to work with our hands in decent occupations, I shall feel it my place to stick to it. You seem to look at it as a sort of amusement, that could be set aside by an effort and done with. Of course it is my duty to do what it is right in my profession, but because a carpenter might expect that he might be tempted to carve wooden idols, there is in that no reason that he should give up carpentering, but rather determine against the carving of idols.

6. Let me not forget to tell you that I have been learning, as you desired, Lyte's very beautiful hymn. This leads you to the extracts from your own life. There is no question that your aggressive position has, through life, exposed you to much discomfort and has been, I am sure, most admirable and honourable. It is possible, however, that something of it is due to the natural colour of your character, and we must not forget this in considering the advisability of similar conduct in others. I can hardly fancy how I should set about it. I am so thoroughly used to speak my mind with entire frankness, that I hardly know what it is to be teased. People are either afraid of my tongue or they agree with me. I am afraid there is no doubt that I have an arrogant temper; perhaps I owe a little of it to you? At all events, I am in the habit of expressing my views quite straightforwardly, for I have a very large circle of acquaintances and enough friends, and if people find me distasteful, they may go away. Nobody, however, now I think of it, ever thinks of laughing at me before my face. Sometimes I am conscious that I surprise people. Some weeks ago I spoke of my work on Sundays to a young poet who, I suppose, is very irreligious; and he said with the most incredulous air, "My dear Fellow, is it really true that you teach in a Sunday-school?" "To be sure," I said, "and in a Plymouth Brothers' Sunday-school too." He stood rather aghast, doubtful whether to be offended or not, but as his opinion was a matter of the completest indifference to me, I said no more. I suppose he considered me a useful acquaintance, in spite of my Methody craze, for he has been very polite

ever since. If he had not been, I should not have cared. It is my good fortune to be so circumstanced that I can do what is right, and what is my work, without the two clashing. As to your saying that I live one life in Tottenham and one in town, it is a mistake. Everybody who cares to know, in London, knows I am Superintendent of a little Dissenting Sunday-School; and everybody who cares to know at Brook Street knows I am a poet, critic and *littérateur*. You only have found these things inconsistent. But I hope you will reconsider your thought on this matter.

7. You refer to your own care in bringing me up. I should like to take this opportunity of offering a just tribute to the excellence of your training. I do not, to be frank, think you were wise in all things, but I do think that the general tenour of your example, especially the deep consciousness I had that you sought with all your heart to bring me up for God, had an immensely beneficial effect on my character. I believe you even suffer now from the effects of your training, for if you had been less unflinching, less logical and firm in your education of me, it would be easier than it now is to lean on other people's opinion and hold two views at once. You did your best to give me a stiff backbone. I am desirous of saying how much I feel I owe to your pious training, lest you should feel that your influence on me had not been wise.

7b. With regard to the question of "reproach." I cannot think that this "very great riches" is one that we have any right to claim from the ordinary conversation of our fellow-beings. Our difference of feeling on this point arises from the different aspect in which we view the bulk of respectable persons. You use this very remarkable expression:—"Their company (that of unbelievers) will be, *ipso facto*, distasteful to you, to be endured, indeed, only when duty makes it imperative." This phrase carries me at once into the presence of profligate, and, still more, infidel persons, whose company is in truth so distasteful to me that no brilliance or wit will tempt me to endure it. But I believe that you do not go so wide as this. I rather imagine that you include in your ban all who have not attained to the Higher Christian Life, all that are commonly called the Unconverted. Among these are thousands of amiable and estimable people who fulfil the laws of righteousness but are not conscious of their own salvation. And here, I know, you will differ from me extremely, nor have I dared before to tell you my belief. Yet since you beg me to tell you all, I must tell you what will displease as well as what will please you. I embrace in the saving arms of the True Church not only those who are happily conscious of peace through Christ, but those myriads also, who, having had dumb motions of the heart towards God, and not having blasphemed against the Holy Ghost, vaguely and ignorantly trust in Christ. I do not believe that one, however faint the desire, however dim the vision, who once has longed for a physician, and glanced at the serpent of brass, will be left out of that prodigious multitude that will sing around the throne. Else, if we do not believe this, how can we find in the great mission of Christ anything but a failure? If only the little knots of the converted out of all the world are to be saved, then indeed might we say that the scheme of God's salvation had failed.

Hence when I walk among my fellow-mortals, I do not feel myself alone among the damned, but as one who owes it to unusual grace that he perceives what is hidden from the bulk of his brothers and sisters, who shall all one day arise into the perfect light of day. I hold the theories of Universalists to be quite opposed to the teaching of Scripture, but I do hold that not a small body of elect but the bulk of professing Christians will be saved by the vicarious sacrifice of Christ.

8. And now, before I close, you want to know what I do believe, what I grasp in this day of perturbation, when all men deeply moved with spiritual instincts are striving to satisfy themselves with so many critical stratagems. This age is a profoundly religious one, and like all religious ages, it is one in which there is rough and unwise handling of creeds. For my own part, I cling to nothing so much as to the Godhead of Christ. If Christ was man and no God, I am driven back into chaos. I can see no scheme of the world's history. Devoutly and firmly do I believe that Jesus Christ was perfect God and perfect Man. I confess it to be an absolute paradox, but I expect what is paradoxical when I judge what is infinite with my own finite senses. I believe also in the need and in the power of the atoning Blood of Christ, that as sin through

the fall of Adam came on all the world, so redemption and immortal life have come into the world through Christ, and stand ready for the acceptance of all. Nay, they are thrust upon all men, and these gifts are not to be given back or thrust away. One touch or prayer gives them, and no relapse can take them away. I believe in Christ, the God-Man, who gave his blood to take away the sins of the world. Beyond this I do not know that I have any creed.

Whilst in the middle of these sheets I received a very sweet and refreshing note from you, for which I owe you many thanks. It strengthened me to pursue what has been a very difficult labour, for it assured me of your patience and interest. And I hope you will not be overmuch surprised or alarmed. When we have the joy of meeting we shall be able to discuss these things with one another, and you will, I am sure, be able to teach me much that I do not understand. I find that, by a quite unintended coincidence, my reply has covered as many pages as your exhortation. Considering then how very busy I am, you will not think this time that I have shown your admonitions neglect. It is very late. I must close.

Accept my tenderest love and respect and believe me to be

Your affectionate Son,

EDMUND W. GOSSE.

It is unfortunate that no written record remains of the impression made on Philip Gosse by this letter, but it will be seen in the next chapter that a brief relaxation of tension which seems to have followed was not of long duration.

In the summer Dr. Fog again visited England. It fell to Edmund Gosse to act as cicerone to the Dean, and he took him to Marychurch. The Dean and Philip Gosse argued as trained theologians, confounding or at any rate puzzling one another with chapter, text, and verse.

So ardently did controversy rage that Gosse, who acted the part of an anxious onlooker, deemed it well on the question of the Atonement to withdraw the Dean from the fight. The visit was marred by the warmth of the polemics; the son, who had excepted much from this meeting, had to recognise that in matters of doctrine his father was hopeless. He and the Dean left on the following day, discomfited; not even with a stranger, however distinguished and authoritative in religious matters, could his father abate one tittle of his argumentative position or curb his fanatical outbursts. Violence in argument carried to such a pitch had the appearance of a breach of hospitality.

CHAPTER FIVE

When Gosse started for his second visit to Denmark he had every reason to be confident. In England he had been already hailed as "one of the most delicate and subtle of living critics." His articles on Scandinavian topics had been translated into Danish and Norwegian. Georg Brandes, and Julius Lange the leading art critic of Denmark, had opened a correspondence with him.

He tells us he was "glowing with the zest of the coming hours." He was approaching his own special preserve, where his supremacy was threatened by no competitor. He was setting out like an ambassador accredited to the literature of a friendly country.

Dr. Fog, who was again his host, received him as a son. Gosse lost no time, and began at once a house-to-house visitation of celebrities. He was welcomed everywhere. All trace of that condition in which he described himself as being when he came to London, "half frozen out of the cold storage of English Puritanism," had vanished: he was thawed. He came now among the Danes, many of them still subject "to the indignant zealotry of earlier times," equipped with a gospel of intellectual emancipation. *Poems and Ballads*, *Dolores*, and *Anactoria* from modern English literature, and *Les Fleurs du Mal* from France, were among the sources from which he sought to invigorate "the exquisite and effete intellectual civilisation of Denmark." If now and then he was as he confesses guilty of "juvenile pertness," this did not lessen the number of his personal conquests. Seldom indeed can a youth visiting a foreign country have gathered so many friends in so short a time: Julius Lange, Holger Drachmann, Exner, Christian Molbeck, Georg Brandes, and many others were attracted, and several of them bound for their lifetime by the charm of his assiduity.

There was much to explain and much to learn. He tripped lightly from one sanctuary to another, he was persevering, he was tireless. His high spirits gave him wings, his intellectual curiosity assurance, and his consecration to literature sincerity. Every hour was packed, he talked and listened, he expounded the word, arguing for the poets and proselytising for a new vision. If he was not one to think that "men of low degree were vanity," still less was he one to consider "men of high degree a lie." It was among thinkers and writers that now, as always, he was most vivacious, most effective, and most at home.

Sometimes in the fulfilment of his mission he was called on to read from the poets. His Danish hearers were mystified by English "lyrical measures and anapæstic rhythms," and Gosse must enlighten them. This explanatory aim confirmed his peculiar method of reading aloud, which was not free from mannerism. It fell at first uncomfortably and a little startlingly on the ear; the rise and fall of his chanting voice, and his singular elaboration of emphasis, sounded like affectation. That was far from being the case. In reading poetry he became oblivious of his audience. He was immediately rapt away by the beauty of the words, and by his delight in rhythm; concerned only like a pianist in evoking every nuance of structure and phrase in the music before him. His enthusiasm became contagious. With those whose hearts were hardened against him the impression of affectation may have remained, others were made aware of new beauties in what he read. It was a style of reading stamped with a date. Mr. Desmond MacCarthy tells me on the authority of W. M. Rosetti that this manner of reading aloud was peculiar to a literary circle of the day, and was started by Swinburne, who would read with ever-increasing emphasis and lilt, as though he must finally be lifted from his chair by his own chanting cadence.

But enjoyment of his Danish holiday was shadowed by a relapse into controversy with his father. A comparatively playful letter of April 20th had been followed by a series of anxious comments on salvation. On April 20th, Philip Gosse had written: "By the way, I lately met with the very best pun I *ever* met with: better even than that admirable one of the postage stamp. I dare say you have seen it, but nevertheless I will give it you. Why is a chrysalis like hot rolls? Because it is the grub that makes the butter fly. I can't even write it down without a burst of delighted laughter. Is it not wonderfully clever? The play on the word 'grub,' on 'butterfly,' on 'makes'—the undercurrent of slang; all are exquisite ——" But for better or worse the lighter mood of the zoologist had not lasted. An article by Gosse in *Fraser's Magazine* had stirred afresh his father's fears. There was indeed a fatality about Philip Gosse's interventions: no sooner did Edmund seem fairly under way and shaping a course full of promise, with an adequate supply of faith, hope and charity on board, than down came a broadside from his father. Occasions were easily found in articles and reviews. In 1873 an essay on Ibsen had been regarded as playing straight into the hands of Satan. "Ah!" the letter of protest concluded, "I fear your heart as yet has but little responded to the wondrous love wherewith He has loved you: or it would be far more sensitive than it is to the claims of His honour and glory. May He give you higher, deeper, truer, holier apprehensions of Him." The year 1874 especially had been a period of agitation, even the statement of March 4th, with its air of finality, had failed to secure immunity. On May 18th, in response to further spiritual condemnation, Gosse, after a brief description of his travels, went on to say:

"I feel a reluctance in giving you any details, however. Your opinion is that 'what I am pursuing will be "wood, hay stubble" by and by.' It is quite useless, I know, to appeal to you against such a letter as your last. What is gracious or courteous or sympathetic becomes absolutely nothing to you when you approach these topics. You have become so permeated with the tone of *Galatians* that the spirit revealed in such an epistle as *Philemon* does not exist for you, when you treat of spiritual things. Why do you do your better nature such a wrong? Why do you insist on stretching every one on your own self-measured bed and cutting off feet and ankles because they push out further than yours do? You insist, more than any professional theologian I have ever met, on your own insight into theology. Why is it that practically you narrow the channels of God's grace to the mere streamlets that can run through your own garden? I cannot understand how you can possibly regard the truth as a thing so *borné*, so stereotyped, so whimsical. You permit the enjoyment of nature in the fields and by the shore; you forbid the exactly kindred pleasure found in the society of one's friends. But it is vain to go into details; I am afraid lest every word I write should be misconstrued, that you should think I write in anger when I write in grief only, and regret; that you should think me irreverent when I only desire to be just in regarding certain attributes of God which you ignore, such as that sympathetic sense of the power and scope of an individual which comes to us (some of us) through the faculty of imagination but which in Him must be intuitive, such as the intellectual breadth of vision which must make visible to Him, what we only guess at and observe, the different effect produced on different minds and consciences by the same food of life. We are not all moulded alike; I do not wish to make you other than what you are, you have your honoured place in the manifold laboratory where God prepares our own souls for his everlasting Kingdom. I also hope He is leading and training me, but in a way and through means excessively opposed to yours, and I feel that it is time that those mutual reproaches which have embittered in past days our correspondence so much, should cease, that you also should consent to treat me, as everyone else does, no longer as a child to be whipped and put in the corner, but as an adult human being for whom the serious questions of life have as intense an importance as they can have for you. If you will but restrain your natural instinct to mould and fashion the character of your own child—it is more indeed than most parents can do, but then I look for greater things from you than I should from most—we may always continue to strengthen and help one another, and we may then lay down one another's letters with a sense of full enjoyment, and not with a disappointed sense of yearning."

He spent the residue of his July leave in Cornwall, and on his return to London wrote an account of it. He seems to have recaptured the zoological ardours of his childhood and to be making the most of them, as one of the links which still bound him to his father.

Tottenham,
August 3rd, 1874.

My darling Father,—

Since you heard last from me I have committed a wild escapade. I have spent the few remaining days of my furlough in a spot that has fascinated my imagination ever since I was a child—the Lizard!

It was not till the arrival of your kind gift made me so rich that I dreamed of this trip, and even then it did not at once occur to me. I wished constantly that you had been with us, we both often expressed the wish—scenery, fauna and flora would alike have delighted you. For never since I was a little boy have I been so ardent a naturalist. I had not been prepared for such a profusion of animal life. Every form seemed a delicious discovery. To you it would have been nothing, but to me it was like a revelation. The rocks are still virginal; the pools and coves have not been in the hands of collectors; the greatest profusion of invertebrate life lies spread at one's feet. At first we did not notice it, but one morning, bathing at very low tide, I swam out to a long knife-life promontory, that became flattened at the end and bisected with a little creek. This creek was hidden with laminaria, and drawing the dark leaves aside, what did I behold? The dark slit was white with a foam of tentacles—it was niven in profusion, packed together end to end. Higher up the pools were starred with miniata, and I saw several specimens that seemed to combine the species, the disk being brown and scarlet, the tentacles white. In the roots of the laminaria were little specimens of ornata. How excited I was! And, marvellous to relate, all the names, that I have not looked at for years and years, sprang one by one to my lips. All the pools were paved with a mosaic of bellis, the brown disk being the common form, but now and then the disk was shot with broad scarlet threads, interwoven. In a larger pool higher up, the edges were fringed with what looked liked a chain of little opals, corynactis swollen with water and transluco-iridescent. I was obliged to tear myself away for fear Miss Otte should think I was drowned, but I have forgotten half the things I saw, troglodytes, cowries, pipe-fishes, all sort of things commonplace enough to a great naturalist like you, but so exciting to me. One anemone I found was quite unknown to me, it was clear pale green, like a safartia in habit, but with obtuse tentacles, slightly knobby, the tentacles banded, the body uniform. What was it? I observed some remarkable crustacean forms, unfamiliar to me. The day before we left we were plagued by a sea-fog so dense that it was useless to plan an excursion; we sauntered down to Polpeer, the most southerly cove in England. The tide happened to be extremely low; a vast stretch of black rocks, studded with pools, was laid bare. The collecting mania seized us both, I rushed back to the inn, borrowed a hammer and a chisel, begged a pickle-bottle, and raced back. I found Miss Otte already on her knees working away with a hairpin and her fingers. We were like intoxicated people! The abundant forms proved to be bellis and gemmacea, these two occurred in thousands. Miss Otte gathered off the rocks. I turned great stones, being rewarded by the strangest echinodermata—queer things like ophicoma and (illegible) that wriggled and heaved, and threw away their legs at a moment's notice—and by little scarlet crabs (ebalia?) and all the slimy doubtful creatures that gladden one's heart. We stuffed our pickle-jar with these (which all died) and with antheas, gemmaceas and niven. We could not get a single bellis. I tore one or two in half in trying to secure them. The serpentine at the Lizard resists the chisel so thoroughly that the attempt to knock off a fine tuft of chondrus crispus resulted in chipping the edge of the chisel. We were thrown on our fingers and the hairpin. Miss Otte was for adding mesembryanthemums and trochi and such things, which I stoutly resisted. She said I showed the instincts of a true naturalist in rejecting "rubbish"! Out on the rocks I came upon an anthea, the green variety, swollen out to such an enormous size that it attracted my wonder. I touched it, and in a moment it ejected a half-digested launce, a fish four or five inches long. Was that not curious? We caught a pipe-fish and brought him home among our treasures. When we got back, instantly we poured everything out into a basin. The pipe-fish was very brisk and merry. We sat down to dinner. The moment the meal was over I rushed to the basin. The pipe-fish's body, stiff and dead, lay drawn taut between a mesemb. and a gemmacea, the former of which had swallowed its head, the latter its tail. I am quite ashamed to tell these little observations, which must seem very commonplace to you. But I think if a real savant, not a mere tyro like me, visited the Lizard, splendid discoveries might be made. I believe I found a haleotis. Is that possible?

We travelled back to town by night, leaving Lizard Town at 1.30 in the afternoon, driving 21 miles to Penrhyn, the nearest railway station, and travelling straight up to town by the mail, arriving between four and five in the morning. The whole visit seems like a dream, it was so sudden, so exhilarating, so brief. I shall never forget those glorious days, in which I became so unexpectedly the "naturalist in petticoats" once more.

Goodbye, my darling father! Let me hear from you soon, and do not laugh at my tyro-raptures.

Ever your loving son,

EDMUND W. GOSSE.

It had once been seriously considered whether Gosse should accept the office of an appointment as a Zoologist in the British Museum: but his literary position was strengthening so rapidly at this time, and the pay of the proposed office presented so little temptation, that the offer was laid aside. In September he began writing for Leslie Stephen in the *Cornhill*.

A few months later Gosse was invited together with R. L. Stevenson to dine with Stephen. Gosse contributed to the *Life of Stephen* by F. W. Maitland an account of this dinner. "We anticipated—I cannot imagine why—a large collection of literary notabilities, and in our eagerness, we were hanging about, outside the house, some time before we could present ourselves. But we were the only guests. Leslie Stephen sat at one end of the table, his wife at the other. Miss Annie Thackeray opposite us two lads. I shall always remember the surprise Leslie Stephen's appearance gave me: the long, thin, bright red beard, radiating in a fan shape; the wrinkled forehead; the curious flatness of the top of the head, accentuated by the fulness of the auburn hair on either side; the long cold hands; the distraught and melancholy eyes. The dinner was extremely quiet. Scarcely a word fell from either of the Stephens, and we two guests, although chatterboxes engrained, were subdued to silence by shyness. Only Miss Thackeray, in her hospitable goodness, did her best to talk for us all, and in the twilight —for the room and table were meagrely illuminated by two or three candles—her voice was heard, holding a sort of dialogue with itself.

"It is characteristic, perhaps, of the impression which he always produced, that this almost unbroken silence of our host—who for a considerable part of the time lay far back in his chair, motionless with his beard on his bosom—though it greatly disconcerted, did not offend or wound either of us at all. . . . We (R. L. S. and I) were taken, I recollect, halfway through the meal, with a terrible simultaneous temptation to giggle, which we withstood; and then for the rest of the evening we waited patiently for the heavenly spark to fall. But it only fell upon kind Miss Thackeray."

CHAPTER SIX

In those concentrations of talent which took place once a fortnight at the house of Ford Madox Brown in Fitzroy Square, there might be seen the main body of the Pre-Raphaelites, William Morris, Holman Hunt, the Rosettis, Swinburne and Burne-Jones, with Whistler, O'Shaughnessy, Theo Marzials, Hueffer, Val Prinsep, and many camp-followers and disciples, as well as occasional celebrities of other worlds such as Mazzini, Turgeneff, Robert Browning and Mark Twain. It was at one of these gatherings that Gosse in 1870 met a gentle girl with a cloud of fair hair. This lady, Miss Nellie Epps, who was destined to be his wife, was the daughter of George Napoleon Epps (1815-1874), half-brother of the better-known John Epps, both active and successful practitioners of homœopathy. In tastes, age, and situation, Gosse and Miss Epps were very near each other. She had some aptitude for art, and was studying at the time in Madox Brown's studio together with the painter's daughter. Gosse, in the early stages of a literary career, had no certain income except his small salary at the British Museum. But hesitations about worldly means were dismissed. The young critic and poet, after a long period of probation, was made welcome by the Epps family, and his courtship was facilitated by his future sister-in-law, Mrs. Charles Pratt. The progress of his attachment, regulated by the code of the day, followed, as the letters show, formalities which have long been brushed aside. His persistence in spite of not being "on visiting terms at the house," enabled him to write on October 24th, 1874:

Tottenham,
Oct. 24, 1874.

My own darling Father,—

Your note this morning reproved and reproached me severely, for I have not, even yet, fulfilled your commission. The fact is I have been in an extremely agitated condition of mind on several regards, partly on account of sundry friends, who have taken it into their heads to get into certain conditions of mind and action which have induced long and exciting confidences. For my intimate friends get into the habit of treating me as a maiden aunt, to whom all secrets are first of all confided, and who is never supposed to have any secrets to confide. Since this day last week, not to mention minor matters, three several friends have sought my sympathy about three several combinations of circumstances of which secrets I am the only repository. These things all excite one and take up one's attention, but add to that that one has a secret of one's own, and life becomes indeed too large for the four and twenty hours to contain it.

I do not pretend that anything, however absorbing, excuses the neglect of a commission which one has promised to fulfil, but I throw myself on your mercy, when I say that in this week of violent interchange of hope and fear, of agitation and anxiety, I have not been able to take your books to Sutton's as I promised to do. But I determinately mean to do so on Monday. Now I shall take for granted that you forgive me, and pass on to particulars.

A certain idea has been gradually forming in my mind for a long while past. It has been obvious to me for months that there was only one woman that I knew that I should ask or wish to be my wife. I have known her slightly for some four years, but as I have not been on visiting terms at the house, it has not been easy for me to know her very well. Still, gradually, I have learned to know her. I must now tell you the lady's name, Miss Nellie Epps, a daughter of a brother of the great homœopathic doctor. There are five daughters, four of whom are married, one to the painter, Alma-Tadema. Four of the daughters are artists, Mad. Tadema, Mrs. Williams (a widow, who lives at home), Mrs. Pratt and Miss Nellie, the latter being by far the most independent talent of them all, Mrs. Williams, though, being much older and understanding the technique best. All this minute biography is that you may be able better to realise the family. They live at Devonshire Street. The family there consists of Mrs. G. Epps (the aunt), Washington Epps, a brother who is a homœopathic doctor, Mrs. Williams and Nellie. The last is aged about 24, is very handsome after a Roman type, like a Claudia, and has been dividing her whole mind between housekeeping, art and her own relatives. Hence though I have been thinking so much about her, she has certainly thought nothing about me.

At last I have been invited to the house, and at a little party there on Thursday I was so situated that what had so long been in my heart rose to my lips, and I said what was, I feel, certainly precipitate.

As soon as ever I got home, I wrote to the aunt saying that I had done so, and begging pardon for such precipitancy, while asking to be allowed to come to the house. That brought a most kind reply from the aunt, saying I might come and talk to her, and begging that, after that, I would stop to tea. I talked it over this afternoon, accordingly, with the aunt, who is an extremely gentle and right-minded person, and she put before me very frankly the difficulties in the way, which are: 1. Miss Nellie's determination of will, she having willed that she will not marry, but prosecute her art with all her might, for, since she has no fortune, she wishes to be indebted to no one for a livelihood, but to work herself into fortune. 2. The fact that she had never thought of me till my abrupt declaration. 3. Her intense attachment to the members of her own family which makes her determined never to leave them.

After being alone with the aunt awhile, down came Mrs. Williams, and invited me to come up and see their paintings.

First, I must tell you that the Aunt confesses to liking me very much, and to thinking that we should suit one another remarkably well, if Nellie could be brought to think so, but her will is so extremely hard to bend. I must add, also, that I have extracted from the young lady the declaration that there is no other man she prefers to me. I believe, however, that she has formed an ideal, and that I am far from approaching it.

Well, I followed Mrs. Williams, who is a great friend of mine, upstairs, where the two girls' pictures were, where Nellie, seated in a corner, welcomed me rather ungraciously. Then Mrs. Williams and I talked a long time about her pictures, till Nellie arose and announced that perhaps I might like to look at hers. So at this juncture Mrs. Williams discovered that she must run down and make the tea. Then followed a *tête-à-tête,* in which we quarrelled horribly. She worried and teased me beyond everything, and yet did not quite say that it was impossible. I would not allow her to give me a final answer; I said I withdrew my declaration, and for the time being we were to be just friends as before. That was quite well, she answered. Then followed a great deal of sparring that I cannot write down. Its import worried and perplexed me; I do not really know what will come of it all, but I mean to fight it out to the last, and perhaps a strong heart may win the fair lady. At all events I am certain that my happiness depends on it. Meanwhile I am to come as often as I like, nor does Miss Nellie make any objection to that. So she will get to know me better, and perhaps in the end may learn to love me. If once she does, that warm, strong, large heart of hers will never change. She is the sweetest and best of girls. The aunt said, "I cannot but commend your choice; she is about the best and truest girl in this world."

So the thing rests at present. I cannot allude to all sorts of other affairs that excite or move me. This is enough for one letter, and, my own darling Father, write me a full and sympathetic letter, and tell me what you think.

Give my best love to Mother and accept the same from

Your devoted Son,

EDMUND W. GOSSE.

Subsequent letters record the fluctuations of his hopes.

British Museum,
Nov. 5, 1874.

MY DEAREST MOTHER,—*

You have both of you such a fixed notion that poor Nellie has "an imperious will." I do not know what I said to give this idea; she undoubtedly has a firm will, but that is quite another thing. If two people love one another with the love of mutual esteem and attachment, under circumstances in which their interests and hopes are identical, I conceive that firmness and distinctness of

* He always addressed his stepmother in these terms.

purpose are no stumbling-blocks in the way of their happiness. In the present case I see no reason why we should differ on any of the great questions of life; our views, as far as I know hers, are singularly alike in matters apart from sentiment or art. Her aunt, in speaking of her character, distinctly asserted that she showed nothing of what is usually called self-will, but (these are the aunt's own words), "a noble and upright determination in acting in the way she believed to be right, and in this she is not to be affected by others."

Certainly she cannot be called "imperious" or "selfwilled" because she did not accept me the first moment I asked her. To have done that would have stamped her as weak and poor-spirited. I think she acted with extraordinary sense and self-control in managing to evade any distinct reply until she knew me better.

One thing I forgot to answer in my Father's letter. He asked if I had been saving money. To which I can answer yes, rather largely I think for so minute an income as mine. You must both be ironical when you talk of my "sumptuous tastes." My tastes may be sumptuous, but I do not gratify them. I do not think I know a young man who spends so little on himself as I do.

With much love I remain,

Affectionately yours,

EDMUND W. GOSSE.

British Museum,
Nov. 21st, 1874.

MY OWN DARLING FATHER,—

You will like to hear my news. I have not much. I remain very anxious, but on the whole a little happier. Every time I go to Devonshire Street Nellie seems a little kinder, and more as though she were struggling against a tendency to like me. She has left off saying that it is on account of her art and her future that she will not marry, and now asserts that it is her duty to keep house for her brother, of whom she is intensely fond, and that she will never leave him. This seems distinct and peremptory enough but, somehow, her manner is less decisive than her words, and I am not forbidden to come and see her, though only once a week. It certainly will need tact and patience. So I must learn to try and exercise both. She has completely dropped the defiant manner she had at first, and is extremely gentle and shy, with sudden pert moments, from which last I hope great things. . . .

Write to me soon. With fondest love to Mother and yourself.

I am,

Your ever tenderly loving Son,

Edmund W. Gosse.

On December 2nd he announced his engagement.

The Library,
British Museum,
Dec. 2nd, 1874.

My dear Parents,—

I have only a minute's space to tell you that my own precious Nellie has suddenly capitulated and without terms! This morning a sweet letter, in answer to a pleading one of mine, comes confessing that she has loved me for some time, and has only held out because her relatives teased her with indiscreet advice.

I am overwhelmed with excitement and joy, and cannot write more now, but send you two *very* inadequate likenesses, one taken at Venice last year, the other in London in 1868, from which you can a little gather what she is—*not* like! Please return them instanter.

Excuse this incoherence, I am so off my head.

Goodbye, dearest Parents,

Your Loving Son,

Edmund W. Gosse.

Tottenham,
Dec. 12, 1874.

My own darling Father,—

Forgive, I beg you, my untimely impatience. I acknowledge fully that it was my own carelessness that caused the unfortunate delay. Now I am quite happy in the assurance of your loving sympathy. I copied out passages of your letter and sent the whole of Mother's to Nellie, knowing they would comfort her. Dear girl, she is so nice in all things, so ready to love everyone I love, so anxious to think of me in the future rather than herself, and so ready to give up all the luxuries of life for comparative poverty with me. "If you will let me fight *side by side* with you," she said the other day, "I shall be happy however hard the fight may be." I long to bring her to you; you will love her at once, she is so gentle, so tender, so womanly, and yet not in the least a fool, as sharp and bright as can be, with a coolness and clearness of judgment that surprises me often. She has not such a massive head (Tadema, who is for ever making studies of it, says it is the grandest he has even seen on an English woman) for nothing. You like to hear my praises of her, do you not? We are completely of one mind, as far as I have discovered yet. We are both on the look-out for subjects of disagreement, as Nellie thinks it will be best to get them over at once, but as yet we have not found any. But, really, I must not be so silly any more. Thank you very lovingly and earnestly, again and again, for your sweet, full words of parental affection. They come so solemnly from you that they sound to us like a benediction; we think they must be prophetic of our exceeding happiness through life. You will, I know, have comfort from the daughter I hope to bring you, and may God in His great mercy spare you many years to us and to the others who need you.

With regard to my hopes of promotion, I find they are very slight this time; it is said to be certain that Mr. Dorset Eccles, who has served the Trustees much longer than I have, and who is in every way eligible, will receive the appointment. And I feel I ought to say, I hope he will. At the same time, I have made the formal petitions to the three principal trustees, and Mr. Kingsley and my kind friend Mr. Kitchin of Oxford, have written, I believe, to the Archbishop. Perhaps on another occasion he may be graciously pleased. The alteration of salary would be £200 p.a. at once, rising £15 a year to £350, a slight but distinct bettering of my position.

Now farewell, and with tenderest love, believe me,

Ever your affectionate son,

EDMUND W. GOSSE.

Thank Mother very warmly for her dear letter.

Congratulations and presents from literary and artistic friends came in abundance. Austin Dobson sent him the works of Joannes Secundus; an odd choice for so decorous a poet and for so domestic an occasion. Nothing indeed could better illustrate the daring lengths to which innocency could lead the Victorians. It ranks with an episode narrated by Henry James of a luncheon party at Aldworth, when Mrs. Greville happened to mention one of her French relatives, Mlle. Laure de Sade. "De Sade?" exclaimed Tennyson with interest. And as James listened, wondering to what lengths the Laureate would go, Tennyson proceeded "to the very greatest length imaginable, as was signally promoted by the fact that clearly no one present, with a single exception, recognised the name or the nature of the scandalous, the long-ignored, the at last all but unnamable author." In such wise did "the conclusive note of the outright all unadorned" sometimes sound in Victorian circles.

Gosse's reply, there is evidence to show, was highly disconcerting to the sender of the volume.

Board of Trade, S.W.
Feb. 25, 1875.

MY DEAR DOBSON,—

How much too good you are! Thank you again and again for this little exquisite Joannes Secundus, and for your delicate verses worthy to be put in Joannes' own best Latin. But what a delicious little book! What an air of fantastic learning and fancy there is in it all! Thank you for introducing me to this delightful poet. From buxom Julia "sculptured by the hand of her own poet-Lover" down to the Manes that put him out of sight with such a full benediction of antiquity, all is characteristic and sweet. Those Propertian elegies, that would not for the world be thought Virgilian,

Per me Maeonides secura dormiet urna,

(Marry come up! what an opinion we have of ourselves) how truly renaissance and joyous and pagan they are, with their sweet sonorous compounds, "frontiserena Venus," "capripedes Sylvani," and the rest! And how the young Dutchman burns and flushes under the Spanish sun and the ladies' eyes in Toledo! And how passionate and tender we are when we are recalled by elegiac reverie "ad expellendum somnum puellae mecum cubanti," rapture that is carefully noted in our day-book "a Palentia—mense Septembri, 1533."

Just fancy that delicious sleep on the cool September morning of 1533, when Joannes puts his head in through the myrtles, and has to kiss several times, *lascivissime*, before *mea Domina* will deign to wake! Realise it, the dark-eyed rogue of a Spaniardess and our ardent Dutchman, just waked up, with those queer dreamy eyes of his, to the mingled magic of Propertius, perfume and *puella*. Is not respectability and school-boards and Sunday clothes a rather dull institution after this? Undoubtedly it was very nice *a Palentia* in September 1533.

Then there is J. S.'s *Basia*, *Liber singularis*. Very singular book surely, how naïve and passionate! I pinch myself to try and recollect Joannes Secundus, but certainly I never heard of him before:—

Alas for him who climbs
Where the Pierids string
The lyre of silver chimes,

for what do I see in front of these same *basia*, but the oracular statement of Hadrianus Junius Hornanus (what names we have in Holland), that J. S.'s *Basia* will be remembered as long as lovers know how to part their lips in kissing. Subtle person this Hornanus, and knowing in the art of love. How fine an oath and how miserably perjured, since J. S.'s *Basia* are not frequently read, I fear.

What sweet kisses they are! Beginning for propriety's sake with Venus and Ascanius, but gradually passing into mysteries, and soon taking us too much into confidence. Julia read no Latin, I take it, else what punishment there would have been for

Componensque meis labella labris
Et morsu petis et gemis remorsa
Et linguam tremulam hinc et inde vibras
Et linguam querulam hinc et inde sugis.

They seem to me so old and forgotten and pathetic, these poems. They seem older by whole ages than the classic elegies they imitate.

Thank you, dear poet, for this exquisite gift.

EDMUND W. GOSSE.

Financial anxieties were to some extent set at rest or at any rate diminished by the offer of better-paid work. In 1875 a translator was required at the Board of Trade. Mr. Farrer, then Permanent Secretary, wished to instal his family governess in the position—but the duties involved an acquaintance with Scandinavian languages, and in these the governess was deficient. The choice fell on Gosse. The vacancy had arisen owing to the death of the previous occupant of the post, a Hungarian. Taken ill, he had been nursed by Simmons, a messenger in the Board of Trade. Simmons thought his ministrations required the daily ablution of his patient—a treatment to which the Hungarian was so unaccustomed that he forthwith expired. In later years his colleagues delighted in reminding Gosse that he owed his success in life to Simmons the messenger. The pay was to be £400 per annum, and the duties not so exacting as to prevent him from pursuing his literary career, just as George Cosmo Monkhouse, Austin Dobson and Samuel Waddington were doing in the same office. On August 4th he wrote to inform his father of the offer.

26, Alfred Place,
August 4th, 1875.

My darling Father,—

A startling offer has been made me.

A middle-aged gentleman called on me at the B.M. to-day, a Mr. H. R. Lack, a first-class clerk in the Board of Trade. He at once made known his mission. He came from the President to offer me the post of Translator to the Board of Trade. The salary £400 a year, fixed—that is to say without rise. The appointment one for life. The rate of superannuation certain, and perhaps higher than that of an ordinary civil servant. Hours 11 to 5. I should be quite independent of others, my own master, a room to myself, and no great pressure of work. I objected the few languages I knew. Mr. Lack replied that the Scandinavian languages were very difficult to secure, and that it was my known knowledge of them that had recommended me to the Board. I objected I did not know Spanish, Portuguese, etc. Those, he said, you can easily get up when you are with us. There is no examination to go through. No exception will be taken to my literary work, which indeed is what has brought this fish to my net in the last instance.

Of course I did not accept on the spot, but I must decide directly. There seems no doubt that the post is an eligible one, and I go down to-morrow to make final enquiries. My prospects at the Museum are absolutely nil, and even if the heavens were to break open and I be promoted to-morrow, it would be ten years before I could get the Assistants' maximum of £360.

There is not one serious point in which the offered appointment does not promise well.

Write and "opinion" me.

Your most loving son,
EDMUND W. GOSSE.

He was to work under Mr. Alfred Bateman (the late Sir Alfred Bateman). By this change in his occupation his salary was at once doubled, his marriage was made possible, and he secured greater leisure for writing. No moment can have stood out for Gosse so charged with bright promises. He had wooed and won, his literary fame was established, friends clamoured for his company, and he was in no common degree framed to enjoy life. Behind a certain gay flippancy of outlook, and an easy wit equally ready for attack or defence, lay a deep seriousness of purpose. As a writer he had both speed and power, airiness and gravity—he knew himself to be exceptionally endowed for the pursuit of literature, nor had he any apparent reason to doubt his ability as a translator for the Board of Trade. But there he was wrong. Thrown among Charter-parties and Bills of Lading, expressed with all their technicalities in the Scandinavian languages, he was soon floundering and at sea. His efforts called forth the gibe, "Ah now, if only Mr. Farrer's governess had been here, how different it would have been!" Mr. Farrer himself appears to have taken a dislike to his new assistant, and declared later on that there were two names that should be spelt with a small "G," God and Gosse. But Farrer habitually looked with disfavour on writers. He once referred in a speech before the London County Council to "certain civil servants who would have been excellent administrators, if they had not been indifferent poets." It was not till Mr. Joseph Chamberlain, as President, took over the Board of Trade in 1880 that Gosse was appreciated by his chief and allowed to extend his literary fame by lecturing in his holidays. Meanwhile under the protection of Sir Alfred Bateman, Gosse with inward rejoicing settled to the work which was to keep him in the Civil Service for twenty-nine years.

In August he was married. On the eve of his marriage he writes:

26, Alfred Place,
Aug. 12, 1875.
9 p.m.

MY DARLING FATHER,—

It seems very, very strange to be sitting in the midst of my half-packed Penates, on the night before my marriage, writing my last letter to you before you have not one child but two. I cannot realize that the moment is so near; time seems so awfully rapid at such serious moments as these. I say so, not meaning that there is anything in my case that makes me dread the future, but only that at such a time as this one longs to review the past and dream of the future more seriously than one has time to do. Yet I wish you could know how quiet, how content, how confident I feel. Nellie's nature is one that soothes, sustains and perfects mine in a manner indescribable. The complete—sometimes too complete forgetfulness of self, the deep and devoted affectionateness (beyond passion) of nature, the sterling good sense and capacity of her mind, always so clear and practical—I am not speaking the foolish language of lovers when I say these adorn her every day and give me promise in her of a wife in a million. I could spend the night in praising her whom you will yourself soon learn to love and to esteem.

I turn to the other great crisis of my life. Sir Charles Adderley signed my appointment yesterday afternoon. I am to enter the Board of Trade on the 24th inst. but I am to have 6 weeks' holidays this year, and shall take a month now. I shall, therefore, hope to be at Whitehall on the 23rd of September, when I shall pocket my first month's salary of £33 for doing nothing! I had a most formidable competitor in a very learned Dutchman, but from Mr. Bullen, and others, the head of the B. of T., Mr. Farrer, received such high testimonials of me that he recommended me at once. Everyone was surprised at the rapidity with which the appointment was made.

The head of the department in which I shall be, Mr. Lack, seems to be a most genial and gentlemanly man, and, under him and Mr. Farrer, I shall be quite my own master. The head of another department is Mr. Austin Dobson, the poet, one of my staunchest literary admirers, so I enter under flying colours.

Uncle George and Miss Buckham have accepted the invitation for tomorrow. Aunt Lizzie and Miss Baker could not come. Aunt Lizzie has sent Nellie a handsome gold bracelet. So many gifts have come to us, so many friends have overwhelmed us with kind words.

I shall feel your prayers and thoughts tomorrow sustaining, calming and solemnizing me. We will send you a telegram from Salisbury.

Thank you for all your dear, precious letters, and for the blessing that they give us, which we deeply and truly value.

Your deeply loving son,

E. W. G.

Gosse's marriage had a soothing influence on his father; it seems to have induced a state of spiritual quiescence. Henceforward in their correspondence little more is heard of the "pit of hell," and the immediate advent of the Lord. Warnings ceased from troubling, and natural affections were no longer distorted by religious misunderstandings. Echoes of the stormy stage of *Father and Son* grew fainter and finally died away.

On September 25th Gosse writes from his new office, and for the first time betrays how heavily the discipline of the British Museum had lain upon his spirit.

Sept. 25th, 1875.

My darling Father,—

I have a comfortable room to myself, looking over Scotland Yard to Charing Cross Station and St. Paul's in the distance. Here with the foreign gazettes round me, I lounge back in a delightful armchair, nobody interferes with me, there is just a murmur of London through the open window, but that is all. This room, however, is not to be my ultimate habitat; certain changes are being made, and after that I am to have a delightfully cosy room upstairs, with an outlook over the river, a fireplace, bookshelves, and everything wanted to make a study comfortable. I shall be in clover indeed. The extraordinary change from the unpleasant severity, the official discourtesy, the irritating surveillance of the B. M. is astonishing. I feel that here there will be a stimulus given to one's sense of honour and duty by the very courtesy and laxity of discipline. It is surely a gross mistake to treat grown-up persons of mature habits as a set of convicts, or, at least, of naughty schoolboys. But enough of the British Museum and its disagreeables.

Goodbye,

Your loving son,

EDMUND W. GOSSE.

P.S.—I have just been supplied with stationery enough of all sorts, for my private use, to satisfy a popular M.P.!

Gosse had now left his work at the British Museum, but while it lasted it had provided material for one of his best-known volumes, *Portraits and Sketches*. It was at the British Museum that he first saw Swinburne, though as we have seen the poet was at the moment in a state of unconsciousness. With Tennyson Gosse was more fortunate. In 1871 when seated in the Den, "the singularly horrible underground cage, made of steel bars," where much of the business of cataloguing was done, he was startled by receiving a whispered summons to "come upstairs at once and be presented to Tennyson." "The feeling of excitement," Gosse wrote in *Portraits and Sketches*, and the account is so characteristic of the epoch and of the writer himself that it is quoted at length, "was almost overwhelming: it was not peculiar to myself: such ardours were common in those years. Some day a philosopher must analyse it—that enthusiasm of the 'seventies, that intoxicating belief in the might of poesy. Tennyson was scarcely a human being to us, he was the God of the Golden Bow: I approached him now like a blank idiot about to be slain, 'or was I a worm too low-crawling for death, O Delphic Apollo?' . . . When I had been presented and shaken his hand, he continued to consider me in a silence which would have been deeply disconcerting if he had not, somehow, seemed kindly, and even, absurd as it sounds, rather shy. The ice was finally broken by the mention of Norway, which Tennyson had visited, and from this the Laureate passed to 'my stammering verses' about which he was 'Vaguely Gracious.' He seemed to accept me as a sheep in the fold of which he was, so magnificently, the shepherd. This completed my undoing, but he did not demand from me speech." Then a remark from Tennyson about the sculpture in the gallery where the introduction took place, and "the gates of heaven were closed and I went down three flights of stairs to my hell of rotten morocco." Gosse is probably right when he says, "proud young spirits of the present day, for whom life opens in adulation, will find it scarcely possible to realise what such a summons meant to me." But in late life he did not regret the evaporation of the enthusiasms of the 'seventies: he impartially recorded them, as a naturalist might an extinct species. In practice he welcomed rather than otherwise the easy approach and the confiding air of "the proud young spirits," and if now and then he allowed himself a gibe at them or an expression of bewilderment, it was in perfect good nature and in no spirit of censoriousness.

It was also at this time that he was brought into touch with Robert Browning and "Orion" Horne at the wedding of O'Shaughnessy. In the early part of 1873 an unlooked-for mystification had fallen on the "nest of singing birds." Gosse had descended on a January day to the bald home of icthyology for a chat with his fellow poet. He found O'Shaughnessy with his head upon his arms folded upon his table. "He raised his face to me," Gosse writes, "in tears, and when I enquired what was the matter he replied by a question, 'Have you not seen the paper? Lord Lytton is dead.' When I hinted my surprise at his emotion he added: 'No one will ever know what he was to me.'" Gosse enquired no further. In June of the same year O'Shaughnessy was married. Marzials and Gosse acted as groomsmen: "All the minor English poets now living, that are recognised, were guests." They were addressed by

Robert Browning, and then there entered "Orion" Horne, a tiny old gentleman who "all uninvited began to sit upon the floor and sing, in a funny little cracked voice, Spanish songs to his own accompaniment on the guitar." The guests grew restless and impatient, but Browning, throwing a protecting arm over the guitarist, exclaimed: "That was charming, Horne! It quite took us to the warm South," and tactfully put an end to the incident. These were casual encounters leading to closer acquaintance, but wholly different in their significance from the chance that brought Gosse in the way of his next new friend.

Early in 1874 he met for the first time Austin Dobson, who in 1873 had published his "Vignettes in Rhyme." In "An Appreciation," printed by Mr. Alban Dobson in his volume, *Austin Dobson, Some Notes,* Gosse has described the circumstances of the meeting so eventful for the two writers. It took place at the house of Mr. Peter Taylor, M.P. for Leicester, whose wife had inaugurated a Pen and Pencil Club to which authors and artists came to read or display their respective contributions. The club evenings were subject to sharp fluctuations in the level of the amusement provided. On the April evening when Gosse, newly admitted to the circle, was present, some dreary readings had led up to the recital by Austin Dobson of a piece which Gosse at once recognised as a "rondeau in the French form elaborately defined by Théodore de Banville in the 1874 reprint of his *Petit Traité de la Poésie Française.*" When the party broke up, Gosse approached the author of the piece, and shyly observed that he noticed that in the verses recited Banville's rules had been followed. They wandered into the night together, and it was only after several hours, passed "in a kind of dream" and absorbed by metrical discussions, that they parted.

It was the beginning of a friendship which lasted forty-eight years, and remained unclouded from the first day to the last. Candid criticism of each other's work passed between them. Disapproval was often expressed, but only where the standard which each had set for the other had not been maintained. Both were devout literary craftsmen, but Dobson had the temperament and all the faculties of the scholar. If he said that Peg Woffington went to Bath on a Tuesday, or that it was Silas Todd who figured in Hogarth's *The*

Idle Prentice executed at Tyburn, none ever ventured to controvert the statement. Gosse, on the other hand, though he had a love of minute accuracy, was too easily excited and too impatient to attain it. He admired and envied his friend's impeccable reliability, and Dobson in his turn appreciated Gosse's illuminating arrangement and interpretation of facts. Again, while Dobson was perfectly content to spend his life in methodical oscillation between a modest office and a quiet suburban home, Gosse's impetuous curiosity, and a certain competitive strain in his nature, ever impelled him to plunge into society and mingle even in the imbroglios of others. Both happily set a very high value on friendship, and it was Gosse's nature to have many friends and many contacts. It is interesting to note that the first two letters he wrote to his friend —by the by a man ten years older than himself—are those of one from whom his correspondent expects advice about practical affairs.

Though for many years the two men occupied in the world of letters positions which brought them into rivalry, each delighted in the successes of the other. They were free from jealousy. They turned to each other in doubt: their relation never varied in its warmth. Dobson has commemorated their association in one of his most characteristic and beautiful poems, written in 1893:

For they had worked together,—been comrades of the Pen;
They had their points at issue, they differed now and then;
But both loved Song and Letters, and each had close at heart
The hopes, the aspirations, the "dear delays" of Art.

They knew not, nor cared greatly, if they were spark or star;
They knew to move is somewhat, although the goal be far;
And larger light or lesser, this thing at least is clear,
They served the Muses truly,—their service was sincere.

And yet they had their office. Though they today are passed,
They marched in that profession where is no first or last;
Though cold is now their hoping, though they no more aspire,
They too had once their ardour—they handed on the fire.

The following is the first letter in a correspondence which failed to be daily only by reason of the two writers meeting so frequently.

British Museum,
Aug. 26th, 1874.

MY DEAR MR. DOBSON,—

I know Mr. Allingham tolerably well, and my experience of him is somewhat out of keeping with his reputation. He is considered cold and unsympathetic; I must say he was the very first person (outside the circle of friends) that saw any merit in my work. My first published article appeared in *Fraser*, and since then the Magazine has always been open to me. At the same time I have never sent poetry to him, and unless he distinctly asked it of me I never should. For in all probability the poetry of younger men is the thing of all others he can least bear. You must remember he is himself one of those who have never reached their Holy Land, but whose bones are strewn in the desert. Naturally the grapes are very sour on the clusters of Eshcol.

Also it is fair I should tell you that I understood that poetry is not paid for in *Fraser*. I heard of a man who insisted on being paid, and who after a great deal of disagreeable correspondence got—7s. 6d. for his pains.

Whether Allingham has yet become editor I do not know.

With your rapidly widening and deepening reputation you ought to have no difficulty in getting your poems printed anywhere. Have you tried *Macmillan's Magazine*? The editor, Mr. Grove, has the reputation of being a genial and sympathetic man. Then there is the *Cornhill*, with Leslie Stephen for editor, for which I have just begun to write (in the Sept. no. on the Danish Theatre) and which pays splendidly.

For a pair of poets we are sufficiently mercantile, are we not? Well, our great progenitor and prototype, Shakespeare, drove an exceedingly hard bargain now and then.

Ever yours truly,
EDMUND W. GOSSE.

The Library,
British Museum,
Oct. 11th, 1874.

DEAR MR. DOBSON,—

You wrote to me that you were wishing to print in some Magazine. Of course a magazine and a weekly newspaper are totally different things. Yet I venture to plead with you for a poem for us in the *Examiner*. The editor, Mr. Minto (who by the way would extremely value your personal acquaintance, and is an admirer of your *Vignettes*), has set me to cater for good poetry. But it has to be done cautiously. Between ourselves, there are a good many, especially of the people who have appeared since Rossetti, whom neither he nor I would choose for a moment to appear in the *Examiner*. In fact, since Minto took the editorship, two sonnets of mine and a little piece by Marzials are all the verses that have appeared. But my friend Mr. Swinburne has promised us a poem, and I hope we shall have one also from Mr. W. B. Scott. But nothing would be more welcome than one of your charming blendings of fun and poetical fancy. It is hardly needful to say that the *Examiner* cannot pay highly, but it pays twice as well for verse as *Fraser* does!

If you feel inclined to indulge us, will you send me something to see whether it will suit?

And believe me to be,

Yours very truly,
EDMUND W. GOSSE.

CHAPTER SEVEN

In February 1875 Gosse took part in an eclectic festival organised by Swinburne to commemorate the centenary of the birth of Walter Savage Landor and the birthday of Charles Lamb, "a Passover feast in honour of a Lamb quite other than Paschal"—as Swinburne designated the occasion. Gosse had reminded Swinburne of the centenary, Swinburne had remembered the birthday. William Minto, Thomas Purnell, Theodore Watts and Gosse met with Swinburne in the chair, a chair so large that his slight form was lost in its recesses. The dinner was made memorable to Gosse at any rate by the careless rapture with which Swinburne had ordered the festivity—and by the expense. In money matters Gosse was exceedingly careful without being parsimonious. He liked spending up to the edge of his means, above all on his friends; but there was no expenditure so minute that he did not record it—even to a sum of 2d. contributed to an offertory in a continental church. He threw off his early training in religious matters, but not in that careful handling of money which necessity imposed on him in boyhood and youth. Inoffensively and unostentatiously meticulous, he had no trace of the alienating obsession known in latter-day language as a money-complex. His great friend Sir Alfred Bateman had more than once to assist him when ways and means were a constant problem, but interest and capital were invariably paid the moment they were due. He recorded in small diaries every penny he spent and earned from 1879 onwards. He was method incarnate. He also kept a ledger in which he entered every guest entertained from the date of his marriage to the last year of his life.

Nothing could look more arid than this ledger with its names and records of social occasions. But like the lists of the occupants of his father's aquaria, every item represents lively anxieties, interested classifications and finally tumultuous enjoyment of the results. Once his agitations were laid aside, Gosse was an admirable host, full of drive and sparkle, courteous, and stimulating laughter, lightness, and levity in his guests.

On their return to London the Gosses lived for a time at Townshend House, the home of the Tademas, moving thence early in 1876 to 29, Delamere Terrace. In their new home Mrs. Gosse's artistic tendencies blended agreeably with the less æsthetic preferences of her husband. The defection from Victorian standards was announced by Morris decorations, and less positively by the monastic simplicity of Gosse's study. The "ledger" now becomes a useful indicator; every phase of literary and artistic culture is represented by some name in it. Swinburne, Andrew Lang, Thornycroft, Onslow Ford, Alfred Parsons, MacColl, Abbey, Comyns Carr, Herkomer, W. D. Howells, Mrs. Humphry Ward, Sidney Colvin, Robert Browning, Marzials—even Churton Collins, so soon to be his severest critic and to threaten his self-confidence—appear constantly among his guests. As time goes on the character of the lists tends to alter: Culture is less prominent, Mayfair intrudes.

He was at this time (1875), as indeed he always continued to be when circumstances allowed, seeing much of Swinburne, who by now had already published besides his poems a monograph on Auguste Vacquerie, *Essays and Studies,* and a pamphlet, *The Devil's Due,* directed against Robert Buchanan. Early in the year, at the request of Georg Brandes, Gosse wrote a critical essay on Swinburne and his poetry. It was translated into Swedish, Danish, German, and Dutch, and was by far the most comprehensive and enlightened estimate that had yet appeared. In 1925 he consented to the essay being privately reprinted by Mr. Norman Gullick, stating in a preface that the only value of the critical sections was "that they reflect the views held in the innermost circle of the poet's intimates half a century ago." Like all he wrote, it is extremely readable. It is a balanced judgment, and for a foreign audience it rang up the curtain on one of the most spectacular figures of contemporary literature; no better introduction to a study of Swinburne's writings could be desired. Gosse did not allow himself to be deflected by the temptation to flatter an eminent living writer or by the even more insidious enticement of showing an obtrusive independence. It is the work of a mature and scholarly critic, widely-read, sensitive, and intimately aware of the excellences and imperfections of Swinburne's genius. In noting the excessive length and the want of concentration in much that Swinburne wrote he anticipated the damaging criticism of later days.

It must, however, have horrified his father to read that in the opinion of his son *Hertha* proclaimed "a pantheism which is at least as comprehensive and reasonable a creed as any other now presented to the human faculty of faith." Of the essay itself and the difficulty he felt in writing it Gosse wrote to Dobson:

"I have been twice to see you, but in vain, and I really cannot venture again into the jaws of the grizzly person who supplants you, and who reminds me of that objectionable Pharaoh who knew not Joseph. I find it excessively difficult to speak about one English poet, and him a living one, to an audience who presumably know nothing of our contemporary literature. It is like learning a language which is not Aryan, one has no roots to help one. It is quite odd—in my own mind I had never decided which of S.'s *Poems and Ballads* were the most important. For this work of course I had to make a little analysis. Accordingly I took the index straight on and marked the poems 1, 2, 3, 4, as I felt them to belong to a high or a low order. It may be my prejudice, but when I came to count up, I found I had only admitted seven to the first class, viz.: *The Triumph of Time, Itylus, Hymn to Proserpine, In Mem. W. S. Landor, Dolores, Garden of Proserpine,* and *Sapphics.* Of these, five do not deal with love at all, and only one, *Dolores,* with the scratching and biting sentiment. Hence it seems as though one would have accepted without murmur one supreme utterance of this frantic kind, but only one, and that the book would have had a quite different and much lovelier character if the rest of the frantic cries had been omitted. Am I right? How divine *Sapphics* is! The very crown and top of all this poet's attainment, I think."

To Swinburne he wrote:

"All these autumn months I have been very much in your spiritual presence, for I have only just finished and sent out the longest piece of prose I have ever written, a study on your works in prose and verse, for Dr. Brandes' magazine. I think on the whole it is tolerably well done. It is loving as becomes your faithful henchman, but at the same time aiming more at analysis and criticism than at laudation. Your achievements are so positive that one is able to treat you already as a classic. I hope this paper, which will probably appear simultaneously in German at Berlin, will do a great deal towards enlightening the Teutons. Of course you know that Ludwig, King of Bavaria, is a great admirer of yours, and that *Chastelard* has been translated at his command?

"Soon I hope to send you my drama. Chatto has taken it from me on very liberal terms, and is bringing it out at once.

"Watts tells me brilliant things of your *Erectheus*, and I am longing to see it. How busy you seem to be. *Vacquerie* is the last thing of yours I have seen, for the epigram in this week's *Examiner* is, surely, one of our old friend Carlyle's property?"

Erectheus was published in the first days of 1876. One critic spoke of the play as "a translation from Euripides"; he could not have found a statement further from the truth or better calculated to exasperate the author. On January 2nd, Swinburne, writing to a friend, said: "I always have maintained it is far easier to overtop Euripides by the head and shoulder than to come up to the waist of Sophocles or the knee of Æschylus."* Swinburne's antipathy to Euripides was well known to his friends, and Gosse in writing to him on January 5th was able to soothe some of the wounds made by ill-informed criticism.

"Your delightful letter made me half glad, half sorry that I had already sent to press a review of *Erectheus*, half glad because I had said several things plainly which you complain have been left unsaid by your other reviewers, half sorry because I should have been glad to steal a few thoughts from your letter to enrich my article. I fear you will find the latter rather dry and bald, but I hope you will confess that it does justice to the spirit and aim of your poem, in however inadequate language. That *Erectheus* is not only un-Euripidean but absolutely anti-Euripidean was the first fact patent to me in reading the opening speech; nor can I understand anyone capable of a rudimentary judgment unable to see so much. Your anger against the unfortunate Euripides I cannot wholly share. When I read Greek at school and had, of course,

* *Algernon Charles Swinburne.* Edmund Gosse, p. 231.

only the crudest canons to guide my judgment, I gained a fondness for him which I have never been able to throw off; I confess to a kind of sneaking kindness for Euripides, for which I know you will have no pity. I had never read the fragments till your book was ready, and then I went down to the British Museum, and spent a couple of hours in reading them. I liked the speech put in the mouth of Praxithea considerably; it seemed to me dignified and pathetic, and not at all sophistical; at the same time, of course, not at all poetical. I cannot bring myself to compare work so thoroughly distinct as his and yours. But you must forgive me for presuming to discuss the subject with one so far my superior in knowledge as yourself.

"You please me very much by the value you set on my opinion in poetic matters. Your commendation is more to me than the praise of twenty reviewers, since I owe so much to your public and personal training, and hold you in special honour as my first and I think only master in the first elements of poetic scholarship. Did you see that the *Contemporary Review*, that Castle Dangerous of clerical libel, accused me the other day, deftly turning some stray words of mine, of having betrayed the cause in attacking you? Mr. Gosse has at last found a *locus pœnitentiæ*! I should have hoped that the most priestly ingenuity could not have claimed for me a shelter among the penitents, a returned prodigal wept over by Peter Bayne!"

The letter of January 9th, 1876, which follows, contains a judgment of Newman's surprising to those familiar with *Viol and Flute*. The "amorousness" of that volume is so mild, so discreet and so restrained that its mixture with religion might have escaped the most sensitive moralist. No one, however, will regret the action of the "friendly but indiscreet person" who sent *Viol and Flute* to the Cardinal.

My dear Swinburne,—

Reading your brilliant and trenchant characterisation of Newman and Carlyle in Yesterday's *Athenæum* has brought to my mind a letter I have from the former to one of the Wilber-forces, passages of which may interest you a little. The friendly but indiscreet person referred to, desiring to reconcile me to the Church and the Church to me, sent my *On Viol and Flute* to Newman without my knowledge, and in process of time had a reply. In the beginning Newman deprecated the fact that he was "likely to write in a fashion which to those who live in the world may seem severe," on the grounds of his sincere conviction that he was right, and then went on to say: "I do not know familiarly the poets of this day, but I do know those of my own youth. Those poets were accustomed to write in a style which, so far from hurting, would benefit their readers." He went on to enumerate these, and named all except Shelley and Keats, including Byron and Moore, "for though they both wrote immoral works, yet it was definite volumes which incurred that disgrace, and one might put them aside, yet read with interest and pleasure the other works of their authors. There are one or two sceptical stanzas in *Childe Harold*, but they are accidental. As far as I can make out from reviews, etc., the case is quite different as regards Swinburne and Rossetti, their poems are soaked in an ethical quality, whatever it is to be called, which would have made it impossible in the last generation for a brother to read them to a sister." So far there is nothing said very remarkable, but he goes on to say that those poets "who are not Catholics, may be quite in good faith in thinking there is no objectionable quality in their poems, because Protestants do not understand, as Catholics do, that not only grave sins of impurity are wrong, but that every thing which savours of or tends towards impurity is wrong too." After some gilding of the bitter pill as regards me personally, he goes on to say that there must be "no mixing up of amorousness with religion, since they are two such very irreconcilable elements." It has struck me that these utterances form a not uninteresting commentary on the text of your beautiful sonnets.

I have told my publishers to send you down a copy of my tragedy as soon as ever it is ready, and I hope you will not be too busy to read it and let me know if it pleases you.

Affectionately yours,

EDMUND W. GOSSE.

On January 15th Gosse makes further comment on Newman's criticisms, and introduces a reference to F. G. Fleay, whose paper on *Metrical Tests as applied to Dramatic Poetry*, published in the first number of *Transactions* of the "New Shakspere Society," had stirred Swinburne to denounce the application of mechanical rules in estimating Shakespeare's work. This was only the opening phase of a controversy between Swinburne and the Society which culminated in a quarrel between the Poet and F. J. Furnivall, the Society's President. The Poet and the President attacked each other with the temper of high-spirited and infuriated schoolboys. The controversy was accompanied by a to-and-fro of vituperation such as Swinburne delighted in, and when Furnivall spoke of Swinburne as "Pigsbrook" and Swinburne retorted with the equally lamentable travesty of "Brothelsdyke," it was clear that the feud had gone about as far as abuse could carry it. Gosse regarded Furnivall as the aggressor, but however that may be, the last and loudest word was, as might be expected, with Swinburne.

Jan. 15, 1876.

My dear Swinburne,—

Do imagine yourself great Ben and me Randolph or Cartwright, and send me those two or three precious commendatory verses that fashion and New Grub Street deny me! I will keep them among my treasures in some Holy of Holies. Be sure you do. Thank you much for your most encouraging and delightful acknowledgment of the book; I care for nothing now I have your sign manual of approval.

It is funny, is it not, that Newman could dare to call amorousness and Catholic religion irreconcilable? From those earliest times when the worship of the physical beauty of Jesus reached such a pitch in Africa that there had to be a special dogma published from the Patriarchate to the effect that Jesus "had no beauty that we should desire him, but was marred more than any man," down to the coquettish hymns of the early Moravians, singing to Jesus as Bathyllus might to Anacreon, the Christian Church has reconciled amorousness and devotion in its celibate sects as much in practice as those you cite have done in writing. Strange that so good and so noble a man as J. H. N. can lend himself to this or any of their soul-quenching paradoxes.

By the way, I must congratulate you on being "one of the sons of God!" You are quite overwhelmed just now with inconvenient compliment and courteous impertinence! I was much amused with your trenchant discussion of Furnivall and your airy anatomy of *Flea.* You know that is what I prophesied from the beginning, that one of these days you would be obliged "to go forth and hunt the *Flea* upon the mountains."

I did not guess that all your reviewers, great or small, would torment you with the "noble fragments" or "droppings," or I would have been original, and said nothing about them.

Very affectly yours,

EDMUND W. GOSSE.

The "book" referred to by Gosse in this letter is *King Erik,* a drama which he published in January. As might be expected, Gosse turned to Scandinavia for his theme, and in the story of a Danish King of the twelfth century found a subject for his one attempt at Tragedy. It is a play that few are now likely to read and none certainly to act. It is not without situations, but just where we should expect the drama to be gathered up in concentrated emotion, it is impoverished by the suavity and elegance of the verse. It runs on an even keel, without adequate contrast of storm and calm, and without sufficient variation of method. Each character expresses his function in the plot rather than a natural response to tragic occurrences. Words are never blown to a sudden flame; the lines fly light across the stage. Gosse, having started his players, watches and controls them from behind the curtain. He is with us talking through his characters in easy and accomplished verse, touching the strings of a melodious harp, but never hurling the javelin. Yet the play is clearly the work of a poet, and contains charming lyrics.

(93)

Autumn closes
Round the roses,
Shatters, strips them, head by head;
Winter passes,
O'er the grasses,
Turns them yellow, brown and red;
Can a lover
E'er recover
When his summer love is dead?
Yet the swallow
Turns to follow
In the northward wake of spring,
To refashion
Wasted passion
With a sweep of his dark wing,
As returning
Love flies burning
To the stricken lips that sing!

CHAPTER EIGHT

THE hopes and frustrations of the next three years are chronicled in Gosse's letters. Each year was consolidating his position as a critic, and it is of interest to note how much he was making by writing:—(1874) £112 2s. 11d.; (1875), £187 9s. 10d.; (1876), £162 6s.; (1877), £165 4s. 9d.; (1878), £244 17s. 10d.; (1879), £268 19s. 10d.

In 1879 he was writing for the *Academy*, *Athenæum*, *Saturday Review*, *Encyclopædia Britannica*, *Examiner*, and various magazines.

This decade in which he was making a name was the high watermark of Victorian criticism. It was certainly a decade of pontifical utterances. The reverberations of the *Origin of Species* were still alive. They had affected and could be traced in every branch of thought, even literary criticism. The established critics in a spirit of exalted seriousness were on the look-out for moral and philosophical significance: their main preoccupations were the origin and intention of the created work, which they usually approached from a metaphysical standpoint. They were earnest and profound, seers and preachers addressing the public from the rock of St. Peter, but while in the 'seventies their fine solemnity and moral elevation were reaching maturity there was growing up a younger and less virile school of writers to whom the apparatus of the older criticism appeared cumbersome and unduly instructive. The criticism which touches lightly through the medium of analogy and allusion, which gossips and becomes confidential, and aims at accelerating enjoyment, was beginning, and Gosse was already one of its accredited spokesmen. The band of writers to which he belonged sought to please and charm by their style, to "gossip in a library," or give the reader "Silhouettes," "Kit-Kats" and "Profiles" rather than the body and deeper substance of their authors. It will be seen that in his letters through these years Gosse never mentions Hutton, Stopford Brooke, the criticism of Matthew Arnold or the essays of Leslie Stephen; he is entirely taken up with the work of his younger contemporaries and his own productions; yet it was the 'seventies which saw *Essays Theological and Literary* by Hutton, *Theology in the English Poets* by Stopford Brooke, *Hours in a Library* by Leslie Stephen, *Literature and Dogma* and *Last Essays on Church and Religion* by Matthew Arnold.

It was beginning to be recognised that criticism of contemporaries was immensely more readable if the critic wrote with first-hand knowledge of his author, if he had stood himself within the temple and could register his observation of the occasion. Gosse was perfectly well aware of his own gift for recording personal impressions and painting in literary terms those whom he saw, and he made it a point that those whom he saw should be those most worth seeing. In this his policy, whether in London or Scandinavia or elsewhere, was deliberate and consistent.

Robert Browning, living at 19, Warwick Crescent, was a near neighbour of Gosse's at this time; both their houses faced the Regent's Park Canal, and Browning used to differentiate their respective aspects by regarding his own as Venetian and Gosse's as Dutch. Browning, with the publication in 1869 of the last volume of *The Ring and the Book*, had touched the summit of his fame. At the beginning of 1875 *Aristophanes' Apology* was passing through the press. In a later letter Gosse wrote to Browning for data for an article he was preparing, and in the course of his letter said, "you know my unfeigned reverence for you, other people may have other gods, you have been to me—ever since I came to years of discretion—the greatest English poet of the age, and I see less reason for changing my view every year I live." Such incense was not burnt in vain; the data were supplied, and resulted in an article in the *Century Magazine* for December 1881.* In 1875 Gosse in the same spirit of pious enthusiasm sought leave to dedicate to Browning his drama *King Erik*. Permission was given, and the fervid verses which precede the play were the result. In a spirit of reciprocity Browning supported Gosse's candidature for the Clark lectureship in 1883 when Leslie Stephen was appointed, and in 1884 backed Gosse's petition to be transferred from the Board of Trade to the British Museum Library.

* Republished in 1890 under the title of *Robert Browning, Personalia,* together with Browning's letter of acknowledgment.

The Library,
British Museum,

To Robert Browning. *Jan. 22, 1875.*

Dear Sir,—

Just a year ago, in a letter which I keep among my best relics, you were good enough to say, after reading *On Viol and Flute*, that you hoped very soon to—well! I scarcely venture to repeat your kind words. I have been working for months past, as steadily as a great deal of prosier literary work would permit me to do, on a tragedy or tragical chronicle on a very romantic story which I found in the *Knythingasaga*, of a Danish King Erik, who, after ruling his people wisely for a time, fell into one deadly sin, and journeyed to Jerusalem to expiate it, but died of a broken heart upon the way,* and was buried in the Valley of Jehoshaphat. I have almost finished my poem, but before I send it to press, I must confess to you the hope I have had from the first, that I might be allowed to write on its first leaf the name which I reverence as the highest of living names. In other words, if my drama has any dedication at all, it must bear, in all the simplicity of genuine homage, the words: To Robert Browning. Will you tell me if I may presume to write this?

Pray believe me to be,

Dear Sir,

Yours very faithfully,

Edmund W. Gosse.

Robert Browning, Esq.

Board of Trade,
S.W.

To Austin Dobson. *February 21, 1877.*

My dear Dobson,—

It has been weighing upon me that I did not at all adequately express to you my thanks at your note on me in your book, or the pleasure and pride I feel in being associated with work so

* In the drama this idea was altered.

admirable and destined, as I thoroughly believe, to be so famous. I assure you I am very pleased indeed.

In reference to certain curious coincidences of correspondence lately I have been inspired with a triolet. Be'old!

Four old women weave æsthetics,
  Toss the web across, across;
Shuttling with a golden tettix,
Four old women weave æsthetics,
Bastard prose in pseud' poetics,
  Symonds, Pater, Dowden, Gosse,
Four old women, weave æsthetics,
  Toss the web across, across.

Damned savage style, isn't it? Worthy of *London*!

Yours always affectionately,

EDMUND W. GOSSE.

The scheme referred to in the letter of June 14th to Swinburne came to nothing; but that Swinburne should have chosen Gosse as a co-partner in such an undertaking argues complete confidence in Gosse as a critic. The view is further confirmed by a letter of July 5th.

Shall we consult Watts? *29, Delamere Terrace,*
To Algernon Swinburne. *June 14, '77.*

MY DEAR SWINBURNE,—

I am delighted with the proposition. Nothing is more needed, and in sympathetic and accurate hands nothing would be more useful. Let us start it at once.

You know, I daresay, "The Companion to the Playhouse," 1764, a book to which the Biog. Dram. is not worthy to hold a candle, and which for its age is really excellent. This, I think, might be the model for our first outline. 2 volumes the first an alphabetical list of authors, and the second of plays.

Next, our limit. You suggest Shirley: but is that not too limited?

What do you say to our taking 1700 as our rough conclusion, as a rule excluding all dramatists who published nothing in the seventeenth century? Rowe, whose first play is dated 1700, might close our list of tragedians, and Farquhar, 1698, our comedians.

The Restoration is a pet period of mine: I have gone into its bibliography, I really believe, more than anyone else living now. I should be unwilling to exclude it from our scheme.

Your work and mine in the *Encyclopædia Brit.* would as you say lighten our labour. You are taking the greatest names there and I the lesser. For instance this last volume has *Davenant* and *Day* by me.

In your second note this moment arrived you speak of "taking a share in possible profit." But this looks like risk. Chatto, I think, ought to do the work at his own risk and pay us for whatever we write, just as publishers of encyclopædias do. Neither you nor I ought to be burdened with the responsibility of the publishing.

It will give me the greatest pleasure, at fairly remunerative terms, to work at this scheme, and to work with you will be most truly delightful. Write to me again to explain the business part of your last note. I am suspicious of these publishers, unless I know what they mean.

Yours ever,
EDMUND W. GOSSE.

29, Delamere Terrace,
To Algernon Swinburne. *July 5, 1877.*

MY DEAR SWINBURNE,—

I send you the no. of the *Cornhill* containing my plea for rondeaux and ballades, and adorned with your exquisite ballades of which I become more and more enamoured. You will, I hope, be interested in the scheme and the purpose of the article, though there may be one thing and another which will meet with your disapproval. I shall take it as a specially friendly favour if you, who are so learned in the history of verse, will point out to me any sins of omission or commission in my historical part. In every case write to me about it, for I am half in despair. In all this battle for form and for pure literature we fight as a mere handful against the whole army of Philistia.

Yours ever,
EDMUND W. GOSSE.

Board of Trade, S.W.
To Austin Dobson. *July 5th, 1877.*

MY DEAR DOBSON,—

The serious necessity of some shifting of meaning in the refrain of a rondeau has so oppressed me of late, that sleep and rest have left me, and it is wholly owing to this disinterested anxiety that I have become the wreck you see me. At last, however, the impossible has been done. Turn the page, old kiddleewink, and enjoy the exquisite distinction of this little *chef-d'œuvre.*

Yours,
E. W. G.

I hope my lines are properly arranged, I have no model to hand.

THE POET AT THE BREAKFAST TABLE

In rose-lit air and light perfume,
The well-appointed breakfast-room
  Delights us as we tread the stair;
  The loaves are beautiful and fair
(As Wordsworth puts it), crust and crumb;
  The coffee hath an odour rare;
  But most I love the sticky stare
Of pickled mackerel, grand and dumb,
          In rows.

And while these dainties we consume
  Let educated youth prepare,
Flushed with new science like a bloom,
  In our rapt hearing to declare,
  How many little eggs there are
          In roes.

29, Delamere Terrace,

To Austin Dobson. *July 24th, 1877.*

My dear Dobson,—

I hope that in the excitement of last night I did not say or do anything rude—ruder than usual? This morning I am very tired and very humble. Saintsbury is very interesting, isn't he, but a little feverish and perfervid. Lang I feel we neither of us did justice to, but he seems very nice. It was right, I hope you think, that we should go individually to see Saintsbury? More comfortable for both of us, surely, than trotting everywhere between the same shafts like a pair of prize ponies. What a plump little cob you are, by the way! What a perambulating sweetness, what a type of amiability that unnamed and untalked-to Fifth was! I ought to have talked to him, but I could not resist the electric Saintsbury.

Write to me, buffer.

Yours,

E. W. G.

Board of Trade,
S.W.

To Austin Dobson. *April 4th, 1876.*

My dear D.,—

I am too ill to write a line to you to-day—such a depressing feverish cold. But I must tell you how happy I was last night, how kind I thought you were, and how nice Locker was. He has certainly all the personal charm of good breeding and modest distinction which ought to mark a poet. Perhaps he is all the more calm and the more tasteful, because there is no strong disturbing influence within, no very decided or volcanic inspiration.

I have tried to copy my sextain for you, but I have not the force to do it. I am in all the anguish of a new bad cold. My Christian name is Sniffles. I wrote a letter of wild mad passion this morning to the charming brunette. I await her reply with the anguish of anxiety, but my prophetic soul tells me she won't reply.

I felt last night so like "engaging Freddy" in the *Bab Ballads*. Do you recollect? "A man all poesy and buzzom."

Sniff.

In a few minutes I am going up to Chatto & Windus to forbid the circulation of my absurd works, and when I get home, I am going to make a bonfire of my MSS. in verse. Sniff. It is perfectly ridiculous to write poetry.

I have forgotten Stedman's letter. You shall have it to-morrow if I can possibly remember. I will—(in blowing my nose I have forgotten what I was going to say) . . . .

Goodbye.

Yours affectionately,

E. W. G.

Sniff.

Emily Pfeiffer's *Gerard's Monument* was published in 1873. It is hardly necessary to state that the "rondel to you" does not appear in the book. The review of *Le Livre des Ballades* appeared in the *Saturday Review* of October 13th, 1877, and dealt with the rules of the "ballade," as to which it averred there was a distinction between those of England and France.

29, Delamere Terrace,

To Austin Dobson. *27.11.1877.*

My dear Dobson,—

Silly old Pfeiffer has sent me—and no doubt also sent you—Mrs. P.'s *Gerard's Monument*. Such a letter, too, from the wicked old sycophant. Of course, I wrote by return of post to thank for the gift as yet unopened. By the living Jingo, there's a rondel to you in the book.

If kin, fame, critics, age, you quote
  As fain to thwart and twit,
Just try to feel your wings and float
  Above the scornful kit:

Oh modern singers, ye who vote
Our times for song unfit!
Oh cacophony! Oh geese! Oh hyenas! Oh pigs!

Send back this parody of her ribaldry: I make you a present of it:

A. D. TO E. P.

O Pfeiffer, try to clear your throat,
You cannot sing one bit;
You've swallowed Hubby's overcoat,
His hat on top of it.

I never heard such discord float
From any bat or tit:
O Pfeiffer, try to clear your throat,
You cannot sing one bit.

If poets true you name and quote,
And coyly try to twit,
You first should breathe along your oat,
And cough and hem and spit:
O Pfeiffer, try to clear your throat
You cannot sing one bit.

Her ballade imitates the very cadences of Swinburne's; her chant royal follows mine like a shorn lamb, tottering, but very close and meek. Her triolet is rather pretty.

I wish you would come in and see me some morning on your way down. I have many things to tell you. I have found out who reviewed the *Livre des Ballades* in the *Saturday*. A certain writer has a collection of form-poems, like the *Odes Funambulesques* presently to appear.

Adieu. Love to Pfeiffer when you write.

Yours,
E. W. G.

The anthology of William Davenport Adams referred to in the letter which follows was published in January 1878. It contains five examples of Gosse's verse. Two lyrics, *Ilicet,* and *I bring a garland.* A villanelle, *Would's't thou not:* a rondeau, *If love should faint:* and a chant royal, *The God of Wine.*

In spite of Gosse's protest, the "false and presumptuous chant royal" closed the book.

Board of Trade,
S.W.
Jan. 31st, 1878.

MY DEAR DOBSON,—

Payne is simply a charlatan. You ought to urge Mr. Davenport Adams not to disgrace his book with such a false and presumptuous chant royal.

In 11.1.2, 4 he rejects his rhyme *blue* altogether.
He uses *King* 3 times.
He uses *wing* twice.
He uses *sing* twice.

The rhymes *are* and *near* to save the rhyme ought to be in *ew.*

These are but a few of the errors.

Mr. Adams will do a great injustice to my chant royal wh. is scrupulously correct, will stultify your essay, and will bring discredit on his book, if he publishes this piece of false art and bad workmanship.

Let him close the book with my chant royal. It cannot be impossible for him to do this, and Mr. Payne is already amply represented by pieces which are what they pretend to be.

I hope you will state this to him, as from me if you like. It would be simply shameful to publish this of Payne's.

Yours,
E. W. G.

CHAPTER NINE

At the beginning of 1879, Gosse published his first book of prose, *Studies in the Literature of Northern Europe*. Stevenson, writing on April 16th, said: "The book is good reading. Your personal notes of those you saw struck me as perhaps most sharp and 'best held.' See as many people as you can and make a book of them before you die. That will be a living book upon my word. You have the touch required. I ask you to put hands to it in private already." The book fell on a public still listless about Scandinavian literature. Names known only to the few and pronounceable only by experts were little calculated to attract popular attention. But the book, while it brought no financial return, increased Gosse's authority in his chosen field.

Board of Trade,
S.W.

To R. L. Stevenson *18.4.1879.*

My dear R. L. S.,—

Thank you for a long and charming letter, which I have already read twice. Notes will only bear one reading, but a letter deserves twice to-day and once more next week before you put it away. But if you correspond with me in word as I make bold to say you do in spirit, pray burden your memory with this brief fair heading.

E. W. G.,
29, Delamere Terrace,
London, W.

Abate no whit of this, for if you do the prophane will write upon it with red ink, as on to-day's letter:

"No such number in Savile Road,
Edinr.
McC."

Who is McC., damn him, that he should scribble on a letter

from thee to me? And that further he should presume to add: try LONDON.

He should try Broadmoor, if we all had our way.

I am very glad you found a nerve of personality in my book, for this is the one vital thing. Not to seem more humble than you would have me, I think I should make a good biographer, of any man, that is, whom I had loved. For all the little fireside ways that distinguish men from one another are easily observed by my temperament, and go far to help me in building up a memory.

When will you be ready with your Cevennes? I look forward to it very eagerly.

I came back last night from Birmingham, whither I went to see the great Meeting at which all the Liberals spoke on Wednesday. Of course I enjoyed a hospitable welcome, or I could not have borne it, and as it was I got into some trouble for begging the citizens to temper their zeal with discretion. The best thing I saw was Bright, inflated with indignation, grow visibly colossal as he denounced the Government. The best thing I heard was Chamberlain's saying that a certain "allegation is false and the alligator knows it." But there is a flavour of trade in Birmingham which is sufferable only because it is so very frank and sincere. They are very liberal in subscriptions, but no flowers will grow in the garden of their souls. Still there is a manliness about their naked politico-athletics which has a charm.

Yours affectionately,

EDMUND W. GOSSE.

None of Gosse's letters have quite the same emotional quality as his correspondence with Hamo Thornycroft. He had got to know the sculptor through Miss Thornycroft, who was a friend of his wife, and a friendship remarkable for the warmth of its devotion had sprung up between the two men. Gosse admired Thornycroft's work, reverenced his genius, and looked on his character and mind as belonging to an order equally exalted. He found in Thornycroft a kindred spirit, and a companionship at once witty, luminous and cultivated. It was to Thornycroft above all others that Gosse revealed his doubts, his fears, and those sensibilities in which he abounded and by which he was so often harassed. Early in their friendship he wrote on New Year's Eve, 1879: "Reviewing 1879 I see that it has been the most prosperous and the happiest year of my life. I have gained several valuable acquaintances, I have published two important books, a son has been born to me; but above all other things I put the fact that *you* have come out of the rank of a common friend into the first place of all, as something better than a brother. You are the inestimable treasure for which I was waiting nearly thirty years, and which, God knows, I long ago thought would never come at all."*

The voice which speaks in these letters is that of a mind tuned to high altitudes of friendship. At heart, Gosse was an idealist and never more so than in his intimacies. His indelible upbringing, for one thing, was continually urging him to seek contrast; to make the most of every experience, and give play to his intrinsic faith in human nature. In this his attitude was exactly antithetical to that of his father, of whom he wrote, "Of friendship as a cardinal virtue, as one of the great elements in a happy life, he had no conception. He could make none of those concessions, those mutual acceptances of the inevitable, without which this, the most spiritual of the passions, cannot exist."† If ever there was a specialist in friendship it was Gosse: here he discarded the role of critic, and gave all he could of approbation and concern. Friendship was a flame, which he would not allow to burn itself out. Highly strung, and sensitive to the point of touchiness, he was, it is true, apt to see slights and offences where none were intended, but he would seize the first chance for reconciliation, and "if he vowed friendship he would perform it to the last article." A phrase of Marie Lecszinska which he wrote in his commonplace book, "L'univers sans mes amis serait un désert pour moi," defined no more than he felt. In 1921, after nearly forty-five years of friendship, he wrote to Thornycroft from Paris.

"How little Paris has changed radically since you and I were so happy there, forty years ago! Everything always reminds me of

* See post p. 128.

† *The Life of Philip Henry Gosse by His Son* (1890).

those admirable days we spent together. How the recollection of them lives and glows!" No man had more tenacity in his affections or fidelity in his sentiment. He was, moreover, delightfully free of the affectation or reserve, whichever our point of view may lead us to call it, which restrains the ordinary Englishman from auditing and avowing by overt expression the benefits which friendship may bring him. Friendship with Gosse was not a light to be hidden under a bushel, or a beatitude to be valued in silence; on the contrary, it was to be regarded and spoken of even to the verge of temerity in expression. "When life is hurrying on so fast, it is silly not to let the few people one is really fond of have the poor little pleasure of knowing it," he wrote to Mrs. Stevenson in 1900. It was the garden he most delighted to cultivate; a storm might destroy it, but it was never to wane for lack of tending. Thus in 1919 he could write to Thomas Hardy: "Dearest and most admired of friends, thank you for the unbroken record of nearly forty-five years of precious intercourse. May we both live on to celebrate our jubilee of Friendship."

A letter to Theodore Watts written in 1879 shows his quickness to rush out when rumour reached him of defection in a friend. The thing had to be tested at once—set right or registered as a proof of decline. He was very slow to condone the venial disloyalty that serves to season conversation.

29, Delamere Terrace,

To Watts-Dunton.

MY DEAR WATTS,—

I am so glad to get your letter, and have no desire but to know exactly how we stand. You are perfectly right that I did feel from the first absolutely sure that whatever you might have said could only have expressed a *mood*. I thought, however, by writing to you to discover the sources of that mood, for I cannot endure to conceal a feeling of this kind. I am totally without discretion in these things, but I most earnestly desire to know what terms I am on with my friends.

As to your questions: the time was alleged as "recently," you were not stated to have said any ill *thing*, that is anything malicious or even condemnatory, but—as I said—to have expressed a personal "dislike or distrust." There is no doubt that the source of this information was a family that can hardly be said to have your interests or mine at heart: and I was inclined at first to put the statement down to random malice, but it was very circumstantial.

Let us, however, leave my informants out of the question for the moment. The position is, either you have no remembrance of anything beyond the fair criticism we always make on our absent friends, or you do recollect *feeling* (let us say nothing about expressing) something that disturbed your permanent feeling of kindness towards me. Should this latter be the case, I will beg you as a great favour to let me know the cause of this disturbance, and if I have been in fault, as is very likely, I will frankly say so.

Yours sincerely,

EDMUND W. GOSSE.

It was sometimes a complaint against Gosse, not that "he mocked in the market-place what he worshipped in the woods," but that he would write to an author who was also a friend, especially to an amateur, enthusiastic praise of his performance, and then sing a different tune in his public criticism of the same work. This was mortifying to the author, and the cause of some embittered speculation. What did it mean, this blowing hot and cold? The probable explanation was that in the first instance affection and the desire to please had stirred Gosse's enthusiasm, and then the sobering influence of public print had reduced it to a cooler level. This got him into personal scrapes, out of which he once lamentably failed to extricate himself. But he was probably sincere, both in his letter and review, though appearances were against him, and the author at any rate found it difficult to think so. It looked on the surface like double dealing. It would be idle to ignore that this was the impression he occasionally created. But discrepancy between promise and fulfilment on such occasions is readily amplified. Such instances of apparent disingenuousness were exceedingly rare, and set against the remarkable quality and endurance of his genuine friendships they amounted to very little. We have only to cite the cases of Austin Dobson and Hamo Thornycroft, and others will emerge from his correspondence.

Thornycroft, born in 1850, was two years younger than Gosse. Both his parents were practising sculptors; but it was not till he was eighteen years old that Hamo turned to art. He passed through the Academy schools, was soon exhibiting his work and securing clients, and in 1880 exhibited *Artemis* (now at Eaton Hall and referred to in the following letters), which established him as a sculptor of note in the classical tradition. He died in 1925, leaving many public monuments as examples of his art, notably the statues of Gladstone, General Gordon, Queen Victoria at the Royal Exchange, and *Teucer* and *The Kiss* now at the Tate. The first letter refers to a statue of Harvey, who had been made the subject of a competition by the Royal College of Physicians. Thornycroft's contribution had been rejected.

29, Delamere Terrace,

To Hamo Thornycroft. *1.4.79.*

My dear Hamo,—

I am as angry and as disappointed as if it had happened to myself. This comes of the damnable practice of letting art questions be settled by outsiders.

" 'Tis profanation of our joys
To tell the laity our love."

Well! I have written a tremendous note about it for the *Academy*, and if they are not afraid of being libellous, in it will go on Saturday. By the way, the *Academy* has thought better of it, and does not mean to die.

But you are right, it would be a thousand times worse to have made B.* than to lose the award. You have genius, and you will impress your mind on the world, even if you die first, like poor

* This refers to a rival statue "B."

Alfred Stevens. But you will not die, but live, and denounce the peddling of the physicians.

Yours always,
EDMUND W. GOSSE.

EPIGRAM ON
THE HARVEY STATUE SUB-COMMITTEE.

Physicians, curb your spreading mesh,
And bills, not statues, garble;
Still murder genius in the flesh,
But spare it in the marble!

April 1, 1879.
All Fools' and Physicians' Day.

Board of Trade,
S.W.

To Hamo Thornycroft. *5.5.79.*

MY DEAR HAMO,—

I was standing on Richmond Bridge yesterday about 1, feeling very much bored with my own society, when I suddenly became three times as much bored with it by seeing you skim under my feet on your delighted little tug. It was the queerest sensation, and if the battlements of the bridge had been lower, I don't know but what I might have thrown myself into the river, and committed suicide out of sheer companionableness.

You must let me congratulate you on your show at the R.A. I am confirmed in all I thought and wrote about your Harvey model. It is extremely fine: I tell the story of your wrongs and the wickedness of medical committees everywhere. But I am anxious to ask you whether your Stepping-Stones was a commission or not; if it was, I am silent, but if it was not, I want to urge on you not to give way to this choice of subjects. Your Warrior & Youth was nobly heroic, your Lot's Wife a poem in marble, but in spite of all the accomplishment and exquisite technique of your Stepping-

Stones, the longer I look at it, the less pleasure it gives. It seems to me that in Sculpture more depends on the subject than in painting: since in painting, you may give real artistic pleasure by rendering the bloom on a cabbage-garden or the light on a bundle of chimney-stacks, but somehow if you employ so splendid and eternal a medium as marble it seems as though you need more than mere admirable workmanship, you want the elevation of some really (and not merely relatively) beautiful idea.

Was it Balaam's ass that came to curse and went away to bless? It seems to me I have done the opposite thing, for I certainly meant to be friendly when I began. However, you know how sincerely I admire you, and you will not take my admonition for more than it is worth. You may put it down to a poet's prejudice against the Pretty.

Yours very sincerely,
My dear Hamo,
EDMUND W. GOSSE.

29, Delamere Terrace,
To Hamo Thornycroft. *22.6.79.*

MY DEAR HAMO,—

I could not tell you truly without seeming to exaggerate how very much I have enjoyed myself and how truly sensible I am of your great and most fraternal kindness. Our days and night on the river have blown away all my cobwebs and taken five years—at least—off my shoulders. To pass through all that rich and lovely country would have been quite a memorable thing to me, even if it had not been enhanced fourfold by my seeing so much of you and getting to know you so well. For this the Ides of June will always be marked white on my calendar. I have come back to find all well and in a flourishing blitheness at home: my colour is pronounced something unprecedented.

I send you my tragedy of *King Erik* which I hope may please you. The public cared less for it than for anything I have published, but some of the élite—and notably Tennyson and Swinburne—have preferred it to all my other work.

Please express to your father my sense of his very kind hospitality; I made such an awkward farewell, lacking readiness of speech at the last moment. Be so good as to send me Wirgman's address, and hold in as affectionate remembrance as you can,

Your friend,
EDMUND W. GOSSE.

Stevenson having seen Gosse in a temporary fit of lameness had christened him Weg after Silas Wegg, the literary gentleman with a wooden leg in *Our Mutual Friend*. Gosse ignores this element in the transposition of initials.

Board of Trade,
1, Whitehall, S.W.

To R. L. Stevenson. *26.7.79.*

MY DEAR R. L. S. (OR RATHER L. R. S.),—

You are the victim of a delusion: you are a self-deceiver: you are like the lady that built up a whole new scheme of prophecy on a misquotation. My initials are not W.E.G.: those are the initials of the infamous People's William. Mine are E.W.G., as you ought to know, Mr. L.R.S.

And so, forsooth, nothing can be made of your initials!

ReLigiouS?

but that's not true.

Rogue of Lothianburn Swanston? true enough, but too ponderous.

I give it up.

So glad you liked the Art article: though the subject lies out of my path, and polemics too. I make a poor fighter. I so easily go over to the other side. I mourn, in ashes, over the sentence you brand: alas! too kind to pretend there is but one such.

If you see the *Saturday Review* of to-day, smile with me over a poor wraith of a novel, a spectral folly, that I have had to blow (but not to puff) away, called *Gloria*.

How is it that thou art feeble? It is a paradox, that you, the General Exhilarator, should feel depressed. I take you for my emblem of Life, and you talk of feeling lifeless. But I am not in fit state to bow down to your Scots passions. Out upon Burns for a fornicator. As to the Twa Dogs, you are one of them, and William Wallace was the other.

Look you here. Would'st earn an eighteenpence in honest fashion? Slay me these three: Shairp, who is a bug, and Masson, who is bugger than Shairp, and Blackie, who is the buggest of all. God's World would be a sunnier one without Blackie and Masson and Shairp. Do the thing cleanly, and we'll call it a florin.

The Savile is dull. Walter Pollock has sombre airs, like a Don in disguise. I suspect him of an ambition to personate Don César. We miss our SaGaCity* almost as much as we do the Rogue of L.S.

Write to me soon: if only to blot out with your tears the monstrous indignity of calling me W.E.G.

The spouse and the offspring and the cat are charmed at being remembered and desire their courtesy to you. Pity me! there'll be another offspring in about a fornight.

Yours affectionately,

EDMUND W. GOSSE.

29, Delamere Terrace,

To Hamo Thornycroft. *15.8.79.*

MY DEAR HAMO,—

I mean to steal round on Monday evening next, on the chance of seeing you to say goodbye. But you are not to stay in or put your arrangements out at all. If I find you in, well, and if not, it can't be helped. The Milo and the Muse give me the greatest pleasure, I look at them constantly; the Muse, especially, sits in my study and looks down at me in a manner that is very encouraging and kind. When the lamp is lit, and she is a little in shadow, she looks so translucent that one can hardly believe she is not marble. I am glad to think that you secured the other head. They will be symbols to each of us of what we feel in common.

I have found a little Greek poem, by Diotimus, which has an

* Sidney Colvin.

interest for you. It is supposed to be inscribed on the pedestal of a statue of Diana. It runs thus:—

"I am Diana. As is meet, I am made of bronze, being daughter of Zeus and of no other god. Behold the vigour and audacity of the young goddess, and confess that the earth itself is too narrow for so swift a huntress."

I am pleased to have come across this, because it is a fine argument in favour of bronze. I find that the famous statue of Diana in the public gymnasium had a light fringed robe descending to the knee.

Farewell,

Yours very really,

Edmund W. Gosse.

I must not say I wish you were not going to Scotland, but I do wish I were going too. But we shall meet for a moment or two between your return and our exodus.

29, Delamere Terrace,

To Hamo Thornycroft. *27.8.79.*

My dear Hamo,—

When I see your handwriting I put it at the bottom of my pile of letters to read it slowly and luxuriously. The delight of having a correspondent whose letters one opens always with a flutter of delight, and never with any apprehension! You must thank Mrs. Wallace for her most courteous and hospitable message, and tell her that though it would give me great pleasure I cannot go so far north just now. It is very tantalizing: I should just like nothing so well as a long walk with you over the springy heather. I am getting thoroughly knocked up with over-work: so I am going down at the end of this week for four days' visit to Alfred Waterhouse in Berkshire.

I am very glad my presence is a stimulus to you in your art. It makes me very proud that this should be so, yet if it were not so, I should be unworthy of your affection in any high sense. I know that you will be very great; but your temperament is so balanced that you are easily discouraged, and it is just here that I may be useful to you, to call upon you to look forward and not around or backward.

I was talking about your work yesterday to some men at the Club, and I was much pleased that Basil Champneys, the architect, remarked that he had noted your work since you began to exhibit, and that he thought much more highly of it than of any other young sculptor's. I think you do not know him? If so, this is pleasant, as quite an extraneous judgment.

This is no letter, but an after-breakfast chat. Adieu!

Always yours,
EDMUND W. GOSSE.

To Algernon Swinburne.

4.10.79.

With Mrs. Hobbs,
Torcross,
Nr. Kingsbridge,

I see your Shakespeare book is announced. I look forward to it.

MY DEAR SWINBURNE,—

Watts has told you of our great desire to induce you to help in this new edition of the British Poets, to which Matthew Arnold writes the Introduction. The working editor, Mr. Ward, has set aside four poets, with whom it is his ambition that you should deal —Chatterton, Blake, Coleridge, Keats. But perhaps having written so intimately of Blake and Coleridge already, you hardly care to go over the same ground again; therefore it is Keats that I particularly urge upon you. A critical study of Keats from your pen would be the jewel of any collection of such essays, not merely from your genius, but also from the fact that the other luminaries of that age have found expositors, but not Keats.

The plan is this. No biographical data are requested, but merely a critical survey of the poet's quality and development, and a statement of his position in comparative literature. To this you are asked to add indications, for the printer's use, of such pieces as you wish extracted in the selection that follows.

I hope you will join the scheme. M. Arnold does Wordsworth

and Gray; Dean Church Spenser; Mark Pattison Pope; the choice of critics has, I think, been carefully made. I have Herrick and Carew as my portion.

Will you be so very kind as to write to me here? The payment, to mention that vile argument, is very good, and would doubtless, in your case, be what you like. My wife joins in kindest remembrances.

Yours always,
E. W. Gosse.

With Mrs. Hobbs,
Torcross,
Nr. Kingsbridge,

To Hamo Thornycroft. *7.10.79.*

My dear Hamo,—

I was thinking rather sadly about you, when your unexpected letter came and gave me a great pleasure. I had no right to expect such a one, for I was in your debt. It disappointed me most acutely that you could not come, although I felt it to be quite right. Yet I had planned more schemes for us than any fortnight could contain, and I fell a victim to my own illusion. I am delighted to think of you worshipping Diana by moonlight. It strikes me as a noble subject for a poem—a great sculptor, born with a Greek heart into bigoted Christian times, and carving for himself, by stealth at night, an image of the glorious goddess. It would mingle the sense of art with the sense of worship. Would that I could see you both—you, I mean, and your Diana. In a little more than a week, I hope, that longing will be satisfied.

This is a strong, breezy place, and has done wonders for us. I never felt so strong, I think, before; every muscle and nerve alive and balanced. It is pleasant to be in a place so unsophisticated. We have made friends with all the simple folk of the hamlet, and there are no ladies and gentlemen to interfere with our quiet. The people of the place are remarkably nice. I have found some of the coastguards very good company, they get to be familiar with nature at unusual moments, and see her when she thinks she is alone.

The morning I got your letter saying you could not manage to come, I set off for a tearing walk, and walked off my vexation after a few hours. I covered 27 miles, taking a round of the coast which astonished these lazy Devonshire people, who never walk if they can help it, and who take a donkey to go to a village two miles off.

We deeply sympathize with Teresa and her black eye. Nellie never ceases to lament that she could not come with you. She would have enjoyed this unique place. Nellie has been painting hard, and will, I hope, have finished three rather elaborate little pictures, giving a good idea of Torcross. Please give our especial love to Teresa.

I have been over to Torquay to see my father, who is not very well. He is only 70, but of late he finds himself much less able than of old to take exertion. It is strange and pathetic that the approach of old age and weakness have softened his temperament. He was, as I think you know, rather severe and unbending to me when I was a child, and I went about the empty house in some dread of him. But now he is clingingly affectionate and apologetic for trouble that he gives. I parted from him yesterday with tears in my eyes; there is something overwhelmingly painful in seeing the peculiar expression of weakness asking for forbearance, in the eyes of a man that has been very high-handed and stubborn. I hope my fears about his health may be unfounded: but I realized yesterday, with terror and for the first time, that his vehement eager life would not last for ever. I wish you could see him once: he has a magnificent head. He is in no feature like me, except the mouth.

I shall write and let you know when we return, for I shall want to come and see you before many hours are past. So, as I shall be very busy, I shall like you to be forewarned of my coming.

Adieu, my Hamo! May Diana graciously protect you,

Yours,

EDMUND W. GOSSE.

"I, like a sad slave, stay and think of nought,
Save, where you are, how happy you make those!"

The following rondeau was sent in a letter to Austin Dobson.

RONDEAU
from the French of Mme. Deshoulières.

"Entre deux draps—"

Between two sheets of linen fair and white
Fresh lavendered, and folded smooth and light,
  The charming Idris of the shining eyes,
  Loyal and prudent, eloquent and wise,
Nestles till noon in downy soft delight.
To censure others' tastes I have no right,
Yet seems it scarcely seemly in my sight
  To loiter lonely in such wanton guise
    Between two sheets,
Since treacherous Love most nimbly wings his flight
To her who, dreaming, squanders day as night;
  For other joys the solitary sighs,
  And soon, without a struggle, virtue dies,
When beauty lets her wandering thoughts alight
    Between two sheets.

8.10.1879. E.W.G.

29, Delamere Terrace,
To Austin Dobson. *21.10.1879.*

My dear Dobson,—

I daresay you have noticed—and if so you must forgive me—how much superior Congreve's Ode to *Mrs. Arabella Hunt Singing* is to his other serious pieces? I hope you will give us a good extract of this admirable poem, pointing out that its beauties are akin to all that is best in the *Mourning Bride*. I do not know whether it is a coincidence or not that the two last lines* are almost exactly the same as the last two of Keats' last sonnet. You should point out the resemblance.

* "Wishing for ever in that state to lie
For ever to be dying so, yet never die."

The style of this ode is the rococo, of course, but I dearly like it. All these tropes and lumbering courtesies remind me of the architectural oddities of that age, the cupid-angels suspended upon wires, the chubby seraphim of wood that blow long metal trumpets, the blowsy allegorical paintings in the heavy organ-lofts. Is it not so?

Yours affectionately,
EDMUND W. GOSSE.

In August of 1879 Stevenson started unexpectedly for California. On board ship he wrote The *Story of a Lie* and the bulk of The *Amateur Emigrant.* The postscript of the following letter refers to the birth of Gosse's only son Philip Gosse M.D.

To R. L. Stevenson. *27.10.1879.*

MY DEAR R. L. S.,—

Your letter met me at the Club to-day and gave me a great delight. The only person to whom I could talk about you, Colvin, has long been away, and I have been gradually fretting myself into a fever of inquietude about you. Many times, in a blue spot, I have lived over again the dismal clammy evening when we bid one another farewell at the corner of Berkeley Square, and have betted sixpence with my soul that I should never see your face again. Monterey, Cal., is so very far off, that I do not feel abashed in telling you that I have found out that your existence is very important to me, and that I could not sustain with any fortitude the idea of never shaking your hand again.

I like the situation of Monterey on the map; it looks north and west over the Pacific in a brisk way. I feel you to be just at hand now I have Monterey on the map. Before, I fancied you weltering in your gore in a New York sponging-house "lying in the dreadful dishonour of death," as it is said so finely in *Paul Ferrol.* But Monterey looks friendly on the map, though a little remote and provincial, I'm afraid. I doubt you don't get your *Daily News* with your breakfast, and that you have fallen off dreadfully in the matter of "Literary Gossip."

Your *Burns* came out this month in the Cornhill. I hear nothing but a chorus of praise of it, in which I join with treble heartiness. I never read any piece of personal criticism more thoroughly excellent. Every page of it is first-rate. The *Story of a Lie* is also out: but I have not yet seen it.

Lang is consumed with curiosity to know where you are. He fancies you have gone to Khiva; but I have dropped a hint that it is really Merv. We all think you are somewhere in Central Asia.

The *Amateur Emigrant* will be first-rate, I am sure. I long to see it. Your *Donkey* continues to be a great success. I was calling at a house the other day, where a handsome kitten was being nursed under the name of Modestine. These people knew nothing of you: yet they were full of your book. This is fame, my good young man.

You tell me to send you my works. Alack and aday, I have none, but my *New Poems* which are coming out next Friday; and you can't abear my verses. Never mind, I'll send them to you: I daresay paper is at a discount in Monterey, and you can use the margins for literary purposes.

By the way, I shall expect you to adopt the Californian orthography and write: "I will sooñ be with you agaiñ."

Your affectionate Friend,

Edmund W. Gosse.

My wife has given me a son, such a nice little bright-eyed boy: she and all of us are extremely well: she sends you her very kind remembrances and wishes.

29, Delamere Terrace,

To Hamo Thornycroft. *29.10.79.*

My dear Hamo,—

Sunday was delicious: you need not imagine that you did not say enough: had you not mentioned the book at all it would not have mattered to me, for I had read your thanks in your eyes and the touch of your hand. But the thanks ought to be all on my side. You do not know what I owe to you: how your friendship has reawakened me, made me young again. Nature, the clouds, the grass, everything takes a new freshness and brightness now I have you to share the world with. You have swept all my cobwebs away, the sort of clubishness that was coming over me; and now I have only one desire, to keep your love and fellowship all my life. After all my dreary, weary youth I have a right, I think, to be happy now.

All your words about the poems are very encouraging. We shall see if they (the poems) bear examination before a colder tribunal.

I must write about Goring, and hope to make it associated in time to come with our names, as Chertsey is with Cowley's and Marlow with Shelley's. I rejoice to hear of the *Waterlily*, and look forward to our cruise in the spring. The "Four Jolly Waterboys and their Skipper" will be our title.

You looked thin and rather sad on Sunday. Three of the Waterboys, you see, are flourishing; their captain must be no less blithe.

May I come and see you and Diana on Saturday afternoon? I shall come unless I hear to the contrary.

Always yours,

Edmund W. Gosse.

29, Delamere Terrace,

To Hamo Thornycroft. *6.11.79.*

My dear Hamo,—

The sunshine to-day—timid though it was—has given me fresh confidence. I had made up my mind that for six months at least we should have this dull sky and nipping air, that makes one's whole blood run slow. But now I am thinking that if some Sunday this month or the next it should be very bright and crisp, you may expect me early in the morning, about 10, and we will go for a walk somewhere in the woods, and smell the damp smell of the beds of leaves before the year quite closes. What do you say?

Was not Monday pleasant? I have lived it over again ever since, the warm firelight and the hollow shadows of your studio, peopled with so much silent beauty. It was at once highly exciting and soothing to me to sit among the ancient people of your dreams, to see their outlines softly in the dimness, and try and fancy all that you have fancied—the hopes and fears, the defeats and victories that you have lived through in your art. I must get over the selfish wish I feel to have all this and you to myself: since when have I become so unsociable?

Diana is now advanced to that stage when I can only recognise her beauty in silence. I don't seem to have anything more to say about her at present. But I must tell you how delighted I am with the Stone Putter. You will make an admirable thing of that: it strikes me as so sinewy and rhythmical, as if with perfect tension of muscle he were performing a single harmonious action. I don't know if you quite understand what I mean, which is, that the figure seems to me so well balanced in strength and grace. I would not have you now attempt any new work just at present. Be content to throw your whole genius into these two, the goddess and the man. These, with your busts, will give you as strong a position next year as anything could.

When shall I see you? I propose we never let a week go by—if this is not a burden on you—without meeting, one week at your house and the next at mine. Do you think of going to Townshend House next Tuesday?

It is nearly midnight. I have been out to the post, and seeing the white face of Selene, wondered if yours was upturned to her also.

Yours,

EDMUND W. G.

Board of Trade,
Whitehall, S.W.1.

To Hamo Thornycroft. *13.11.79.*

MY DEAR HAMO,—

May Sunday be like unto to-day in sunshine. Ever since Tuesday I've been in a whirl of bustle, the Book beginning to feel the public's pulse. Gabriel Rossetti heads the tide of congratulation with a most generous and ardent letter. No fear of my not being egotistical on Sunday. You will have to listen to all my news.

Laura mentioned you to Nellie yesterday, saying that Tadema was afraid I should be angry with him for having been so dilatory, but that, as a matter of fact, Leslie and the President had put their names down before I first suggested the thing to Tadema. She said Tadema had a very high opinion of your art—and I know he has, when female Machiavellis (whom may God confound) do not seduce him from his better judgment.

Pray tell Teresa that Laura would dearly like to act Venus in our play, if the doctor will allow it.

I stepped across the Park this morning in an ecstasy. There was a silver bloom upon the grass, the sun was walking through real blue sky, and I held an animated imaginary conversation with you about all sorts of bright and open-air matters.

Till Sunday, farewell,
Your affectionate
E. W. G.

Don't you love this brisk and tingling weather?

Board of Trade,
S.W.

To Hamo Thornycroft. *18.12.79.*

My dear Hamo,—

Were you not rather tired on Saturday? I ached in every bone, and lay in bed till 12 next day. After getting off my skates, I came and stood above you at the head of the lake. It was too dark for me to distinguish anyone but you: I stayed there watching you talking and meditatively pirouetting on the ice till I made up my mind to go. I hope you saw the splendid bar of crimson in the west, behind the trees.

You have been busy this week, I expect. I have been doing a great deal since I saw you. I shall have—I hope, rather an important poem to read you when we meet next in any quietude. For the moment, I send you a sonnet, fantastic and very unintelligible, I daresay, to most people.

Be sure you don't forget that you dine with us next Monday, about 6. Come in your grey velveteen coat, if you will, and we will make as much mess as we like over the Milo and the bust.

I miss the skating very sadly, but it would probably make it impossible for me to work at all if I saw you so often. Absent, you make me work—present, there seems nothing worth working for.

Two terrible wet blankets are hanging over me: I have to make an analysis of an Icelandic saga for the *Cornhill,* and I have to write a long survey of Dutch literature for the Encyclopædia Britannica. Both are wanted by the middle of January, and neither is begun; while I spend my evenings in writing poetry. Isn't that intellectual profligacy?

Think ever kindly of

Thine

EDMUND W. G.

To H. T.

When by the fire we sit with hand in hand,
  My spirit seems to watch beside your knee,
Alert and eager, at your least command,
  To do your bidding over land and sea.
You sigh—and, of that dubious message fain,
  I scour the world to bring you what you lack,
Till from some island of the spicy main
  The pressure of your fingers calls me back;
You smile—and I, who love to be your slave,
  Post round the orb at your fantastic will,
Though, while my fancy skims the laughing wave,
  My hand lies happy in your hand, and still;
Nor more from fortune or from life would crave
  Than that dear silent service to fulfil.

29, Delamere Terrace,

To R. L. Stevenson. *Dec. 29th, 1879.*

MY DEAR R. L. S.,—

Why do you write such letters to wring my heart? Here am I, who though determined that nothing signified to such an old party as me, as nearly as possible disgracing myself with crying over your letter just received. It is too bad of you. Come straight back to us from that Monterey. You will be all right again on

British ground. I cannot bear to think of you all alone in the midst of strangers, fretting and tiring yourself to pieces. Do come home. You don't know how glad we shall all be to see you, how delightfully dull and humdrum everything is here. We haven't the originality to think of dying. It's never done here, in our set. I hate you for making me so miserable.

Are you really so bad, dear child? I try to persuade myself that it only is that you are lonely and out of spirits. You must not lose your pluck. How can you say that I am not "to believe half the bad I hear of you"? First place, I never do and never have heard anything bad of you, and second, if I did, there is this to be remembered, that I admire, honour and love you right through, and should be as ready to believe ill of you as of any one of the six best people in my world.

Whether you live or die, you will live for ever in our hearts and in the roll of men of genius. Nothing that anyone can say or do can darken the bright name you have made for yourself.

Thank you for your messages. I have just given my little rosy girl the kiss you sent her, and she has pronounced your name as sententiously as unintelligibly. 'Twas a poor attempt at enunciation, but confidently and courageously made. My wife is as sad as I am about you, and she and I and everybody says nothing but Come home straight.

Write to me soon again, telling me truly how you are, better or worse. Meanwhile be sure of my constant and solicitous thought of you.

Your friend,
(Sgd.) EDMUND W. GOSSE.

Hepworth Dixon is just dead: I take it as a good omen, they evidently want the bad writers, not the good ones, up there.

29, Delamere Terrace,
To Hamo Thornycroft. *31.12.79.*

MY DEAR HAMO,—

I have been as busy as possible all the evening with proofs, letters, etc., and now having cleaned up everything, and made clear decks, I mean to spend the last half hour of 1879 with you. I have a pleasant fancy that you are at this very moment writing to me, but I daresay that is only superstition.

I have been rather sad since I saw you. You remember my often speaking to you of Robert Louis Stevenson (By the way, he is the wayward youth who brings mischief on the wanderers in my poem). Well, I have had a letter from him from a little town in California, where he lies very ill. He does not think he will recover; he says his health is broken altogether. You cannot think how this has upset me. He is such a charming creature, all instinct with genius and power. He is absolutely one of the best prose-writers we possess; he has but to die and people will at once say "the best." He is only our age, or a little less. He is exactly like Hamlet's description of Yorick—"a fellow of infinite jest, of most excellent fancy." We never thought of the death of so bright a creature, yet no one could suppose he could live long. He has that restless ardent temperament of Keats and Fred Walker, all energy with nothing to fall back upon. He took this last mad journey to America in despite of all his friends. I had a presentiment of trouble when he went, and, as it was a mere freak of his to go, I told him so. Now it is more than one can bear, to think of his dying alone in a little town in California.

But this is melancholy, and not fit for New Year's Eve. It is moreover the only dark spot I have. Reviewing 1879, I see that it has been the most prosperous and the happiest in my life. I have gained several valuable acquaintances; I have published two important books; a son has been born to me; but above all these things I put the fact that *you* have come up out of the rank of a common friend into the first place of all, as something better than a brother. You are the inestimable treasure for which I was waiting nearly thirty years, and which, God knows, I long ago thought would never come at all.

1880 must be a great year for you. Diana will unveil her charms to the world, and bring you only too many admirers. It will not be your fault, and it shall not be mine, if you are not a roaring lion by next New Year's Day. But this is not our object, is it? and shall not be our wish. Rather may you be inspired with great and beautiful thoughts, and rise, quite careless of what the world thinks, into still higher flights of art. I am astounded when I think what progress you have made this year; and I do not think there is any peak or alp of the sculptor's art that you may not reach if you husband your powers and are true to the strong simplicity with which you have begun. Don't be too social, and don't work too late anights, these are the only warnings I presume to give you.

You see I venture to watch over you. Do the same good office to me, in another way. I am sadly conscious of my faults, dear Hamo! Beside your serenity and seriousness, my ugly temper and frivolity show off in colours that are anything but pretty. I speak of this for this once only, because I am often deeply ashamed, and shall feel happier if it is understood between us that I perfectly well know my own ugly ways. By and by, I hope to conquer my faults and grow more like you and worthy of you. Help me to do this, like a true friend.

Will you dine here at 6 next Monday? Do. If you positively cannot, tell me a day soon that I may come and spend an evening with you, when *you have no company*. But I hope you will come on Monday.

If I write any longer, it will be 1880. My last thoughts in this year and my first thoughts in next year will be of you.

May you enjoy every desirable and happy wish of your heart through 1880, may your work grow steadily better and better, and if you must have any troubles may they only be such as you can share with

Thy

EDMUND W. G.

At this time he made the acquaintance of Irving, and in a letter to Dobson he records with satisfaction that he had been invited by Irving to the Lyceum, adding in a spirit of flippant apprehension, "Conceive how my poor volatile heart is beating. I shall wear simple white with a rose in my hair. Or do you think my amber satin will be more in tone with tragedy?" He followed up his visit to the theatre by publishing a poem to Irving in the *Athenæum.*

Let gorgeous shapes of tragedy pass on at thy command,
And leave the Phrygian flutes to thrill the uplands of the
Strand.

He was an enthusiast for the theatre, but in his writings there are singularly few references to actors and acting. His interest lay in the literary values of the stage, rather than in the way they were rendered. But his will to be interested and his readiness to be amused gave an evening spent with him at the theatre a special zest. His criticisms multiplied the enjoyment of those who accompanied him, though whether his more audible comments always had the same effect on those for whose ears they were not intended is doubtful. He was by all the laws of mind a critic, but also Charles Lamb's "genuine spectator" rippling "with honest titillations of mirth and generous chucklings of applause."

But words were more to him than acting, language than a dramatic situation. When listening to Congreve's *Way of the World*, he turned to Mr. Marsh with tears in his eyes exclaiming, "The *excruciating* beauty of the language!"

CHAPTER TEN

1879 saw the end of Swinburne's constant visits to Delamere Terrace—visits which had given immense intellectual stimulus to Gosse, and provided him with rare opportunities for observing and recording the idiosyncrasies of the poet. In that year Swinburne finally withdrew to his retreat at Putney under the care of Watts-Dunton. Thenceforward Gosse saw him at rare intervals only. A paper left by Gosse, and (so far as I have been able to discover) not hitherto published, gives a curious account of some of Swinburne's personal characteristics.

SWINBURNE'S AGITATION

During the years when I was most frequently in the company of Swinburne, that is to say from 1871 to 1879, what was most remarkable about him was his extreme intellectual vivacity. He seemed to be moved to external excitement by an interior explosiveness, which he was unable to repress. I observe in reading Perrault's memoir of the French-Latin poet, Santeuil (1631-1697), that this writer was violently upset by his own enthusiastic inspiration, and Perrault uses a curious expression, "s'il y en eut jamais un *agité de cet emportement*, c'est celui dont je parle." I have never met with a phrase which so exactly describes Swinburne, who under the agitation of his own thoughts became like a man possessed, with quivering hands, eyes thrown up, and voice hollowed to a kind of echoing chant. This strange possession was entirely unconscious; no one less than Swinburne was an actor; he was wholly unaware that he was behaving in an unusual manner; and he would be on his guard against such effusions in general company. It was the more noticeable because he was habitually rather still and often entirely rigid. I used to look at him furtively in these last-mentioned moments, in order not to disturb him. His eyes would be fixed on nothingness, his lips alone would be moving without a sound; until occasional tremors through his limbs would presently announce that he was waking up to speech. Then he would begin in a very low voice, still not looking at me, with some such sentence as "Down all the vista of literary history it is impossible to see a figure &c. &c." as though he were reading out of a book; and then he would turn to recite with an almost excruciating ardour some lines of Æschylus or Marlowe, or a French lyric. In the midst of this melodious fury, if other persons entered the room he would suddenly return to ordinary life, asking a question, or making a joke, with transitions so abrupt as to disconcert even those who were most often in his company.

E. G.

Gosse had a striking gift for imitating Swinburne, and reproducing his agitation and diction. His mimicry went some way towards making good the deficiency of those who had missed the chance of seeing the poet. Among these imitations was a conversation about a difference which arose between Emerson and the poet. Emerson had visited England soon after the publication of *Poems and Ballads*. In an interview with a journalist he was reported to have said things about the volume which gave deep offence to Swinburne. Swinburne wrote a mild protest, saying he felt sure that Emerson could not have used the words attributed to him. No reply was received. Swinburne was incensed. Some time afterwards Gosse and Swinburne were resting in the Green Park and the conversation turned on Emerson. Gosse learnt for the first time that Swinburne had again written to him. He said, "I hope you said nothing rash." "Oh no." "But what did you say?" "I kept my temper, I preserved my equanimity." "Yes, but what did you say?" "I called him," replied Swinburne in his chanting voice, "a wrinkled and toothless baboon who, first hoisted into notoriety on the shoulders of Carlyle, now spits and sputters on a filthier platform of his own finding and fouling." The letter like its predecessor received no answer.

At Delamere Terrace Swinburne would call and remain for hours at a time. On one occasion he arrived obviously unwell, complaining that he was suffering from a surfeit of mineral waters. He remained for three days desperately ill, watched over by Gosse and

Mrs. Gosse in turns. He was completely at ease in the Gosses' home, sometimes gentle, exhausted, silent, sometimes ecstatic, or voluble and inspired as the mood drove him. Of an evening spent at Delamere Terrace, Gosse wrote: "When he and I were alone he closed up to the fire: his great head bowed, his knees held tight together and his finger-tips pressed to his chest, in what I call his 'penitential' attitude, and he began a long tale, plaintive and rather vague, about his loneliness, the sadness of his life, the suffering he experiences from the slanders of others."* He was privileged, he was under no social compulsion; humoured by Gosse, he became domesticated, his ways were understood, his whims catered for. His silences were often difficult to interpret. Once after being unusually quiet, gazing at Mrs. Gosse, he crackled out, "All day long I've been wondering who ought to have painted you, and at first I thought it was Palma Vecchio, but now I know it should be Paris Bordone." At Delamere Terrace too he indulged his effusive delight in tiny children, not as Gosse is at pains to point out because Victor Hugo had written about them, as sometimes alleged, but from a spontaneous and unfeigned pleasure in their company.

Swinburne's removal to Putney meant the end of hours of incomparable converse.

In 1880 Gosse was appointed the London agent for Scribners. His income from writing was showing satisfactory progress. 1881, £442. 1882, £647. 1883, £702. At the beginning of each year he mapped out a course of buying as a student might a course of reading, and made a list of plays he wished to acquire. For a large number of these he paid as many pence as the buyer of to-day would be called on to pay sovereigns. He was an adroit purchaser, with a specialist's flair for title-pages and editions. Taxation and the American buyer had not yet driven collectors to look on first editions and works of art as lucrative investments. Gosse was guided by what he could afford rather than by what he could gain. He loved everything to do with books. Catalogues were like windows opening on to promised lands, some corner of which he might hope to possess. By-streets and sale-rooms, the quays in Paris and all the haunts of booklovers were scenes for excited discovery and high

* *Portraits and Sketches*, 1912, p. 15.

enjoyment. Put him in a room with a shelf of books, and like Dr. Johnson he would at once "pore over them almost brushing them with his eyelashes from near examination." He ran to books as a painter to pictures. He handled them with the care and gusto of a connoisseur, expert not only in the matter of contents, but "enamoured as a swain" of binding, print and provenance. To the end of his days he kept up an imaginative attachment to his books, buying better even than he knew and accumulating by small annual outlays a library which after his death realised £26,000.

The routine of the Board of Trade was not exacting. It provided some of the things most wanted by a man of letters, an assured income, a state of comparative isolation, quiet, and unlimited stationery. Moreover, and this was the very thing Gosse needed, the work kept him in touch with foreign countries and foreign languages. In his room several storeys high in Whitehall looking over the Thames, he had a refuge, where he could shut himself off and work even over time at the articles and reviews by which he was week by week winning the esteem of the reading public. He was pushing his way to the front rank of critics, thanks to his pellucid style, his natural and now highly-trained discernment, and his engaging metaphors. He worked hard and he worked quickly and at the same time methodically. In all directions he was busy pushing out lines of communications. He had set himself to know everyone of note: and he was insatiably anxious to be in the thick of things literary, to be recognised and applauded, and rank high among writers.

His taste had few exclusions, and in his preferences he was just and sincere. Criticism to Gosse was not the diffusion of accurate knowledge, or the imposition of an æsthetic: to him as to the newer school of critics, its principal purpose was to spread the love of literature, to intensify interest, steady judgment, and broaden appreciation. That purpose he was successfully fulfilling. It might even be said that in these years his fame was growing a little too fast: that he was actually being outpaced by his reputation. Success, as he wrote to Howells in 1886, had come to him too easily. This had many beneficial consequences, but it had less obvious drawbacks. He was, as a result, credited with the authority of a learned scholar, a position which his knowledge, various and discriminating though it was, never really justified and at this time was very far from supporting. It was assumed that one who wrote so well and ranged so far must be erudite in the most specialised sense of the term. Scholarship was in fact being thrust upon him, he was driven to living beyond his intellectual capital. The result was to emerge later, but it has to be borne in mind when the attacks come to be considered.

But his occupations were not solely intellectual; in summer he missed no opportunity of swimming and boating, and in those far-off winters when safe ice seems to have been a less rare phenomenon he was an enthusiastic skater. Leslie Stephen's saying of Swift, "He had the characteristic passion of the good and wise for walking," and applied by Charles Whibley to W. P. Ker, was applicable also to Gosse. He had plenty of physical courage, and though through his nervous temperament very much aware of fear, controlled it like an evil passion by reason. In the early days of bicycling he was run away with down a long incline and in describing the event in a letter to Mr. Marsh, he wrote, "I experienced Fear, the most rousing of the passions." He could be actor and onlooker, agent and observer, as if applying inwards and towards himself those habits of observation which in childhood he had been trained to direct upon the lesser creatures of the sea.

Thornycroft had directed Gosse's mind to the technicalities of art. In 1881 Gosse was commissioned by John Morley to visit Paris and write articles on the Salon for the *Pall Mall Gazette*. Having tasted blood, he returned to London and appeared in the *Fortnightly Review* as a critic of the Academy, scattering judicious praise, but in conflict with popular opinion denouncing Poynter's *Helen of Troy*. His art criticism, which he kept up for a few years only, was "safe" and painstaking, in line with the taste of the day, and concerned for the most part with the personnel and tendencies of the Royal Academy. It was of course an entirely unimportant deviation from his true vocation, but left him with the necessary means for gauging the pretensions of others in a similar line.

29, Delamere Terrace,
Friday night.

To Hamo Thornycroft. *16.1.80*

My dear Hamo,—

Will you dine here next Monday at 6? If you can't, fix any day you like next week. Write, in either case, to 1, Whitehall so that I get it on Monday, as I go there from Reading without first going home.

I have a great longing to talk to you, and nothing to say. What a foolish person, you will say—but I have long given up trying to make you think me anything else. It was such a delight to me on Wednesday to see you so prosperous: I mean, that I felt you were advancing in all respects just as we should wish. It gave me an indefinite sense of satisfaction, like looking at a plant after a day or two's absence, and finding it slightly but sensibly grown. Your putting in of that drapery is superb. I have now no fears of any kind. I just throw up my hat and sing when I think of the *Artemis*.

Please throw the skirt of your prosperity over me, for I want it. Besides the official worries I told you of, since I saw you I have had a tiresome misunderstanding with the *Saturday Review*. At first I thought it would be very serious: now I hope it may be got over, but it has been enough to give me half a dozen sleepless hours last night. Then I have such a bad rheumatism in my right arm that I cannot write without pain, and I have had to write for three hours this evening. So altogether my horizon is rather leaden, and the only sunlight I find just at present is when I absorb myself in the thoughts of you, grand and serious, face to face with your goddess, putting on her robes for her, like Apollo when he winds the body of the Dawn in fleecy raiment of clouds. You are Apollo to me: how glumpy and wretched was I when I began this note, and already your far-reaching beams have pierced my darkness. But you must expect to find me excessively dull and spiritless on Monday.

Shall we ever go up the Colne? I can't believe it, to-day. It seems as though it were a very far-away memory of my childhood, that you and I, little tiny boys, paddled up to Uxbridge in a washing-tub, or something of that kind, and got whipped for our pains. I can't believe that anything pleasant will ever happen to me again. Why can't fortune let us alone, when we want so little, just a nest of domestic quietude in which to brood over our two blue eggs, Friendship and Art, till they hatch two fledgeling immortalities?

This is mere jabbering; but I write on because I am too tired to leave off, and because the only thing that would really quiet me would be to drop my head into the paws of some feline creature—a jaguar for instance—and sleep a dreamless sleep.

Goodnight: I wonder if I shall sleep. About 4 in the morning it begins to be so dreadful.

Thy
E. W.

29, Delamere Terrace,
To Hamo Thornycroft. *Saturday.*

DEAR DR. HAMO,—

The patient was troubled yesterday with a very large sore lip and a general feeling of brains having been well-shaken. But otherwise he did great credit to his physician; and is better still to-day.

I was excessively annoyed to find the thermometer hopeless yesterday morning. I wanted to show you that I was not a bit daunted by my accident, but more devoted to the edge than ever. As it is, you must take my pluck for granted. No more ice this season, I am afraid. You agree with me, I hope, in spite of the tumbles, that Thursday was by far the best of the good days we have had on the ice. The glow of the sun as we sat on the bench, how it thrilled us. Did you notice how naturally it set us talking of the dear old "Waterlily," Fanny Balls and the comfortable country Cumfrey? Few people know how moving a sunshiny day in mid-winter is; it sets all the summer veins pulsing, welling up blood from the heart in the great throb of the arteries, till the whole body is in a sort of melting ravishment, ready to take in every hint of colour and perfume and bodily touch. I could say many curious things about that bask we had in the sun on Thursday; but I saw in your eyes that you were thinking them too, so I will not waste my speech.

Do you not perceive that, like the bees, we are storing a great deal of the honey of memory for our old age? Strange, that people don't do this more; but I suspect few people live quite so much at their own finger-tips as we do. It is a power to thank God for and to cultivate, to roll the moments on one's tongue, and keep the flavour of them. When we had been talking the other day of riding and shooting—do you recollect?—I could not help thinking as I skated about what a poor thing all the matters I used to boast myself of—I mean mere acquirement of knowledge and book-learning—are in comparison with living one's life while one is young. It seems to me much more worth doing to be able to ride a colt across a rough piece of country than to be able to read a page of Thucydides. Ten years ago it would have seemed blank idiocy to me to have said that, but now the long months and months I have spent in stuffing the inside of my sheet of brown paper seem to me almost wasted. I think I could be quite happy to go with you to some place in the Back Woods, where we could make a clearing, build ourselves a hut, grow our own food, and go off with our rifles into the forest when we wanted a change of employment. Do you know that you are a great wizard? I am very oddly bewitched; I scarcely know myself.

Last week I sent you some very bad verses which I honestly wish you to destroy, if you have not yet done so. To-day I send you, to take the taste out of your mouth, a sonnet which I fancy is more worthy of me, and of you. Be sure you tell me what you think of it: it expresses exactly what I have once or twice tried to say to you. There are some things I can say to you in verse that I find it impossible to express in prose.

If I can finish my *Island of the Blest*, I have had an offer to put it into the April number of the *New Quarterly Magazine*. It is very unusual to get so long a work brought out in a magazine. But I want to know whether the description of your *Artemis* is sufficiently full to give you any annoyance, if it came out *before* the Academy exhibition. I expect you to tell me your real feeling.

EDMUND GOSSE ÆTAT 30

Moreover, I cannot screw myself up to finish the piece. The end ought to be very dramatic and spirited, and I hardly know whether I can reach back into the feeling. A poem ought to be written straight off, poured out while the metal is blazing hot, or else it sticks.

I had no idea I was writing you so long a letter. I hurry to close it.

Your

E. W. G.

If the size of this budget frightens you, keep it to read in bed on Sunday morning, for it is about nothing in particular.

Board of Trade,
S.W.

To Hamo Thornycroft. *23.3.80.*

How good of you, Hamo, to write to me! I was longing for a letter, yet giving myself a dozen reasons why, of course, you were too busy to write one.

We had a goodbye gathering on Sunday, and missed you much. I hope Helen told you something of what occurred. Swinburne in light blue trousers and with a little peak—unknown in anatomy—in the pit of his stomach, was the feature of the afternoon. It was very strange to me to see the broken body of *Artemis.* I never realized before what the human face would look like seen from inside.

How more than fortunate that the injury of the Little Man is unimportant: I was fidgeting inwardly over that.

You must be very tired, my poor Child. Will the summer and the canoeing time never come? I long to be paddling up the river, and looking sideways down a meadow-land all shining with buttercups and bloomy grasses, in that way that one catches the long things, such as sorrel and meadow-sweet, silhouetted against the sky; and with all around us a murmur and perfume of June.

Thursday at 6.

Ton

E. W. G.

3.30 p.m.

I have just been lunching with Sidney Colvin: he asked after you and said he was glad we had not come to Cambridge in February. He thinks it will be much nicer in May, and he will then have more time to show us about.

ISOLATION

We press so near, yet fall so far asunder,
  The lightning cleaves us from the abyss above,
And though, like rolling clouds, we meet in thunder,
  Between us lies the mystery of love.

I wrote the verse opposite this morning and thought it very fine. Now I don't know what it means. Do you?

The following letter refers to an article in *Fraser* reviewing the poetry of Gosse, Andrew Lang and Dr. Hake. Gosse's *New Poems* published in 1879 contained, as well as a selection of poems already printed, a number of new lyrics. Here Gosse has cast out the crude lusciousness of his earlier verses, and exercises a restraint and delicacy of observation which give a more cultivated quality to his poems. His outlook on life has undergone a change; contemporary influences are less apparent; he is himself—accomplished, sensitive, exquisitely aware of nature, and rendering the new and deeper significances which life has brought him in a manner of his own. The sentiment is true and no longer flushed with artificial throbs and tremors; here and there in pure poetry he shadows forth a reality he has experienced and observed. The best of the lyrics in this volume whenever they are read will be read with pleasure.

Board of Trade,
S.W.

My dear Hamo,— *2.11.80.*

As usual I split the interlunar darkness of my week—long obscuration between one Friday flash and the next—by a consolatory chat with you. How many years I lived without having anyone to write to in this cosy way!

I had a nice time down at Reading. Sunday was a superb day.

Waterhouse and I walked to church at Sonning, and after church crossed the river for a walk. The meadows, however, between Sonning and Shiplake were completely flooded. There was indeed a punt for passengers, but the punt was gone to its dinner on the Shiplake side. After yelling and whistling in vain, we just took off our boots and stockings, rolled up our trousers, and waded about half a mile. Then we had to strike out smartly to get up our circulation, and reached Henley in good style, went on to Fawley Court, back again, over the bridge at Henley, through Wargrave, to Twyford, where we got a trap to take us home. A good walk, wasn't it? 15 or 16 miles at the least.

The magazines are much occupied with me this month. My poems are praised, incidentally, in four of them, and in *Fraser* there is the best notice of my entire work as a poet that I have ever received, by a perfect stranger. I must show it you: it has given me great pleasure. It is so very pleasant to have a man survey your work, not piecemeal, but in its entirety. It gives one a glimpse of what, if one is very fortunate, posterity may say about one.

The ghastly pipey skeleton of your bowman is covered with flesh I suppose. Who will you find for a model? Is he to be draped or naked? I have just been amused to see how Foley feels constrained to belt his nude Caractacus, and draw a sort of pocket-handkerchief down through the belt to hide what it would have been much more innocent to leave un-noticed and un-noticeable. By the way Armstead's figure that I was describing to you is too plainly suggested by this same Caractacus.

Dinner at 6 on Friday.

Your loving,

EDMUND W. GOSSE.

CHAPTER ELEVEN

Early in the new decade, a decade the first years of which saw the deaths of Carlyle, George Eliot and Borrow, Gosse made the acquaintance of Thomas Hardy and W. D. Howells (1837-1920), and he quickly formed friendships with them which lasted for the remainder of their lives. It was in 1881 too that he paid the first of many visits to Coventry Patmore (1823-1896) at Milward House, Hastings. "The old poet," he wrote to Thornycroft, "is very genial and most interesting, with a fresh and original mind, with strong individual sides which come out in unfamiliar forms of prejudice." The "old poet," ranging in verbal rhapsodies through realms of mysticism, and "descending every now and then to earth in some fierce eccentric jest," provided Gosse with a pure intellectual enjoyment, as keen as any he had ever tasted. Long walks over the downs, struggles with wet winds along the sea front, talks by the poet's fireside, brought prophet and enquirer into close sympathy. Gosse observed and noted. He remembered Stevenson's precept.* Thirty-five years later in his life of Coventry Patmore he recorded his recollection of the poet's characteristics with that fine skill and vivid touch of which he was master.

W. D. Howells, to whom letters that follow are addressed, in England is now a name—in the 'eighties he was a vogue. At his death in 1920 his repute as a popular novelist had already dissolved into thin air, he had ceased to be discussed or read. "The 'best seller,'" Gosse remarks in his volume *Silhouettes*, "never recovers from the ordeal of Kensal Green, unless his work contains extraordinary qualities of solid merit." Howells had been a best seller. In the 'eighties, *A Foregone Conclusion, The Lady of the Aroostook* and *The Rise of Silas Lapham* were familiar to the generality of readers. They were suited to the taste of the day. Anti-romantic in tendency, they gracefully introduced a type of realistic writing, but

* See ante p. 105.

so winnowed by prudery and so refined by evasive selection that it amounted almost to a negation of realism. They lingered on, enjoying a considerable measure of popularity. But the new realism with its robuster methods was fatal to writing so purely elegant and making such a delicate approach to life. Howells was some ten years older than Gosse: he had recently arrived from Boston. He came at a period of lull; Andrew Lang's *Ballads in Blue China* had appeared in 1880; Swinburne, having published *Tristam of Lyonesse*, seemed for the moment to have fallen on a time of exhaustion; Banville's "feats of graceful metrical gymnastics" had set a fashion for the younger poets who were now busy with "French forms," with rondeaux, villanelles, triolets, and chant-royals, allusions to which abound in Gosse's letters; the Muses of Tennyson and Browning appeared quiescent; Meredith in 1883 was bringing out *Poems and Lyrics of the Joy of the Earth*—but *Diana of the Crossways* had still to begin its career as a serial in the *Fortnightly*. Thomas Hardy was publishing *Two on a Tower* in the *Atlantic Monthly*. Andrew Lang, Austin Dobson and Gosse were pressing the claims of the younger poets. Gosse, now a prominent literary figure, prolific in output, accepted as an authority, and widely sought after as contributor and lecturer, was preparing, in response to an invitation, to visit the United States. These were busy years; clouds blew up only to scatter and leave as they passed a new gift of light on his days; the coming storm still lay unsuspected below the horizon. How, it may be asked, did he manage to gather friends, as he seemingly did, at will? Certainly one spell by which he brought them into the fold was his conversation. Talk was one of his essential virtues, an asset that never wasted and whose excellence none would be found to deny. No one had listened to him with greater pleasure than Stevenson. In his essay *Talk and Talkers* published in the *Cornhill Magazine* 1882, and now included in *Memories and Portraits*, he has once and for all conveyed exactly the living spirit of Gosse's conversation. "Purcel," he writes, and Purcel is Gosse, "is in another class from any I have mentioned. He is no debater, but appears in conversation, as occasion rises, in two distinct characters, one of which I admire and fear, and the other love. In the first he is radiantly civil, and rather silent, sits on a high courtly hill-top, and from that vantage-ground drops you his remarks like favours. He seems not to share in our sublunary contentions; he wears no sign of interest; when on a sudden there falls in a crystal of wit, so polished that the dull do not perceive it, but so right that the sensitive are silenced. True talk should have more body and blood, should be louder, vainer and more declaratory of the man: the true talker should not hold so steady an advantage over whom he speaks with; and that is one reason out of a score why I prefer my Purcel in his second character, when he unbends into a strain of graceful gossip, singing like the fireside kettle. In these moods he has an elegant homeliness that rings of the true Queen Anne." That was Gosse; "singing like the fireside kettle" or "letting fall a crystal of wit"; and as it was in 1882, so it was in 1927. But it was not only with his intellectual equals that Gosse could talk, and talk exceedingly well; he was just as vivacious and interested in discussing sheep-shearing with a shepherd, horse-shoeing with a blacksmith, or vintages and local topics with an innkeeper. In writing to Howells he says, referring to a remark of his correspondent about Delamere Terrace, "You shall be welcomed, Oh! how gladly, into the Home of the Gigglers. In that home there are no *corvées* to be done, and no errands to be run. It is giggle and make giggle from morning to night." In childhood, he had been taught, and not to much purpose, to look for sermons in stones and elsewhere, in maturity he made up for it by perpetually finding laughter in folly, in incongruities, and the unintended import of words. His humour was related to Charles Lamb's; they would have chuckled together at the same jokes; Lamb would have rejoiced over a conversation at the Luttrell Arms,* where the landlord used to talk so frequently of one Ell as a local infliction, and much looked down on, that when he informed Gosse that a Mr. Snooks had been elected as a Local Government representative Gosse said, "They will be having Ell next." "Yes, Sir," said the landlord, "they *will* be having *Ell*," fully believing that Gosse had meant to refer to the Infernal Re-

* At Dunster, where Gosse was a frequent visitor till the death of the landlord.

gions. Equally can one picture Lamb's delight over a visit of Gosse and Arthur Benson to the premises of the gamekeeper at Addington, who invited them to inspect some rabbits. As they were leaving Gosse said, "Look at the poor things, they are so sorry we are going that their eyes are quite pink with crying," upon which the keeper gravely remarked, "No, sir, it's the nature of the animal"; or over Gosse's recollection of his voyage back from Stockholm when a Swede on seeing the liqueur *anisette* at lunch, asked Gosse if he knew what it was made of. *"Aniseed,"* said Gosse. "No," replied the Swede, "it's made of some particular seed." He had an insatiable appetite for the ridiculous, for bagatelles thrown up from the underworld of nonsense, and, relishing humour in many keys, nothing was too trifling for his laughter, and few things too grave for his wit.

In a letter of this year (1881) he refers to a ball at the Tademas' and Oscar Wilde's refusal to conceal his features behind a mask. It must have been on this occasion that Wilde on being introduced to Gosse said how glad he was to meet him—Gosse said, "I was afraid you would be disappointed." "I am never," Wilde replied, "disappointed in literary men, I think they are perfectly charming. It is their works I find so disappointing——"

The Grove,
Great Stanmore,

To Hamo Thornycroft. *March 11, 81.*

My dear Hamo,—

It would be a pity that you should hamper yourself at all on my account: and so we have arranged that our little crisis shall take place next Thursday, wh. is your in-evening. Don't make any preparation: I'll just drop in about 10 p.m.

You wonder why I am here. It was quite an improvisation. I was feeling rather done up, and so came out here early this morning. It has been a radiant day, reminding me very vividly of our day here together last year, eleven months ago.

As I walked up from the station it was all so fresh and radiant that I put it into verse for you. It was the woodpecker burring and tapping that set me off:—

Where are you, Hamo, where?
For our own bird the woodpecker, is here,
Calling on you with cheerful tappings loud;
The breathing heavens are full of liquid light;
The dew is on the meadow like a cloud;
The earth is moving in her green delight,
Her spiritual crocuses shoot through,
And rathe hepaticas of rose and blue;
But snowdrops that awaited you so long,
Died at the thrush's song.

"Adieu! adieu!" they said,
"We saw the skirts of glory, and we fade;
We were the hopeless lovers of the spring,
Too young as yet for any love of ours;
She is harsh, not having heard the whitethroat's song,
She is cold, not knowing the tender April showers;
Yet have we felt her as the buried grain
May feel the whisper of the unfallen rain,
We have known her as the star that sets too soon
Bows to the unseen moon."

This afternoon, in sunshine as warm as June, we drove to see Herkomer. We found him charming, full of cordiality and zeal, holding us with his glittering eye, painting a colossal picture with one hand and designing a giant advertisement with the other, practising mezzotint with his left foot and printing off portraits of himself with his right—you know his eager way? But very charming—and I think he has got into a wholesome groove again with his work.

But I can't get off this beneficent miracle of warm air and flowers and birds. I have been so elate and excited all day, pacing about this lovely grass garden, half laughing, half crying. The smell of the earth seems intoxicating, the life in one's own veins seems to respond to the teeming warmth in the ground. Very soon, if this lasts, we must go into the country for a walk together. I have been turning all day to mingle my exultation with yours, and found you not.

Did you see yourself in the forefront of the *Daily News* this morning? Herkomer has given me one of the original advertisement bills of *The Woman in White* by Walker. Is not that a nice thing to have?

Expect me at 6 on Monday.

Your loving,
EDMUND W. GOSSE.

29, Delamere Terrace,
23.4.81.

To Austin Dobson.

MY DEAR DOBSON,—

What is to be said unto you, you writer of sweet words? Your little critique is a model of grace and thoughtful considerateness. Where I am tearing my hair is at the thought of what a fool I was not to ask you to read through that curst preface!

What a dreadful year this is for deaths! I have just been indescribably shocked to hear of the sudden death by paralysis of my old friend Burges, the A.R.A. He was almost the first artist I ever knew. You should ask Monkhouse whether he can't write a nice appreciative notice of him somewhere. He used to give the quaintest little tea-parties in his bare bachelor chambers, all very dowdy, but the meal served in beaten gold, the cream poured out of a single onyx, and the tea strictured in its descent on account of real rubies inside the pot. He was much blinder than any near-sighted man I ever knew, and once when with me in the country, mistook a peacock seen *en face* for a man. His work was really more jewel-work than architecture, just because he was so blind, but he had real genius, I am sure. I have a sort of impression that you knew him or he knew you: if I am wrong, forgive these impertinent reminiscences.

Thank you again, my dear, for your charming notice; when shall I see you?

Your affectionate
EDMUND W. GOSSE.

29, *Delamere Terrace,*

To Hamo Thornycroft. *Oct. 26. 81.*

MY DEAR HAMO,—

I have just finished my oriental poem* and turn to you, with rather an excited head. Perhaps what I have written to-night will be read after my death! I never felt more inclined to think so of anything of mine. I should really like you to hear these closing fifty lines—they are certainly the best. Have you this queer unsettled feeling when you have finished a statuette? I feel in so odd a minglement of discouragement and conceit. A thing done, as well as one knows how to do it, and yet so many fathoms below how one knows it should be done.

I dined at Townshend House last night; it was very dull. All Germans, except the lank and melancholy painter called Wigglin† or Wriggling, you know the man? How is he spelt? . . . .

. . . .

Your loving
EDMUND W. GOSSE.

29, *Delamere Terrace,*
W.

To R. L. Stevenson. *7.11.81.*

MY DEAR LOUIS,—

I have been in correspondence with my New York friends about you, and they wholly agree with me that you ought to be secured hard and fast, and towed with the other immortals down the golden river of the *Century* which used to defy metaphor by calling itself *Scribner.*

But what the editor says regarding my first proposition is this:—"He would have to say something remarkably fresh about our

* *Firdausi in Exile.* † Weguelin.

dear old household divinity Franklin to justify him in tackling that exhausted subject."

Well, I admit that there is a good deal in that.

Now, they propose that I ask you to write an article on the Course of the Thames, to be copiously illustrated. That would, of course, be most delightful, but could hardly be managed at Davos.

Will you write me as sober and business-like a letter as you can contrive, and let me know what you are at work upon, and what you could propose for us of a bright and fresh kind.

Our pay is £2 a page, but when we get hold of a tip-top swell like you we can manage £3 10s. a page. Which is, I think, pretty decent.

Yours affectionately

EDMUND W. GOSSE.

To Austin Dobson. *Jan. 18, 1882.*

MY DEAR DOBSON,—

I wish you many happy returns of the day which gave England so fine a poet and me so dear a friend. I have no news to tell you of any kind whatever, except that Mr. Gray, of Peterhouse, has just printed, with Mr. Dodsley, a paper of Reflections in a Country Church-yard, and that the town is mightily taken with it. But you must absolutely not name the author. Mr. Walpole was so busy as to do so, and it went near losing him the gentleman's acquaintance. 'Tis a proud little person, they tell me, and faugh! what has a poor poet to do with pride? He might leave it, like the vapours, for quality alone.

I am, dear child, very much

your servant,

EDMUND W. GOSSE.

29, Delamere Terrace, W.

To R. L. Stevenson. *17.3.82.*

MY DEAR LOUIS,—

My wife has divulged, with sobs and cries, concealing her crimson face in the hollows of her hair, that she wrote you a little timid letter that was meant to be funny, and that you have withered her with well-deserved sarcastic silence. It was not for her, a mere guardian of babes, to bandy jokes with a professed wit, and that on the very body and bones of Holy Scripture. But she is very deeply sensible of her fault, will never jest again, and will walk veiled in a pink flush of her own composition, till she hears, through me, that you have quite overlooked the indiscretion. "Woman," I said gently to her, on receiving this confession, "return to your spindle." "That is a plagiarism," she modestly replied, but returned nevertheless. You are not very angry, I hope? It was not really anything very dreadful that she said?

It seems a very long time since I had any news of you. I saw Colvin the other night, only for a few moments, on the first night of *Romeo and Juliet.* Irving made a beautiful Romeo, 55 at least, with wrinkles painted in his neck, and altogether a wonderfully careful presentment of amorous old age. In the noblest art of the actor, however, something is wanting, and it seemed to me that a more shaky hand and more marked weakness of the hams would have emphasized his conception of the part. And a few white hairs carelessly stealing from under the black wig would have given a fine touch. Yet he did old wrinkled Romeo finely. He and the nurse seemed formed to make one another happy: yet nothing came of it.

Do you get on with your Glencoe Tragedy for us? I look forward to something in your best style.

My Gray for John Morley is almost finished. I shall be very anxious to see what you think of it. It is very human: I fear I have said too much about the man and not enough about the works: I like the man best.

Please give my kindest regards to Symonds. Do not let him hasten over his Philip Sidney. The subject wants digestion. I know why he chose him for a hero, but they would send me to the Tower if I wrote the reason in a letter! O naughty world!

Yours always sincerely,

EDMUND W. GOSSE.

EDMUND GOSSE AND AUSTIN DOBSON AT THE BOARD OF TRADE

FROM A CARICATURE BY MAX BEERBOHM

29, Delamere Terrace,

To R. L. Stevenson. *4.4.82.*

My dear Louis,—

Your letter gives me inexpressible joy, for I *knew* (peccavi!) that Purcel meant me,* but dared not say so in the face of its being appropriated elsewhere.

Congreve—Baxter.

Opalstein—Symonds.

Are these not right? I have made Baxter's acquaintance, with very great satisfaction and appreciation.

I am bound to tell you that my wife was the first to detect Purcel. She thinks it inimitable as a description of my talk. I am excessively pleased and flattered to be thus crystallized in your writing. I did not for one moment (O forgive me!) take it for anyone else.

The point of Erasmus is that he bore about in him "the orient and the occident," that is the instinct for the old faith and a feeling for the new—he was, it seems to me, the Janus of the Reformation, Mr. Looking-both-Ways (*sic*), preternaturally intelligent, but too clairvoyant to be at all happy either way. This is the key to my verses, the present sense of which can be obscure to no one, who turns from the Rev. Orby Shipley or the Rev. Newman Hall to Bradlaugh & Co.

Buccaneers, hell take them, are waiting the pleasure of Mr. Illustrator Lucas.

Bravo the Emblems! Thou second Alciati, Quarles was but a quip upon thee, thou walking Cato!

Yours affectionately,

Edmund W. Gosse.

Hôtel de la Hure,
Laon.

To Hamo Thornycroft. *7.4.82.*

My dear Hamo,—

It seems quite incredible that one breakfasted in London yesterday. We seem days and weeks from home. We crossed over to

* See ante p. 143.

Boulogne with an infinite crowd of tourists from whom we parted by simply leaving the train at Amiens. I think you know this delicious place, with its pure cathedral, its exterior full of lovely Gothic sculpture. We slept there, and passed on this morning to Noyon, which I feel sure you do not know. Fancy a little town of 6000 inhabitants in which every house is a picture, and which carries in its centre the loveliest Romanesque cathedral scarcely touched by restoration, full of the boldest and most original work I ever saw. All this under a sky of unclouded blue. The town is a cluster of irregular *places* and winding streets, almost all the houses timbered in the richest style, not a few quite as elaborate as that old Cheshire hall of which you have a drawing. When the houses are not of this kind, they are of lovely old brick, the colour of a freshly plucked mushroom. Up into the air at every angle go quaint fantastic gables, full of colour and fancy. Not a corner, not a lane but would make a picture; and all this without a touch of the sight-seer or the itinerary; nobody has yet discovered Noyon, and the people seemed as surprised to see us as if we had dropped from the moon. Yet the beauty of one feature alone, a library of the 15th century, in exquisite preservation, would be enough to call attention to the place if the sublime cathedral were not there with its rich apse and incredible buttresses filling the scene. Positively you and I must see Noyon.

We did not stay more than a few hours at Noyon, and came on to this place. Laon is a city set on a hill; it has a fine cathedral, also, but one which has been in the hands of the restorers. The real point of Laon is its position on the small top of an abrupt hill in a plain; you walk round the ramparts, and take an almost infinite view of the country on all sides.

Our party consists of four men besides myself, all much older than me. We are a very merry party, and make the most of our little holiday. How I wish to go over every step of the country in your company! I shall have much to tell you. We go on to Rheims to-morrow.

Yours,

EDMUND W. GOSSE.

29, Delamere Terrace,

To Algernon Swinburne. *22.6.82.*

My dear Swinburne,—

Will you accept the accompanying copy of a little book I have written on Gray? I am anxious to send it to you at once, before you hear from anyone else that I have ventured in it, in one or two points, to differ from your expressed judgment. I hope you will not think that I have done so in an unbecoming spirit or in forgetfulness of your position. When I have grown to the utmost bound of my nature, you will surpass me still by all the vast difference which separates genius from mere talent. Do not believe that I shall ever forget that. But Stromboli may dispute with Vesuvius, I hope, on abstract questions, if he does it in a proper spirit, and I am, believe me, not less certain that you are usually right than I am convinced that you are in this one instance wrong.

The little book represents a great labour of compilation and even of discovery. I hope the story, now told for the first time, is not unamusing.

Believe me,
Yours very sincerely,
Edmund W. Gosse.

29, Delamere Terrace,

To Algernon Swinburne. *26.6.82.*

My dear Swinburne,—

Your kind words about my *Gray* and some of a similar tenour which I just received from Matthew Arnold are inexpressibly encouraging. With such suffrages I am quite careless what the critics may say.

Your anecdote about Wordsworth is new to me, and of very great personal interest. I did not even know that you had ever seen Wordsworth.

It gives me particular pleasure to find you at one with me on the curious merit of the Norse fragments.

Thank you for your kind letter and believe me,

Ever sincerely yours,

EDMUND W. GOSSE.

29, Delamere Terrace,

To R. L. Stevenson. *23.6.82.*

MY DEAR LOUIS,—

Read this little gray opuscule, and tell me truly if it bores you. I want to know if you feel the *man* to have been a fine soul—if not, I have failed.

Meanwhile Edmund

is all yours.

29, Delamere Terrace,

To W. D. Howells. *12.10.82.*

DEAR HOWELLS,—

Your angel-visit was so bright and brief that I hardly know whether it really took place. Perhaps I only dreamed of meeting you, and am now startling a distinguished stranger with the audacious familiarity of my address. I won't, however, even pretend that an event which left me permanently richer never happened at all. But I will warn you, for your instant satisfaction, and that you may not be cursing deep and free, that I don't expect any answer whatever to this letter. It is simply to relieve my own feelings that I do it. It is an epistolary run-away knock; don't trouble to answer the bell. Unless I can get you any books about reefs or coolies, or send you anything you want for yr novel, in which case I shall be much offended if you don't write.

We are all talking about you. I see ladies giggling over little books in the train, and then I know they must be reading *The Parlour Car*. A quantity of cads have sworn to behave like gentlemen in consequence of meeting *The Lady of the Aroostook*, and the question, Have you read *A Wedding Journey*? is one of those tiresome things that make one loathe one's fellow-creatures. I really cannot but think that Douglas' edition must be very successful. My wife gave me the whole series on my birthday: they really are charming little books—I mean in their physical aspect.

I have been so busy ever since I came back that I can't find time to write my necessary business notes: which gives the fact of my writing this needless letter to you almost the zest of a vice. I was very glad you went down to Stoke Poges and that you felt the delicious sentiment of the place: it is wonderfully ancient and secluded for a spot so near London. I have just entered into treaty with Macmillans to edit Gray's Works for them in handsome form. It has never been done before.

If you are really writing much about Hong Kong, you had better let me send you some blue-books lately published here, on the atrocious tyrannies of the local police, quite a Zolaesque study of the life in the low quarter of the town. But perhaps your hero is careful not to get into bad company, and keeps his ethics gilt-edged till he is thrown up upon the atoll. I want to read it very much.

With kindest remembrances to Mrs. Howells and Miss Howells.

I am, we are,

Yours very sincerely,

EDMUND W. GOSSE AND FAMILY.

29, Delamere Terrace,

To Hamo Thornycroft. *2.7.83.*

MY DEAR HAMO,—

We are blind creatures, and although I have often teazed you about Tonbridge, I had no notion that it was serious. You describe a sculptor's wife, and if your sketch of her is only fairly like, she must be a most charming, a most lovable creature. I pray God with all my heart to bless you both, to teach her to love you as you deserve to be loved, and to give you a long sunny life together. If she is worthy of you, and I cannot help hoping that she may be, you will be a splendid pair.

I feel so serious and agitated about it that I cannot indulge in any of the gentle chaff which is proper to these occasions. Perhaps that is never in very good taste, and for me it is about as possible as if I was your mother. The grand event has happened, the greatest in the world, the moon has suddenly turned round—as she always does once and only once—and what is on the other side? Who knows? Happiness, tenderly reciprocal affection, a thousand quiet blessings, I hope.

You are not so young now as to be treated as if you were the sublimely selfish first-lover of 22. I may even venture to speak to you of myself, for at this crisis of our lives my one great thought is one of gratitude to you for these four wonderful years, the summer of my life, which I have spent in a sort of morning-glory walking by your side. You will not think about this at first, and I should be sorry if you did. But as time goes on and we grow older still, it will all come back to you.

I can say nothing but what is stupid. God bless you and be good to you. When you find a spare moment you must try and prepare your future wife to like me. I am so very anxious to like her.

Your loving Friend,

EDMUND W. GOSSE.

Let me entreat you not to prolong your engagement. Marry soon.

Shirehall Lane,

Dorchester,

To Hamo Thornycroft. *July 23, 1883.*

DEAR HAMO,—

Hardy has taken a rambling house in this town, a house of which a townsman said, "He have but one window and she do look into Gaol Lane." It is indeed a kind of mole, for the entrance is almost invisible and its burrow extends to the back of everything. Dorchester is an enchanting little county-town, with several handsome churches, old fortifications turned into elm-avenues, and bits of Roman wall and vallum everywhere. It is, moreover, as bright and clean as a pin, and full of life; a cavalry and an infantry regiment are stationed in it, and bugling and marching, and the loitering coloured military give it quite a foreign air.

Hardy and I walked last afternoon through fields of rye 5 and even 6 feet high to the village of Winterbourne-Came, of which

Mr. Barnes the poet is Rector. We were ushered up into the choir, behind a delicious old carved screen, among 17th-cent. marble monuments of the Earls of Portarlington. The church is a tiny little affair, that you could put in your pock; the congregation seemed to fill it pretty well, and yet we were only 45 souls in all. Barnes is a wonderful figure; he is in his 83rd year. He has long thin silky white hair flowing down and mingling with a full beard and moustache also as white as milk, a grand dome of forehead over a long thin pendulous nose, not at all a handsome face, but full of intelligence, and a beauty of vigour in extreme old age. He undertook the entire service himself, and preached rather a long sermon. Then he stayed behind to hear the school-children practise their singing, and walked to the rectory, as he had walked from it, rather over a mile. We waited in Came Park and he caught us up. His dress is interesting, black knee-breeches and silk stockings, without gaiters, and buckled shoes. I hear he is the last person in Dorset to keep up this dress. He was extremely hospitable, and seemed untirable; we stayed four hours with him, and all that time he was hurrying us from place to place to show us his treasures. His mind runs chiefly on British antiquities and philology; it was difficult to induce him to talk much about his poems. I was extremely gratified and interested by my visit.

Expect me on Wednesday morning.

Your affectionate

E. W. G.

To Lady Tadema. *28.7.83.*

Dearest Laura,—

I think that you call to-morrow your copper-wedding, and though, as an antiquarian, I deny the existence of a copper-wedding, I wish all the same to congratulate you warmly on the anniversary. The fifth is called the "wooden-wedding"; the seventh the "woollen-wedding"; the tenth the "tin-wedding"; and custom recognises no other until the twelfth, the "silk-wedding," and the fifteenth, the "crystal-wedding." So that I don't know where you get your copper-wedding from, but wherever it was, I wish that you may enjoy it no less than all those that have preceded it, and that you will pass on in due time, through the "crystal" and the "porcelain" and the "silver" and the "ruby," to your 50th "golden" wedding-day, and that I may be there to see.

And I will hope to drink your health to-morrow at breakfast in a bottle of *vin fin* at the ancient city of Troyes, whither it seems hardly credible that one night's journey will carry us.

The wind is high for such a queasy stomach as mine is, but you, I recollect, have no sympathy for such weakness.

My aunt at Stanmore has had her beehives decimated by the tit-mice, so she told her gardener that he ought to stick a potato full of feathers and hang it up close to the hive to frighten the little marauders. "Why! so I did, Ma'am, and no sooner had I done it, than the tits came and sat on the potato and looked at me!" Such is the march of modern scepticism!

Good-bye for a month, dearest Sis,

Your affecte brother,

EDMUND GOSSE.

I have written a second letter to Tad. to Townshend.

CHAPTER TWELVE

Before Howells left Europe again he had persuaded Gosse to cross the Atlantic and try his fortune lecturing in the United States. The Board of Trade acquiesced, and with the prospect of nine weeks' leave in the winter of 1884 Gosse set to work to prepare a course of lectures to be entitled *From Shakespeare to Pope: a History of the Decline of Romantic Poetry,* "which will be—let me boast to you," he wrote to Howells, "the best things I have ever written." "It would fill a gap," he continued in another letter, "in English criticism, and my reading for fifteen years has prepared me to fill it. It would be no *réchauffé* of other people's notions. I can promise original research, and the time is romantic to a surprising degree." The payment he was to receive was modest. Gosse was never mercenary. In spite of his book-keeping habits, he was incapable of bargaining. His tendency was always to take the terms that were offered, without exploring further the market value of his wares. He appeared perfectly content with the results. In the case of his American tour he regarded an assurance of £400 as sufficient to cover his expenses, his loss of earning power in England, and the cost of finding a substitute to do the work of *The Century* during his absence. The balance was to be made good by the excitement of the venture and the novelty of the experience. He was certain, too, to forge fresh links, and he was curious to see and learn more of a country whose heiresses at this time were invading Europe in great numbers, but whose less opulent literature and culture were finding their way across the Atlantic with hesitation.

Lecturing in America was a less-exploited source of revenue than it is to-day. It was a whirlwind ordeal, as agitating as a well-contested by-election, with much the same publicity and hustle, and supported by a boisterous Press and the scenario of a circus. Matthew Arnold had toured the States in 1884 in a train set apart by his managers for the *Matthew Arnold Troupe*, travelling at reduced rates with theatrical tickets bearing the same superscription. Gosse had no similar experience, but like Arnold he was feasted and fêted, tossed hither and thither on the wave of publicity and exhausted by the calls of hospitality and the claims of acquaintances. Arnold stooping to read his manuscript while lecturing, was likened by a Detroit newspaper to "an elderly bird pecking at grapes on a trellis." About Gosse the newspapers were less graphically personal; but preserved cuttings make it clear that his success was incontestable, and his letters leave no doubt as to the delight with which he responded to the excitement. At Baltimore he was offered the chair of English Literature in the University with a salary of £1000 a year.

To R. L. Stevenson. *20 Feb., 1884.*

Dear Louis,—

. . . . I have seen the proofs of your children's poems. I think them very unequal, but the best are simply splendid. Wherever you work out the notion of children being serious, and grown-up people idle persons who play at nothing, you are first-rate—most original because most true. The young gentleman who hunts upon the forest-track behind the sofa-back is a tender memory of ME. I used to do that—and I daresay lots of other I's, for I see that to this hour my own children never eat their porridge nor paint their prints nor even play with their bricks without pretending that they are doing something else. They live in an unbroken vision through which they prosecute the most ardent adventures, in which their mother and I are sometimes allowed to take part, but always on sufferance—merely because we are useful as Dramatis Personæ. When we have played our part we are coolly dismissed.

And it greatly amuses me to see how mutely indignant they are when the happy illusion has to be broken by a constitutional walk or a washing of face and hands or any of those tiresome things which only grown-up idiots would think of wanting done. The other day in a fit of annoyance at some trick or other, I called my son "a pig." A glow of gratified vanity swam across his face, instead of the shame I expected to find there. We found after a good deal of cross-examination that to become a pig (in reality) had long time been his young heart's dream!

(I have dropped my tiresome W, and am going to let it appear on no future title pages. So W. E. G. is E. W. G. no more.)

Ever your affectionate

EDMUND GOSSE.

Board of Trade,

To Mrs. Philip Gosse. *9.4.*

MY DARLING MOTHER,—

Once more I have the gladness of congratulating you and myself on another of your birthdays. How fast they seem to come, these birthdays! Each makes you more dear to me, and renews my prayer that you may have many more, and health given you to enjoy them.

Since I wrote to Father in the beginning of the week, I have taken an important step. The Trustees of the Lowell Institute at Boston have been asking me to come over next winter to deliver a course of 6 lectures at their Institute, and they offered me £150 for the course. I asked for a little time to think about it, and they seemed to suppose that the money made me hesitate, for they have repeated their invitation, this time offering £200. My friends out there have greatly pressed me to accept, and the authorities of the Johns Hopkins University have made a vague offer to me to repeat the same six lectures at Baltimore. They talk of £100. So that I believe myself justified in accepting. Yesterday I saw the authorities in this place, and asked for special leave of absence, which was granted at once, with the utmost courtesy and readiness. I therefore wrote to the Lowell Trustees yesterday, accepting their offer for next December. I think I shall probably start about the last week in November, and return early in February, with a total absence of ten weeks, six of which will be my total annual holiday of this year, three weeks of extra leave granted me, and one week of next year's holidays.

Nellie will go with me.

This matter has occupied our thoughts greatly during the last month, and I feel a certain relief now that our action is finally decided.

My friends in America are hoping to secure for me an invitation to Cornell University at Syracuse, to deliver the same series, for perhaps £100 more. If I could pocket £400, I should spend a very pleasant holiday without expense, and yet have something to put by when I come back.

The subject of my lectures will be "From Shakespeare to Pope"; an enquiry into the causes and character of the change from the Romantic to the so-called Classical School of Poetry in the 17th-century. The subject is important in the history of criticism, and has scarcely been touched. I propose simply to write a book on this subject, which I shall read on six consecutive nights, and print on returning to England.

This is quite a budget of birthday news for you, is it not?

With fond love,

Your affectionate son,

Edmund William Gosse.

While negotiations for his American tour were proceeding Gosse was appointed Clark Lecturer at Cambridge in succession to Leslie Stephen.

To R. L. Stevenson. *7th May, 1884.*

My dear Louis,—

I feel disgusted with my long silence, which has followed so ungraciously upon one of the most charming letters ever written. No! I cannot boast a potted hawthorn, but I am training infancy in the shape of sweet peas to trail along my leads, and I am watching pots of mignonette and eschscholtzia as though they were Scottish families from which fantastic poets might be expected to burst forth. Moreover, I have adults as well as infants [word illegible], grown-up wallflowers, a little the worse for wear, indignant primulas each bloom of which is paler than the one before, auriculas which have wiped all their dust away upon the tails of cats.

I am writing to you to-day because I have just—ten minutes ago—become Professor of English Literature in the University of Cambridge. What do you think of that, my boy? I knew nothing of all this, absolutely nothing, when last night there came a letter from the grim old Master of Pleasantries* (the author of "We are all of us liable to error, even the youngest of us") announcing that Leslie Stephen had resigned and that I had been unanimously elected to succeed him. Now, do not think I deceive myself. It is not my genius or my great deserts that have done this, but the goodness and affectionate zeal of Colvin, than whom a truer or more adroit friend, though perhaps a little inclined to exaggerate the merit of his protégés. I hope you recognize the style in which the last sentence is written: it is a very beautiful example of "Nicholasism."

My wife and I assisted yesterday, in company with a distinguished body, at ——'s triumph at the new Museum. It was a charming occasion. —— behaved with more discretion than usual, but came to pieces very sadly—played cup and ball with his teeth, chucked his eyes about and lost his hands—in the usual way. His speech was very clever and monstrous, and left upon the most innocent spectator the impression of his being a very naughty old man. When he was not actually speaking, he was sleeping the sleep of inebriation and eld in ——'s arms,—looking the picture of indignant distress. The more serious and learned speakers left less impression upon my mind. I think —. such an unique object, an 18th-cent. relic, such as we have no other example of. His intense wickedness, his slumber, his wit, his attitude of childlike confidence as regards the future, his courage and cowardice, his abject attitude towards the Church of England, his intense elderly frivolity, combine to make a character that one deplores, I suppose, but that one likes. It is a wonderful thing for such a wreck as he is to preserve the same cautious affability towards God and towards the Devil.

I must stop this chatter. I wanted just to tell you of my pro-

* William Thompson: Master of Trinity.

fessoriate, because I am as proud as a learned peacock and must have you know it. . . . .

Ever your affectionate friend,

EDMUND GOSSE.

Board of Trade,
7, Whitehall Gardens,
S.W.

To R. L. Stevenson. *1.7.84.*

DEAR LOUIS,—

Will you not kindly arrange to come and spend as many hours as you can spare *here* in quiet. No one shall disturb you. I will go on with my work, and you shall sit among my books, or have a chair out on my leads, whenever you feel tired of talking. And we would have our luncheon brought up to us whenever you begin to get hungry.

A folio Beaumont & Fletcher tilted against the stomach is a great solace, at times. I have all sorts here, grave and gay, divine and pornographical, elegant and balderdash. Do come. I would call for you and fetch you if you would.

Please write here, for we are supposed to be out of Town.

Ever your affectionate,

EDMUND GOSSE.

To W. D. Howells. *July 8, 1884.*

MY DEAR HOWELLS,—

I wish to explain to you that only this minute has the Johns Hopkins University completed its arrangements with me. I am to lecture there during the first two weeks in January, which is very convenient, as I am very anxious to get back here before the month of February begins.

I have been wanting to tell you how much I have enjoyed the lovely little book you have sent my wife. It is all new to me, except, of course, your English child, the Lexington. The style all through is so delicate, so pure, so appropriate that it awakes my envy. No, my sympathetic admiration. I think it wonderful that you, and the few that write well when they have attained their eminence, should be able to do so. A person like myself, still hanging by my eyelids to the outer cliff of fame, is nerved and stimulated to write well, or sink into oblivion amid the titters of exasperated relatives. But you, who might write like a waart-pig (have you ever seen a waart-pig?—ugh!) if you chose, and would still be certain of praise —for you to put in those little touches, fairy-bells at the tips of your sentences, tiny wafts of perfumed wit, which only about a dozen of your readers ever perceive, this is very creditable, my dear fellow; it shows that you are an artist down to the tips of your toes. Do you notice that women never can do this? All of them, the best of them, George Sand herself, calls her work her *métier*, never her art.

I have got the works of Capt. John Smith, all about Pocahontas, etc., for you, if you care to have them. It is a new reprint, not likely to have reached America, being privately issued. It is very taking reading, nutty and old. Say on a postcard if you care to have it.

I have heard of you from Aldrich, Pennell and others. You have taken a new house, I hear, at the back of the Bay.

My wife desires her love to Mrs. Howells and I mine to you.

Yours very cordially,

EDMUND GOSSE.

Nevill's Court,
Trinity College,

To Hamo Thornycroft. *25.10.84.*

MY DEAR HAMO,—

You will want to know how my affairs went off. I had a splendid audience, of about 200, in the Hall, and was very well received. The Master came, and sat aloof in a kind of remote silver grandeur, and smiled benignly. The young men were particularly sympathetic, and as far as I can gather, approved. I have had one great conquest, in young Chamberlain, the eldest son of the Birmingham tribune, who upheld to me, all the hour through, a luminous face of attention, adorned with dimples whenever I approached the confines of a joke. He came this evening, in the dusk, like Nicodemus, and talked in the most engaging way. He seems the cleverest young fellow here, by what people say.

My roofs! such a fairy place. You positively must come up while I am here. You ought to see the Master of Pembroke about the bust, and you must do it while I am here. By the way, will you arrange it, and come a fortnight from to-day? The rooms are in Nevill's Court, and look across at the Hall, and the lovely florid corridors. I look out now, and see the gray traceries pale against a sky almost as gray, and the long orange lights of the windows in the just-lighted hall.

Nellie and Laura have gone back to town. They had a first-rate time, Colvin took them all about, and did the honours of the University. Agatha should have come. Give her my love, and accept the same yourself from

Yours,

EDMUND GOSSE.

With W. D. Howells,
302, Barcon Street,
Boston.

To Hamo Thornycroft. *2.12.84.*

MY DEAR HAMO,—

We have been three days in this country, and it seems like three weeks. We arrived at New York on Saturday afternoon, and came on here last night. Our reception has been something I never dreamed of. But I have no time to tell you all. I will just tell you of one episode.

On Sunday afternoon I was taken to the studio of St. Gaudens. When we came in four men were playing a quartette of Schubert, dark against the whitish draperies hung at the end of the studio —rough blue pots, casts in plaster, etc., etc.—such a refined subject it made. St. Gaudens himself looks about 35, a strong silent sort of man, with a very sweet expression, quantities of red hair and full red beard, a thorough sculptor-man, poetical and inarticulate. Bits of his Farragut round the place, lots of moulds of his work in relief. He does an enormous lot of low relief; the new school of architects work with him in the decoration of the houses of millionaires, such lovely decorative panels, fireplaces, etc. I wish you got that sort of thing to do; mostly bronze, into which he is free to let his imagination go out. His late things are wonderful, but he has just suffered a terrible blow. Three marble angels, Donatellesque, which he was carving for a sarcophagus to an admiral, have been burned with the moulds and casts—the whole thing irreparably lost, all but a few fragments. We saw a photograph of it, a most enchanting thing. It is not to be done over again; is it not a pity? He has the most reverential feeling about you; when I told him how interested you were in his work he seemed quite in a glow. The people here are all so simple and enthusiastic. If you want to be amiable, you should send, on receipt of this, a photograph of your Mower to me at the Century Office, with a scrap of paper by way of greeting. It would gratify St. Gaudens extremely.

Howells asked after you at once, and sends kindest messages. We are overwhelmed with kindness and appreciation. My first lecture is this evening.

Our love to you both.

Yours affectionately,

Edmund Gosse.

America.

To Hamo Thornycroft. *Sunday, 14.12.84.*

My dear Hamo,—

We are pounding away in one of the quickest trains in the world—the afternoon express that goes from New York to Boston in six hours. This country would amuse and surprise you beyond measure, and we are always saying to one another that this or that is just what would interest you. The people who are not pleased with America must be those whose sympathies are fossilized or whose eyes have no power of observation. Such delightful and entertaining schemes for hoodwinking nature you never saw, such ingenuities for beating the terrible forces of the seasons, such daring inventions and heroic tricks of luxury. The people are bluff and good-natured, civil if you are civil to them, as sharp as needles to detect and defy pretension. Come with a simple civility and an obvious desire to be pleased, and you will be surprised at the good time you will have.

Saturday, 20.12.84.

I wrote the above a week ago and could not finish it. Now we are on the return journey from Boston to New York. It has been impossible to manage a letter all this week, so crowded with every species of excitement and entertainment. My Lowell Lectures are over, and have been a great success. Last night's was delivered to an audience diminished from the 850 of other nights to 500 by the intense cold. Last night was the coldest which has been felt in New England for 8 years. The temperature fell to 6 degrees below zero. You will easily think how interesting this was to us, and, oddly enough, we did not experience the same intense distress from it as the inhabitants themselves. Howells' son, John, a boy of 16, had his ears frost-bitten. All day a cloudless sky of Italian blue hung over an earth of adamant. It was very interesting, especially as the city, tho' unprepared for the "snap," as they call it, was able in a very few hours to adapt itself to the change in a way which is quite unknown in Europe. Every house is heated by one or more furnaces, so that you turn out of the terrible parching Arctic horror of the streets into a delicate tropic climate at a step.

We have heard very little from Europe, except from you, whose two dear letters have been most welcome, and eagerly devoured. I grieve to hear that Watts is so ill; his pictures have decidedly enjoyed a success in New York. You will laugh to hear that we have been introduced to more than 600 people already. I try to remember their names and faces, and by dint of tremendous effort should perhaps recollect more or less vaguely 150 of them. Nellie gives up trying to remember any but the most celebrated and the most agreeable.

We have enjoyed—but I must not be reported to have said it—the greatest social success that any Englishman of letters has enjoyed since Thackeray lectured in Boston. Old Dr. Wendell Holmes, who has been the intellectual king of Boston all his life, told me that we must not suppose that all English lecturers were greeted as we have been. He said that he had never known a stranger make such a conquest as I have made. He wrote me, "we are all a little in love with you."

We have just crossed the vast shining levels of the Connecticut River. The lines of nature strike us as wonderfully large—slow broad planes such as Watts discovers on the Gods of Phidias. The landscape is monotonous, great woods of black-green spruce, brindled with snow, and lower down brown bunches of arbor-vitæ, and ruddy thickets of the non-deciduous oak. All else white, deadly white, like a lunar landscape, under the fleckless blue dome of soft mockery, the insupportable sun blinding you, but not warming you at all.

I do not know what to tell you about, where all is strange. The train, I suppose you know, consists of a long series of cars, connected by platforms, so that you can walk from end to end of the train, although in this formidable weather it is not inviting to do so. Each parlour-car passenger has an armchair, on a revolving pivot, so arranged that it can be swung right round without trespassing on anyone else's domain. The cars are lighted by very large windows, and heated, and everything is done to lighten the tedium of these enormous journeys. We have just dined very agreeably in a restaurant at the other end of the train, sailing along through the frosty glitter as if we were in the saloon of a steamer and the sea on either side of us.

I must now bring this very scrappy note to a close. We are specially glad to hear that Agatha is so well. We shall be constantly thinking of her with anxious affection. Nellie unites with me in love to you both; and I am,

My dearest Hamo,

Your very affectionate

EDMUND GOSSE.

Philadelphia.

To Robert Browning. *Jan. 2, 1885.*

My dear Mr. Browning,—

I cannot go to bed without telling you of the performance at which I have just "assisted," the presentment of *A Blot in the 'Scutcheon* by Lawrence Barrett at the Opera House in this city. There was a very full house, the leading Philadelphians were all present; the first act was listened to quietly, the second went enthusiastically, with great applause, and the third was going excellently, when a mechanical accident, such as you know is incidental to first nights, somewhat obscured the close. The electric light went out, and left the group in so much obscurity as confused the audience a little. Nevertheless, it was a decided success. The admirable way in which Barrett declaimed your blank verse, with that swing and cadence without which the best elocutionists can never hope to please the poets, would have gratified you. He interpreted Tresham with the utmost delicacy and scholarly grace; he will gain force, I daresay, as the novelty of the performance passes away, and his utterance will grow less rapid as he becomes more sure that he holds the text. But I wanted to tell you, while the impression was quite strong upon me, how entirely delightful the play had been to me as a play—as a poem you know it has always been delightful to me. I suppose that the critics may declare that Barrett has thought more of you than of the public. He has not lopped any of your branches (except the Song *There's a woman*), to make the action clearer to the vulgar. But this is a merit in my eyes, and the action is as clear, and as momentous, as anyone can wish. He had a sweet, little, trembling Mildred, who *almost* achieved a real success in the part. No doubt it will all improve. I wanted to tell you at once that the thing was done all through in a reverent spirit.

I shared the best box with General Sherman, which seemed like sharing it with Alexander the Great, and not a whit less romantic. The old tiger, now reduced to the most agreeable purring cat, sat well forward listening to your poetry, and turning back every now and then to explain the action to me in a very loud whisper.

Forgive this long letter. I have seen Thorndike Rice, who sends his best regards to Miss Browning and yourself.

Believe me to be,

Affectionately yours,

EDMUND GOSSE.

The American trip must not be dismissed without mention of two visits paid by Gosse to distinguished American writers. Hero-worship was a frank and genuine emotion with him, inseparable from his passion for literature. He felt with Swinburne who wrote, "I am not sure that any other emotion is so enduring and persistently delicious as that of worship, when your god is indubitable and incarnate before your eyes." As a youth Gosse had approached more than one of the prophets and tested them with the incense of an unknown admirer. The result had invariably answered his expectation. And now he was about to establish contact with one of the species whom he had addressed in an impulse of admiration more than ten years before, when a clerk at the British Museum. In 1873 he had written to Walt Whitman.

Library of the British Museum,
London.
Dec. 12th, 1873.

DEAR SIR,—

When my friend Mr. Linton* was here last, I asked him, during one of our conversations about you, whether I might venture to send you a book I was then writing, as soon as it came out. If he had not encouraged me to do so, I should hardly have liked to trouble you with it, and yet there is no one living by whom I am more desirous to be known than you. The *Leaves of Grass* have become a part of my everyday thought and experience. I have considered myself as "the new person drawn toward" you: I have taken your warning, I have weighed all the doubts and dangers, and the result is that I draw only closer and closer towards you.

As I write this I consider how little it can matter to you in America, how you are regarded by a young man in England, of whom you have never heard. And yet I cannot believe that you, the poet

* William James Linton, 1812-1897.

of comrades, will refuse the sympathy I lay at your feet. In any case I can but thank you for all that I have learned from you, all the beauty you have taught me to see in the common life of healthy men and women, and all the pleasure there is in the mere humanity of other people. The sense of all this was in me, but it was you, and you alone, who really gave it power to express itself. Often when I have been alone in the company of one or other of my dearest friends, in the very deliciousness of nearness and sympathy, it has seemed to me that you were somewhere invisibly with us. Accept the homage and love, and forgive the importunity, of your sincere disciple.

EDMUND W. GOSSE.

In January 1885 the disciple, in response to a letter, received the desired invitation. It was midwinter—the cold intense—the journey arduous, and the weeks ahead studded with engagements. But his intellectual curiosity prevailed. He found the poet in a "dreary little two-storey tenement" in Camden, New Jersey. Greeted with the exclamation, "Is that my friend?" he was quickly at his ease, and with his unrivalled aptitude for situations, lost no time in inducing a corresponding state in the poet. Gosse was a born medium. His eagerness was contagious, his sympathy compelling, and his gift for letting fall the right word at the right moment instantaneously effective. Whitman, seated in the one chair in a large empty room, "with a small poker in his hand, spent much of his leisure feeding and irritating the stove." Gosse, on a box from which he had cleared away a jumble of papers, sat listening to a "flow of elemental talk," or the reading of extracts from the poet's works. When the pilgrim departed from the shrine he carried in his mind another portrait, and another personal interview, to appear later in *Critical Kit-Kats*. This interview had been preceded by a visit to the poet Whittier, then seventy-seven years of age, who received Gosse with "all that report had ever told of gentle sweetness and dignified cordial courtesy." He gave lively satisfaction by saying of Gosse's books, "I am grateful to thee for all that enjoyment." Speaking of the *Life of Gray*, he said, "Thee were very fortunate to have that beautiful, restful story left to tell after almost all the histories of great men had been made so fully known to readers." This meeting is recorded in *Portraits and Sketches* (1912).

Maryland Club,
Baltimore.

To W. D. Howells. *Jan. 7th, 1885.*

My dear Howells,—

I have been wanting to write to you for days past. But in this flagrant sort of life it is quite difficult to settle to a quiet pleasure. I had three remarkably showy days at Philadelphia. Imagine the interest of an evening spent with Gen. Sherman, and of hearing from his own lips why he burned Columbia and what he really did at Atlanta. He struck me as an affable kind of tiger, reduced to purring good-nature by peace and praise, but with a tremendous clawsomeness somewhere down under the fur. He was monstrously good-natured to me, and on parting, at 2 in the morning, invited me to come and see him at St. Louis. Then I saw Booker—a handsome sort of barber's image, I thought—waxy, self-contented and dumb out of sheer satisfaction with his own silence—Furness, who is one of the most lovely souls I ever met, perfectly sweet and patient under the burdens of his bereavement and his deafness, full of literature, gay, unaffected, in short a lovely person—Walt Whitman, with whom I was immensely pleased, I had a really enchanting visit to Camden to the dear old man, with his beautiful head and sweet, smiling, calm, affectionate ways. I am going to begin admiring Walt over again, his person is so attractive. Other people were civil at Philadelphia—Dr. and Mrs. Whister, Gov. Curtin, the Journalists' Club—what memories I shall bear away of this thrice-delightful country—but Boston was the best of it.

We are going for three days to Washington, then back here, then to lecture (probably) in New York, and then, possibly to Aurora, Yale and Princeton. How will it be possible to squeeze all this in before we sail on the 27th?

If you see Dr. Holmes give him my love. I see that to-day's papers telegraph bits of my review of his *Emerson* in the *Pall Mall Gazette*.

Our most affectionate remembrances to you all. Thank Mrs.

Howells for her letter. Our address for at least a week will be Mt. Vernon Hotel, Baltimore.

Ever your affect'e Friend,

EDMUND GOSSE.

To Hamo Thornycroft. *14.1.85.*

MY DEAR HAMO,—

I never seem to find time to write letters except in the train. To-day I shall be travelling more or less all day, for I am going straight from Baltimore, where I lectured last night, to New York, where I lecture this evening, and back to-night to Baltimore, where I lecture to-morrow. If you glance at the map you will see that this represents a respectable amount of globe-trotting for a single day. We are now at Wilmington, in Delaware; I mean at this moment—every now and then we cross one of the immense lustrous estuaries of the great cluster of rivers flowing into Chesapeake Bay, and we have just passed one of the most ancient buildings in the country, the little church built by the first Swedish settlers. The weather is absolutely summery: we sit with open windows, in a temperature of 60°. Since we have been in America, we have experienced a range of at least 80°. It is nearly as hot to-day as we have had it; in New England it fell to many degrees below zero.

We are beginning to retrace our steps. My southernmost point has been Arlington, in Virginia, and now we are back at Baltimore, in Maryland. How much we shall have to tell you of our lovely tour—all sunshine and delight, without as yet a single touch of acid. On the whole, I think our *excitement* culminated at Washington, where the fashionable people took us up. We went to reception after reception, saw the most interesting military and political personages, and were summoned to the White House to a private audience by the President, which was a tremendous compliment, but frightened us almost out of our senses. Perhaps the two most extraordinary people I have seen are General Sherman and General Sheridan, the two great leaders of the Civil War. I met the former at Philadelphia, the latter at Washington, and had the most curious and interesting conversations with each of them.

We wanted to transplant Agatha to Baltimore. It is a lovely society. Boston is slightly priggish, New York vague, vast and bustling, Philadelphia solid but dull, Washington dazzling but too fatiguing. On the whole Baltimore would be the place to live at. It is a lovely southern city, full of light, like one of our favourite French towns, reminding me the least in the world of Périgueux, the society is brilliant, but easy and refined, full of grace and charm, lots of lovely women, balls, parties and receptions going on all the time, the very Paradise of young people, without any parade of wealth. It is amusing to move in a thoroughly Southern society, after so much Northern experience.

It is rather extraordinary that with all our engagements and hurrying hither and thither, lecturing almost every night, and constantly at parties and receptions, we remain remarkably well. Nellie is looking lovely; at the Charity Ball last night, which was held in the Opera House at Baltimore, she made quite a sensation. Red hair is very unusual here: Nellie puffed hers out so as to make a great mass of it, and then fastened a wreath of asparagus-foliage (like fennel) around it, and adorned it further with three blossoms of a lilac orchid—it was most daring and most successful. Among all the flashing Baltimore beauties she quite held her own, with an originality and an individuality. She has enjoyed the whole affair like a child; we have had the most delicious time together, it has been quite a honeymoon.

Fare thee well,
Ton,
E. G.

CHAPTER THIRTEEN

The Letters to "My darling Mother" and "My beloved Parents" show the affectionate relation that existed between Gosse and his stepmother. Philip Gosse had married his second wife, Eliza Brightwen, in 1860. In *Father and Son* Gosse has described how on a December evening at Marychurch, after a "scene" with Miss Marks the governess, who had herself hoped to figure as Mrs. Philip Gosse, he as a lad of twelve all smiles and caresses welcomed the bride and bridegroom "on the doorstep as politely as if I had been a valued old family retainer." From that day his stepmother had remained as a beneficent factor in his life, always promoting harmony, and often, when the lists were set for some embattled theological wrangle between him and his father, unobtrusively intervening on the side of moderation. In later years, after the death of her husband in 1889, she continued to live in Devonshire, where Edmund Gosse and his wife used to visit her. A Quakeress by birth and upbringing, she continued all her life to use "thee" as her accustomed mode of address. She was devout and cultivated, and liberal-minded enough to recognise other roads to salvation than those laid down by the Plymouth Brotherhood. She would strain a point of doctrine in favour of a silk dress or a lace cap, and disregard a whole code of her husband's inhibitions in her regard for food. But she shared his ignorance of wine, and Gosse related that on one occasion when his wife was visiting her, Mrs. Philip Gosse invited her to partake of a bottle of claret which was standing on the dinner table. Noticing that, when tasted, the wine did not seem to be appreciated, Mrs. Philip said: "Is there anything wrong?" "It seems to taste a little odd," was the reply. "My dear Nellie, that only shows how little you can judge, because it is the identical bottle you tasted last year and liked so much." Not that Gosse himself was either a connoisseur or even a discriminating critic in these matters. The fare he provided at his own table was disconcertingly elaborate, while outside his home nothing short of the uneatable would elicit from him a complaint.

Little of Gosse's later correspondence with his father has been preserved. Enough, however, remains to show that a change in the spirit of their relations had been brought about by time. Affection, which at recurrent periods had been kept alive only by the recognition that relationship had duties, now flourished in a richer soil. By degrees the gulf which divided their habits of mind had been bridged. The rigid framework of Philip Gosse's religious faith had relaxed. His beliefs which had been so positive and expectant, which had looked so exactingly for crucial manifestations in his son, were now penetrated by a softer and more generous vision. Vicariously he had been living life afresh in the experience of his son, tasting new pleasures through his success. He had seen him stray from the fold and yet he was not lost. Was, then, the contagion of the world, of which he knew so little himself, as fatal as he had thought? Was it after all possible to consort with men of different faith, and even with those professing no definite creed, and still walk towards the light? There, at any rate, was his son, in whom the sense of duty glowed like a lamp, whose affection never failed, and whose intellectual and even worldly conquests were bringing comfort to the autumn years of his life. All this tended to liberalise his outlook on things which in old days he would have denounced. Then, again, prophecies had failed for the moment to materialise. The coming of the Lord was long overdue, if the Scriptures had been rightly interpreted; the "saints" at Marychurch and elsewhere were continuing their worldly avocations, and no cataclysm had swept them from the earth. Modifications in certain of his beliefs, concessions to experience, hesitations which the fiery dogmatism of his youth would have consumed, increased with his years. His faith had not weakened, but the humanities fostered by his son had grown stronger. He still hoped that his son "would come back with mourning and confession and a true change of heart." But such hopes he no longer supported with menaces or references to the wrath to come.

The year 1885 was entirely uneventful: and none of Gosse's letters through the greater part of the year have more than a limited personal interest. He published no book, being busy with his Clark lectures, his usual quota of magazine articles, and critical reviews.

29, Delamere Terrace,

To W. D. Howells. *15.2.85.*

My dear Howells,—

Our inner selves have come together too closely for you to mistake my silence, or I yours, if ever you should be silent, and so I will not pretend to apologize for my forced silence. Since I came back to England I have been ill, tired, bothered and overworked, the proper penalty for having enjoyed myself too much. Now I am getting over the change, and renaturalizing myself, and yesterday I sent you a leaf of olive in the form of the first edition of the *Pastor Fido*, which is more fit for your library than mine, and which you will please accept with my love.

Last week I dined with Henry James at the Reform Club, to satisfy his craving for gossip, which proved insatiable. You will be perfectly charmed to hear that the very first question he asked, over the soup, was, "And how is poor Howells?" But the other part of your prophecy was unfulfilled, for he was eager to know every little tiny thing that had befallen us, and what "poor" everybody said and was doing, and in fact was a most agreeable recipient of all that I was primed with.

There is not much news. Poor Mrs. Lowell has been raving mad for a month past, and dying for a week past. The news last night was that she seemed a little better, which no one can in pity wish her to be. Lowell is very much overstrained, I hear. James has been dismayed to be told, first by Lowell, next by me, and next by a quite independent third witness, that everybody in Boston will take his Miss Birdseye* for a portrait of Elizabeth Peabody. Is there a stir about it? Is the Devil to pay on Jamaica Plains? You may tell the Ear of Renown that the portrait of Miss Birdseye is intended to be flattering in the extreme, and that she is presently (about May or June) to die in an odour of white roses. Tadema has prob-

* In *The Bostonians.*

ably written to tell you that he was charmed with his Cincinnati pot, and still more with your thought of him.

By the way, I hope you have invested those $2 I left with you in some good thing. I gave them to you to buy photographs of Boston for me, but if you were tempted to put them for your children's sake into some excellent speculation, I can't blame you. But at a less interest than 6% it would be sheer vulgar peculation; your only real excuse is that you are turning off a handsome profit. Lord knows I don't grudge it to you, if it really will put Pilla out of the fear of penury.

A great many friends asked news of you. I find a great deal of admiration excited by your *Silas Lapham*, as I knew would be the case. I believe you are going to hear from a certain actor of the name of Beerbohm Tree about the possibility of bringing out your Venetian play here in London. But I cannot give you the particulars. On the other hand I am very anxious to hear what was the result of the rehearsal of your opera. Osgood told me that he was quite sanguine about it.

You took so complete an interest in my American affairs that I think you will let me tell you that the total result of my lectures was far more important than you had suggested it would be in your first and most sanguine idea. Altogether I made £490 in America. The New York drawing-room lectures were very lucrative, they were crowded, and tickets were $5 for the course. If I could have stopped another two months, I could have been busy all the time, for invitations kept flowing in upon me to the very last.

Nothing is yet settled about my future. For the present I linger on at the Board of Trade, and if I can only manage to make myself invisible there for a few months more, I think it very possible I may be spared for a year or two. I should like to scrape on until 1887, and then retire altogether from the service.

I constantly think of what you so affectionately confided to me at Concord, and without any curiosity of a vulgar kind, I am solicitous to know as much as you ever feel inclined to tell me of your troubles and anxieties.

With our united love to you all, but with my special love to you specially, I am,

My very dear Friend,
Yours,
EDMUND GOSSE.

29, Delamere Terrace,
W.

To R. L. Stevenson. *22.11.85.*

MY DEAR LOUIS,—

It was very grateful to you for the gift of "Prince Otto," which arrived just when my college work for the term was beginning. It is the only book I have allowed myself to read, outside my range of labour.

Of course I read it right through at a rush, and then I read it slowly. My opinion about it is expressed with such surprising exactitude by a gentleman in last night's *Athenæum* that I feel as if he must be me or I must be he—though this is not so.

The book has given me intense pleasure, and it will take a high place among your works. I suppose it was written in a time of suffering and weakness, but there is no sense of this, it is bubbling with energy and fullness of life, and its faults, where it has faults, are those of youth.

I hope it is not impertinent of me to allude to these faults, or rather to the one I have noted. That is a lack of simplicity. Perhaps I should limit down my accusation to the particular passage of the Fight of Seraphina. I don't know whether you have already been upbraided for this piece of fine writing. Forgive me for saying that it is not worthy of you. It is a wilful and monstrous sacrifice on the altar of George Meredith, whose errors you should be the last to imitate and exaggerate. In this passage you inflate your chest and toss back your hair, and are, in fact, devilish brilliant and all that, by Gad. The reader that has followed you all entranced, and who has forgotten you entirely, in the excitement of the narrative, becomes conscious of you again, and is amazed to find you so offensively clever and original. And then back you go to the beautiful old simplicity that makes you so easily the master of us all.

There are many things, I believe, that could be said about your ethics. I find myself, however, after some inward argument, inclined to believe that you know best. You are a great magician, and not least in this that you make one acquiesce in what is naturally unpleasant to one. The gentlemanliness of the Prince is intended, I take it, to be rather the reverse of real gentility sometimes? He is delightfully exasperating and Scotch.

You will not gather from these few foolish words how much I have enjoyed the book or how much it has occupied my thoughts. I hear you are simply breaking out on all sides into penny dreadfuls. They are sure to send me with a gooseskin to bed. It is one of the great advantages of a married life that one can go to bed after a soul-devouring tale of blood without the awful solitude of darkness around one.

It is so long—this is not a reproach—since you wrote to me that I do not know the name of your new house. Pray remember me very kindly to Mrs. Stevenson—to either Mrs. Stevenson, please—and believe me,

Very sincerely yours,

EDMUND GOSSE.

Your dedication to Otto is a masterpiece of tenderness and delicate grace.

29, Delamere Terrace,

To Mr. & Mrs. Philip Gosse. *17.12.85.*

MY BELOVED PARENTS,—

Accept my warmest and most loving congratulations on the close of your quarter-century of married life. How well I remember the first evening twenty-five years ago—the setting out of the new lamp, the gift of the brethren at the Room, in the unfamiliar drawing-room—poor Sarah Andrews alternately weeping and scolding around, all in her bonnet, if I remember right, as a symbol of her fugitive status—and then the noise of the carriage arriving in the dark, and the flutter of my shyness as the gracious new Mamma came in—in a grey silk dress, I think, am I wrong?—and kissed me—the beginning of so sweet a new life for me, under fresh and unspeakably favourable auspices. I think of all this, and I applaud the very clever act performed by my Papa twenty-five years ago to-day, at Frome in Somerset.

We rejoice to think and hear that you are both so well. We learn from dearest Mother that you get up at 5.30 these terrible mornings. It seems to us that if you go on in this way, you will soon give up going to bed at all, or else take out your sleep in the afternoons and evenings, and rise at midnight. I do not know anything that gives me so fine an idea of your indomitable vigour as this notion of your getting up at half-past five on a fine frosty morning.

Take care of yourselves, at all events, through these long hours of darkness, and accept a fresh testimony of the fond love of your son.

EDMUND WILLIAM GOSSE.

Cowley House,
Broadway,
Worcestershire.

To Hamo Thornycroft. 7.9.85.

MY DEAR HAMO,—

Your very welcome letter from Walberswick was given me in my bed this morning, and had the reception which is given to things unexpected, for no London letters were delivered here to-day. I suppose it found its way over from Southwold geographically, without being sucked into St. Martin's le Grand.

I gather from what you say about Moreton House that it has been left to your brother. Of course I hoped it might have been eventually left to you, after a life-interest to your mother. But I suppose it will make no difference to your plans; you will continue to rent your studio from your brother as you did from your father, and he is sure to be a considerate landlord. I should be sorry to think you were disturbed, for the studio suits you admirably. You

EDMUND GOSSE

FROM A PAINTING BY JOHN SARGENT, 1885

will need all the room you can get, too, with this great new commission.

We are enjoying ourselves very much. It is nice to have pleasant neighbours, and we see a great deal of one another in an informal way, and play like schoolchildren. Nothing we do scandalises the villagers. Fred Barnard, with an enormous stage slouch-hat over his shoulders, chased one of the Americans down the village street, the man chased screaming all the time and trying to escape up lamp-posts and down wells. Not a villager smiled. Miss Millet, yesterday, in the middle of the village green, was reposing on a bench when the wood gave way and threw her into Fred Barnard's lap. Not a villager smiled. Whatever we do or say or wear or sing they only say, "them Americans is out again."

Yours always,

EDMUND GOSSE.

29, Delamere Terrace,

To R. L. Stevenson. *Xmas Day, '85.*

MY DEAR R. L. S.,—

May I write you a Christmas letter about nothing at all, merely to recall myself to your existence? We have been adding to the natural gloom of the season by reading your admirable study of remorse in *Unwin's Annual*. Do you know an early monograph of Zola's on the same subject, *Thérèse Raquin*? It is many years since I read it, but I remember greatly admiring it at the time. I have been staying in Birmingham with Shorthouse, who always stimulates me. We were talking of you; he fancies that there are relations, not of resemblance but of sympathy, between *Prince Otto* and *Little Schoolmaster Mark*. I see what he means: I should like to know whether you also see. I hope you are not one of those who stiffen the nape-muscle against Shorthouse, because he is beloved of deans and premiers. You are beloved of premiers also, for Miss Gladstone was telling me the other day that her father had read *Treasure Island* over and over, and had tried to make Lord Hartington read it—but complained "He won't read anything—not even

Treasure Island and *Sister Dora*." I give you this conjunction with my blessing.

I have burst into correspondence with Symonds again. He is a most charming letter-writer, certainly; his letters seem always pitched in the exact note of sympathy, and he ripens with years, undoubtedly, grows more good and human. It is very curious how acquaintances lie dormant for years, like mummy-wheat, and then spring into blade.

I don't think there are any two people of whom my wife and I more often talk than of Mrs. Stevenson and you. We know all your pains and troubles, or vaguely divine them, and never expect you to write to us. But if she or you would sometimes drop us a post-card, it would be very welcome. Nellie unites with me in affectionate greetings to you both.

My dear Louis,
Yours,
EDMUND GOSSE.

29, Delamere Terrace,
To W. D. Howells. *28.12.85.*

MY DEAR HOWELLS,—

I really thought you were going to allow me to go down to Oblivion on the arm of Obloquy. When one has a friend who writes the very best letters in the world, one is apt to be exacting. How busy you must be at Auburn (loveliest village of the—dale). I cannot help thinking you will want to get back to Boston again. You must have slipped away like a Boojum, for Dr. Holmes, who writes frequently to me (you see, some of the distinguished *do* write to me—turbans *are* worn, as the lady said in *Cranford*), complains that he does not know what has become of you. I am in a mournful frame of mind, for I have come in for a veritable vendetta of criticism*—the storm has long been brooding—and my new books this winter have caught it from the crawling things of criticism. It is extraordinary how offensive the small reviewer

* See post Chapter XIV.

can be. I have never suffered from him before. He is not sufficiently educated to discuss one's book, and so makes it a peg for insulting one on the score of one's friends, one's politics, one's manners, one's very travels—for one of the proofs brought to show that I am a poetaster and criticaster is that I have been to America! In several cases I can trace the direct personal enmity; in others, I see no reason for attack. I suppose, in a sort of negative way, these things show the result of success. But they are nasty, my dear, and they embitter existence. Enough of this.

It is just a year since the dearest of friends and refreshingest of gigglers made Boston more than a city of palm-trees to us. What a lovely time! But it has made all the rest of life seem rather flat since. With all our love to you all,

I am ever,

Dearest Howells,

Yours affectionately,

Edmund Gosse.

29, Delamere Terrace,

To R. L. Stevenson. *Jan. 4, 1886.*

My dear Louis,—

If I answer you at once, it is not to drag you into a correspondence, for no one is so much as yourself to be held excused from letter-writing, but to thank you for a letter that has given me a great deal to think about, if the volatile movements of my brain can be called thinking. It interests me very much to find you succumbing to this general tendency to take life so very seriously. I suppose you are right, you must be, you have the majority of the lost on your side. But I cannot pretend that I follow you, except civilly and for sympathy's sake. I do not know how it is that you and so many others—indeed it seems to me most people except labourers and maidservants—have a gift entirely denied to me, the gift of thought. If I can be said to think at all, it is flashingly, along the tip of the tongue or the pen; and when I hear people talk of a sustained exercise of thought it is of a thing unknown to me.

We learn to be very hypocritical about the attitude of our minds. If I am strenuously honest, I should have to confess that when I am not working my mind is absolutely idle. I have no anxiety about my soul—I am infinitely and sufficiently amused by the look of people, by the physical movement of things; out of doors I stare at the girls—one of the pleasures of life, which I had always expected to cease or change, but which shows no signs as yet; at home I think of my meals, of little personal ambitions, of what my children say and do, little palpable things that carry me over the pleasant blanks of non-working time. I am not without terror, sometimes, at the idea of this sensual sufficiency in life coming to an end; I have no idea how the spiritual world would look to me, for I have never glanced at it since I was a child and was gorged with it. You will perhaps see how oddly your serious letter has affected me; I am made rather sullen, frightened a little, by your earnestness; I have only two ambitions, to do my work well, and to be present when John Gilpin rides by. I feel that these are not enough, but how to rouse myself? I pitifully agree with you about the unimportance of the man of letters—only let us only whisper it among ourselves; for God's sake don't go blowing on the whole thing in public. If once they, The Many-Headed, find out that our Mission is all humbug, where will our cheques come from?

I think you are a little unjust to the trade. This Mission is an outward and intelligible symbol to the public of that inward and inexplicable thing, the essential greatness of Literature. The individual *littérateur* is nothing, but Literature is everything. I grow a deeper idolator of this deity every day—the great books, the phrases of the great men, give me a more thrilling pleasure the older I live, seem more supernatural than ever, satisfy my nature more completely. And to touch the skirts of this glory, live in the repletion of it, be conductors of the warmth of it, this is quite as much as religion!—again, I speak as augur to augur.

I did not write the review of *Prince Otto*; if it pleased you, I wish I had. I have quite broken with the newspapers, and as long as I can struggle along this side of beggary without them, I shall not be back. My last bond was broken when the P.M.G. burst into its Romance of the Brothel.* I wrote on the first day of those spurious revelations, and said I could write no more for the paper. They have since done their dirty best to punish me.

Don't give way to being too didactic in literature. It is the curse of the age, everybody from Ruskin and Matt. Arnold down to Vernon Lee scolding and preaching away. If you also take to preaching I shall sit down and howl.

EDMUND GOSSE.†

Write to 29 D.T. *Trinity College,*
Cambridge.

To Hamo Thornycroft. *12.6.86*

MY DEAR HAMO,—

You will be glad to hear that I was re-elected‡ yesterday for 3 more years. It makes life much more pleasant and I feel very happy and satisfied.

I came up here this morning with dear little Dr. Oliver Wendell Holmes. He is the most charming guest, like inviting up a delightful elderly bird, that sings whenever you ask it to. He is rather fragile, but has the most delightful readiness in going to bed—has been there twice already to-day—before dinner. I took him to see the Master. It was a great success.

Yours always,
EDMUND GOSSE.

To R. L. Stevenson. *15th July, 1886.*

MY DEAR LOUIS,—

Thank you for the most welcome gift of *Kidnapped*. I consumed a great deal of the night in reading it, and got up earlier than usual in order to finish it, reading it very carefully, every word; so that

* This refers to W. T. Stead's exposure of the White Slave Traffic.

† The letter to which this is an answer is printed in *The Letters of Robert Louis Stevenson*. Edited by Sidney Colvin. A new Edition Rearranged in Four Volumes, Methuen & Co. Vol. II, p. 265. Jan. 2, 1886.

‡ As Clark Lecturer.

you see it does at least arrest the attention. I think on the whole it is the best piece of fiction that you have done. *Treasure Island* was more of a surprise, because we did not expect it; but, putting aside that first rapture which you "never can recapture," I think *Kidnapped* is more strong throughout and better sustained. It is certainly much more human and convincing. It is one of the most human books I ever read. The only romance I know in which the persons have stomach-aches and sore-throats and have not cast-iron physiques that feel nothing. There are passages that are quite superb—the attempted murder on the tower-stair, the scene on Earraid, in all its details—the scene in the cage (but this you should have made a little more of, I think, because in that terrible journey through the heather the reader would be glad of a longer episode more picturesquely emphasized)—the scene in the ale-house opposite Queensferry. The language is exceedingly pure and true, sometimes the answers crack like a whip. I feel sure that you have never done such good dialogue before. Pages and pages might have come out of some lost book of Smollett's. You are very close to the Smollett manner sometimes, but better, because you have none of the Smollett violence. Your 18th-century is extraordinarily good; I read the whole book through, every word, and although there were of course plenty of little things in it not said exactly as Balfour would have said them, there was only one phrase that actually shocked me. That was in the Appin part, "ferny dells." This strikes me as purely post-Wordsworthian.

This morning a little thing happened which I will finish this sheet by telling you. I met a dark dwarf, a sort of Malay, carrying a long bird-cage in his hand, with bald canaries and elderly Java sparrows inside. He put this down to retire and I went to have a look at it. On the upper part, above the birds, these words were printed in faded red letters:

LADIES AND GENTLEMEN
TAKE ADVANTAGE (OCCASION)
OF THESE INDIAN BIRDS
TO SELECT ONE AT MODERATE PRICE
TO BE THE PLANET OF YOUR FORTUNES.

Is this not delightful? Talk of style! What could it mean, too? I copied it on the spot for fear of being betrayed by memory. How could you not take advantage (occasion) of this little circumstance and weave a story round it? I give it to you.

I am your affectionate Friend,

EDMUND GOSSE.

CHAPTER FOURTEEN

Writing to Dobson on March 13th, 1882, Gosse said, "I am in a great state of agitation; I have just written the death of Gray, with inexpressible excitement: I have been crying so that my tears blinded the page—how ridiculous—tears for a little man who died more than a hundred years ago—how ridiculous!" This life was written for the *Men of Letters* series edited by John Morley. Begun on December 8th, 1881, Gosse's first attempt at biography was finished March 28th, 1882. It has proved one of his most popular writings, having been reprinted as many as five times and passed through various cheap editions. He followed it up in 1884 by publishing for Macmillans a complete edition of Gray's Works.

In his Preface to that edition he was deluded into putting forward a claim which turned out not to be justified. "As far, then," he wrote, "as regards the largest section of Gray's prose writings—the letters which he addressed to Thomas Wharton—I am relieved from the responsibility of reference to any previous text, for I have scrupulously printed these, as though they never had been published before, direct from the originals, which exist in a thick volume, among the MSS in the Manuscript Department of the British Museum." Unfortunately Gosse had employed some one else to copy the letters in the Egerton MSS, and the copyist, wearying of the script and finding that the letters had been published by Mitford, soon began to copy from the printed word in preference to the MSS. Mitford's edition of the letters differed from the originals, and those differences faithfully reappeared in the work of the copyist. Gosse's amanuensis had let him down. In 1901 the Rev. Duncan Tovey, in his edition of Gray's Letters, called attention to these errors reproduced in Gosse's edition; and in 1915 Mr. Paget Toynbee, in his two volumes of the Letters of Gray, Walpole, West and Ashton, pointed out further inaccuracies and showed that Mr. Tovey himself was not impeccable. Moreover on Gosse's authority minor mistakes have crept into the *Dictionary of National*

Biography and other works. Error breeds error, and one office of the scholar, which Gosse did not always fulfil, is to prevent error from multiplying itself. His natural gifts lay in another direction. But those who seek a living portrait of Gray, and who wish to know the man, and his relation to his environment and epoch, will continue to read Gosse's Life.

Between the "Gray opuscule" of 1882 and *The Works of Gray* 1884, Gosse published in 1883 *Seventeenth Century Studies.* This volume reflected the width of his reading. It included monographs on Webster and Etheredge previously published and new essays on "the rank and file" of the century, Lodge, Rowlands, Captain Dover's Cotswold Games, Herrick, Crashaw, Cowley, Katherine Fowler ("The Matchless Orinda") and Otway. It was praised by the reviewers and applauded for its style and scholarship. The *Academy* likened him to Leigh Hunt. In the same year Gosse also published a *Life of Cecil Lawson* with etchings by Herkomer and Whistler.

In the summer of 1885 Gosse joined a colony of artists who had established themselves at Broadway. This village, one of the beauty spots of Worcestershire, is now the goal of excursionists and a rendezvous of holiday makers; in 1885 it was remote from railways, little known and less frequented, a street of grey Jacobean houses and mullioned windows running like a quiet river down the sloping foot of the Cotswolds into the plain of Evesham. During the early 'eighties there had been a considerable influx of American artists into London, Edwin Abbey, George Boughton, Frank Millet and others. They were friends, and given to a genial sort of semi-Bohemian hospitality. Having started as black-and-white draughtsmen for the New York Magazines, so far more brilliant in those days than anything of the kind on this side of the Atlantic, they were now all in process of becoming painters, and had pitched on Broadway as their camping-ground. Here they were joined by Henry James, John Sargent, and later by Gosse, who, during August, had been acting as a juror at the Antwerp exhibition.

It was a curiously assorted company, with Henry James as benevolent onlooker and amused observer, and Sargent sympathetic and inexhaustibly industrious, "standing a little at the edge of the wild riot, not objecting in the very slightest, but not able, with equal high spirits, to swell the revel." Here was scope for Gosse's own high spirits, overflowing as they were at this time under the provocation of his success. "I should like," he wrote to Sir Alfred Bateman, "to have £600 a year and a tricycle. I should never bother about London again. I hate the notion of coming up to town: everything here seems so calm and cool and lazy." He was still glowing from his progress through the States; he had been chosen by Cambridge from the world of letters to fill the place of Clark Lecturer: a comfortable income from literature seemed assured, so much so that he was even contemplating retirement from the Board of Trade: he was supremely happy in his family life and his many friendships. But he had published three books. *Firdausi in Exile*, *The Masque of Painters*, and a collection of the lectures he had delivered in America and repeated at Cambridge, under the title *From Shakespeare to Pope*. This volume was to haunt him to his dying day.

It will have been seen that in a letter* to Howells he complains with some resentment of the criticism to which his books had been subject. Hitherto critics and reviewers had been so much on his side, that there had been no rift in the unanimity of praise. He had been sailing with a fair wind. He had had as yet no experience of the ordinary vicissitudes of authors. But now, and it shows better than any assertion the position he occupied, the *Academy* began an unfavourable review of *From Shakespeare to Pope* with "This is not quite the book we were awaiting from the hands of one whose words on this subject have come to be invested with an air of authority and whose verdict is presumably to be accepted as one approaching finality. . . . It is mature in its scholarship, delicate and judicious in its criticism, brilliant in its illustration, easy and pointed in its style . . . it embodies the research and the judgment of a scholar who knows his subject intimately." The reviewer continued by politely drawing attention to a few blemishes. No author who had not been brought up on honeydew would have detected malice in this. Yet to Gosse it was gall in its purest form. That was

* See ante p. 184.

in November 1885. In December the same Magazine devoted four columns to *Firdausi in Exile*, Gosse's most ambitious poetic work. Even here there was hardly more than a momentary faltering in the chorus which had been accustomed to welcome his verse. The conclusion of the reviewer, George Cotterell, was that "Mr. Gosse . . . can produce polished verse but he cannot 'build the lofty rhyme.'" At the same time he admitted that two or three of the sonnets in the volume might be said to be perfect, and went on to praise the beauty of other poems, which dealt with nature, the affections, and domestic and rustic life.

But a very different note was struck by the *Quarterly Review* in October 1886.

Among Gosse's friends and at one time most frequent guests at Delamere Terrace was John Churton Collins (1848-1908), who, like Gosse, was a friend of Browning and Swinburne. At certain points the two men were rivals, and if an element of jealousy was present it did not proceed from Gosse. Both were experts in the same field of literature, and while the writings of Collins were not comparable in charm or brilliance to those of Gosse, yet in accuracy of scholarship and width of knowledge Collins was at that time greatly his superior. Educated at Balliol, he had been in 1885 disappointed by his failure to secure the Merton Professorship of English at the University of Oxford. On the other hand Gosse, unconnected with the Universities, had, as we have seen, been appointed Clark Lecturer at Cambridge. There was nothing in the situation to suggest that the friendly feelings of Collins towards Gosse had changed. The criticisms on *From Shakespeare to Pope* had ceased, the volume itself had slipped into oblivion, when without warning in the October *Quarterly* there appeared an article by Churton Collins, written with the ferocity of a scholar's contempt for offhand inaccuracies, intensified by jealousy of a successful man of letters. Never were "conscientious criticism" and "a painful duty" so obviously combined with enjoyment. It was Gosse's first reverse, and it was serious. He was struck in his pride and prestige, the foundations of his learning were challenged, his reputation derided, and his right to instruct the youth of Cambridge denied. And the blow had been delivered by a friend. To Gosse it was

> Transparent as a glass of poisoned water
> Through which the drinker sees his murderer smiling.

In an essay on Camden's *Britannia*, and published in one of the most delightful of his works, *Gossip in a Library* (1891), Gosse referred to Camden's treatment at the hands of Ralph Brooke. The parallel is too apparent to be missed. "Suddenly," Gosse writes, "about twelve years after its first unchallenged appearance, there was issued, like a bolt out of the blue, a very nasty pamphlet called *Discovery of certain Errors Published in the much commended Britannia*, which created a fine storm in the antiquarian teapot. This attack was the work of a man who would otherwise be forgotten, Ralph Brooke, the York Herald. He had formerly been an admirer of Camden's, his 'humble friend,' he called himself: but when Camden was promoted over his head to be Clarenceux King of Arms, it seemed to Ralph Brooke that it became his duty to denounce the too successful antiquary as a charlatan. He accordingly fired off the unpleasant little gun already mentioned, and, for the moment, he hit Camden rather hard." If for "Camden" we read Gosse, for "Ralph Brooke" Churton Collins, for "Clarenceux King of Arms" Clark Lecturer, and for "a very nasty pamphlet" the *Quarterly Review*, the resemblance requires little to make it complete. Like Camden, Gosse was hit hard, so hard that he carried the scar through the rest of his life.

It is impossible to give an idea of what this controversy meant to Gosse, without referring in a little detail to the personal element in the assault.

Collins began by assailing the condition of current literature, the practice of hurrying into the world books which owe their existence to "the paltry vanity which thrives on the sort of homage of which society of a certain kind is not grudging and which knows no distinction between notoriety and fame" . . . "As the general public," he continued, "are the willing dupes of puffers, it is no more difficult to palm off on them the spurious wares of literary charlatans, than it is to beguile them into purchasing the wares of any other sort of charlatan." . . . "It is shocking, it is disgusting, to contemplate the devices to which many men of letters will stoop for the sake of exalting themselves into a factitious reputation." After more of the same sort he turns to the book itself, *From Shakespeare to Pope*, "not the least mischievous characteristic of which is the skill with which its worthlessness is disguised." He then makes definite charges, a few of which may be summarised. He points out that Gosse did not know apparently whether the *Arcadia* of Sidney and the *Oceana* of Harrington were in prose or verse; that he had confounded James Harrington the prose writer born in 1611 with Sir John Harington the poet born in 1561; that he had described Henry More's philosophical allegory, the *Psychozoia*, as an epic poem; had said that Hobbes' translation of Homer into the heroic quatrain was followed a dozen years later by Dryden's *Annus Mirabilis*, whereas Dryden's *Annus Mirabilis* was published in 1667, seven years before the first instalment of Hobbes' Homer; had mistaken the Shaftesbury of the Cabal for the Shaftesbury of the *Characteristics*; had claimed that Waller made the first experiment in distich in 1621, a quarter of a century before anyone else in England, forgetting that the heroic couplet had been used by Nicholas Grimoald in 1557, Robert Greene in 1593, and Joseph Hall in 1597; and had confused George Savile, Lord Halifax, with Henry Savile, a son of Sir William Savile, and so on.

Each charge in this formidable indictment was dwelt on with animosity, every instance of carelessness cited with gusto. It was a gauntlet thrown down in face of the whole literary world. What would Gosse do? Would he or could he enter the lists, and break a lance? This was the question everyone was asking. The answer was not long in coming.

On October 19th Gosse wrote from Trinity College, Cambridge. His back was to the wall and he was at bay. To such accusations as permitted an answer he replied effectively, some he parried, the truth of others he acknowledged, and where he could he countered with vigour and success. Collins had accused him of having written about Garth's poem *Claremont* without having read it. Gosse concluded his reply, "I first read Garth's *Claremont* in the company of my *Quarterly* Reviewer that same summer, in the garden of a Berkshire house where he was staying as my guest."

Collins replied at considerable length in the *Athenæum* of Oct. 30. By way of proving his impartiality and absence of malice, he cited the terms in which he had attacked "one of the kindest friends I ever had, Mr. Swinburne," in the *Quarterly* in 1884. "I have yet to learn," he went on, "that Mr. Swinburne considers me 'no gentleman,' or complains of 'mortal wounds given by an estranged friend,' etc. . . . I have no doubt that if Mr. Swinburne had answered it, it would have been without any allusions to 'old days' and 'stabs in the dark.' "

This was the first that Swinburne had heard of the article. His reply in the *Athenæum* of Nov. 6th left no doubt in the mind of any reader as to what he thought of the *Quarterly Review* or what he was prepared to say of Churton Collins. It is true that there were no allusions to "old days," "stabs in the dark," or "no gentleman," but the phrases by which these were replaced were sufficiently full-blooded substitutes to give ineradicable offence to Collins and immeasurable satisfaction to Gosse.

Gosse was in no sense crushed, but he was humbled. His letters give only a faint impression of the extent to which he suffered. His self-confidence was undermined, his personality reduced. Firm ground had turned into quicksand. Was not everyone watching his struggles, and regarding him as doomed? At the rival University it became a stock saying for anyone who had made a "howler," that "he had made a Gosse of himself."

His own account of his sensations was that he went about feeling that he had been flayed alive. He had accepted beforehand an invitation to stay with Tennyson at Aldworth, and he felt a strong desire to get out of it; but he pulled himself together and went. He arrived in the afternoon and was sent out into the garden, where he found a large party; tea spread out at a trestle table, Tennyson at one end of it, and an empty chair near the other. To this he crept, hoping to escape notice, but in vain. Tennyson boomed out at him, "Well, Gosse, would you like to know what I think of Churton Collins?" This was worse than anything he had anticipated. He managed to mumble that he would. "I think,"

Tennyson went on, "he's a Louse on the Locks of Literature." The phrase from such a source was infinitely restoring.*

What was thought of the affair at Cambridge, where Gosse in the meanwhile had been for the second time elected as Clark Lecturer? In the *Athenæum* of Nov. 6th a letter appeared, above the signature of W. R. S. Ralston, giving an answer to the question. Mr. Ralston wrote that the general feeling at Trinity was that it would have been better to have taken no notice of the *Quarterly* Article. The preface to *Alzire* was quoted: "Un voyageur était importuné dans son chemin du bruit des cigales: il s'arrêta pour les tuer; il n'en vint pas à bout, et ne fit que s'écarter de sa route. Il n'avait qu'à continuer paisiblement son voyage: les cigales seraient mortes d'elles mêmes au bout de huit jours." On the other hand it was recognised that the *Quarterly* Reviewer had pointed out a "number of blemishes, chiefly due to carelessness," and that it behoved the author of *From Shakespeare to Pope* to be more careful in future. The manner in which the blow had been struck was universally condemned. Intense interest was felt in Gosse's first appearance after the controversy. Cambridge was agog. Would he refer to what happened? Twice in his lecture he began sentences which seemed to herald an approach to the subject. He said something had happened since he last addressed an audience at Trinity which was of great interest to him and of some interest to the College. "A thrill ran through the hall: it was supposed that he was about to be incautious. He was only about to allude to his re-election as Clark Lecturer." Later he referred to something which had occurred recently that had given him personally great pain and had cast a shadow on the College. "Once more curiosity sprang into life: once more it was doomed to disappointment. Mr. Gosse was only alluding to the death of the late Master of Trinity." Mr. Ralston, who attended the lecture, continues, "I have listened to many lectures: but I do not remember ever having heard any on a literary subject more intrinsically good, and delivered in a more excellent style."

* If malice were a failing among literary men, it might be supposed that Churton Collins had heard of this remark before he published *Illustrations of Tennyson*, 1891, a work which, in showing coincidences between Tennyson and his predecessors, also gave proof of Churton Collins' profound learning.

In public at any rate Gosse was able to hide the "sick fatigue, the languid doubt," and intrigue his audience with a humour not wanting in puckish flavour. But his self-confidence had been badly shaken, and his claim, too lightly asserted, to be considered a scholar had been gravely impugned. During the period immediately following he endured many minor humiliations. William Hazlitt after an attack in *Blackwood* could not enter a coffee-house without supposing the waiters were pointing him out as "the gentleman who was so abused last month in *Blackwood's Magazine*," nor arrive at the house of a friend without being convinced that the servant who opened the door had read the article. For a while at any rate Gosse was no less sensitive. He was on the look-out for lower temperatures, he was uneasy, ready to think that those he met were in league with Collins, and that the quality of his reputation had deteriorated to the point of jeopardising his whole career. Such reflections ate into his sensitive nature, and time is slow to purge such poison from the system.

But these things could not affect the charm of his writing, nor could carelessness impair his judgment, his taste, his fresh and illuminating critical gifts. He had far less claim to scholarship than the public had thought, that was all. But he was still what he was always to remain, a fine man of letters, pre-eminent in the service of literature.

It would be of interest to fathom the causes of his carelessness. Even to the profane it is clear that Gosse was hasty and impulsive, and once armed with an *a priori* notion was tempted to regard too uncritically all facts which fitted. It has been seen that, in a letter to Stevenson, he declares that a sustained exercise of thought was a thing unknown to him. This, without being literally true, points to a certain lukewarmness in research and a certain distaste for collecting all the factors of a problem. He had the impatience of the imaginative man. He possessed the dangerous boon of a powerful but not always accurate memory, and he trusted it with the eager alacrity of a poet. But at this period of his career the main cause of these unfortunate blunders was that he was educating himself and teaching at the same time. He was acquiring *ad hoc* knowledge as he proceeded, without leisure to saturate himself in any branch of learning. He never had the discipline of examinations and "schools," no don had drilled his mind, he was pitchforked into the world; he awoke at a bound, he careered at his own will in the fields of literature. His knowledge was wide and stimulating but it was not minute. His mind was vividly alert but not meticulous. He had "emulation," but with him it was not "the scholar's melancholy."

When his Professorship at Cambridge came to an end in 1889 he was rewarded by an unusual tribute. Undergraduates, some of whom were to occupy distinguished positions in politics and literature presented him with a piece of plate and added their signatures to the address that follows:

London,
August 3rd, 1889.

Dear Gosse,—

We, whose names are subscribed, are among those who at one time or another have had the privilege of attending the CLARK LECTURES delivered by you at Trinity. It has also been our good fortune to become your friends, and thus to enjoy a less formal intercourse with you during your five years' work at Cambridge. Our friendship outlives your term of office; and we desire to mark in some lasting way our sense of the twofold gain we have received from you. In the hope that our gift may serve to remind you of a pleasant episode in your life, and of those whom you alike charmed and stimulated,

We remain,
Yours sincerely,

Arthur B. Cane.
Austen Chamberlain.
Ernest R. Debenham.
Frank Gillson.
L. N. Guillemard.
Stanley M. Leathes.
Theodore Morison.
F. S. Oliver.
Arthur Platt.
W. A. Raleigh.
R. Ll. B. Rathbone.
A. H. Smith.
H. Babington Smith.
H. F. Stewart.
Arthur H. Studd.
C. S. Whibley.
H. F. Wilson.

A series of uneventful years followed. He had much leeway to make up; patience and assiduity were needed. He turned with redoubled eagerness to his friends, courting, and not in vain, encouragement and support. For the rest, he continued his literary activities and his lectures, visiting the Continent in his holidays, and indulging, whenever the occasion allowed, his passion for the byways of France. He was much in the self sufficing and exclusive society of the surviving Pre-Raphaelites, sauntering in that fenced and Olympian circle, equally at ease with high priest and acolyte. He abounded in recollections of their idiosyncrasies, their passionate dedication to art, and their sectional differences of opinion. It was a time when anarchist was as much on people's lips as Bolshevik in the present day; soft dark hats, cloaks and spreading neckties, were common to artist and revolutionary. Gosse entering a crowded omnibus found himself opposite W. M. Rossetti and his daughter—"I understand you are an anarchist," said Gosse, urged to the remark by the appearance of his friend. "I must differentiate," replied Rossetti in the loud tones that seem to have been habitual with the Brotherhood. "*I* am an atheist: my daughter is an anarchist." An answer that led to a speedy evacuation of the conveyance by the other passengers. But of Swinburne in his Putney fastness Gosse had been seeing less and less. A rift had started in the relations between Gosse and Watts-Dunton, and though they maintained an ostensible friendliness in their communications, below the surface the two men had become hostile to one another, "cold in amity and painted peace." Frequent breaks were repaired by fictitious joins; rubs were smoothed over and friendship professed—but neither was convinced.* The Putney portcullis was seldom raised, Watts-Dunton maintained his vigil on the battlements.

29, Delamere Terrace,

To Thomas Hardy. *17.10.86.*

My dear Hardy,—

Your account of Barnes is splendid—it puts all others in the shade. What a biographer was lost when nature stamped Novelist on your brow!

* *E.g.*, see "post letter" of May 26th, 1902, p. 282

You have heard or will hear that the *Quarterly Review* has felled, flayed, eviscerated, pulverized and blown to the winds poor Me in thirty pages of good round abuse, "charlatan," "gross ignorance," "impostor," and the like. It is rather shocking, and keeps me awake o'nights and affects my liver. But I hope to live it down. The article is written by an old friend, one J. Churton Collins, which makes it more painful but less afflicting, if you know what I mean? You will see my answer in the *Athenæum*.

Yours sincerely,

EDMUND GOSSE.

Board of Trade, S.W.

To W. D. Howells. *Nov. 19, 1886.*

MY DEAR HOWELLS,—

I was exceedingly glad this morning to receive your delightful letter, and I seize a very large sheet to tell you so. The storm roused by the *Quarterly* continues to rumble away in quarters like the *Pall Mall Gazette, World* and *Truth*, but the rest of the public is thoroughly tired of it, I think. I do not suppose that it has done me much harm: everybody has to run the gauntlet some time or other. No doubt it has been a blow—that I would not for a moment pretend to deny, but it is a blow which has not knocked me down, and which I may even receive benefit from.

Your charming Hawaiian friends the Mott Smiths are here. Nellie has seen a good deal of them, but unfortunately I have been at Cambridge almost all the time, and have hitherto seen but little of them. Very aggravatingly Dr. Mott Smith dined one day in Hall at Trinity, but as the guest of a non-resident clergyman who did not know who anybody was, and so, although I was sitting opposite to him, and although he asked who I was, he did not know me. A day or two afterwards he was calling on Nellie, and saw Sargent's portrait of me on the wall, and recognised it at once as the man he had been dining with at Trinity. I was very much annoyed about it.

It is very good of you to like my Raleigh. You can't think how nice a little praise is after 5 weeks' unlimited abuse! I shall look forward to December's *Harper*, and your public praise will do me public good, by cheering up my friends, who feel my persecution, I think, more than I do.

To W. D. Howells. *Nov. 19, 1886.*

I was sure you would like the Creightons. They are delightful people, and he is one of the salt of the earth. I should think he was a man whom Americans would like, he is so sincere and genial, underneath a certain brusqueness of manner. He is one of our most rising churchmen, with a bishop's mitre in his pocket.

People here were frightfully grieved at the Lowell outrage; sympathy, I think, is all with him. There is one point which I should like to clear up, if possible. Thomas Hardy, our greatest novelist over here, as I think, was very much wounded by what Lowell was reported to have said about him. There are circumstances in the case which would make the sneer at Hardy's personal appearance singularly cruel: I cannot myself believe that Lowell said all that—it is quite in the Julian Hawthorne vein. Hardy, who has always been a great supporter and admirer of Lowell, is wretched at this supposed snub. I wonder if you happened to see Lowell whether you could not get from him a verbal assurance that he did not say all this? You may, of course, feel it too delicate a mission. The article is decidedly a serious blow to Lowell's position here: he ought, I think, to have repudiated it all more thoroughly, much more thoroughly.

With our love,
Ever yours very sincerely,
Edmund Gosse.

In these years he was much with his friends Lord de Tabley, Henry James, and Walter Pater. In a letter which follows there is introduced on the scene Mr. George Alison Armour, an American citizen, bibliophile, and patron of letters, who together with Mrs. Armour was visiting England and beginning at this time a lifelong friendship with Gosse. In 1887 Gosse and Mr. Armour were on the Continent together. "Your husband," Gosse wrote from Nuremberg to Mrs. Armour, "is one of those perfect travellers with whom everything turns as smoothly as on a lathe, and I would trust him with a lark's egg through a field of battle." On his return to America, Mr. Armour received frequent reproaches for not answering Gosse's letters, but with a strong distaste for correspondence, he had a more magnificent method of reply by arriving in person at unexpected seasons. Another American in England in 1886 was Oliver Wendell Holmes, who stayed with Gosse at Cambridge, and later in his *Our Hundred Days in Europe* singled out this visit to Trinity as one of his most enviable experiences.

29, Delamere Terrace,

To Mr. George Armour. *Dec. 4, 1886.*

My dear Mr. Armour,—

I was exceedingly touched as well as gratified by your kind letter of this morning. Your gift is princely, but it is almost obscured for the moment, by your delicate and generous sympathy shown in the manner of giving it. I am telling you the simplest truth when I say that no present could have pleased me more, nor have been more calculated to flatter and soothe my susceptibilities.

I am truly sorry that you failed to find me at Trinity and here. If I could have found you here in my library I should have shown you a lasting memorial of our earlier correspondence, for I have a letter of yours bound up in a volume of MSS, respecting the Gray Monument at Pembroke.

Mrs. Gosse, who was no less charmed with your letter than I was, joins with me in hoping that you will let us know beforehand of your coming in April, that she may call at once on Mrs. Armour, and in the wish that we may see you both at this house. Perhaps I might have the pleasure of going with you to Cambridge for a day or two: we must see: at all events I shall not at that time be lecturing there. In April and May the undergraduate mind is too much disturbed by examinations to get much good from lectures.

I feel that you ought not to have robbed yourself of Langbourne. But you will at least know that no one in London will appreciate the book more than I. It is the very apex of the collection of

Restoration drama which I have been forming for so many years. Some day I shall bore you by making you look at my books. By the way, I have been commissioned by the *Independent* of New York to write a series of fortnightly gossips on my books. You will not mind, I hope, if I make Langbourne the subject of one of them?

You allude, with exquisite tact and feeling, to the worry I have been undergoing. I will not pretend to you that I have not felt it. One does not stand in the pillory of the Press for eight weeks, daily being pelted with rotten eggs, without beginning to be rather tired of it. It becomes monotonous looked upon merely as a performance. But I have had a great deal of sympathy from almost all the first literary men in the country, even from some who were previously complete strangers to me, and my own University is splendidly staunch. I hope to make the blow a matter of real advantage to me. I mean to pull myself together, and do work so sound and good that the very fools and knaves that are hooting now shall be forced to listen to me with respect. Such sympathy as yours is of inestimable service to me, and I thank you for it with all my heart. I hope you will write to me again.

Yours very sincerely,

EDMUND GOSSE.

Board of Trade, S.W.

To W. D. Howells. *30.11.86.*

MY DEAR HOWELLS,—

We are all grateful to you for the *Mouse-Trap*. My sister-in-law read it aloud to us last night, and when she had finished we all, and she included, had laughed so much that we voted the performance incomplete, and I had to read it, as gravely as I could, right through a second time. I assure you I never read anything more laughable in my life. I congratulate you on a success of the very freshest and most sprightly kind.

Coming upon the mouse-trap was an accident, for what I really got *Harper's* for was to read your praise of me. It is very kind, and very generous: I hope it may not lay you open to any mean attacks. The degree to which I am still made the victim here of pails of journalistic slops is really extraordinary. The attack occurred six weeks ago, and the reverberations of obloquy are going on still, in the seventh week. I am anxious to keep up my spirits so as to get the real benefit of this blow, and not be paralyzed by it. It would be childish to pretend that it is not a blow. But I am tolerably young still, and I have plenty of work to do. Work must tell, even in our hurried generation. I have been too easily successful, I suppose; I have glided on, and I can see that I have been negligent and have taken for granted that everything will come right. I think that so long as one is not absolutely crushed out of competition, a blow of this kind is very useful. It makes one draw one's self together, and strengthens one's face against the world. In a hundred little ways, of course, I feel the sting of it at present; it is like being struck a blow in the face, and then tickled with nettles over the spot. But I must pray for health and vigour of brain, and live it down. And it may even turn out the best thing that ever happened to me.

Bear me in affection, as I always bear you in grateful and loving remembrance.

Yours very sincerely,

EDMUND GOSSE.

CHAPTER FIFTEEN

In the period immediately following the Churton Collins encounter, Gosse's gaiety and assurance were under eclipse. He had lost something of his buoyancy and confidence, and this can be traced in his letters. At the beginning of '87 he writes to Thomas Hardy: "I wish you would drop me a postcard a few days before the publication of the *Woodlanders*. I think I might do a stroke of log-rolling, although my little influence for good is almost gone. We are passing I think into Ragnarok where the law is to be that all that is good in literature shall be cursed and all that is bad shall be blessed. I am as downcast about the future as possible." In the same vein of despondency he writes again in September: "I hope your spirits have been pretty good this summer. I have been scarcely fit for human society, I have been so deep in the dumps. I wonder whether climate has anything to do with it? It is the proper thing nowadays to attribute to physical causes all the phenomena which people used to call spiritual. But I am not sure. One may be dyspeptic and yet perfectly cheerful, and one may be quite well and yet no fit company for a churchyard worm. For the last week I should not have ventured to say unto the louse 'thou art my sister.' I am right sick of London." He was in the position of a man who has been warned by his doctor and become chary of taking risks. In 1888 he published his life of Congreve.* The Reviewers, now aware that Gosse was vulnerable, were on the look-out for slips in fact and judgment, but they were unable to find in the volume anything but matter for praise. Thirty-three years later in *A Note on Congreve* Gosse wrote: "In this kingdom

* Years later he wrote to Mr. C. S. Evans with regard to the copyright of this book. "In 1887 I was very down on my luck, and could get no work. A Mr. Eric Robertson, who I think must be dead now, was very kind to me, and said that he thought he could induce Messrs. Walter Scott to publish the book about Congreve which I had written. They did so and ultimately gave me a *very* small sum of money, but I don't think there was any agreement and I never heard any more about it from that day (1888) to this (1923)."

of the blind,* however one-eyed, I continue to be king, since in the thirty-three years succeeding the issue of my biography, no one has essayed to do better what I did as well as I could." In his *Note* he calls attention to some minor discoveries since the Life was written, chief among them the error into which both he and Congreve had fallen in regarding Grace Lady Gethin's *Reliquiæ Gethinianæ* (1699) as original compositions, whereas they were in reality the guileless gleanings of her ladyship's commonplace book. Leslie Stephen was the first to call Gosse's attention to what had happened with the remark, "I wonder neither you nor Congreve spotted 'reading makes a full man'!" The Life is a genial and vivacious piece of writing, expressing the revised estimate of Congreve. The stage from which Gosse addresses his audience is small, but it is wanting in no appliance which can enhance its attractions. The *Spectator* described the book as "a masterpiece of fine prose and of sound comprehensive and conscientious criticism." Congreve's life was so entirely uneventful and so little else but a succession of literary experiences that it was no small accomplishment to write his biography without a single dull page. The book is equipped with the wealth of allusion and the range of comparison available only to a man of wide and assimilated reading, and whether Gosse's estimates of Congreve's work are final or not, they have so far at any rate remained little disturbed. Second only to his gift of portraiture was his power of following with humour and felicity the ebb and flow of literary movements, their origins and developments, the controversies which they started, and the protagonists they engaged. His chapter on the famous crusade of Jeremy Collier against the profanity of the stage twinkles with pleasantry and scholarship; it is balanced and discriminating, compact in expression, and graceful and nimble in movement in spite of its academic robes. His income from his literary work had increased since 1883, when it stood at £702: it was now £915, the highest he had yet received except in 1885, when it was £970. For each series of Clark Lectures he was paid £200.

* But since the publication of *The Complete Works of William Congreve*, Edited by Montague Summers (1923), and the brilliant essay of Mr. Bonamy Dobree in *Restoration Comedy*, 1660-1720 (1924), no longer a "Kingdom of the blind."

In 1889 he was elected a member of the National Club. Unlike other social clubs, the National did and indeed does still require concurrence on the part of candidates with certain "Fundamental Principles" connected with the "Protestant Reformed Faith." These principles indicated the anti-papal purpose with which the Club was founded in 1845. At the time of Gosse's election it was evangelical in tone, "family" prayers which members were invited to attend were held every morning at 8.45 for the spiritual enlightenment of the domestic staff, no fish was served on Fridays, and to ensure the spiritual character of the Club, special terms were offered to the clergy. It had agreeable premises in Whitehall (now the Cabinet Office) with a long cool green garden stretching down to the Embankment. Several Civil Servants, prompted by the opportunities which the Club offered for a luncheon under congenial conditions near at hand, rather than by any desire to combat the doctrines of Rome, became members. Gosse was soon a power in the Club, collected a little group of followers, and got others to join, telling them they need not be perturbed by the "tepid Erastianism" of the principles to which members were required to adhere. There was a corner-table exclusively set for Gosse and his friends, and as years went by the "corner" acquired the status of an institution in the neighbourhood of which the stranger increasingly feared to tread. Here Gosse, Sir Alfred Bateman, Sir Thomas Elliott, Austin Dobson, Hon. Thomas Pelham, Sir Chauncey Cartwright, and a little later Maurice Hewlett, Victor Lytton, "Eddie" Marsh, W. E. Norris and Hall Caine, would meet and at the luncheon hour present a convivial if formidable phalanx to the rest of the Club. The company later suffered a loss in the person of Hall Caine who was asked to resign because he had opened a Roman Catholic bazaar in the Isle of Man, otherwise they held tenaciously together for a number of years. Gosse was quite at his best in these surroundings. His gaiety and sparkle were inexhaustible. He was on easy and affectionate terms with all the company. He was appreciated, applauded and looked up to as a benevolent despot. In such a group it was inevitable that jokes and anecdotes should give rise to current expressions. There was the story of the showman of birds all of which had many clever tricks, except one, a very small bird which was his favourite and was possessed of only one accomplishment, namely, to ruffle up its neck feathers in imitation of an owl. "Do your little owl," the showman would say encouragingly. This became a stock phrase in the "corner" for spurring on the indolent. Another showman of performing fleas, when a lady in the audience was moved to exclaim "Poor little things!" was said to have retorted, "Pity your own fleas." This provided another colloquialism.

Indeed nothing was so absurd that Gosse could not enlist it for the service of lightness and high spirits. An advertisement caught his fancy of "So-and-So's 'Celebrated Invalid Turtle' which could be sent at a moment's notice to any part of the country." Gosse pictured the unfortunate animal constantly starting off at a "moment's notice" and arriving in a decrepit condition with lack-lustre eye at some remote destination. In an American Dictionary of Biography under the title of *Highcock, Laurens Persius,* he found as the sole entry "The style of Laurens Persius Highcock lacks distinction," not another word. He rejoiced in trifles of the kind, they floated lightly through and about his conversation and wit, like coloured bubbles, blown on a laugh, things of a second, dissolved as soon as seen.

Gosse's letters have many references to his children. For children as a species apart it is doubtful if he had much sympathy. But he had at least a shrewd power of estimating the appreciation shown by fellow-adults, and could measure their professions with the eye of a connoisseur. He could distinguish between the feelings of Hans Christian Andersen, who would never tell stories to little children unless there was a background of adults, and those of Swinburne for whom "the sirens sang behind the curtain of every wandering perambulator," and again those of R. L. Stevenson, who wrote the *Child's Garden of Verses* for fathers and mothers, and only saw in a child one who was experiencing "the panic fears and adventurous pleasures" of which he had himself a memory abnormal and comprehending. Gosse's own attitude was correct rather than impulsive. In the early years he took infinite delight in their tricks and precocities, and was at pains to foster childish idiosyncrasies; but his attitude was more akin to that of Stevenson than to Swinburne's. It is highly improbable that he heard the siren singing or was even aware of "a wandering perambulator." Working so often at high pressure, with the nervous irritation that accompanies such a state of activity, he must have appeared not infrequently an impatient and rather alarming figure to his offspring and their contemporaries. But once his work was laid aside, in holiday time, by the shore of the sea, or in the freedom of the moors and fields, or when winter brought ice and snow, he was their leader and companion. His recollections of his own grave and isolated childhood were too vivid to allow of his running the risk of reviving any such regime for others.

Gosse had three children, Tessa (b. 1877), Philip (b. 1879), and Sylvia (b. 1881). As they grew up, he found unalloyed pleasure in the companionship of Tessa, and the artistic and literary successes of Sylvia and Philip. All three played a large part in his life. At home he could be incomparably amusing and devoted, gay and sympathetic, but he could also be alarming from the fact that his disapprovals, rare as they may have been, fell naturally into terms of irony and sarcasm. But such verbal departives from pure harmony, never hid the opulence of his affection and solicitude; and it was with these after all that he made his home an abiding place for his children.

Bayerischer Hotel,
Nuremberg.
12.7.87.

My dear Hamo,—

I never wished for your company more than here, although there would be no moving you about—you and your pocketbook would be glued to every corner. Think of a town where there is nothing extraordinary in seeing fifteen oriel windows in one little line of street-way, and where mediæval houses are not the exception but the rule. It would be perfectly vain to attempt to describe it. The centre, the presiding genius of it all to me is not A. Dürer so much as Peter Visscher, and he as revealed in the Shrine of St. Sebald.

This is pure Gilbert, only glorified and enlarged—tiers on tiers of bronze figures, all exquisitely finished, all moving, not any gesture or form repeated, and invention, fancy, beauty, truth in every line of the great composition. It rests, for feet, on gigantic snails, so wonderfully realistic, so shelly in the shell and so soft in the flesh that no Japanese could do better. Out in the streets one comes upon sculpture everywhere. Outside the great Laurence Church, the townsfolk help themselves to water from the Fountain of the Virtues, by a disciple of Visscher. This is a pyramid of figures, each about 2½ ft. high, at top Justice, with jets of water streaming from her breasts, below her a tier of infants blowing trumpets ending in jets of water, below them the ring of Virtues, slim delicate women in long draperies, with their bosoms open and the water arching from their breasts. Then the whole thing, close to the surface of the pool below, suddenly narrows to a stem of bronze, as if it were a great bronze flower starting from the water; round the whole, to protect it, runs a light screen of hammered iron, flying off into points and tendrils everywhere. Another jewel—a thing you could put under your arm and walk away with—is the Ganzmännchen or Little Goose Man of Labenwolf, outside the Church of Our Lady. This you know, of course, but you can scarcely have realised how small it is, how exquisitely finished in its entire realism. The whole population here are picturesque. As we were looking at the Ganzmännchen there came up a sturdy young butcher, in high boots, close-fitting breeches, a broad belt studded with silver bosses, a sort of quiver full of knives hanging from his belt, and his only other garment a loose shirt open at the throat and pulled out a little from the belt. If he could have been struck into black bronze then and there, and set on a pedestal, no one could question that Labenwolf or Visscher had made him. I shall have much to tell you about our travels next week. We hope to return on Monday night.

Did you see the *Saturday* for July 9th? My belated article on this year's sculpture is there. I should be glad to know whether you agree with what I have said about Ford.

With best love to Agatha, ever your affec^te

EDMUND GOSSE.

Stanley Villa,
Sands Road,
Paignton.
22.9.87.

My dear Hamo,—

Thank you and Agatha, especially Agatha, for your very delightful and welcome letters. We rejoice in your brilliant Scotch tour, which must have been truly refreshing and invigorating. We have been very quiet down here. I have had one or two long walks, but otherwise our time has been spent on the beach, in indolent play with the children. I never had so much of the company of my family before, and I find that with middle life (I was 38 yesterday!) a new pleasure comes that I had never thought of, the delight of seeing one's children delighted. We have had such excitements as collecting cockles, catching prawns in pools, bathing on the sands and climbing over the strange crimson promontories; and Philip has been my companion in longer excursions along the coast.

My mother is our guest here, and we go over frequently to Marychurch to see my father. The latter is very sweet and gentle, wonderfully mellowed at last by the softening hand of age; and I have felt an affection for him and a pleasure in his company, this visit, that I am afraid I never really felt before. And so, in the evening there is light.

We have had no "sprees" of any kind. So to-morrow we are going a regular plunger. We are going (if it is fine) to start off quite early in the morning for a 40-mile drive on to Dartmoor—by Totnes, Buckfastleigh, Ashburton, up to Hey Tor, on the summit of which we mean to dine, and come back in the late afternoon by Bovey Tracy, Newton and Torquay. My dear mother, who is a regular death-watch, has been regaling us with so many stories of awful calamities to carriage-parties on Dartmoor, that I feel quite scared and eerie. As, however, the old lady herself is all agog for the excursion, I must hope it will be all right.

Yours ever sincerely,

Edmund Gosse.

On Goodrington Sands.
11.9.87.

To Mrs. G. Armour.

The landward breeze is soft and brisk,
And frets the feathery tamarisk,
Beneath whose pale green hedge we lie
Up where the golden sands are dry,
And hear the train roll grumbling by.
Along the line of Roundham Head
The crumbling cliffs are crimson-red,
And just beyond their point we see—
Light in the mist, with headlands 3,—
The villa-sprinkled town, Torquay.
The sea is rather grey than blue,
And rippled o'er with neutral hue,
The balmy sky is lightly spread
With pillowy cloud, and overhead
Lace-curtains on a faint blue bed.
No other creature shares his beach;
We scatter, shouting each to each;
One ancient horse stands quite apart,
Eased from his week-day seaweed cart,
But all too stiff and dull to rest
His (illegible) ribs and jaded chest;
He is the only thing in sight
That interferes with our delight,
And with his suffering, dumb and rude,
Breaks in upon our solitude.
The children, now, with falling locks,
Begin to paddle round the rocks,
And far away their father sees
Their ruddy feet and pale pink knees
Searching for cold anemones.
Tessa* is dressed in faded pink,
And squeaketh when her ankles sink
In weeded holes where gobies wink;

* Gosse's eldest daughter.

Philip in trousers blue and slack,
With artless braces down his back,
Hurls rocks about that splash and thwack;
While shyer Sylvia curls her toes
About the seaweeds as she goes,
And holds her petticoats with taste
Up to the region of her waist.
What time, with one accord, all three
How and wherever they may be
Make noise enough for thirty-three,
Nellie,* in most degagé dress,
High up above the tide's distress,
Upon her lap of watchet-blue
Unfurls the *Saturday Review*,
And I who write this artless rhyme
While go-to-meeting bells do chime,
Am so extremely stiff with sitting
That I must now be up and flitting.
So now my fine Chicago charmer
Goodbye to you, good Mrs. Armour,
And when this pretty note you get it,
Remember please and don't forget it,
That it was written on a rock,
    On Sunday by a boss
Whose thoughts to you-ward fly and flock,
    A certain

EDMUND GOSSE.

Stanley Villa,
Sands Road,
Paignton.

To Mr. G. Armour. *13.9.87.*

MY DEAR ARMOUR,—

Don't talk to me of "disturbing me in my country rest," by a letter. Good gracious me! It is always a pleasure to hear from you, but in seaside lodgings it becomes a perfect treat. I was very glad

* Mrs. Gosse.

to get your screed, though it was meanly brief; and thank you for the too-flattering extract from the *Scribner* young man. I wish they would ask me to contribute my "beautiful English" to their magazine: but in this world, etc.

Seaside lodgings in wet weather are the Devil. In other words, they are THE DEVIL. As long as it is bright and one can be out all day, very good; one sits on the rocks and indites doggerel verses to Chicago dudes. But let it rain steadily, and then you find out that you have not brought your books with you, that there is no one to swop stories with, and that London is after all the only place in the world. It is when it rains that one finds out what an extraordinary smell of bilge cheap seaside lodgings have, how gritty the stairs are, and then when one goes to bed, much too early, one notices that the springs of the bed, which is too narrow, are broken on one side. But to talk like this is to be a beastly cynic, and to-day the sea is like an amethyst, the sun bakes generously down, and there is no excuse for being indoors. I take long walks—what Philip calls "really most 'normous walks"—through distant little houseleekly hamlets that smell of sows and cider. I walk with the Ordnance Survey in my pocket, which is the only way in this country. If you were here, ah! that it could be so, we would go over to Dean Priory, which is only seven miles from here. But I haven't the energy.

Love to Mrs. Armour and George. Take care of yourselves. This is a lovely place, I wish you could see it in sunshine. But 'tis always midnight in my guilty heart. Tessa sends her love: no one else is here, or all would. I am sunk to reading a novel of Paul de Kock.

Ever thine,

E. G.

Stanley Villa,
Sands Road,
Paignton.
22.9.87.

My dear Armour,—

We have had ten delightful days. I came down in a feverish and agitated mood, not very well in soul or body. I seem to have been blown through and through by the strong sea wind. I never enjoyed so much the society of my children, and my intercourse with my father has been entirely pleasant. I find him gentle and approachable, he is wonderfully mellowed and I do not think that ever before I had such sincere (as opposed to conventional) pleasure in being with him. But he is certainly weaker and older, and wears his 78th year with a new appearance of venerableness. My stepmother, who is one of the most lovable of mankind, has been our guest here all this week—the parental abode being about 4 miles off. So you see, altogether, we have been very domestic.

Since I have been down here I have read a long Russian novel (in French of course), by Dostoievsky—"Le Crime et le Châtiment." Do you know it? It is a masterpiece of psychological study. On the whole I think it is the most powerful, the most successfully daring, domestic novel I have ever read. The subject—a murder and robbery by an educated man, and the conduct of his mind after the event—is distressing enough, but most thrilling and entrancing in its carrying out. I should like you to read it.

I am ever, My dear Friend,

Yours sincerely,

EDMUND GOSSE.

Gosse has described in *Critical Kit-Kats* (p. 297) his last meeting with Stevenson referred to in the following letter. Stevenson for the sake of economy had taken his passage to America in a tramp vessel, the *Ludgate Hill*, carrying among other things a cargo of stallions and monkeys. "I was so happy," he wrote from America, "on board that ship, I could not have believed it possible. . . . I had literally forgotten what happiness was, and the full mind—full of external and physical things, not full of cares and labours and rot about a fellow's behaviour." This in spite of the fact that the ship rolled like a rocking-horse and the stallions "protruded their noses in an unmannerly way between the passengers at dinner."

29, *Delamere Terrace,*
To Mr. G. Armour. *21.8.87.*

My dear Armour,—

I have just come back, much excited, from saying farewell to R. L. S. I did not in the least expect to see him, but I had a summons last night. He is in a quiet family hotel (he calls it the Real Todgers) in Finsbury, ready to sail early to-morrow morning. I went over directly after breakfast, not expecting to see himself, except for a moment in bed. But when I got there, after waiting ½ an hour, suddenly he came into the room, looking rather white, and a little dazzled in the eyes, but otherwise much better and less emaciated than I feared. I was allowed to be with him for a whole hour. He is in mourning for his father, and he was quite stylishly dressed in a black velvet coat and waistcoat, a black silk neck-tie and dark trousers, so that instead of looking like a Lascar out of employment, as he generally does, he looked extremely elegant and refined, his hair over his shoulders, but very tidy, and burnished like brass with brushing. He prowled about the room, in his usual noiseless panther fashion, talking all the time, full of wit and feeling and sweetness, as charming as ever he was, but with a little more sadness and sense of crisis than usual. I had to be one witness to his will, the housekeeper of the hotel being summoned to be the other. No one else, except his wife, was there; there was absolute Sunday peace all around; it was very interesting and very affecting.

Yours sincerely,
Edmund Gosse.

29, *Delamere Terrace,*
To Monsieur Sarrazin. *Dec. 17, 1887.*

My dear Sir,—

A month ago I received your charming letter, and now also reaches me your essay on Wordsworth in the "Langues Vivantes." I have hastened to read this *latter* and with the greatest pleasure.

You have felt with remarkable sympathy and have seen with

complete clearness the central qualities of Wordsworth's poetry: its artistic purity and its moral elevation. No truer appreciation of this great genius exists than that which in so few pages you have contrived to give. Accept my congratulations on an essay, which, unless I am greatly mistaken, is the most masterly which you have yet written.

It interests me very much that you live in the Dordogne. There is no part of France which has a greater interest to me. I once stayed at Périgueux for some days under circumstances peculiarly and romantically delightful. In my last volume of verses I have dedicated a sonnet to the exquisite city of St. Front; it pleases me to think that your home is in the valley of the limpid and crystal Dronne.

I anticipate with very great pleasure a sight of the forthcoming essays which you promise me. It will always be a delight to me to see your handwriting.

Believe me to be,

My dear Sir,

Yours very sincerely,

EDMUND GOSSE.

CHAPTER SIXTEEN

WHILE studying the stars on a winter night of 1887 Philip Gosse contracted bronchitis; by January it had settled into a serious illness from which he never recovered. Towards the close of his life the stars had been his constant subject of study, leading him night after night in all temperatures to his telescope by the open window, his vision ranging over the firmament with something more than an astronomer's curiosity. His letters show that the expectation of the personal coming of the Lord was embedded in his mind, not understood in a symbolic or metaphysical sense, but anticipated as the fulfilment of a divine promise which at its destined moment would become a visible reality. With such expectations the heavens were inevitably associated. It is not clear from his letters in what manner he apprehended that the event would occur or by what means it would be effected, nor how upon its occurrence it would first be communicated to the world. But entertaining the belief he persisted in it, heeding neither the discoveries of science nor the lessons of his own biological studies, and disregarding alike the publication of *Vestiges of Creation* and the advances of Biblical criticism. Indeed, nothing is more remarkable in the spiritual life of Philip Gosse than his continuance in this expectation, based on a literal interpretation of certain passages in Scripture, and held in defiance of successive disappointments. For there had been moments in the past when its fulfilment seemed to be imminent; but when those moments passed without any manifestation being vouchsafed, some of the weaker brethren among the "saints" had faltered by the way. Philip Gosse had been differently affected by these failures; his faith, being cast in bronze and unassailable, did not suffer; but his dogmatism grew less vociferous, a new gentleness tempered his outlook towards the opinions of others and blent with his affection for his son. "We go over frequently," Gosse wrote from Paignton in October 1887, "to see my father. He is very sweet and gentle, wonderfully mellowed at last by the softening hand of age; and I have felt an affection for him and a pleasure in his company, this visit, that I am afraid I never really felt before—and so in the evening there is light." And then in these last months of Philip Gosse's life the great expectation, surpassing for him all else in its wonder and significance, flamed up illuminating the darkness which was closing round him. When it became evident that he could not long survive, he said, turning to his wife in her distress, "Oh darling, do not trouble. It is not too late; even now the Blessed Lord may come and take us both up together." Harbouring this hope to the end, Philip Gosse passed away on August 7th, 1888.

The hope which had brought so much consolation to him had reacted in unforeseen ways on his son. In Gosse's childhood it had formed one of the articles of belief which his father had sought to impose on him, and, as we have seen, he had at one period, under the stress of a sudden movement of faith, entertained the expectation himself; but that interlude passing away there had grown up in its place a habit of scepticism not merely towards that particular belief, but towards other dogmas with which it was connected. Writing of Arthur Clough, Walter Bagehot said:

"A susceptible, serious, intellectual boy may be injured by the incessant inculcation of the awfulness of life and the magnitude of the great problems. It is not desirable to take this world too much *au sérieux*: most person will not; and the one in a thousand who will, should not. . . . As soon as an inquisitive mind was thrown into a new intellectual atmosphere, and was obliged to naturalise itself in it, to consider the creed it had learned with reference to the facts it encountered and met, much of that creed must fade away." If anything about Gosse is to be learnt from his letters written in youth it is that he was a "susceptible" and "intellectual" boy with an "inquisitive mind." To launch him on his career, to throw him "into a new intellectual atmosphere" with notions about the invisible world so definite as those his father had tried to teach him, was setting him to run a race encased in armour. A rigid creed suited neither his kind of intellect, nor the problems floating in men's minds during his adolescence. His faith in that creed was foredoomed. Its rigidity was its weakness. A more elastic mould might have continued to hold the spiritual consciousness which, though not definitely associated with dogma and not susceptible of exact statement, was a feature in Gosse's character. But with things as they were the belief in the Second Coming was soon thrown aside, and with it went much else. Had this not happened, English literature would have lost an enlightened critic.

Yet these violent fluctuations of religious experience were of value to him. They opened many windows, broadening his vision; enabling him to approach certain varieties of literature with sympathy and understanding, and relegating moral preoccupations to a secondary position. He had been behind the scenes, in the very sanctuaries of sincerity and bigotry, actually wearing for a time the vestments of the faith. After that, no spiritual eccentricity could be beyond his sympathy, none too extravagant for his comprehension. And he had gained other things by his intercourse with Philip Gosse. He had certainly not acquired from his father liberality of thought or moderation in opinion, still less worldly ambition or zest for the variegated pattern of life; but he had gained from him his passion for writing, and learnt the importance of minutely observing and recording what he saw, whether it were the submarine wonders of the pools on the rocks, the frolics of tiny rotifera, or his own emotions and sensations. With Gosse everything observed was literary material. He had the artist's impulse towards expression, and in his father's exact and easy style he had an excellent early model.

In June 1889 he gave the last of his Clark lectures and brought his official connection with Cambridge to an end. University life had thrown its spell over him. Coming to him comparatively late, it found him all the more susceptible to the charm of its scholarship, and "its visible and ever-glittering prestige and excitement."* And in his battle with the *Quarterly*, the most formidable crisis of his life, Cambridge, loyal to an adopted son, had stood by him and encouraged him to patch up his reputation in the quiet of her quadrangles and the serenity of her lawns. His obligation was deep and never forgotten. To Mr. Armour he wrote: "I have been very happy there for five delicious years, but something whispered to me that I ought to make way for some other man—so I bravely an-

* Letter to Mr. G. Armour.

nounced to the Council that I should not be a candidate for re-election. . . . It was a living interest in my life."

The following year he published the *Life* of his father. Taking it to be the truest piety to represent him exactly as he had known him, Gosse avoided the pitfalls waiting for a son who writes of his parent. He brushed aside the tradition of Victorian biography with its richly furnished monuments and lapidary inscriptions, and took a notable step in the direction of modern methods. Detaching himself from his subject, he looked at his father objectively, studying the incongruities and the complex psychology of his character, and presenting a portrait, which satisfies the reader that he has been shown the truth. Nothing even in *Father and Son* makes us understand one aspect of Philip Gosse's character better than for example this passage from the last chapter of the *Life*.

"No question," the author writes, "is more often put to me regarding my father than this—How did he reconcile his religious with his scientific views? . . . The word 'reconcile' is scarcely the right one, because the idea of reconciliation was hardly entertained by my father. He had no notion of striking a happy mean between his impressions of nature and his convictions of religion. If the former offered any opposition they were swept away. The rising tide is reconciled in the same fashion to a child's battlements of sand along the shore. . . . It was certainly not through vagueness of mind or lack of a logical habit that he took up this strange position, as of an intellectual ostrich with his head in a bush, since his intelligence, if narrow, was as clear as crystal, and his mind eminently logical. It was because a 'spiritual awe' overshadowed his conscience, and he could not venture to take the first step in a downward course of scepticism. He was not one who could accept half-truths or see in the twilight. It must be high noon or else utter midnight with a character so positive as his." The passage is worth quotation if only to emphasise that the description gives the exact antithesis to Gosse's own character, with its recoil on the one side from dogma and cocksureness, and with its leaning on the other side to the *via media*, and temperance in opinion.

R. L. Stevenson writing to Gosse described the book as "a very delicate task very delicately done." "There were," he went on, "two or three flabbinesses of style which (in your work) amazed me. . . . I was the more interested in your *Life* of your father, because I meditate one of mine, or rather of my family. I have no such materials as you, and your attack fills me with despair; it is direct and elegant, and your style is always admirable to me—lenity, lucidity, usually a high strain of breeding, an elegance that has a pleasant air of the accidental. But beware of purple passages. I wonder if you think as well of your purple passages as I do of mine? I wonder if you think as ill of mine as I do of yours? I wonder: I can tell you at least what is wrong with yours—they are treated in the spirit of verse. The spirit—I don't mean the measure, I don't mean you fall into bastard cadences: what I mean is they seem vacant and smoothed out, ironed if you like. And in a style which (like yours) aims more and more successfully at the academic, one purple word is already much; three—a whole phrase—is inadmissible. Wed yourself to a clean austerity: that is your force. Wear a linen ephod, splendidly candid. Arrange its folds but do not fasten it with any brooch. I swear to you, in your talking robes, there should be no patch of adornment; and where the subject forces, let it force you no further than it must; and be ready with a twinkle of your pleasantry."*

29, Delamere Terrace,

To William Archer.

9.3.88.

Dear Mr. Archer,—

The little anecdote you referred to this afternoon is as follows: In 1870 I was at Trondhjem as a common tourist. I strolled into the principal book-shop to buy a Tauchnitz. The foreman (Braeksted), who was unfastening a huge parcel, talked to me in English, and I asked him if there were any Norwegian poets. He said, with indignation, yes, indeed! And added that the parcel before him, just arrived from Copenhagen, contained the last new book of the greatest Norwegian poet, Ibsen. I bought it. It was the *Digte* of 1870; I sent for other books, and finally in the autumn, I reviewed

* Letters of R. L. Stevenson (ed. 1911), III, p. 257.

the *Digte* (very ignorantly, in the *Spectator*). That was the first time Ibsen's name was printed in any English publication.

Yours very truly,

EDMUND GOSSE.

Board of Trade,

To Mrs. Alexander Waugh. *July 26th, '88.*

MY DEAR COUSIN,—

The great stress of business lately will be my excuse with you, I hope, for not having sooner answered your kind letter of the 9th inst. I did not wish to reply until I could read your son's poem. I think *Gordon in Africa* an eminently graceful and accomplished piece of work. It seems to me to rank high among the long regiment of Newdigates. It is too soon, of course, to say that Arthur will be a poet, but I think we may safely augur from so very refined and polished a poem that he will always use his mother-tongue with skill.

You are very kind to ask after my poor father. He has hung on ever since his attack in March in the same melancholy and precarious condition. His spirits are very bad, and he requires constant attention. We have to be prepared for the worst at any moment, and yet he may linger on in his melancholy condition for months.

May I send my best congratulations to Arthur as well as to yourself and sign myself

Yours sincerely,

EDMUND GOSSE.

29, Delamere Terrace,

To Mr. Armour. *31.1.91.*

MY DEAR G. A. A.,—

What do you think of Stevenson's *Ballads*? I confess we are all disappointed here. The effort to become a Polynesian Walter Scott is a little too obvious, the inspiration a little too mechanical. And—between you and me and Lake Michigan—the versification is atrocious. Nor is his prose above reproach. There has been a good deal of disappointment among the few who have read the approaching *South Sea Letters*. The fact seems to be that it is very nice to *live* in Samoa, but not healthy to *write* there. Within a three-mile radius of Charing Cross is the literary atmosphere, I suspect.

Kipling, our last much over-advertised but not I think over-appreciated genius, goes on. He is a thorough artist, absorbed in his work, a little maddened but not poisoned yet by praise, and wants but health to be astoundingly great. You would be struck with him.

Affectionately yours,
E. G.

29, Delamere Terrace,
To Thomas Hardy. *19.1.92.*

My dear Hardy,—

I am very glad that you have written to me. The review of *Tess* in the S. R. was a positive scandal. I expressed a wish to write about the book, and reminded Walter Pollock that I had done so in the case of *The Woodlanders*. But no reply. I vaguely think some one of the horrid women that live about the Albany is guilty of this deed. There are certain traces I think I recognize of a female hand that has done this sort of thing before. But there—I have raged around, and felt inclined to do all sorts of silly things, and what does it matter?

Your letter helps me to see what I cannot see when one of these vultures swoops down on myself and tears my liver, but what in your case I can plainly see. A review like this, in which the bad faith is manifest, and the want of literary gumption not less manifest, and in which the opinion is diametrically opposed to that otherwise generally expressed, *is of no importance whatever*. I go further, and say that it is a positive boon. If you are praised everywhere, with a nauseous uniformity of compliment, even those who naturally like your work get impatient. A review like this in the S. R. puts them back upon their mettle.

My dear Child, listen now to me!

In *Tess of the Ds.* you have achieved the biggest success you have made since *The Return of the Native.* Your book is simply magnificent, and wherever I go I hear its praises. If you could have listened to the things that I have heard said about it, by Walter Besant, by Mrs. Humphry Ward, by Henry James, by I know not whom else, you would not,—you could not care what the *Saturday's* ape-leading and shrivelled spinster said or thought. Your success has been phenomenal. I have not heard a book so earnestly and honestly praised by word of mouth (and that is the praise that tells) for years. You have strengthened your position tremendously, among your own confrères and the serious male public. Let them rave.

Your affectionate Friend,

EDMUND GOSSE.

29, Delamere Terrace,

To Mr. G. B. Foote. *8.12.92.*

MY DEAR FOOTE,—

Yesterday we had a curious little excitement. This new Ibsen play had to be nominally performed here to save copyright, it not having yet been played or published even in its own country. So Heinemann rented the Haymarket Theatre, put a bill outside, and inside, with an audience of 4 persons, we read the play in Norwegian. I send you the bill (of which 12 copies only were printed); it marks my solitary appearance as an actor! It was odd to think that all this could go on in the very heart of London, where everybody thirsts for something new, and yet totally escape the newspapers. One journalist did discover the bill and wanted to make "copy" of the affair, but was promptly nobbled.

E. G.

April 3, '93.

35 rue de Lubeck,

To Hamo Thornycroft. *Paris.*

MY DEAREST HAMO,—

Coming home early this morning after a very noisy party in the Latin Quarter, I found your delightful letter. I have been drinking absinthe with poets and their loves. Bobbinette—isn't that a lovely name?—is a lovely creature, as delicate and innocent-looking and playful as if no such thing as the marriage-bond existed, and as if Latin Quarter manners set the code of morals for the world. I have been having a most amusing time with these queer people—all so gracious and friendly to me. I never really touched the life of Paris before.

To-day I have a breakfast-party at St. Germain. My guests will be arriving—poets in straw hats and pink shirts.

Ever your loving,

E.

To William Heinemann. *Friday, April 6th, '93.*
In the train between Creil & Amiens.

My dear W. H.,—

My week in Paris has been a great success, tho' quite unlike what I expected. We were mostly in the Latin Quarter, and I saw a great deal of the Symbolist poets. Mallarmé was ill, but all the rest, from Verlaine and Moréas downward, were on show, and they were extremely cordial to me. I did none of the swell things you had suggested, but instead haunted the Brasserie d'Harcourt and Gambrinus and Bullier; the violent converse of all this was the austere and melancholy James, who was ensconced in great splendour in the Rue de la Paix. James was positively decoyed once up into the Latin Quarter, and was to be seen by mortal eyes descending the Boulevard with a certain "Reine de Golconde" on one arm and a certain "Bobbinette" on the other.

Ever yrs mon chien de chou,

E. G.

29, Delamere Terrace,
To A. W. Pinero. *27.5.'93.*

My dear Mr. Pinero,—

I could not easily exaggerate the impression made upon me last night by *The Second Mrs. Tanqueray.* No recent English play that

I know anything of has been so solidly constructed, so greatly conceived, so delicately finished as this. I really consider the first performance as a signal event in English dramatic literature, and I congratulate you on this great triumph with all my heart. I was agitated with interest and emotion all through, and indeed am not even yet rid of the intellectual excitement it produced.

Mrs. Gosse joins with me in thanking you most cordially for your kindness in letting us be present upon so delightful and indeed momentous an occasion, and with warm expressions of admiration and congratulation,

I am,
Yours very sincerely,
EDMUND GOSSE.

P.S.—I believe it is you who are destined, as Ben Jonson put it, "to raise the despised head of drama again, and strip her of those rotten and base rags wherewith the times have adultered her form." I could not help thinking last night that perhaps this was the first swallow of a new summer of English tragic poetry.

E. G.

29, Delamere Terrace,

To R. L. Stevenson. *7.7.93.*

MY DEAR STEVENSON,—

You got, I hope, a book of essays I sent you the other day? You have been very vividly brought before me the last week from three circumstances, 1. that Colvin and I dined together and went to the play—and really seemed (as usual) to have nothing but you to talk about, 2. that I have been sent from America a very fine photograph of Augustus St. Gaudens' relief taken of you in '87, which I had never seen before, and which I think exceedingly admirable; and 3. because I have finished reading for the third time your *Island Nights' Entertainments*. When I read these stories first I was a little puzzled by the exotic air of them—not exceedingly attracted, I must say. But I read them a second time, and the charm fell upon me, and now a third time, and I am tempted to think them your best work, or a bit of it. The writing was never more delicately right, more rare without preciousness, more picturesque without loss of nature. I include all three stories, although I believe the *Beach of Falesa* the most heroic performance of the three—the most difficult to carry through.

But there! I don't know that this will ever reach you, or that you will care if it does, or that I shall ever know if you care. Writing to you is like writing to the Man in the Moon or to Kubla Khan. Did I tell you how greatly we enjoyed seeing your dear mother?

I am, O thou mysterious dweller in coral groves,

Your affectionate Friend,

EDMUND GOSSE.

29, Delamere Terrace,

To R. L. Stevenson.

19.8.93.

MY DEAR LOUIS,—

It does indeed bring you close, on the 17th of August to receive a letter dated the 17th of July. Thank you for this, and for your delightful letter of a month earlier. It is quite like old times.

My wife and children are down in Devonshire, where I have taken for seven weeks a remote old house called Cherubims—corrupted by the natives into Cherufims. The servants are gone too, and I am in charge of a fierce old woman, who believes me to be mad, and sees evidences of it in my most deprecating remarks. She cooks very well, but brings up each meal with the air of one who knows that she may never cook again.

Tom Hardy has been sharing one of these sad feasts with me to-day—the presence of a guest being a momentary relief to my afflicted guardian. His ideas about fiction are curiously interesting, but I am on your side, not his. By the way, about poor Symonds. You ask me questions about him, which I will try to answer. The obituary in the *Saturday* was mine: I am glad you liked it. It was not so adequate as I wished, and was much altered editorially; still I am glad you liked it.

Symonds was a very dear and charming creature, a loyal friend, courageous in the face of piteous troubles from within and from without, by the very nature of his isolation singularly free from prejudice—I think of him with genuine affection and most real regret.

It makes me rather anxious to read of wars in your pacific paradise. Will you become H.M. King Louis I? Louis the Ingenious—no monarch, I think, has ever borne that title. Seriously I hope these disturbances, the nature of which is as vague to me as the Wars of the Roses, will not break y'r rest o' nights.

By the way, I spent last Sunday with one of y'r greatest admirers, Lord Houghton. He thinks, when the Government goes out, and he is no longer Lord Lieutenant, of taking a Pacific voyage, and his Mecca will be Apia. If he comes, you will find him one of the most delightful of mankind, and y'r ladies will agree one of the best-looking. I humbly apologise for not sending you *The Secret of Narcisse*. It was a kind of shyness, of which I promise to have no second accession. For good or bad you shall have my books in future; you can give them to the missionaries, for they are very harmless. I understand that it is useless to send you the S. of N. now, for you have ordered it.

I am very glad *Questions at Issue* has amused you a little. The public seems to like it better than anything I have published before. People like the contemporaneous: I am not sure that I do.

Ever sincerely yours,

EDMUND GOSSE.

29, Delamere Terrace,

To R. L. Stevenson. *13th Nov., 1893.*

MY DEAR R. L. S.,—

It is rather late in the day to thank you for the gift of *Catriona*, but I can't set to to anything else before getting that off my mind. We were down in Devonshire when it came out, and the family pestered me so much about it that I bought a copy the very day it was published, for the sake of peace. When we were half through it, for we read it aloud in full conclave, o' evenings, your gift came, which we have kept in silver paper and lavender for posterity and great occasions. The whole family knew its *Kidnapped*, so the audience was prepared. I think we were all too much excited with the story to criticize. When we cooled down, and I had time to think it over again in our professional way, it was borne in upon me, as the holy say, that *Catriona* is about the best—the sanest and truest—bit of narrative you have done.

I have one criticism to make, which is purely personal to myself, and which you will very likely pooh-pooh. To me the charm of your writings is yourself, is the personal accent. Now, in no book of yours is the dramatization so complete as in *Catriona.* David seldom betrays himself—he is consistently and persistently the brave, honest, priggish, moral Scot that you intend him to be. And that is well enough, and vastly proper from the novelist's point of view. But you—to my thinking—were pre-eminently sent into God's earth to be an essayist, the best in my humble opinion (without one soul to approach you) since Lamb. To me you always seem an essayist writing stories rather than a born novelist. That may or may not be sound judgment, but, given that that is my conviction, you see how I resent that a book of yours should extinguish the essayist altogether.

A hideous twopenny print, edited by that strange little man Jerome K. Jerome (have you ever seen him? He has bright red hair, a bullet head, and tight little legs set far apart—looks like a stable-man in Sunday clothes), has come out this week with an instalment of your *Ebb Tide.* I wish you luck thereof, but no Christian man can read it till it comes out in book form.

Have you read Lowell's Letters? It is the best piece of pure literature the Autumn has given us. The letters are highly personal and vivid, revealing the man in his shirtsleeves with his vigour and his vanity, his provincial limitations and his power of growing far beyond them. And so funny with bursts of real boyish spirits and scholarly nonsense. On the whole I think, the most delicious recent letters, in English at all events. The book has revolutionized my idea of Lowell, whom I faintly disliked in the flesh.

We have been hearing of your visit to Honolulu, which I suppose is true? I say that, because the gossip-columns of the newspapers pullulate with gossip about you that cannot be true, such as:

"All our readers will rejoice to learn that the aged fictionist R. L.

Stevenson has ascended the throne of Tahiti of which island he is now a native";

or

"We regret to announce the death, in Cairo, of the well-known author, Mr. Stevenson."

or

"Mr. Stevenson is now in Paris."

or

"The vineyards which are cultivated in the island of Samoa by Mr. Stevenson, have been visited by desolating storms; the gifted romance-writer fears that he will, this season, export none but elderberry wine."

"Mr. R. L. Stevenson, who is thirty-one years of age, is still partial to periwinkles, which he eats with a silver pin, presented to him by the German population of Samoa."

We are quite disappointed if the newspapers pass a single day without a paragraph of this kind, and I am sorry I do not know how your future biography is to be compiled from the enormous mass of conflicting material. Since Byron was in Greece, nothing has appealed to the ordinary literary man as so picturesque as that you should be in the South Seas. And I partly agree.

Poor dear Symonds used to be so indignant with you for being so respectable. Fancy, he used to say, having the chance to lounge about in palmy coves with a few hibiscus flowers on, with the most beautiful people in the world, and then building oneself a sort of Scotch manse in a wilderness.

What would Symonds have been in Samoa? I think he fancied the joys of becoming a kind of æsthetic beachcomber. I expect he would soon have pined for the Scotch manse.

Your affectionate friend,

E. G.

29, Delamere Terrace,

To Algernon Swinburne. *Feb. 8, '94.*

My dear Swinburne,—

Will you think me very tiresome if I cannot refrain from pouring out upon you a little of the poignant and complex emotion that your noble poem to Morris, in to-night's *Athenæum*, has roused in me? It is little that I think it, seriously, one of the very finest, most dignified and strenuous poems of personal occasion in this or any language known to me; this conviction would not excuse me for troubling you with a letter. But the *vox humana* stop in it, the tender elevation, the loyalty to the oldest faiths and the highest ideals, these are something, I think, extraordinary. I feel I must thank you for a word so strong and pure on behalf of poetic friendship in these days when envy seems to gnaw the pedestal of every reputation. Most of what you say to Morris is what I feel to you, I

"the boy
Who heard and exulted in hearing
The songs of the sunrise of youth
Ring radiant above me, unfearing
And joyous as truth."

It is 27 years since I received my first letter from you, 24 since first you took my hand. No second light has arisen during all that time that has been to me what the lamp of your great passion for poetry has been. Forgive me, if—while you spoke of Morris—I could but think of yourself. And forgive this indiscreet and uncalled-for burst of a letter!

Ever sincerely yrs,

EDMUND GOSSE.

To Austin Dobson. *25.10.94.*

MY DEAR DOBSON,—

I hope you will write and tell me—quite truthfully how the book* strikes you. If that insolent notice in to-day's *Times* is true, if I really have not learned the mere technical business of the trade, if I have not risen above the commonest level of mediocrity—it is better I should know it, and make no more ridiculous attempts. I don't know when I was more cast down. This sort of verdict—

* *In Russet and Silver.*

"pretty fair, but might have taken more pains"—after such an infinitude of pains, after thirty years of practically thinking or caring about nothing else, is crushing. I feel I shall never have the heart to write another sentence. If, therefore, you can conscientiously comfort me a little, it will be the work of a friend.

Yours affectionately,

E. G.

Henley's hostility to Gosse was never explained, indeed was probably not susceptible of explanation, being founded on a personal dislike, without any misunderstanding capable of dispersion. Henley was a formidable enemy, not only as himself a scholar, and truculent critic, but as leader of a band of young literary braves who were bound to him by a loyalty as devoted as that of the musketeers to D'Artagnan. He inspired a kind of idolatry in his followers, and to count Henley as an enemy meant that at any moment you might be attacked by half a dozen highly accomplished swordsmen only too keen to find a suitable objective.

Board of Trade,

To William Heinemann. *7.12.94.*

My dear W. H.,—

I thank you warmly for your kind note. I congratulate you on having secured so powerful a man as Henley to be the editor of the *New Review*. Of course it is rather a shock, at the first moment, to find you so closely connected with a man who has shown me bitter enmity in the past. My position towards Henley is singular; I do not know—I cannot guess—why he has been so violently my enemy. As a rule I enjoy hating, and hate back with energy. But I have never been able to hate Henley. I admire his genius and have always supported it. I am not aware of any reason for dislike on either side, unless wicked Tongues have been at work. We are, no doubt, extremely different in temperament, but I can't see why that should prevent us from being Civil.

At all events, I appreciate very warmly indeed the kind and delicate way in which you have written to me about the matter.

I am very sorry for poor Waugh, who has worked so hard and cleverly. Do try and find him something good. He will do conscientiously and rapidly any task given to him.

What fun our dramatic performance was this morning!

Yours always,

EDMUND GOSSE.

CHAPTER SEVENTEEN

So far Gosse had been interested in his contemporaries and seniors. At forty he was reaching that time of life when a man becomes conscious of the new generation as "the young." The young in the 'nineties were showing some impatience with the Victorian spirit, and some were crying 'a truce to this seriousness, enough of the solemn and pontifical, the academic and conventional, let us startle and amuse.' And they proceeded to do both with much brilliance; their *fin-de-siècle* moods afforded means with which to startle, and their defiance of convention opportunities to amuse. The intellectual activity of the decade makes it memorable in the history of literature. "It was an era of hope and action," writes Mr. Holbrook Jackson in his volume, *The Eighteen Nineties*. "People thought anything might happen. . . . Dissatisfied with the long ages of convention, and action which arose out of precedent, many set about testing life for themselves. The new man wished to be himself, the new woman threatened to live her own life. . . . The experimental life went on in a swirl of song and dialectics. Ideas were in the air. Things were not what they seemed, and there were visions about. The Eighteen Nineties was the decade of a thousand 'movements.' People said it was a 'period of transition,' and they were convinced that they were passing not only from one social system to another, but from one morality to another, from one culture to another, and from one religion to a dozen or none! But as a matter of fact there was no concerted action. Everybody, mentally and emotionally, was running about in a hundred different directions." It is unfortunate that so little reference to what was passing is to be found in the correspondence of Gosse: he was in the centre of it, and no man was more aware of what went on around him. In a letter to Stevenson* he declared that he had no liking for the contemporaneous. In these early years he was diffident about the movements in the making—he was always reluctant to rush in

* See ante p. 231.

with praise or reproof of tendencies which needed time to mature. If you did not know the figures of a country dance it was better to wait till you could see how the dance progressed before expressing a criticism. In *Gossip in a Library*, he does make a charming protest against one characteristic of the decade. "We are," he writes, "wholly given up to realism; we are harshly pressed upon all sides by the importunities of excess of knowledge. If we talk of gryphons, the zoologists are upon us; of Golb or Aklis, the geographers flourish their maps at us in defiance. . . . Little by little, even our children are losing this happy gift of believing the incredible, and that class of writing which seems to require less effort than any other, and to be a mere spinning of gold thread out of the poet's inner consciousness, is less and less at command, and when executed gives less and less satisfaction. The gnomes of Pope, the fays and 'trilbys' of Victor Hugo, even the fairy world of Doyle, are breathed upon by a race that has grown up habituated to science." He belonged as early as the 'nineties to what was fast becoming the old guard of writers, and his main preoccupation was with the past. In 1890 he published *A History of Eighteenth-Century Literature* and *The Life of Philip Henry Gosse, F.R.S.*, in 1891 *Gossip in a Library*, in 1892 *The Secret of Narcisse: a Romance,* in 1893 *Questions at Issue*, in 1896 *Critical Kit-Kats*, in 1897 *A Short History of Modern English Literature*; all these were remote from and unconcerned with the movements developing around him. It was after all in this decade that George Moore, Barrie, Shaw, H. G. Wells, Kipling, Francis Thompson, W. B. Yeats, Max Beerbohm and Housman emerged into full light, that Oscar Wilde startled, delighted, and then vanished in the tragedy of 1895, and that Aubrey Beardsley dazzled London with the novelty of his brilliant audacity, was received into the Catholic Church (in this also representative of one aspect of the period), and in 1898 died at the age of twenty-six, repenting his *Lysistrata* and *Under the Hill.*

But though Gosse says little about the English writers of the 'nineties, he was an enthusiastic student of the French poets and authors in whom the young æsthetes of the decade were finding inspiration. Notably, Verlaine, Mallarmé, the Belgian poet Verhæren, and at this date we must also include Anatole France. When, for example, Maurice Baring contributed an essay to the *Yellow Book* on France's fairy stories, the latter was only known to the esoteric and inquisitive few. Gosse's own letters to Maurice Baring are among the most lively and engaging he ever wrote. Here he wrote at ease and at the same time as one having authority. His best letters were always written from a position of equality or a coign of vantage. Deference, self-consciousness, or an underlying motive are liable at any time to spoil letters; "naturalness" vanishes and idiosyncrasies are ironed out. This was noticeable in the case of Gosse. In his correspondence he had, more than most writers, lively variations of temper and manner, dependent on occasion, and, as in the case of all good letters, on the reader whom he was addressing. Provocation made him artificial, and deference robbed him of dignity. But letters so coloured have biographical value; it is enlightening to see when and why the mask is assumed, and to follow human weakness in sudden deflections of character.

From now onwards his attitude to the younger generation is more in evidence; there is a new orientation of his interests. The young begin to benefit by his friendship. No appeal to Gosse could be made in vain. He was an unrivalled counsellor in literary matters; he would take endless pains to give advice and encouragement. He was out to help, and for that end would lay aside work of his own or sacrifice his leisure. In listening to a friend reading aloud a dull manuscript Gosse might have been supposed to be indulging in one of the supreme pleasures of his life—he would throw himself back in his chair, his hands folded in front of him, and if there was any hesitation in the reader to start, he would wave aside diffidence, saying, "Now begin, I'm listening," and remain with his attention fixed till the ordeal was over—interrupting now and again to insist on the repetition of a sentence, to correct or commend. And when the reading was finished, he praised with exquisite tact, where praise was possible, or disapproved in a way that encouraged further effort. The experience for the reader was unforgettable as a manifestation of authority, judgment and active kindness. Then the "crystals of wit" would begin to sparkle; he would talk of other things. Out of a whirl of high spirits and drifting enjoyment, his conversation would play and flash, gild or wither; hints and lights falling upon every kind of literary personality, and with amused laughter as a background. Mr. Baring has given an account of the impression which Gosse made on a young man of the 'nineties. "I first met Gosse at the end of July in 1893. I had just left Eton and was going to Cambridge that autumn. I was staying with the Cornishes at their old house, Holland House. I was asked to go round to Arthur Benson's after dinner. The room in which we sat was on the ground floor, Gosse was sitting in a leather armchair smoking a cigarette. He was told I was going to Cambridge, and so he talked about Cambridge. He had been there lately, he said he had been like a father to a little band of what he called mild 'decadents'—the word then in vogue for the ultra-modern literary—whom he had found very intelligent and amiable. They would have been justly annoyed if they had been told at the time that he called them 'decadents,' as they were a group of earnest intellectuals consisting of Oswald Sickert, Sanger, Makower, and E. Marsh, who had been editing a serious newspaper called the *Cambridge Observer*, and regarded the so-called 'decadents' of the day with contempt.

"The conversation veered through Verlaine to French poetry in general, and Arthur Benson said that it meant nothing to him. Words of a foreign language, he said, to him were symbols, like the figures of a Noah's Ark, whereas in English every word fired a train of association, and sometimes a single word was enough to redeem a whole page. I said I thought Racine's verse was enchanting, and Gosse gave me a look of piercing benignity through his spectacles and said, ' "enchanting," that's just the word.'

"And here you had the whole secret of his manner and fascination to the young. He was subtly flattering to them by giving them to understand that they understood as much as he did, that they were in the secret, while it was patent to them that he was intoxicated with the fun of appreciation and that there was nothing he didn't understand, no point of view that eluded him, no joke at which he couldn't laugh.

"From Racine we got to Baudelaire. Swinburne's elegy on Baudelaire was mentioned, and Gosse said that that poem had been written in a Turkish bath, and A. C. B. said he was not surprised that a poem should be written in a Turkish bath about a man whose whole work seemed to have been written in a Turkish bath. 'Of course it's howibly good,' he added.

"He then talked of Swinburne, and I thought it was like having the gates of fairy-land opened to hear Swinburne and others of that calibre, Morris and Tennyson for instance, mentioned as casual acquaintances. I remember his saying that the poem *Faustine* first appeared in the 'Virgin *Spectator*.' From modern poets we got on to older, and among others to Collins. Upon which A. C. B. thrust into his hand a typewritten essay which I had just written and given him to read. A. C. B. sent it (before or later) to Mowbray Morris, who had refused it, but refused with a really encouraging letter. Gosse took it in his hands and scanned it searchingly, all his critical feathers alert, as they always were whenever literature and especially the literary efforts of beginners were in question, and he glanced through it, turning over page after page and seeming to absorb what was on it at a glance. He came to a sentence describing Collins' mental plight, something about 'a creeping deficiency and gradual eclipse,' I forget the words, but whatever they were Gosse rolled them out in the voice he kept for reading aloud and quotation and said, that exactly describes the case of X.—some contemporary. Then, turning to me, he said, 'I see you do not mention Collins' *Ode on Greek Music*.' This is the ode which Collins is known to have written and which has disappeared. It was characteristic of Gosse that in so cursory a glance he should have been able to pick out at once a missing link. He was encouraging and highly flattering, using the most subtle form of flattery, not praising, but reading out a sentence here and there, as if conferring the matter and the manner. We talked on till late, and when I said goodnight to Gosse, who was leaving the next morning, he told me to be sure of going to see him at his office in the Board of Trade. The next day I saw A. C. B., who said to me: 'Wasn't Gosse delightful?' I thought indeed that never had I heard such intoxicating talk, and was amazed at the dexterity and ease of his diction, his fund of amusing illustration and episode, and his deft descriptions and living thumb-nail portraits. Later in the year I sent him a privately printed book of *Triolets* which he at once acknowledged, saying one of them was already a family catch-word, and this began a correspondence which lasted till he died."

In 1895, the *Saturday Review* changed hands and Gosse began writing for *The Realm*. "The *Saturday Review*," he wrote to Mr. Foote, "has been bought by a wild kind of Sioux or Apache called Frank Harris, who has driven all the old staff out into the street with cuffs and kicks, and is trying to run it with young braves and scalp-hunters of his own. Many of us are taking refuge in a new weekly called *The Realm*, which starts next week under good auspices." Gosse, however, continued to write for the *Saturday Review* as well. Each journal paid him £70 in 1895. His connection with *The Realm* then came to an end. His income from literature was now averaging something like £850, royalties bringing in about £120 per annum. About the same time he became a lecturer in West End drawing-rooms. The general increase of intellectual excitement in these years had penetrated the sanctuaries of fashion and produced a revival, if not of learning, at least of curiosity about learning, many wishing to know what they ought to think on literary problems, others already with ideas of their own being anxious for further guidance. Gosse and Churton Collins were again brought into rivalry, and while Gosse was lecturing in Bruton Street, Churton Collins might be heard instructing distinguished audiences at a house in St. James's Square. So close a contact with the world of fashion had the effect of whetting Gosse's appetite for social life. He becomes a much more frequent guest in Mayfair. New names come to figure in his roll of hospitality, the glamour of titles and prestige begins to exercise a certain sway: he makes lasting and rewarding friendships, with Lady Dorothy Nevill, Lady Ponsonby, and Lady Londonderry, and later on with Lady Newton and Lady Charnwood, amongst others. Nothing, however, was allowed to abate his prodigious industry, he was merely filling in some of his leisure time with the liabilities of a new role, that of a welcome guest in a score of fashionable houses. Nothing was allowed to interfere with his daily walk to the Board of Trade—no engagement was permitted to affect the regularity of his literary work, which was forthcoming at the moment promised, without exception. Here his training with its order and precision and subordination of distraction proved itself of value, leaving him free to drop a safety curtain between work and leisure. But every party he went to was an event of significance and invested with excitement. Carrying an outfit of high spirits and abnormal powers of enjoyment, he was able to find even in the most forbidding social functions unexpected sources of amusement and interest. He held the secret of finding and evoking diversion on every possible occasion. Even those inconclusive snatches of conversation, so apt to be the dust and ashes of intercourse in assemblies of jostling humanity, were to Gosse stimulations of an inveterate curiosity and zest. Party for party's sake might have been a formula to cover and even explain some of his enthusiasms. He liked to be invited, he liked to accept; and once there, his interest in human beings kept him in an agitated ecstasy. He would edge his way through crowded rooms, heading for a decisive point, never failing to greet an acquaintance or dart to a friend some observation unexpected and alight with humour. In Society, it is true, he could be perverse and peevish; but the one thing he could not be was dull; and from his setting so much store by "the world," it became the one sphere in which he was inclined to pedantry, seeing a certain sanctity in etiquette and rules of procedure. These things mattered; they were part of the machinery by which an institution of which he delighted to be a member was kept together. There was something almost transcendental about them, and it was not for profane hands to put them on one side. In his own house he aimed at the same conformity which he was himself prepared to observe in Society. It implied a high standard of scrupulosity in regard to the objects which were the ends of social life. His ideas of hospitality were chivalrous and convivial. He enters in his commonplace book a quotation from Brillat-Savarin, "Un maître de maison est chargé du bonheur de ses invités pendant tout le temps qu'ils sont chez lui," and adds, "I never met with this passage till to-day, but I have always tried to live up to it. E. G. 27.5.90."

It will be remembered that in a letter already given* he complains bitterly of a review of *In Russet and Silver* (1894). Here again his

* See p. 234.

extreme sensitiveness is evident; the review was slight and might justly indeed be described as inadequate, but the *Times* critic had nothing worse to say than this: "There is no piece which strikes us as inevitable and supreme, none, on the other hand, which falls conspicuously below a worthy standard of conception and execution, and there is much graceful fancy and much delicate sentiment. There are, however, some awkward verses and some unpoetic expressions, and we confess we are not a little in the dark as to the meaning of the title *Neurasthenia*, as well as of the poem to which it is assigned." The review is certainly not illuminating, and it ignores *Tusitala*, one of the happiest examples of Gosse's poetic gift: on the other hand, "some awkward verses," "some unpoetic expressions," hack generalities of any reviewer for any poet, seem wanting in the poison which Gosse found in them.

They were at any rate accusations which he could have afforded to disregard. *In Russet and Silver* are poems of his maturity and devoid of mannerism; they are clear-cut with the sharpness of careful and chiselled workmanship. "There is," he said to Sir Arthur Pinero in answer to congratulations, "so little careful verse published now. At any rate it is careful."

At forty-five he has become retrospective, the shadows have lengthened, and the future begins to wear a more sober hue. He writes of the dying down of "battling hopes," of "the pain of growing old," and exclaims:

"I ask no longer to enjoy,
But ah! to muse and feel."

A new mood runs through his verse, contrasting with his earlier buoyancy, but seldom betraying depth and seldom sustained. His spirits were too quick and mercurial, he was too little meditative by temperament. The transitoriness of all things human, always vividly present to his mind, was met with a cheerful philosophy, its sting was blunted by playful mockery. "I want to renew my youth like the eagle. What a clever bird! How does he do it? On the contrary, I waste away like the crane and become unpleasant like the albatross," he wrote to Maarten Maartens, and later, "Oh my gods and gaiters, what a dreary thing I am." He was always ready to take up the challenge of time, without visions or illusion, and to view its operations with smiling detachment. Just how far such an attitude can be productive of high poetry may be questioned. The mood, at any rate, as it filtered through his mind, gave rise to verse of high accomplishment, and poems of the quality of *Revelation* and *Tusitala* will always claim a place in anthologies.

The volume was sent to Stevenson, who in reply wrote on December 1st, 1894, to acknowledge the dedication, "I am afraid, my dear Weg, that this must be the result of bribery and corruption! The volume to which the dedication stands as preface seems to me to stand alone in your work; it is so natural, so personal, so sincere, so articulate in substance, and—what you always were sure of—so rich in adornment. Let me speak first of the dedication. I thank you for it from the heart. It is beautifully said, beautifully and kindly felt: and I should be a churl indeed if I were not grateful, and an ass if I were not proud. . . . I must own an especial liking to

> I yearn not for the fighting fate,
> That holds and hath achieved;
> I live to watch and meditate
> And dream—and be deceived.

You take the change gallantly. Not I, I must confess. . . . I do like to be deceived and to dream, but I have very little use for either watching or meditation. I was not born for age." And at the close of his letter Stevenson wrote, "May you write many more books as good as this one—only there's one thing impossible, you can never write another dedication that can give the same pleasure to the vanished Tusitala."

Two days later Stevenson was dead. The last letter he had written had been to Gosse, and so the end of twenty years of friendship found them testifying to one another in the same close fraternity. Time and distance had not altered their relation, which had run vital and excited through the many years it had lasted. "There was not such a gracious creature born," Gosse used, quoting from the speech of Queen Constance, to say of Stevenson; and in the desolation spread by the news of his death, few were rendered as desolate as Gosse. "It makes me cold and sick," wrote Henry James, "and with the absolute, almost alarmed sense, of the visible material quenching of an indispensable light. That he's silent for ever will be a fact hard, for a long time, to live with. To-day at any rate it is a cruel wringing emotion. One feels how one cared for him—what a place he took: and as if suddenly into that place there had descended a great avalanche of ice . . . for us the loss of charm, of suspense, of 'fun' is unutterable."*

Gosse's readers, though not his critics, had long forgotten the Churton Collins episode. He had resumed his position in public favour, he was sprouting literary leaves in copious abundance. Periodicals in America were clamouring for his contributions. He was in demand as a lecturer, and no public dinner where literature was involved was complete without Gosse to propose or return thanks for the cause. He was the doyen of the pioneers who had introduced readers to the writers of Scandinavia. The Norwegian Club in London had elected him their President, and his many links with Scandinavia marked him out as the natural host for distinguished visitors from the North; for Max Nordau, "like a hair-brush worked by machinery," for Georg Brandes the eminent critic, and Holger Drachmann, the Danish poet with the aspect of a Viking, and the evasive timidity of a deer. One of my earliest recollections of Gosse is a luncheon given by him at the National Club in honour of Drachmann. At the end of the meal, the poet, who was dressed in nautical apparel and had about him the very tang of the sea, bore down on me and to my great embarrassment said, "I have not yet been to see your play at the Lyceum": I could only murmur some bewildered regret, when Gosse, who had overheard, approached us, and said in his tone of slyest humour, "I'm afraid Mr. Charteris' play has not yet been produced." The Viking was not convinced, and renewed the attack by asking me questions about my poetry; again Gosse came to the rescue, pointing out that Mr. Drachmann was wrong in assuming that all his guests were poets and that I at any rate was not Stephen Phillips. Later—but this is to anticipate—when Gosse was Librarian at the House of Lords, I attended a luncheon given by him to Georg Brandes. We were a party of six, and at the end we were all

* Letters of Henry James: To Edmund Gosse, Dec. 17, 1894. Vol. I., p. 228.

confounded by Brandes rising to his feet and giving us an address, which lasted some ten minutes, on the delights of visiting the country of Shakespeare. To this Gosse listened with an expression of agitated amusement, and when the oration was finished, said with mellifluous courtesy, "Now I think we had better join the ladies," and we filed off to the smoking-room. There had evidently been a mistake. Brandes, receiving an invitation with 'House of Lords' stamped on the paper, had anticipated a reception—a ceremony—and the call for a speech: the fact that there had been no call was no reason for wasting the speech.

29, Delamere Terrace,

To Mrs. Patrick Campbell. *1st February, 1895.*

Dear Mrs. Patrick Campbell,—

You must let me tell you how much pleasure your letter has given me, and how good of you I think it to read my verses. You are one of the most genuine artists, in the blood and bone, that I have ever met, and you know how much we poor strummers on the lute appreciate praise from those very few whose praise means anything.

I hope Pinero is preparing for you a part well worthy of you in his new play. My most cordial wishes are with you.

Very sincerely yours,

Edmund Gosse.

29, Delamere Terrace,

To Mrs. Patrick Campbell. *1st April, 1895.*

My dear Mrs. Campbell,—

"What I thought of the play?"* Well, I have a great difficulty in saying, for, to tell the truth, you swamped the play for me. The play was—you. I tell you without exaggeration, that I never saw on the English stage a piece of acting which seemed to me so brilliantly sustained, varied and vivified. Almost the only thing which seemed to me wrong was the whole business about the Bible. What was that book doing *dans cette galère*? It jarred upon me as an

* *The Notorious Mrs. Ebbsmith.*

incoherent and stagy, and therefore disturbing, element in an otherwise splendid mental and interior drama—I mean the drama of Mrs. Ebbsmith's inward movings—vicissitudes, apprehensions, whirlwind of battling instincts—all mirrored and translated by you in a manner transcendently poetical and thrilling. When it dawned upon you that Lucas was no real comrade, and the project of retaining him by commoner attractions was floating in your mind—now repulsed, now again projected—your acting was so magnificent that the strain of it on me was almost maddening. I wanted to scream. In this (I think—but I am no dramatic critic, only a recorder of personal impressions) your greatness lies. You can interpret—you alone on our present stage—the flash and gloom, the swirl and the eddy, of a soul torn by suppressed intellectual emotion.

"What did I think of the play?" I am afraid I was thinking only of you.

Yours very sincerely,
EDMUND GOSSE.

29, Delamere Terrace,

To Robert Ross. *17.5.95.*

MY DEAR ROBBIE,—

I am very glad indeed to hear from you, because I wanted to write to you and hate sending off letters to vague addresses. The recent intolerable events* have vexed my soul—mainly (I confess) on your account, my regard for you turning what would else (perhaps) have been comedy, or satiric drama, into pure tragedy.

Now the great thing is to forget. Your action throughout, so far as I understand it, has been quixotic and silly but honourable. In this dark world no one can do more than walk by the light of his conscience. If it is any pleasure to you to know it, you preserve all our regard (my wife's and mine), and in future, calmer times we shall both rejoice to see you and give you any support we can, if ever you want support. I miss your charming company, in which I have always delighted, and we all miss it, for you are a favourite

* The trial and condemnation of Oscar Wilde.

with every member of this family. I would say to you—be calm, be reasonable, turn for consolation to the infinite resources of literature, which, to your great good fortune, are open to you more than to most men. Write to me when you feel inclined, and however busy I am I will write in reply, and in a more happy season you must come back, to be truly welcomed in this house.

My wife unites with me in joy that you have written to us, and in the expression of true and warm sympathy.

I am, my dear Robbie, now and always,

Sincerely yours,

EDMUND GOSSE.

Bel Alp,
Aug. 15.'95.

To Lewis Benjamin.*

MY DEAR SIR,—

I am very sorry that you should have been kept waiting so long for an answer to the letter which now finds me here. And I am very much more sorry that you should have such bad news to give me about your MS. I not only wrote to Mr. Heinemann, but I called on him specially to commend you to him. I am quite certain, therefore, that he has not neglected your MS.

Perhaps, as you have written to me several times, you will not think me disagreeable if I ask you whether you are not a little rash in supposing that you can, without training, at once write in such a way as to be successful. No one expects to be a painter or a lawyer or an engineer in a couple of months. These professions require long training and laborious attention: why should not literature? My own experience is that years and years of study, concentrated on the particular purpose of eventually learning to write well, are needed to result in anything like success. Now, I hope you will not be offended if I say that I was struck in your first letter to me by several indications of want of skill, of simplicity, even of correctness in the turn of the phrases. If you do not yet write a letter well, may it not be that you have not mastered the technical art of book-writing? I must not venture to say that this is the case; but

* Lewis Melville.

if you are so very anxious to write, would it not be well to read much and study the manner of writing before you make another attempt on the publishers?

Believe me,
Yours very faithfully,
EDMUND GOSSE.

Hôtel Bel Alp,
Valais,
To Maurice Baring. *21.8.95.*

MY DEAR MAURICE,—

Your charming letter has given a great deal of pleasure to Arthur, my wife, Tessa and Tatham, as well as pre-eminently to me. We have all been here a week. At first we clung together, with noisy evidence of Aunt Sister,* refusing to mingle with our fellows. Now, we have reached the other extreme, and wallow in social laxities. Arthur and Tatham are very proud and go off on solitary expeditions. Tessa and I go with extravagant chains of clergymen and the like, trapesing over the glacier. There is a formidable lady here, known as The Second Witch, who pinches her lips together and does unparalleled feats on the ice; when she returns to the hotel, she settles down to absolute immobility, with a hymn-book. We enjoyed all the accounts you give of your carpet†; it must be very delightful to have Marsh with you to help you to play the fool. Nellie has sprained her ankle, which is very tiresome, and delivers her up into the hands of the fussy matrons that bask around the hotel. We liked this place immensely until so many people came that there are beds in the sitting-rooms, the bath-room and the smoking-room. Last night we heard a sort of rumble outside our bedroom door, and peeping out in the dusk saw rows of people, sleeping on shake-downs, in the passage itself. Arthur is rather large and remote, reading Shakespeare and *Anna Karenina*, and writing lots of sonnets on the Marmot, and the Mountain Goat, and the Gentian and the After Glow, you know. Seriously, he is

* "Aunt Sister" expresses an indisposition to exertion.

† An expression drawn from a vocabulary invented by the Ponsonby and Baring families signifying (roughly) a humdrum atmosphere.

writing some exceedingly beautiful things, though his fluency and continuance are alarming* to me, whose tiny vein always, even in its voluminous days, oozed drop by drop.

There has been a most shocking accident here since we came. A. W. Eyre, who was quite a social personage in the hotel, handsome and genial, did not come home on Friday night, and was found on Saturday morning horribly smashed, on the rocks almost within sight. The accident has had the curious effect of making a number of visitors unwilling to go out of sight of the hotel, and you see people going round and round as if for a wager. There are 88 English and 2 French people in the house. The two French amuse me very much; they are the Vicomte and Vicomtesse de . . . . . . Madame certainly had black hair once, but it is coppery-red now, and she has a pallid, hooked countenance like that of a small parrot. She is portentously grave till you speak to her, and then, instantly, without a moment's transition, she shrieks with laughter and shakes her food-box. Every now and then the Vicomte chases her into their bedroom (which has a very public position) and you hear him beat her and then kill her; when the last moan has died away the Vicomtesse enters from another door, with plumage absolutely unruffled. There is also an Infanticide, who, dressed in black, with white gloves and a large white weeper round his top hat, steals out at night with a large basket, out of which we (think we) see sticking the legs of Swiss children he has killed during the day. With kindest remembrances to Marsh and our love to you,

Yours always,

EDMUND GOSSE.

Board of Trade,
S.W.

To Sir Alfred Bateman. 25.9.95.

DEAR A. E. B.,—

Max Nordau is in London for a few days, but refuses to be lionized, which is a good thing as there is nobody here. Heine-

* Added in another handwriting: "he means disgusting, A.C.B."

mann brought him to lunch to-day. He is only 45, but has a mass of harsh white hair and beard which makes him look old. He talks very fluent English, and very intelligently, but I should think he might become a frightful bore. He has got hold of a new formula for crime, for ill-doing of every sort—it is "parasitism." A burglar robs you and knocks you down, because he is a parasite. Well, that you can follow. But a man that has a prostitute is a parasite also, because he does to her, for money, what she does not want to have done. That is more difficult. In short, he seems a learned empiric, a kind (really) of brilliant humbug, and I should think had possibilities of boredom quite stupendous.

The Y.V.* who has only had 24 hours of him yet, looks pale with exhaustion (he won't go to bed, and then rises at 5!) already, and he is to stay a week.

Ever yours sincerely,

E. G.

29, Delamere Terrace,

To Henry James. *14.6.96.*

My dear James,—

For the last fortnight my life has been in such a whirl that I have not had time for the plainest duties, one of which certainly was to write and tell you that Philip† is now definitely attached to Edw. FitzGerald's expedition.‡ We are conscious—and we give you our affectionate thanks for it—that your cordial words, spoken at the right moment, had a great deal to do with this happy arrangement. We have received great kindness all round. The people at the Zoological Gardens, in the most charming and surprising way, have put their best dissector at his service to teach him the whole art of preserving birds, and even Thiselton Dyer, the rebarbative and formidable Dyer, who chivies Royal Princesses off

* W. Heinemann, who was nicknamed the Young Voluptuary.

† Dr. Philip Gosse.

‡ To climb Aconcagua.

the grass, and repulses the amiable advances of Cabinet Ministers, has been amicability itself, and gives the boy the run of Kew. The naturalists are amused at what they think an atavism, the grandpapa reapparent. At all events the boy has a superb chance, and all must now depend on his own brains and character.

I am giving weekly lectures on Matt Arnold at Mrs. S. Dugdale's to some of the smartest ladies in London, to whom the presence of one another evidently supplies a complete confidence in the importance of the lecturer. The Duchess of Bedford is convinced that dear Lady Carnarvon would not come if it were a second-rate article, and the presence of Mrs. Asquith gives everybody security—"she's so clever." They are all ladies, except a bearded figure at the back, semi-recumbent on a sofa, like a water-god—Sir Wilfrid Lawson. Unless Mrs. Dugdale muffs it fearfully, I ought to get quite a nice lot of money, but the countesses come streaming up, and whether anyone takes their guineas is what is unknown to me and to Lady Audrey Buller (my faithful familiar, who has really got up the whole thing). But this, you will justly say, is vulgar without being amusing.

In an evil hour I was overpressed to write an article about Barbey d'Aurévilly, and I am in the Valley of the Shadows of Boredom in consequence. Every page I read makes him seem more insignificant and more impertinent. I believe that as a person he lent himself to comic biography, but I have no details. Did you not, years and years ago, meet him at Edmond de Goncourt's, and did he not say to you "Je n'aime que les femmes stériles"? It seems to me that I have a vague recollection of it, which has been recalled by a fatuous passage in one of his stories, where he declares that those who deeply love always sterilize their passion. He was a poor mouldy affair, I'm afraid.

Still, I don't know your address. Artful creeper into rabbit-holes, you shall, nevertheless, not escape detection.

We all send our love to you and I am ever affectionately,

Yrs,

EDMUND GOSSE.

Great Northern Hotel,
Bundoran,
Co. Donegal.

To Maurice Baring. *Sept. 7, 1897.*

My dear Maurice,—

What delightful letters you write! You shall be appointed Correspondent in Ordinary to the Great Cham, and that shall settle the difficulty of your professional career. We delighted in every clause of your letter, and I can only repay you in a poorer key. We have been nearly 3 weeks in this extraordinarily brisk and bracing place—quite the nicest British seaside affair I have ever known. The hotel stands on a headland pushing right out into the Atlantic, and the scenery is incredibly fresh and clean.

The great event has been the return of Philip,* who appeared, quite suddenly, like Robinson Crusoe, in rags, with a cockatoo on his shoulder and a macaw on his wrist, and mice in all his pockets. He is extremely well, seems to have made interesting collections, is curiously adult in judgment, and singularly sweet and modest in manner. But, apparently, without a spark of ambition, even for his zoology. He has had extraordinary adventures, which he has to be pressed before he will recount, and has been (among other things) within an ace of being murdered by the mutinous peons of whom he was left in charge. But he seems to have cowed them with that "dominant race" instinct which is so curious—a dozen jackals or cats kept at bay by one bull-pup of Britain. But you shall see him. He is terribly illiterate, but the very best of good company—and I am a doting idiot.

> "As foolish parents on their offspring dote,
> Each idiot author loves the brat he got."

(That is the only couplet of Nicholas Rowe, Queen Anne's Poet Laureate, that I know.) I have finished here reading the proofs of

* Dr. Philip Gosse, who had recently returned with the FitzGerald expedition from S. America.

my last brat, the *Short History of English Literature*. But I don't love it—I am tired to death of it: it seems to have turned to ashes. I wonder if anybody will read it. This is an infernally stupid letter, and a wretched return for yours, but my brains are baked and salted. We stay here another week. We all unite in love to you, and all want badly to see you again.

Yours,

L'Exilé de Bundoran.

Somebody writes to Nellie to-day and says, "Mr. Gosse seems to be enraging all the critics." What about? We see no papers, and I can't imagine what I have done now to stir the bile of the penny-a-liner. Do you?

Excuse this foolish enfolding of sheets. This is how we write letters on the Celtic Fringe.

29, Delamere Terrace,

To Robert Ross. *21.2.98.*

My dear Robbie,—

I must apologise for leaving your kind letter unacknowledged, and the two Ibsen* guineas from Mr. Adey (what are his initials?) and yourself.

The *Ballad of Reading Gaol* pleased me much more as a literary production than it did you. I thought that it contained—with mystical and exaggerated passages—several stanzas of penetrating and convinced emotion. I never read anything more steeped in despair, it is like the poem of a nature whose mainspring is broken. But where it is simple and direct it is poignantly effective.

Yours ever sincerely,

Edmund Gosse.

* Gosse was organising a tribute to Ibsen.

"Vikingness,"
Hardanger,
Norway.

To Maurice Baring. *July 11, 1898.*

DEAR MAURICE,—

As we walked over to Ljönsvanger this afternoon from Ljöndestangen, I gathered a posy of flowers in the forest, and when we reached the shore I gave it to my wife, saying, "Il est bon de faire des collections." She smartly replied, "Il est meilleur de faire des promenades," and so we turned and walked back to Ljöndestangen, that I might write to you.

Ljöndestangen is the real old name of this place, which has been called "Vikingness" to attract tourists. They are not attracted. The only people here, besides ourselves, are an old captain from British Guiana, and a perfectly innocent English clergyman and his wife, who skip in the meadows like silly children. We are perfectly happy. The place is deliciously beautiful, fresh, fragrant and solitary; the weather glorious beyond words, and the dear Norwegian people, with their pale, cold faces, and yellow spun-silk hair, cluster round us with civility—half sympathetic and half entertained, for they know that we are mad. As I talk a little Norwegian, they think my case less desperate, but they wonder that the English Clergyman's wife, who has adopted Norse stage-peasant's costume (a fact!), is allowed out of the asylum. They are so sweet, with their cold, pale faces, and they take us out to row and sail upon the lake, and they feed us with rödgröd and fladbröd and lax and saft and delicatessen till we cry to Baal and Bellygod to save us.

We have never been at a place we liked so much, or one where we were more perfectly happy. I wish you and Marsh could come out and join us. How people can go to Switzerland, when there is so much greener and cleaner a country with such vastly sweeter and neater inhabitants, I can't imagine.

Write me a little line as at the top of this sheet.

Ever yours in the Lord,

EDMUND GOSSE.

The clergyman's wife, who can't speak a word of Norwegian, rigged herself out in her stage-peasant's costume, and went this afternoon to call (uninvited) on the principal peasant proprietor of the district, a grim rich old lady rather like old Lady Stanley of Alderley, and talked gibberish at her and gave her a tract, and behaved like an absolute evangelical lunatic. Poor Nellie had to accompany her, and nearly died of shame. The stately courtesy of the old peasant-woman and her family was splendid. But as she went out behind the clergyman's wife, Nellie shook her head at the old lady and touched her forehead with her forefinger, that the Norwegians might thoroughly understand that the clergyman's wife *was* a lunatic.

CHAPTER EIGHTEEN

In 1899 Gosse published his *Life of Donne*. Twenty years earlier he had announced his intention of undertaking "what was perhaps the most imposing task left to the student of Elizabethan and Jacobean literature." Dr. Augustus Jessopp had entertained the same design, and for many years had been collecting material for a life of the Dean of St. Paul's: he insisted that Gosse should collaborate with him. The work hung fire. Dr. Jessopp was "never able to feel much enthusiasm for Donne as a poet, whereas to Gosse even to his last seraphical hour in his bedchamber at St. Paul's, Donne was quintessentially a poet." Suddenly in 1897 Dr. Jessopp transferred the whole responsibility to Gosse's shoulders.

The difficulties of the subject were undeniable. Much in Donne's life was incapable of elucidation, the field for scholarly and ingenious conjecture was unusually wide, and theological questions of a complex nature had to be dealt with. By temperament and certainly by inclination Gosse was much more likely to succeed single-handed than in collaboration with even the most accomplished scholar. It was a happy chance to vindicate his own authority by showing the world that accurate scholarship was his province and that he could be as painstaking as the most pedantic. In the Preface he approached the public with disarming modesty, planting his standard on an eminence more lowly than readers of his edition of the Works of Gray might have looked for. He acknowledged that the subject was beset with pitfalls, and, if we read between the lines, he was equally aware that ambushed on many sides hostile forces were waiting ready to pounce on any signs of carelessness.

When the book appeared it was received with a chorus of praise. The *Athenæum* acknowledged that "the little demon of inaccuracy, who occasionally takes his stand at Mr. Gosse's elbow," had in this case been foiled: a few slips, inevitable having regard to the size and nature of the undertaking, being all that the critic could point to. So far so good. But when the wave of approval was spent there appeared in the *Athenæum* for December a letter above the signature of Arthur Vincent, calling attention to what appeared to be a serious error, serious because it related to a statement of fact on which Gosse had founded a view of Donne's character and conduct.

Gosse had alleged that in the nullity suit of the Earl of Essex and Lady Frances Howard, Donne had played an active and discreditable part. Gosse, doing his best to palliate the offence of Donne, found himself driven to take refuge under the shelter of Dean Church's opinion that all the Jacobean churchmen were subjected to a sort of fate, which obliged them to become base at least once in their lives.

Donne however was innocent of any such direct complicity. The source of the trouble was a document among the Ashburnham MSS. which Gosse took to be a compendium of the nullity suit drawn up by Donne in the course of 1613. Upon this he had assumed that Donne was an active and influential coadjutor in procuring the decree of nullity. Mr. Vincent pointed out that the Harleian MS., of which the compendium was a copy, was drawn up not by Donne but by "Sre. Danell Dunn, Doctor of the Civill Law," one of the commissioners who tried the case. The error was unfortunate, serving to prolong unjustly the tradition that Gosse was too careless to be regarded as a scholar, and for the moment diverting attention from the erudition and research on which the book was founded. In point of fact, it was an error that did small injustice to the Dean, and could not vitiate the inferences to be drawn from the circumstances that Donne did actually take an interest in the process, expressed his willingness to help, and subsequently wrote an elaborate epithalamium for the wedding which followed. Donne was therefore at the least, in the spirit of a worldly wise churchman, an accessory after the fact. As was so often the case with Gosse where error was concerned, the portrait drawn was true in spite of the error. He had the intuitions of an artist, and an artist's instinct for the essential. A high authority* considers that Gosse has given the best extant portrait of the Dean, and that he was the earliest writer to afford a view of Donne in correct perspective, showing for the first time how gradual and unwilling

* Professor H. J. E. Grierson in a letter to the writer.

his "Steps to the Altar" had been, and how much of the unregenerate Donne had survived till the final step was taken.

In his *Life of Donne* Gosse is answering a challenge which had largely to be met by the weight and number of facts which he could produce. He was determined that this time there should be no question of slackness in original research. His writing consequently is weighted with a heavy cargo, again and again his progress is impeded by the abundance of his information, the narrative —and it is mainly a work of direct narrative—bristles with facts, and is constantly held up by the very excess of its learning. We get less than usual of his illuminating judgments and his lightness of touch; his vivacity and wit are too often buried under the stuff of scholarship, the finished article under the raw material. To this day, however, it remains the definitive *Life*.

Board of Trade,

To Maurice Baring. *24.3.99.*

My dear Maurice,—

Philip tells me you were extremely kind in looking after him. So good and like you.

I am sending you another proof, because it fits in with what Philip brought you. I want to know whether you don't think the *Ignatius his Conclave* amusing? No one has ever looked at it before, as far as I know. But still more, I want your careful judgment on my treatment of the *Biathanatos*. Without exception everyone who has written about Donne has said that this is a joke, or a mystification, or that he could not possibly have meant anything particular by it. You will see my theory is that he was sorely tempted to commit suicide and wanted to persuade himself that it would not be mortal sin if he did. I have read the book with extreme care—which I don't believe five other living people have done. Do tell me—unicus semper lector meus—whether the analysis amuses you.

Ever yours affectionately,

E. G.

Yes! D. *was* a correspondent. I think I must try to write you a letter in that style!

29, Delamere Terrace,

To Sir Arthur Pinero. *13.4.99.*

MY DEAR PINERO,—

I have just seen *The Gay Lord Quex.* May I bore you by expressing my enthusiastic admiration? That third act is one of the most magnificent pieces of stagecraft in our literature. I look upon this play as the finest specimen of pure comedy that you (and therefore any one in our time) has produced. I could say many things, but I should only weary you. But I am still a little under the dazzlement of your great play—so vigorous and beneficent and gay.

Do stick to COMEDY now you have got safe to it—no more melodrama or farce or Ibsen, or anything but the pure heroic comedy which is the very child of the gods—the laughing child, the child of *April.* I feel very strongly about this; *Comedy* is what we want.

Ever sincerely yours,

EDMUND GOSSE.

29, Delamere Terrace,

To Max Beerbohm. *April 29, 1899.*

MY DEAR MAX,—

You will, I hope, forgive my delay in thanking you for the kind thought you had in sending me your new volume of essays. I wanted to read and re-read them before I wrote to you. Now, let me say to you how very highly I think of them. I weigh this little book against its predecessor, and I am astonished at the growth from the petulant, amusing, clever boy to the finished man. I do not think that there is an essayist living who is your equal now, *at your best.* But, bless me, how unequal you are! What rejoices me about the little book is that I find you throughout (or almost throughout) the rigid censor of your own things. You select for permanent form only your best, and I observe the revisions made since the first periodical appearance of the essays—always for the better.

Well, this really answers my anxiety and my indignation. The bad things don't matter, if you only reprint good ones. The newspaper is lost, the book remains. Our duty is towards our books. A little essay of yours is a sonnet, really; no one turns out the classic "*sonnet sans défaut*" every time. The fatuous essayist thinks they are all equally good, and his are all equally bad.

Now, about *More*. I should bore you if I told you all the reflections which have occurred to me in reading it. You are now a finished master in the form of your best groups of phrases. I am in despair: I have been trying to see where the magic of some of your sentences comes in, have even (for purely self-educational purposes) been trying to imitate some of them privately. Your constructions, at their best, have now become miraculously characteristic, in their solidity and lightness. You have an instrument quite your own, and you know how to use it. Beware—oh! good gracious, what is the good of being ware of anything, when one writes so well as you do?

Still, in pure priggishness, I will give you one or two warnings:—

In these delicious little affairs of yours the balance is so exquisite that the least failure in tact vexes the reader. However, one or two little unfitting projections of yourself make me wince. You speak of yourself *humorously* with absolute success. But sometimes I am hurt when you speak of yourself *seriously*. You say your reviews of Ouida and again of Mrs. Meynell caused in each case a revolution of taste. This is not the voice of Max, but that of ——. Ah, how much more delicately Max could indicate what here has a touch of coarse vanity. Do you think of this, and of the rare sensitiveness of the ear to the proper sounding of the ego.

Then, sometimes, you—whose whole function is to be on the side of the angels—fight abruptly with the fools. The essay in *More* which I like least is the Edile one. I don't like you to be obvious. Now, there are a thousand journalists in London whose ignorance and whose insensibility to impressions render them entirely capable of approving or of signing your remarks on sculpture, which you will forgive me, my dear Max, if I tell you are quite unworthy of you. If you are insensible to form, sculpture may give you no pleasure, as music gives me none who am insensible to tune, but I have always refrained from saying that there is no difference between good and bad music, and that all music is insufferable. Don't let us insult the arts; it is such a stupid thing to do.

I could go on long talking about your delightful little book: but I must weary you.

Most truly yours,

EDMUND GOSSE.

29, Delamere Terrace,

To Gordon Bottomley. *June 3rd, 1899.*

MY DEAR SIR,—

I am sorry that I have allowed a month to pass without acknowledging the kind gift of your poems, *At White-Nights*. I have read them with a great deal of pleasure. I remember your earlier book of verse very distinctly, and the sense of promise which it gave me, and that promise seems now fulfilled in these beautiful lyrics, with their high sense of moral and physical beauty.

Believe me,

My dear Sir,

Very faithfully yours,

EDMUND GOSSE.

29, Delamere Terrace,

To Mr. Foote. *28.6.99.*

MY DEAR FOOTE,—

You have a funny Press in America! I don't think an English paper would print an attack, headed "Edmund Gosse's Errors," without making some slight attempt to see whether the accusation was founded or not. As a fact, the letter is a tissue of blunders, and the outcome of naïvest ignorance on the part of the writer. The idea of a man writing in that way about a subject so excessively complex as the bibliography of the *Dunciad* without looking at a single authority, but grossly attacking another man who has given his life to these things, is (I confess) to my mind a disgraceful feature of journalism.

It seems a long time since I had the pleasure of a letter from you. I hope you are well. I am almost tired to death by my great *Life and Letters of John Donne*, but the second volume is now nearly thro' the press. Kindest regards from

Ever sincerely yours,

EDMUND GOSSE.

Byglandssommerhjemmet,
Soetersdalen, Norway.

To Maurice Baring. *Aug. 12th, 1899.*

MY DEAR MAURICE,—

We have been speculating, my wife and I, how you would like being here. We decide that it would depend on the company. We depend entirely on our own. This is an hotel miles and miles away from anything, reached by a steamer once a day. It is rather large, and we have an extremely nice room overlooking the fjord, from which we watch milk-blond girls, with yellow tails, playing croquet in the dust, and excessively Early Victorian Norse mammas (hair drawn tightly back, with a flat knob behind, heavy gold chain, brooch at throat) knitting in the skeletons of what were meant for *laubes*. There are quantities of Norwegians (some of them talk English *to one another* at meals, for practice), some Danes and two or three of the usual dull English. We get quite away from all sight or sound of all of them by walking one minute 30 seconds in any direction whatever, and we are very happy. There is an Elysian garden islet in the shape of a promontory running out into the fjord, where we sit for hours under the birch-trees, and sniff the junipers and rosemaries. I have been reading the *Life of William Morris*, which Eddie Marsh most kindly sent us just as we were leaving town. It is well written, but I am entirely consoled by it for any disappointment I might have felt in never having really known him at all well. Don't you, more and more, like *personal* people? It seems to me that "abysmal personality" is what one can't do without. Now W. M. was excessively *im*personal. With his picturesqueness, and his violent temper and his art and all, he had no real touch with humanity, at least not with mine. And while I like inconsistency, I don't like incoherency. Morris was incoherent—the romantic poetry, and the carpets, and the Socialism, and the collecting of missals don't hold together. Mackail says that Morris was extremely like Dr. Johnson in character! Save the mark. He was a strongish kind of man, and we owe him a great revival of beauty, but I didn't like him when he was alive, and I like him no better now that he is dead.

Is not this funny letter-paper? It is *tout ce qu'il y a de plus norvégien.* I could write reams of it to you, but that I fear to bore you. You would be amused with the country-people here. Soetersdalen is the most remote, unfriended, melancholy and slow province of Norway, and the only one now where the ancient dress is habitually worn. It is not like the tourist-haunted places where waitresses put on a scarlet bodice and call it their "costume." You wander here high up among the woods, and you hear a tinkle of bells, and three kids and a lamb gallop out, and suddenly there stands at your side a being as dark as an Indian and dressed like a hoplite, with a kind of white fustinella showing her long black legs, and a fringe of black shawl waving like feathers about her iron forehead. She is not at all shy—it is you who are shy, and she comes quite close to you and asks questions in a loud, harsh voice and a strange Norrona-dialect as old as the hills. They are the kindest people in Europe, but they frighten me to death. If the kind and indulgent whim should seize you of writing to me during the next 28 days, address to me

Adr. Hr. O. Thommessen,
"Verdens Gang,"
Christiania.

I am always, my dear Maurice,
affectionately yours,
E. G.

Noesset, Soetersdalen,
Norway.

To Henry James. *Aug. 12, 1899.*

My dear James,—

We have been talking so much about you this morning, that I feel that I must talk *to* you. We have been here (Sommerhjemme) nearly a fortnight, very restful, with the eternal freshness which is the great pull Norway has over all other countries known to me. It is not that the scenery is handsome, indeed it is often rather monotonous—but it sparkles, it twinkles, there is a sort of radiant dewiness stirring through the very hottest hours. And the heat has been dog-star, never was such a summer known in Norway. I am sitting in a most delicate and Elysian peninsula of birch-trees where we come every day in the middle of the heat. It runs right out into the fjord, and there is always a breeze here. Through the stems of the birches I see the blazing lake, and the mountain reddish-purple behind it. The heat sucks out all the odours, the resin and the birch-sap, and the junipers baking at our feet, and a little invisible rosemary that fills the air with perfume—a regular orchestra of hot smells. There is never anyone else on this little delicate Sirmio of ours, except a flock of eight great Royston crows, with their little grey shawls thrown over their shoulders; they can't understand our intrusion at all, and stalk forward to gaze; and they fly into the birches to discuss us. One has now been deputed to expostulate with us, and he has come forward and sits on the dead bough of a birch, shaking with indignation. But, although I give him every courteous encouragement, now he has come he can't think what to say. Our friend Sparkes was with us here for a day or two, and we made up to a cultivated and very agreeable old Norse captain and his wife. But they are gone, and the rest of the people in the hostel offer us no prospect of pleasure. We left this absurd little fragment of civilisation, and went up to the head of the valley, posting 100 miles in stolkjarres (carriols for two) in three days. This was highly delightful; and the primitive people received us gladly. At one place, Viken i Valle, we stayed at the house of the principal village-man, and at night we sat round the open fire of logs, while the daughters and a young son—a youth like the young Achilles—sang staves to us in dialect, some very ancient, some their own composition. Folk-poetry is still alive in these remotest mountain valleys. The costume of the people here in Soetersdalen is most surprising and amusing. Instead of its being a sort of race survival, encouraged by the hotels on Sundays, it is universal, and the dress, which is peculiar to this valley, is as extraordinary as it is picturesque. The women look like hoplites; they stalk about in a sort of white fustinella or crinoline of padded woollen, which shows their black-stockinged legs from the knee; in the upper dress a good deal of bright colour, and a strange feathery fringe round the head. The weight of the short, crinolined skirt forces them to walk slowly, and you see them stalk slowly across the landscape, often with incomparable dignity of gesture. One would not have supposed anything so queer survived in western Europe. The men wear immense trousers, which come up to their necks, and are beautifully embroidered on the breast, with (on gala days) the funniest little perfunctory coat, also embroidered, and looking like moths' wings; the vast black trousers are suddenly drawn close about the ankles with bright-green leather gaiters. I can't think why nobody comes here to paint the peasants: they are marvellous. Very high up, at Viken i Valle for instance, where the landhandler's son sang to us as I told you, the men's dress differs again—a jerkin, tight to the shape, close breeches and stockings, more like the Irish people in *Punch*.

Nellie has been busy sketching. She sits a few yards from me now, half buried in whortleberry-bushes, with a comical expression of intense seriousness and one eye shut, trying to get the tone of the white birch-trunks against the blue of the fjord. It is a pleasure to see her so perfectly well, and rested.

Nellie sends her love to you, and we are both,

My dear James,

Affectionately yours,

EDMUND GOSSE.

SYLVIA GOSSE TESSA GOSSE MRS. GOSSE EDMUND GOSSE

THE GOSSE FAMILY IN DELAMERE TERRACE

29 (*not* 28)
Delamere Terrace, W.

To Maurice Baring. *20.11.99.*

My dear Maurice,—

I have made a few slight suggestions, mainly prosodical, for the text of your beautiful and melodious poem. Is it this which is going to Lady Randolph's review?* We may appear together, for she has asked me for some poems for her Christmas number.

Have you read the wonderful *Letters of R.L.S.*? I can think of nothing else. They are ineffable. Get them at once, and tell me what you think of them.

I have been staying at Rye with Henry James. He was telling me that some young actresses, staying at Winchelsea, had expressed a desire to see him, and had come over to tea. I asked, "Were they pretty?" He replied, "Pretty! Good heavens!!" and then with the air of one who will be scrupulously just, he added:—"One of the poor wantons had a certain cadaverous grace."

Write to me again. I may not be with you long.

Yours affectionately,

Edmund G.

29, *Delamere Terrace,*

To Maurice Baring. *27.12.99.*

My very dear Maurice,—

I was just sitting down to write you a New Year's letter when I had a note from Eddie to tell me that a present was on its way to me; and now it has come. Thank you very much indeed. But I am so sorry you have no proper title-page. I think that it will look best in scarlet morocco. What do you say? Rivière? Yes, I think so, I am very proud of having one of the 3 only vellum copies. *Altera Circe* is the only piece I had not seen before. It is extremely melodious and delicate. The last line is like a sea-scape on a Japanese fan. I like the old sonnets more and more, *Le Calice* is without

* *The Anglo-Saxon.*

question one of the most beautiful sonnets of our age. It is absolutely perfect, not a flaw in it from first to last. By degrees you will have a little sheaf of pure winnowed wheat, no chaff in it at all; and the world will wake, perhaps, to an English Heredia.

I was exceedingly amused the other day, in a letter from George Leveson-Gower, to receive a quotation from *Hildesheim*, with an elaborate explanation for my ignorance of who you are and what "H" was. He is a great admirer.

Have you seen Arthur's life of the Primate?* It is very much more interesting than I ever expected it would be, and presents a more workmanlike appearance. There are many pages in it which you would read with great appreciation.

Lytton flashed upon us last week, a delightful apparition. He looks very much stronger in health, and he is steadying down into a very sane, intelligent and graceful fellow. I think he will be a remarkable man, perhaps a great one.

There is a perfectly appalling quantity of illness about. The Bacillus Demon waves his purple crest and gnashes his green teeth. We had no servants on Xmas Day, and Tessa had to lay the fires and make the beds! We all rather enjoyed it for a change, a sort of picnic. But, golly! what a Christmas!

You don't know how much I enjoyed that little sight of you. It broke the continuity of absence, and that is such an immense thing. It is so difficult for Doubting Peters—the children of Mrs. Gummidge—to be quite sure that l'Ami Chose is just the same, if months go by and you see nothing of him. One fancies that the pride of life and the poison of youth must have produced some sort of change. And friendship is so absurdly intolerant of change. But if one touches the brow and feels the print of the nails every now and then, faith revives and continues.

Did I tell you that I have a little cycle of four poems coming out in the *Anglo-Saxon*? The edition was mainly burned in the Ballantyne fire, but the thing is said to be going to rise from its ashes in the middle of January. I wonder what poem of yours is going to be in it?

* A. C. Benson. *Life of Archbishop Benson.*

This is a frightfully dull letter; but I am a dull dog, congenitally. We all unite in love to you.

Your affectionate

E. G.

In 1900 there appeared in the April *Quarterly* an article on Queen Victoria. The author was Gosse. He had been supplied with some of the material by Lady Ponsonby, the widow of Sir Henry Ponsonby, Queen Victoria's Private Secretary. It was written within three months of Her Majesty's death. No idea of the sensation it created can be formed without recapturing the state of the public mind at the time. To-day the article reads as a blameless and successful attempt to estimate some of the personal qualities of the Queen. In April 1901, the attempt hardly escaped the charge of sacrilege. More than twenty years later Gosse, in reviewing the *Life of Queen Victoria* by Lytton Strachey, reminded his readers of the feeling which found expression at the time. "Her phantom took divine proportions; she was clothed with the most extravagant and the most incongruous attributes, and anyone who endeavoured, in however respectful and even affectionate terms, to separate the fabulous from the historic elements and reduce the vast idol to human proportions, was regarded as libellous and cruel." Had Gosse been detected in the act of cutting a caper at the august lady's most memorable funeral, he could hardly have earned more reprobation than by the questions which he set himself to answer in the *Quarterly Review*. "Was it a human being at all?" he asked. "Was it worthy of the idolatry it awakened? How much of the worship was paid to a woman and how much to a fetish?" To ask such questions, no matter how they were answered, was to lay hands on the sacred ark; there was no getting away from it, his audacity was regarded as an exercise in profanity. And yet in reality he had rendered a service to the memory of the Queen; he had arrested the growth of a myth, it is true, but he had replaced it by the delineation of an extremely human and sovereign woman. *Queen Victoria as I knew her*, by Sir Theodore Martin, which Gosse said should have been entitled, *Victoria as Martin failed to see her*, was an effort in 1908 to restore the haze of adulation, but it was in vain. Gosse's article had sounded the knell to the impossible, the inhuman, the sanctified creation of popular esteem and dissolved it once and for all. The lowly adage defining the privilege of a cat in relation to a King had been extended to the consideration of a Queen by a critic, and in the process the way had been thrown open for the historian.

He described her three cardinal qualities as shrewdness, simplicity and sympathy, and proceeded to show the benefits which had flowed from the tactful exercise of these attributes. So far as the possession of higher or different endowments was claimed for Her Majesty, he desired that the question should be considered in no *ex parte* spirit, but as one open to honest and respectful discussion. "Such shining qualities as hers," he wrote, "could not but have their defects, and it is the poorest-spirited obsequiousness to pretend that they had not." The analysis which followed was shrewd, and in the then state of public opinion, bold. In considering "one of the most remarkable personalities of the nineteenth century," he claimed that legend and fable should be discarded and the character of the Queen examined by the light of truth and the standards of common humanity. With touches of decorous and scarcely perceptible irony he went on to put into more exact perspective the extravagant titles with which she had been invested by the popular imagination. While detracting nothing from the basic greatness of her character, he succeeded in evoking a portrait differing little from the most modern delineations of which the Queen has been the subject.

29, Delamere Terrace,

To W. Heinemann. *12.5.'900.*

My dear W. H.,—

Very many thanks for the d'Annunzio brochure.* It is prepared in the most interesting way, and I could not help reading it through at once. I see that the play has the same odious thesis that d'Annunzio always affects—namely, that merely physical infatuation, sheer lust in short, is a sufficient excuse for every species of ingratitude,

* A translation of *La Città Morta.*

disloyalty, cruelty. This runs through every book he writes, and makes him, to my mind, the most odiously immoral and disgraceful of modern authors. Not one of the worst Frenchmen has gone so far as he in the deification of mere cowardly sexuality.

Ever sincerely yours,

EDMUND GOSSE.

29, Delamere Terrace,

To Sir Gilbert Parker. *23.11.'900.*

MY DEAR PARKER,—

I am delighted. Your absence would have been a real disappointment to me.

The great man*—who is eccentricity itself—has disappeared! Melted, like a long genie out of a bottle! But he shall reanimate his picturesque clay by the 30th. Poor Mr. Braekstad is rather alarmed:—He sees in vision:—

SUDDEN DISAPPEARANCE OF A DANISH POET

but I am not anxious. The most ethereal of Bards becomes materialised when a Dinner is being given in his honour. Even Stephen Phillips would write a letter or Andrew Lang give a civil answer on so very exceptional an occasion.

Ever yours,

EDMUND GOSSE.

29, Delamere Terrace,

To George Armour. *8.4.'901.*

MY DEAR GEORGE,—

We thought of you and drank your health on the 27th, but I did not write to you because I waited to make a certain announcement. I feel that you and Harriet ought to be among the very first to be told that you will never see us again (unless you look very sharp)

* Holger Drachmann, the Danish Poet: see ante p. 243.

in this old house that you have known so long. The great piece of news which overshadows everything else is that I have bought a house! It is No. 17, Hanover Terrace. It is a large, solid house in an old Georgian Terrace jutting into and overlooking Regent's Park on the western side. It is a good deal out of repair, and Mr. John Belcher, A.R.A., is going to make some structural changes and put it fully into a modern state for us. The builders go in this week, and we hope that by July at latest we may be settled in. I hope and think you will like it. The situation and aspect are delightful; there is no view in London more beautiful than from our upper windows. There is a vast balcony where we hope to live entirely in summer, where I shall work by day, and sit on fine nights with the electric light delicately shaded, and enjoy long talks. How happy a day when those talks shall be again with both of you.

I have been and am extremely busy. Besides more humdrum things I have finished a fantastic sort of poem, very modern and antique, of quite a new kind. I cannot describe it, but I hope you will like to read it. It makes a little volume. It has gone to press to-day, but is to be delayed until this tedious war is over.

Ever yours affectionately,

E. G.

29, Delamere Terrace,

To the Revd. William Hunt. *16.5.'901.*

My dear Hunt,—

You have written me the charmingest and cheeriest letter. So many thanks.

This thing* is pleasant because of the way in which it came. It was all kept perfectly dark from me—it was an absolute surprise. But it appears that the Norwegian Government, in a Memorandum signed by all the Ministers, asked King Oscar to give it me "in recognition of my services to Norwegian Literature." Is not that nice?

I must show you the insignia—extremely pretty. The "Seraphim"

* The insignia as Knight of the Royal Norwegian Order of St. Olaf, First Class, 1901.

is not Norwegian, but Swedish. The thing to do now is to live for that! *L'un n'empêche pas l'autre.* But the more the Norwegians love me the more the Swedes eye me with suspicion.

I hope you will be at the Club on Saturday.

Always yours, with very sincere thanks for your jolly letter,

EDMUND THE SERAPH.

CHAPTER NINETEEN

In 1901 Gosse moved from Delamere Terrace to 17, Hanover Terrace, which was to be his home till he died. He had lived in "the house overlooking a canal with a screen of poplar-trees between it and the barges" for twenty-six years. He had crowded it with literary memories, every notable man of letters of the day having been his guest there at one time or another. In early days George Moore on one of his adventures from the Nouvelle Athènes had brought there his youthful drama in blank verse *Martin Luther*, and thither since those early days had come a host of authors with their MSS. for the edification of trying them on Gosse. That was the price he paid for his sympathy with young authors, getting back full measure through the enjoyment he derived from encouraging and directing.

And here too in Delamere Terrace he had been indefatigable in hospitality—a warm and vital hospitality—reflecting the glow of his own delight at contact with his friends. It was the custom for the Gosses to be "at home" on Sundays. The procedure was well known to their friends. At four o'clock people would begin to arrive, Gosse would play the watchful shepherd, even in his agitation at times overplaying the part, herding together, willy-nilly, those who were not always too sympathetic, and forming conversational units which would to his despair often enough indulge in a break-away. At five, tea was brought in, giving a new impetus to regrouping of guests. The affair was not without a ritual of its own—it was organised on a pattern; there was an ideal to be realised, the *salon* model to be aimed at, and Gosse probably went as near to achieve it as the refractory conditions of English social life would allow. The critical moment arrived when he had to head off those guests whom he wanted to stay for supper. When that was successfully accomplished his anxieties were at an end, the Victorian intentness was relaxed, he was at his best, sure of his audience, sunned and basking, his good humour simmering, his conversational armoury polished, and his talk exhilarating and responsive, shining out in the nimbleness of its wit, and its faculty of evading dead-ends and dull conclusions. For the symposium of laughter which followed the familiars were to be found among Henry James, George Moore, Arthur Symons, W. B. Yeats, Max Beerbohm, Aubrey Beardsley, Maurice Baring, Arthur Benson, Maarten Maartens, Andrew Lang, Eddie Marsh and many others. The evening would as often as not be prolonged till the early morning, till it might have been said "the huntsmen are up in Arabia: and they have already passed their first sleep in Persia."

He was a warm upholder of the traditional Christmas—nothing would have induced him to spend it away from his wife and children—all the forms were observed, the modern fashion of commercialising the occasion, the *do ut des*, almost the *rogo ut des*, would have been in the highest degree distasteful to him: he translated Christmas into its most simple and familiar manifestation. The impressions of his childhood had never forsaken him. Readers of *Father and Son* will remember that scene where the child, having eaten of Christmas fare, was driven to exclaim, "Oh Papa! I have eaten of flesh offered to idols," the Father saying sternly, "Where is the accursed thing?" then plunging into the kitchen, seizing the "idolatrous confectionery," and so holding the child tight with one hand and the plate in the other, proceeding to the dust-heap in outer darkness and there burying it out of sight. Such recollections—and they abounded—were beacons in Gosse's mind, directing him away almost automatically from the things which had darkened his childhood. Far more than might be supposed of his conduct in life was due to unconscious protest against that childhood, and far more was determined by the consistency and completeness of the reaction to which he was in continual response. It would perhaps be safe to say that the only recognisable survival of direct influence from his upbringing was his fear of what at Marychurch was invariably spoken of as "the so-called Church of Rome." He no longer denounced it, as in childhood he had been instructed to do; but he maintained towards it an attitude of curiously sustained antagonism—breaking into open censoriousness when any member of the community to which he belonged was enrolled as a convert.

On New Year's Eve he used to keep open house for his friends, marking the occasion by some entertainment usually of excellent quality. But the entertainment was often necessarily a leap into the unknown and seldom without risk. He was once misled into an unlucky choice of marionettes, which turned out to be very poor. The show was in a rather small upstairs room, packed with celebrities. Eddie Marsh found himself squeezed against the wall next to Henry James. As the entertainment proceeded there was a growing sense of failure; Henry James, whose capacity for being bored, and it was a capacity never to be ignored, was stretched to the utmost, laying his hand (that gesture so familiar to those who knew him) on Marsh's shoulder, said, "An interesting example of economy, my dear Marsh, economy of means—and ur—ur" (with a fine gleam of malice coming into his eye) "—economy of *effect*." But such *contretemps* were foreign to the genial atmosphere that usually prevailed.

The new house, 17, Hanover Terrace, was a pleasant and comfortably spacious structure, entered from an arcade which runs the length of the Terrace and supports the continuous balcony of the individual houses. Henry James compared it to Bologna. A narrow hall opened directly on the staircase; on the first floor was an L-shaped drawing-room communicating with a broad balcony, having a fine view over Regent's Park. In the longer limb of the L, divisible from the front room by a curtain, bookcases and bays held Gosse's library, and the table at which he wrote. The comfort was adequate but by no means excessive. Everywhere on tables and walls and staircase were traces of the Victorian era, including Japanese prints to illustrate the vogue of the 'seventies, photographs by Mrs. Cameron, sculpture by Thornycroft, Frampton, Onslow Ford and Goscombe John, drawings by Rossetti and Alfred East, William Rothenstein and Max Beerbohm, paintings by Sargent, Alfred Parsons, Tadema and Cecil Lawson; and works by many other hands, each illustrative of an epoch and a reminder of a personal relation. He liked to be surrounded by the evidences of his sympathies and tastes, by things which recalled an experience

EDMUND GOSSE IN HIS LIBRARY, 17, HANOVER TERRACE

FROM AN ETCHING BY SYLVIA GOSSE

or a friendship. He carried the chattels of his past as in a caravan, regarding them with sentiment, and treating them as companions with a biographical interest, and as guests with a history. Here he continued the traditions and conventions of Delamere Terrace, dispensing the same free hospitality.

There was a sense of unity and consistency about the character of the dwelling: one could tell at a glance that it was the house of a man of letters, who had been in touch with the development of his epoch. Every author of note seemed to be represented, and as time went by the house became the record of a bygone age, with everywhere the relics of great personalities—to which Gosse himself furnished an explanatory and illuminating footnote: his memories vivid and light, not easily drawn, but once started of entrancing freshness and humour. With his regard for the great and what they had accomplished went a discriminating appreciation of their weaknesses, whether those of Browning, Tennyson, Swinburne, George Eliot or Pater. By his exquisite conversational craft he could give those of them he had known substantive form and reincarnate them before the eye of the listener. That was one of his supreme gifts: under a dancing levity of words to convey a profound sense of reality and truth, to be the glorified showman of experience, lending art to reminiscence and differentiating it from anecdote.

At the time when he moved from Delamere Terrace to Regent's Park he was fifty-three years of age, but looked considerably younger. The almost airy quickness of his movements, his crest of fair hair, the intense mobility of his expression, the piercing intelligence of his eye, all denoted a surviving spirit of youthfulness. Laments at the advance of years, forecasts of decrepitude ("Still in the body," he would say in a Marychurch phrase to enquiries after his health) and flippant references to the hungry generations without, were no more than a domino at a masked ball, thinly disguising a dauntless determination to continue as he was, an invincible optimist, an insatiable lover of life. "If it amuses him," wrote Mr. John Drinkwater in 1912 in a review of Gosse's poetry, "to talk of himself as a back number, none of his friends would wish to cross him in his little amiabilities. None of us believe him and he very well knows that none of us believe him. But we join in the fun the more readily since it has on more than one occasion achieved a poetic expression as lovely as anything he has written."

Gosse saved himself much "expense of spirit" by conforming to a daily time-table. Every morning he breakfasted at eight and afterwards wrote till the moment came for him to set out on foot for his office: again, on his return in the evening he would write till dinner time. He allowed nothing to disturb the pattern according to which he regulated his hours of work. Punctuality was a hobby with him. To keep a luncheon engagement he would often arrive so early that he deemed it necessary to walk to and fro in the street, studying his watch till the appointed hour had struck. He was never known to be a day late with an MS., whether of a book or an article. He was always well in advance of his commitments. Such a thing as a letter remaining unanswered was too foreign to his sense of courtesy to be tolerated. He replied on the instant. The result was that he found time for everything, for his friends, his recreations, his correspondence, and his omnivorous reading. But the very variety and multiplicity of his interests, coupled with his peculiarly exposed sensibilities, would inevitably have landed him in a break-down, had he not lived within the shelter of a recognised routine.

No one did more to maintain the sanctity of the routine than Parker, that friend and dependent of the family, who in fulfilment of her duties admitted guests and callers to the house. By applying a drastic process of selection at the front door, she constituted a bulwark against intruders. Possessed of a voice at times stentorian, a sibilant accent, and a diction adaptable to the occasion, she seemed able, in the very announcement of a name or a prefix, to indicate to the guest his place in Gosse's esteem. The sonorous intonation with which the introduction of *Lord* Haldane would be made, would be succeeded by a gentle sibilant as she announced *Mister X* who was following on his heels. Faithful, friendly and efficient, she had bound herself to the fortunes of the family, regarding Gosse himself as the special object of her care and protection. Her equanimity was never at fault—it might be a guest who had come to dinner on the wrong night, or a German air-raid, or an outbreak of influenza, or a Scandinavian celebrity with a conundrum for a name—she took them all in her even stride. When a Zeppelin was hovering over London and after answering a call on the telephone, she opened the dining room door and in a level, unfaltering voice said, "Miss Sitwell, sir, says she will *not* be an Aunt Sally for the Germans, so she is not coming to dinner."

Villa Marguerite,
Dieppe.

To Lady Gosse. *Sunday, June 9, 1901*

My Dearest,—

Your letter has just arrived: so many thanks. Please send the *Revue Critique*—something about Shirten Collars,* I suppose. I was in excellent time at Victoria. The sea was rather rough in the middle of the Channel, and broke over the ship rather unpleasantly. I was soaked several times from head to foot. But I lay back in a long chair and managed to live it through without being quite ill, and on the French side it was calm and I recovered.

Harland missed me at the pier, and I was just bargaining about a *voiture* to drive me up here when a gay apparition—in very elegant grey clothes and a fly-away tie—shouted "cher maître, cher maître!" over the heads of the crowd, pressed through and folded me in his arms. This is a wonderful little place—a sort of tiny sham château at the top of a garden full of trees, all vocal with birds; small descending terraces, a tiny meadow, a charming brook regulated by a tap, short winding avenues made to look interminable, and roses, roses, roses everywhere—roses that climb to the chimneys, and flop about the paths, and race up gimcrack pavilions, and grow up in solemn bushes pretending to be oleanders. The air is full of the scent of them. We feel the sea air all the time, for right behind the trees falls the cliff. The host and hostess are like two enchanted children—in fact the whole thing is like an enchant-

* Churton Collins.

ment, I imagine somebody saying "Konx Ompax,"* and suddenly there would be nothing here.

Ever your loving

E.

17, Hanover Terrace,

To Mrs. Patrick Campbell. *6th November, 1901.*

DEAR MRS. PATRICK CAMPBELL,—

Permit me to congratulate you very warmly on your wonderfully delicate and spiritual performance of this afternoon.† We have come back dazed, like people who have seen a vision. I am quite sure that your rendering of the part of Klara would give exquisite pleasure to my friend the poet. I greatly wish that he could see it.

The first act was in every way beautifully staged, but don't you think that the arrangement of the furniture might be a little simplified in the second act? I thought your marvellously beautiful entrance at the end was spoiled by chairs and tables in the way. Klara and Sang should seem (I think) to be drawn irresistibly together, she drawn to him like steel to a magnet, with no clergyman or other piece of furniture impeding. Forgive my ignorant meddling.

Quite apart from the transcendent beauty of your personal part in the piece, you claim the highest applause from every serious-minded person for your courage in presenting a poem, the interest of which is so unusual and so intellectual.

Just behind where we sat, the critic of one of the biggest newspapers sat snuffling and wriggling, and I heard him mutter (just at the most exquisite point of your first scene) "Fancy coming to a thing like this—it is about as amusing as a funeral!" I thought the imbecility of this remark, from such a pretended authority, quite worth recording.

Thank you again for an immense pleasure, in which, and in kindest remembrances, my wife joins me.

Yours very sincerely,

EDMUND GOSSE.

* "I have said *Konx ompax* and it is finished" (see Hogg's *Life of Shelley,* vol. I, p. 226).

† The play was Björnson's *Beyond Human Power.*

17, Hanover Terrace,

To George Armour. *8.11.1901.*

My dear George,—

. . . .

I have published a little sort of masque called *Hypolympia* which has the oddest effect upon people. Some persons, chary of praise—like Henry James and Pinero, for instance—eulogize it as a masterpiece, and cannot say enough about it, and some of the newspapers too. Other readers ask blankly what it "means," and the Press generally is treating it as absolute imbecility and rot unparalleled. I think—in my long experience—I never managed to awaken by one production such violent extremes of opinion.

Ever yours affectionately,

E. G.

17, Hanover Terrace,

To Thomas Hardy. *23.11.1901.*

My dear Hardy,—

Thank you for the most kind gift of your new Poems. I have been reading them eagerly to myself, and every now and then, when I could not keep them to myself any longer, reading one and another to my wife. You go straight to the very heart. Your poems on the War are not only the best that have been published, from a technical point of view, but they are the only ones which have gone below the drum and the tinsel. I cannot tell you how great a thing I think *The Souls of the Slain* to be. I like—of the others—immensely *The Well-Beloved* and *Lizbie Browne* and *The Darkling Thrush* and oh! so many more. It would be impertinent to praise some others where the feeling is almost too penetrating and poignant, and where, as I read, my eyes grow clouded with the waters of self-pity. That is really how lyrical poetry affects me, isn't it? I will not give myself away by telling you which affected me most in this way, but I daresay you can guess.

What an admirable ballad is the *Lost Pyx*! But where I like so much and where all speaks to me in the accents of a voice I love so much—in the accents of the man whom of all my living contemporaries I admire and delight in the most—how can I specify?

This is a wretched letter, but I cannot help it. I should make a fool of myself if I told you—told you again!—what your work is to me, how I turn back and back, how helplessly uncritical about it I have become by the sheer intensity of my sympathy. And it is not so with other writers whom I have admired and shall always esteem. I esteem them still, but I can't read them. But you—till I am blind and deaf and dull, I shall always read you with the old tingling pulse.

Your affectionate old admirer,

EDMUND GOSSE.

National Club,

To Sir Alfred Bateman. *13.12.'01.*

DEAR BATEMAN,—

It is inexpressibly painful to me to rest, even for ten minutes, under the stigma of seeming to forget, or to under-value, my immense debt to you for kindness during the long years of the past. No sense of want of appreciation, or having become hopelessly and undeservedly stranded in an official backwater, will ever in the smallest degree lessen my lasting gratitude to you.

Yours sincerely,

EDMUND GOSSE.

17, Hanover Terrace,

To Theodore Watts-Dunton. *May 26, 1902.*

DEAR WATTS-DUNTON,—

Mrs. Gosse and I were away in the south of France when your letter reached my house, and it was not forwarded.

When I received it at length, I should certainly have acknowledged it, had I not been much embarrassed by it.

I was not able to understand why you favoured me with the particular statements it contained, which should—I could not help thinking—have been made to me by Swinburne, if they were made at all.

Again, I did not know how to approach the rather distasteful fact that on occasion of my having put myself out to reassert and define Swinburne's position at a moment when the fickleness of taste has for the time being retired from him, Swinburne himself should have no word of affection, or of sympathy or of the very barest civility, to address to one of the oldest personal friends he possesses.

Yours faithfully,
EDMUND GOSSE.

With regard to the letter which follows, Mr. Birrell has supplied the accompanying note:

"The letter is about Mr. Birrell's *Life of Hazlitt* in Macmillan's Men of Letters Series, 1902. The Doll Tearsheet allusion relates to Hazlitt's book *Liber Amoris*, a small semi-insane volume that purports to relate an amorous adventure with one of the daughters of Hazlitt's landlady in Southampton Row. The book largely consists of actual letters written by Hazlitt to Mr. P. G. Patmore (the father of Coventry Patmore) and Mr. Sheridan Knowles. In 1902 Mr. Birrell did not know of the correspondence in 1893, to which Gosse refers."

17, Hanover Terrace,
To Augustine Birrell. *28.6.'902.*

DEAR BIRRELL,—

I have been reading, with a great deal of enjoyment, your book about Hazlitt which seems to me—if I may in humility say so—the best thing yet said about this rather tousled hero. I delight in your common sense and general sympathy and humorous alacrity to catch the point of view. Quite delightful from beginning to end.

As it is holiday time, I allow myself to chat with you for a minute or two—button-holing you and wasting your time—on one or two things so trifling that they are hardly worth mentioning.

1. How the Patmore Letters about the Doll Tearsheet business came to be preserved is hardly "beyond guessing," because it was told in full in the *Times*, in 1893, by Coventry Patmore, who, in

quite a blaze of indignation with the Hazlitt family, seemed to ignore the very poor figure his own father cut in the matter.

2. P. 208. You rather give the impression (justified by the Hazlitt Memoirs, I think) that R. H. Horne was personally known to Hazlitt. But he never saw him alive. In my youth I knew old Horne very well. He told me that at this time (1830) he had a great curiosity to see Hazlitt, and teased Wells, who saw a good deal of H., to take him to see him. But Wells would not do so, on the ground that Hazlitt was difficult, and disliked strange faces. But on the day that Hazlitt died, Wells, who seems to have been with him (partly nursing him?), came hurriedly round to Horne and hurried him off to Frith Street. They found the door open, and pushed in and up the stairs, and entered a bedroom, where Hazlitt lay dead, quite alone. Horne described to me his long hair "like bunches of grey snakes," he said—strewn in disorder on the pillow, and the strong features. The monument and epitaph at St. Anne's, which you attribute to Horne, were attributed by Horne to Wells, who, he told me, did them entirely at his own expense, as a tribute. All this may have some faint interest for you and has never (I think) been published.

3. What you say on p. 217 about R. L. S. and Hazlitt, I should like some day to talk to you about. People give different reasons for the same act to different people, and it may be that R. L. S. told Colvin that he refused to write the life of Hazlitt because of the *Liber Amoris*. But at the time—I think it must have been about 1880—when R. L. S. was so full of Hazlitt, he talked a great deal to me about the project, and never gave that as a reason. The reason he gave was that he did not feel in Hazlitt the substance of a biography, that when you took the writer from the man, there seemed so very little left.

I don't think R. L. S. was the man to be shocked at the *Liber Amoris*. He would see the vulgarity, and, what is worse, the slight insanity of it all. But the processes of desire are so mysterious, and Stevenson so fully realized that, in the case of an artist, it is what art he deposits, not what desire he takes in, which is of interest, and he was, moreover, so devoid of the least touch of cant, that I rather resent your words on this subject, although I perfectly understand your writing them on your knowledge, and on Colvin's evidence. Only to my ear, they sound false of R. L. S.

But if you have got so far as this in this elephant of a letter, you must be tired to death. Don't dream of acknowledging it, but excuse it, and believe me always,

Very sincerely yours,

EDMUND GOSSE.

Thank you for your kinds words in the book about myself. I like them very much, so human am I!

National Club,

To Maurice Baring. *11.7.1902.*

MY DEAR MAURICE,—

I was very glad indeed to get your letter, and to learn that all is settled about your poems. Would it be any satisfaction at all to you if I looked through the proofs? I would do so, if you really wished it, with the very greatest pleasure, and a fresh eye sometimes catches harvest-mice in the standing corn.

It is a long time since I had any direct news of you, but I hear of you every now and then from your enchanting Aunt* at Ascot, which whom indeed I had a fortnight ago a discreet lunch which was a revel of philosophy and wit. I don't know whether you know that I was rather badly ill in March and April? I was afraid that I was going to break down altogether, but I was slowly dragged through by a course of Swedish treatment (passive massage), and now I am almost well. On the 1st of August we go off to Sweden, where I am to complete my cure by three weeks at Saltsjöbaden, on the Baltic, which—as I daresay you know—is the great cure-place. It has been a tedious year for me, hitherto—languid and dispiriting, and I have had a good deal of pain, which I am not used to. But I try to remember that I have had on the whole a life of wonderful health, and that it can't last for ever.

I have seen several of your people quite lately, Mrs. Spencer,†

* Lady Ponsonby.

† The late Viscountess Althorp.

looking radiantly well, at a dinner Eddie Marsh gave, and John* (at Lord Cowper's), very affable. He referred—with great openness—to certain events not unconnected with the United States. I said, "It must have kept you in such a fret," and John instantly added, "which you, among the leaves, have never known!"

Yours,
E. G.

Board of Trade,
To Sir Alfred Bateman. *Jan. 1, 1903.*

Dear Bateman,—

I enclose my customary statement of the work I have done during the past year for the other departments.

Will you permit me to draw your attention to the steady and not inconsiderable increase in the amount of the work? This last year I have had 342 pieces of translation to do, as against 311 in 1901, itself the largest number up to that date.

There is at least as steady an increase in the *bulk* of the work, which amounted in 1902 to 822 foolscap pages, as against 643 in 1901.

Believe me truly yours,
Edmund Gosse.

Summary for 1902.

German	107
Dutch	61
Danish	55
Swedish	49
Italian	38
Spanish	18
Portuguese	5
French	5
Icelandic	4
	342

1.1.'03. E. G.

* The late Lord Revelstoke.

To Miss Louisa Moyra Guiney. *17, Hanover Terrace,*
15.1.'903.

My dear Miss Guiney,—

I am greatly delighted to receive your kind and enthusiastic letter. I must explain to you that my *Life* is to be no more than a volume of the English Men of Letters series, occupying 200 pp. I shall therefore have no room to quote documents in detail. But the personal facts about Jeremy Taylor are very scanty. They are almost all included, so far as present knowledge goes, in the article in the *Dic. of Nat. Biog.* to which I would refer you as to a guide, showing what I do *not* want, as the mere amplification of data there correctly given is not within my range.

But I shall be very glad if you will look thro' the State Papers' Cats. to see if anything has been overlooked by the *D.N.B.* And the Bodelia, of course. In the 1849-50 edition of Heber's *Life* prefixed to the works, a great many useful documents are given in notes, and of course those I don't want. Unprinted *letters*, anecdotes, records of movements—those are what I long for.

Of course, he stayed after the Civil War with the Vaughans (Carberys) at Golden Grove. Any links between the Battle of Cardigan and Golden Grove, or any details of his life there as Chaplain, would be more precious to me than rubies. And so on, and so on!

I shall be greatly indebted to you if you will keep a careful note of the time you spend in these investigations, and will allow me to settle with you on your own terms and at your own convenience.

It will be very interesting if you can trace back to Siluria the ancestry of West. But I was not able to discover the Father of the Chancellor, who was born about 1691.*

Yours very sincerely,

Edmund Gosse.

* Miss Guiney had undertaken to collect data for Gosse's *Life of Jeremy Taylor*.

Hôtel de la Paix,
Marvejols,
Lozère,
To Sir Alfred Bateman. *Whitmonday, 1903.*

My dear Lordie,—

I hope you are having—somewhere—as jolly a time as we are. You would be amused to see us, sitting together in a far-away café of a meridional *chef-lieu d'arrondissement*, with two soldiers and two farmers in *blouses* playing *le billard* in front of us. I am no judge of billiards, but I don't think the ball ought to be struck with such violence. There should surely be a distinctive nuance between billiards and skittles. I should like you eminent statisticians to explain the difference of manners between a mountainous and a lowland country. We have come from the rich rolling country of the Aveyron—where all the people smile a soft smile, and lisp caressingly when they speak to you—to this rough hill-side country, with its chestnut-forests up steep limestone cliffs, and here the people shout at you in absolutely opaque patois, and offer you asparagus as if they were chopping your head off. We have had an absolutely lovely time, and are, both of us, in perfect health. It is wonderful how one responds to this sort of thing, and the incessant railway travelling, and the rough inns, and the violent contrasts of heat and cold, seem to have done us nothing but good.

What dear people these French are! We have met absolutely nothing but cordiality and politeness and gentle civilized courtesy from everybody in Town and Country. The English, *mirabile dictu*, are tremendous favourites here; all the little newspapers are naïvely full of articles full of friendliness. What mercurial spirits! But I love it—I would be mercurial myself if my age and infirmities permitted.

I thought there must be a difference between billiards and skittles: they have now smashed something. How violent people are in mountainous countries! Did you ever hear of anybody coming to Marvejols before? It is not a Monte Carlo, but it has walks around it more beautiful than I ever saw elsewhere, and its nightingales are first-class. You need not read this silly old letter till you have

"ATOSSA"

FROM A DRAWING BY ALMA TADEMA

nothing better to do. I shall be back in harness on the 8th, but I hope you will take a longer holiday.

Ever your affectionate,

E. G.

17, Hanover Terrace,

To Edward Marsh. *12.1.04.*

My dear Eddie,—

I must pretend to keep promise, although I have no news to give you. On Saturday I spent an hour and a half in very charming battledore-and-shuttlecock conversation *tête-à-tête* with the Countess.* Henry James could report it in the manner of *The Ambassadors*. I can't. Admirable and extraordinary woman—the more confidential she is, the more she baffles me. Next day Maurice was here for hours—quite delightful, but again luminously dark. He and she, however, agree in one point that "it will certainly be best for him to live in Moscow." Very well! In sheer mental weariness I agree, it will be best for him, and for you and me and Mr. Chamberlain and King Edward to live in Moscow. But, good heavens, why Moscow?

You saw Cartwright, I hear: that was capital. I am hoping acutely that you will have good weather. I suppose at Brescia there are lots of Morettos? Cartwright seems to have been uncommonly pleased with a place called Salé on the Lake of Garda. Shall you go to olive-silvery Sirmio?

I have burst forth in a controversy in the *Times* to-day, 10,000 strong. So tiresome to have you and Elliott away. I miss your mild reproof. It's about the extravagant advertisement of cricket and the neglect of Herbert Spencer.†

There is no other news, so I shut up.

Yours affect^{ly},

E. Gosse.

* Countess Benckendorff.

† Mr. Marsh remembers answering by imagining the posters of the evening papers in a better-ordered world, in which the chief public excitement would be a match between teams of Oxford and Cambridge metaphysicians, culminating in TOTAL COLLAPSE OF MACTAGGART.

Mountstewart,
Newtownards,
Co. Down,
Easter Sunday, 1904.

To Lady Gosse.

We went to the North Downshire Steeplechase Races yesterday in the omnibus motor. They are held close to the town of Combar. Two of the party, our hostess and the Solicitor-General, had toothache and didn't come; the rest of us had great fun. Arriving in the square of Combar, Lord Londonderry, who as Lord Lieutenant of the county had to start the races, got on his horse and rode down. The rest of us went to the course in an omnibus. The rain blew in gusts out of a slaty sky, and the wind was cruel. But that didn't prevent a huge crowd from gathering, and the humours of the field were like those in the Irish Magistrate stories. A large party arrived in a hearse. Close to us a huge old woman, in a very tasty bonnet, with an artificial cabbage-rose and a great feather, set up a roulette-table and did a roaring trade. The "bookies" stood gesticulating at their boards, and writing down bets as if they were playing the harp. There were county ladies who rode up on every description of steed, or arrived in compact masses in cars and shandrydans and gigs and waggons. The races themselves were rather pretty, watched from a distance over a rolling green landscape, and when they were actually on, we all scrambled up outside and sat on the top of the omnibus. In the middle of it, we were taken to an immense lunch at the house of the principal citizen of Combar—the whole of which town Lord Londonderry owns—and he and Lady Fingall sat in state at the top of the table, with the rest of us and a most amazing conglomeration of squireens and horsy ladies and the racing world of County Down. We were met at the door with the immense Irish hospitality, everybody seemed welcome, and there was a splendid spread—salmon and cold lamb and champagne unlimited and pale jellies trembling in cream and everything that makes the liver a burden. Then out in the pitiless rain to the races again. Lady Fingall and I had enough of it after a while, and sat inside the omnibus and chatted. The rest all kept on the top till the races were over, when a plausible old humbug in white breeches, scarlet waistcoat and top hat, came up and made a speech in honour of Lord Londonderry. Everybody crowded round and cheered, and then silver cups that had been won were brought, and handed one by one to Lady Annesley up on the roof of the omnibus, who gracefully presented them to the winners (foxy-looking men, very smiling and shy), sipping a little champagne out of each as she handed them down. And then we all drove home in the motor, drowsy with the rain and with having laughed so much, and on the way passed all sorts of quaint figures, male and female, returning home from the races, flushed and happy, and a good many of the former in a very uproarious state of animal spirits.

So that was a good typical experience, wasn't it?

Just before we started, I got your perfectly delightful first letter from Folkestone. So nice to know of you as safe there, and to be able to *realize* you. I enjoyed every scrap of your letter. It is a pity for all of us that the weather is so piggy, but we must hope it will improve.

Much love to Sylvia. How she would have enjoyed the Races! At every turn there were things one longed to sketch.

Ever your loving,

E.

CHAPTER TWENTY

In 1904 by the death of Arthur Strong the post of Librarian to the House of Lords became vacant. For some years Gosse had felt that in the Board of Trade fate had pushed him into an official backwater, where his prospects were *nil*, the rule seeming to be, once a translator always a translator, and the work increasing. The stationary stipend of four hundred a year attached to the office, with no chance of increase, was a monotonous vista. He was showing signs of fever and fret. Austin Dobson earned his momentary displeasure by composing an epitaph:

"This person died of discontent;
He never had an increment."

The Board of Trade had served its purpose as a haven, but its efficacy was exhausted. When therefore he was invited by the House of Lords to act as their Librarian he had no hesitation about severing his link with a Government office. The change of anchorage revolutionised his prospects, providing him at once with an adequate salary of £1000 a year, and a congenial base of operations. The precincts of the institution had an irresistible attraction for him, the large quiet rooms overlooking the river, the Library itself with all that it implied to a book-lover, the prestige attaching to an expert among those less familiar with the subject of his knowledge, and not least the easy personal contact with their Lordships which would inevitably result from his tenure of the office. In his witty delineation of Gosse as Professor Criscross in *Triple Fugue*, which, though it delighted Gosse by its literary felicity, is certainly not strained by the quality of mercy, Mr. Osbert Sitwell writes: "Here the Professor's two genuine, sincere, and perhaps not un-English affections—one for a title the other for an amateur—the force of which is quadrupled by the combination of the two—nearly overcame him." The infirmity here indicated can scarcely be referred to without lending to it an importance not altogether warranted, without in fact suggesting that it was in itself an expression of character related to deeper qualities. It had no such significance, it had no such relation, being no more than an amiable and superficial weakness—linked with the desire to know everyone, to associate with those of *prima facie* importance, to respond to the lure of "the top of the tree," whatever the nature of that tree might be. In such a response he had had great predecessors. Writing of Congreve, Lord Macaulay said: "Two kinds of ambition early took possession of his mind and often pulled in opposite directions. . . . He longed to be a great writer. He longed to be a man of fashion. The history of his life is the history of a conflict between the two impulses." And in a letter quoted by Mr. Herbert Read in *The Sense of Glory*, Swift, writing to Pope, says: "All my endeavours from a boy, to distinguish myself, were only for want of a great title and fortune, that I might be used like a Lord, by those who have an opinion of my parts—whether right or wrong, it is no great matter, and so the reputation of wit or great learning does the office of a blue ribbon, or a coach and six horses." Instances could be multiplied, and they are as wine to water when contrasted with the artless and venial impulses of Gosse in a cognate field. Indeed we can sympathise with the blameless gusto underlying the first entries in the journal which he kept as Librarian.

"Feb. 12, 1904. Lord Knutsford introduced himself to me and very courteously spoke of my books, said he had just finished *Jeremy Taylor*. Lds. Ribblesdale and Beauchamp paid me visits of congratulation.

"Feb. 15th, Calls from Lds. Aldenham, Stanhope, Bishop of Rochester, Lytton, Northampton, Burghclere, and Avebury. Was introduced to L. Barrington and L. Balfour of Burleigh. Heard L. Newton lead off debate on Bulgaria. He is a fluent rough speaker with a good deal of humour, and some odd laughable turns of speech. Ld. Percy came in to listen, and talked to me. L. Lytton extraordinarily good, with great simplicity and elegance, excellent choice of words, deliberate and telling, with a gravity beyond his years."

This shows no more than his determination to play the part for which he was now cast, and make the most of every aspect it presented. It was a new world, and he had no idea of stultifying himself by ignoring any one of its implications. Like Mr. Meagles in *Little Dorrit*, he respected a genealogical tree. As long as he was in the world he wished to be of it—at any moment he could have withdrawn from it with complete happiness and ensconced himself in literature and friendship—but so long as it was the arena of his activities, *status* and every agency contributing to its maintenance was of importance.

This year he received his first public recognition from France. In Paris he delivered an address, *L'Influence de la France sur la Poésie anglaise*, and was entertained at a banquet at the Restaurant Durand, given in his honour by French authors; on each occasion he showed a scholar's familiarity with French literature, and delighted audiences which comprised some of the most critical of French *littérateurs*. There was more than a rhetorical flourish in his final compliment when he declared, *"votre bienveillance couronne ce soir le plus heureux jour de ma vie."*

Hotel de France,
Arcachon,
To Edward Marsh. *Sept. 29, '04.*

My dear Eddie,—

Thank you for your delightful letter, which reached me at Aix. You apologized for it—but it served for three readings, and after that seemed savorous. I was very much obliged for news of Elliott, but I fear he has had a relapse, for instead of his being at Bournemouth, I got a day or two ago a low-spirited letter in pencil from him, speaking of the hospital as quasi-permanent.

We have had a wonderfully successful and varied holiday; from the extreme Pyrenees (we actually got, by dint of rising at 5, and driving with three horses, into the Republic of Andorra), we went down to Toulouse and again down the whole length of the Garonne to Bordeaux, and we have finally come here to be braced up for London again. Have you ever been to Arcachon? It must be hateful in the season, when the place is thick with people, but the crowds have all gone back, and *il n'y a presque personne.* The beauty of the place is beyond description—it is so pale and exquisite—all dotted with boats at anchor, and the blue rim of the sand-dunes all round the Basin. It is extraordinarily Japanese, and we are constantly reminded of some old Hokusai sort of colour-print. It has been rather curious to begin our holiday with a blazing Atlantic (at Biarritz) and come back to it cold and ashen, though with beautiful fiery lights, here in Arcachon.

I want you to be aware that we expect to be in London on the night of Wednesday, the 5th of October. I would be sure to come to the Club, if you were to be there for certain, on Thursday. But let me have a line to say, when I arrive at 17, Hanover Terrace. You probably know the latest of Maurice. The last I have heard is that after a skirmish, about the 15th of this month, he telegraphed cryptically to Mrs. Grenfell, "All through the battle: Bird."* I suppose the providence which hangs over mad minstrels will protect him, but it makes me terribly anxious.

Your phrase about Swinburne's "nonsense" pleased me very much indeed. It is just the right word. There has always been, with so much splendour and exaltation and beauty, that element of stuff and nonsense. Oh! bosh! one feels inclined to say. Shelley began it, I think, but it now pervades all new poetry. Especially the French and Yeats. But Swinburne most of all.

Bless you! Hoping soon to see you.

Ever yrs. affectionately,

E. G.

Grand Hôtel Brun,

Bologna.

To Evan Charteris.

Sept. 29, 1905.

My dear Evan,—

We have been out of England just a month, and you have probably forgotten my existence. It is time, however, to remind you of it, as the autumn Session is approaching. Have you ever been here?

* Mr. Baring was acting as War Correspondent with the Russians: see *With the Russians in Manchuria. Bird:* Baring word for happy.

Nicest hotel I was ever in, bar none; in spite of the ghastly work-house picture above.*

"I wonder what the inn-engravers buy
One half so ugly as the prints they sell."—O.K.

We are settled in it, in most balmy repose, after having been sorely banged and bruised in many very bad Italian hotels—Bergamo, Brescia, Parma, Modena, which God confound. The places themselves are lovely (I mean the cities), especially Parma, which is a real Little Sarras or golden Paradise of the saints. But when you are not well (see *infra*), and the weather is broken, you want good comfort in your inn. Note in yr. tablets that you will always find it at Bologna.

Not well. No, even you—a heart of tin—might melt to think how many nasty little maladies I have had. An abscess in my jaw, which drove me daily to a foolish dentist in Pallanza for nearly a week, a chill in my little stomach, a wrench in my ankle. I will not dwell on these, all of which are better, but the process of holiday-making and the Hunting of the Arts are made difficult by such things. But the Arts have really triumphed: I pushed on with indefatigable zeal, and already, in looking back, I see far more pleasures than pangs.

I have nothing to tell you to amuse you. I see in a belated *Times* downstairs that Dr. Barnardo is dead. I suppose this has no interest for you. But it has a good deal for me. When I first came up to town, in 1868, I fell in with Barnardo, who was young then, and like a flame, and beginning vaguely his philanthropic work. He drew me in with him, and for a little while I "worked" with him in the East End. I did not make a success of it: the people intimidated me, which was fatal. One curious incident of that period of my life I may have told you. It was in the Summer of 1868, on a Sunday night, Barnardo and I went to a service in a penny gaff, which was to be held by a well-known Primitive Methodist preacher. But he did not come, and after a certain delay, it was announced that "a brother from the country, brother Booth," would preach, and so he did, very noisily and badly. This was the

* Refers to a picture of the hotel at the head of the writing-paper.

then entirely unknown person who soon after started the germ of the Salvation Army, and is now "Generalissimo" Booth. I remember him very distinctly, with a crest of jet-black hair and a wisp of jet-black beard, which he pulled violently, alternately.

We went, in the wake of the Divine Being,* to Villa Serbelloni above Bellagio, and it is a shrine well worthy of her presence. I could perfectly well imagine her there, among the fountains and the laurels. But for common mortals it is too confined, and we fell into a *piège* of horrid "intellectual" English people, male and female, who wished to cluster round, and be intense, and talk about "literature." I disgraced myself by being frightfully rude, and then we fled away. George Eliot's rather preposterous husband was leading the "brainy" revels. If there is anything I hate on my travels, it is this kind of thing. Rather the facchino in his blindness than a circle of chattering academical English people.

Well, write to me. Write to me in pity, because I am old and dull and cross, and near the end, and not at all "intellectual." Write to

Hôtel Bellini,
Florence

(an address which a babe-in-arms might recollect), whither, when we can tear ourselves from this divine brown Bologna of arcades, we are going.

Did you see Walkley on the guitar-play of F. E. Fyffe? Exquisite! And can F. E. Fyffe really be her Grace of S——d?

Ever yours sincerely,
EDMUND GOSSE.

To Thomas Hardy.

17, Hanover Terrace,
Nov. 5, '05.

MY DEAR HARDY,—

It is a most enormous time since I heard from you, and I should like very much to know how you are, and what you are up to, and how the *Dynasts* progresses. We have just come back from seven weeks' wandering in Italy, which was exciting and pleasing, but

* Lady Desborough.

rendered very fatiguing by the awful chaos of the Italian railways. But we finished up with Florence, and Florence is always restful.

George Meredith told me in the summer of your visit to him, which he had enjoyed very much. Rather quaintly he said that your "pessimism" had grieved him. I wonder whether you were not saddened by his optimism? There is something to me almost flighty in his cheerfulness. You know he has broken his ankle? He appears to be quite cheerful about that too. What a very curious thing temperament is—there seems no reason at all why G. M. should be so happy, and in some irrational way one almost resents it.

Have you taken to cycling again? Do you remember my plungings in your back lane—I blush to think of them. If you set up a motor you must really let me know, for I am keeping a list of the bloated novelists who keep motors—I know of three at least; Hall Caine is not one.

You have nothing to do all day, and so there is no excuse for your not writing me a full account of how you do it, with every particular. "My God, Sir," R. L. S. used to say, "your famous novelist is the most pampered pet in Europe." And be particular to tell me when (if at all) you are coming up to town before Xmas: I want you to keep at least one evening for me.

You are a neglectful creature, but—bless you. Write a nice letter to your importunate and aged

Edmund G.

17, Hanover Terrace,
26.2.'06.

To Thomas Hardy.

My dear Hardy,—

I have now been able to read every word in *Dynasts*, Vol. II, and I can do no less than express to you my hearty congratulations. It is a magnificent success. I do not know whether it is partly that I myself have grown accustomed to the novel medium, but I think your imagination flows with greater freedom in II than it did in I. In that volume there seemed occasionally to be something tentative, as if you were feeling your way. Here, you out your wings and speed along.

As I closed this volume, I thought to myself there could hardly be a better test of the genuine—as opposed to the reflected and fictitious—appreciation of literature, than to put a reader down to *The Dynasts* and see what he thinks of it. I hold myself that it will be, that it is becoming, the most important piece of creative art that the young 20th century has yet seen, and that when we get far enough away from now, we shall see it soaring above everything round it.

So, I have but to pray you to go on. Slacken not in winding this glorious poem up to a noble and thrilling conclusion. I cannot express to you how I look forward to it. It is nearer, to my mind, to being a real historical *epos*, in the true sense, than anything else in the production of modern Europe.

How proud I am to think that I have been allowed to stand a little nearer than the crowd, and to see your gifts unfold like the aloe-blossom. You have always been to me among the first, and since the dear R. L. S.'s death you have been without any rival, the very first in the stimulating army of my contemporaries and betters. If I could render back to you one-tenth part of the glow and flush your works have given, and continue to give, to my life, you would be quite a merry man.

I did not mean to write you such a long letter. "La! how I dew run on!" as the servant-girl said.

Your old friend and affectionate admirer,

EDMUND GOSSE.

In 1906 it occurred to those responsible for the production of the *Daily Mail* that it would add to the prestige if not to the circulation of the paper, if like the *Times* it was reinforced by a weekly literary supplement. It was believed that among readers of the journal there might be found persons sufficiently interested in literary topics to welcome such an innovation. In the event the belief proved to be without solid foundation. But with admirable judgment Gosse was invited to act as Director of the Supplement, with Mr. Archibald Marshall as Editor, at a salary of £400 per annum. He assented not without hesitation, but *Father and Son* was finished, he had no immediate literary work on hand, and £400 a year was a welcome addition to his income.

It was something of an escapade, taking him into the heart of a new country; but having once made up his mind he threw himself into the venture with all his intellectual *brio* and conscientious thoroughness. He had no difficulty in finding recruits to support his enterprise, and for a brief period the *Daily Mail* became an organ of literary as well as journalistic authority. Possibly the alliance was too artificial to succeed, anyway the "supplement" under the title of "Books" trotting fastidiously beside its more robust parent, found itself by degrees outpaced, and its activities more and more restricted. It met with little encouragement, and after eighteen months its precarious career was brought to an end. "I was considerably surprised an hour ago," he wrote to William Heinemann,* "by being sent for by Marlowe, and told that my services would not be required after next week. No complaints: expense given as sole reason."

17, Hanover Terrace,
11.8.'06.

To Robert Ross.

My dear Robbie,—

The articles have given me a great deal of pleasure. They show that you only need free space—I mean the good will of an admiring and tolerant editor—to make you an excellent writer. What is peculiar to your own mind and nature comes out most agreeably here and there, and I hope you will cultivate it.

The article on Pater is excellently written, and with the greater part of it I agree. I do not know that I mind the end. That is a sound expression of opinion, and I do not feel that it goes too far. You lightly, but justly, sweep over, with an indicating finger, what those who replied to you seem to think wants a mattock and a spade.

In the matter of style, the only thing that jars upon me is the "vivisection" passage. This marks the difference between what is effective in speech and in writing. If people had been sitting round

* May 6, 1907.

a table, this *boutade* would have been highly successful—we should all have laughed. But for *written* irony, it is too heavy. The mind is not stimulated, but troubled by it, and is thrown off the track of ideas. Irony is a most delicate artifice and it should always be used so as to aid and illuminate, not to obscure, the line of thought. Your paragraph is too startling, and attracts attention to *itself*, and not to the general trend of your argument. Will you forgive me?

The article on Wilde is very interesting, sober and true. I am surprised anyone should fail to see that you wrote it: to me that would have been palpable. Except that I should have asked myself what made you praise, and in such rich terms, one of the most degraded and most crapulous of recent biography-mongers. I think you should be more chary of your praise, and keep it, like your irony, for more excellent purposes.

But I am delighted that you are writing so much, and doing it so well. You ought to aim at the highest distinction, and I don't see why you should not get it. You have qualities of satiric humour and whimsical independence which are altogether your own. Your courage is extraordinary, in fact it is a snare to you. But these are lines on which you should go far.

Yours always sincerely, and affectionately,

E. G.

17, Hanover Terrace,
Regent's Park, N.W.

To Professor Bliss Perry. *March 6, '07.*

My dear Mr. Bliss Perry,—

It is truly good of you to wish me to write for you about Tolstoi as I did about Ibsen. The proposal is tempting, especially as I have read Tolstoi with care for many years.

But I do not know him in the original, which must be a very great drawback. And I am less and less a believer in him. In his two great romances, of course, my faith is firmly settled. But his miscellaneous writings, especially his pseudo-theological and pseudo-political tracts, fill me with a growing languor, and even some disgust. This gigantic Tartar of a Tolstoi does really settle the problems of mankind with too brutal a positivism. If his system were accepted by mankind, it would mean the adoption of the most outrageous bondage that the human spirit and body have ever languished under.

My private belief is that Tolstoi is a nodule of pure imaginative genius floating about in a quite barbarous cocoon of folly, preposterous idealism and even (not a little) insincerity. I could not speak of him in the terms one would wish to use for a great artist dead. But thank you very much all the same.

I came across your really delightful volume on Walt Whitman, and read it with such pleasure that I had to *review* it also, to try and share my pleasure with others. But I don't believe in those "children"! For reasons, of course, precisely opposite to those put forward by the servers of pillows to all armholes. The real psychology of W. W. would be enormously interesting. I think the keynote to it would be found to be a staggering ignorance, a perhaps wilful non-perception, of the real physical conditions of his nature. But the truth about him (the innermost truth) escapes from almost every page for those who can read.

Very faithfully yours,

EDMUND GOSSE.

Professor Bliss Perry.

House of Lords,
S.W.

To Maurice Baring. *21.3.'07.*

MY DEAR MAURICE,—

I was delighted to get your nice long letter.

This winter has been a very trying one to me. I have not been at all well, and the labour of bringing out "Books" every week has been a very trying one, largely because I am an old dog to be set at a new trick. I am very glad indeed to know that you read it, and I think there must every now and then come little flashes to you that may amuse and please you.

I don't know how long I shall be able to keep it up. The dilemma is one which I heard put by a perfectly awful old woman, years ago, who was describing with horror the exposure of her person which some maiden had to make at a music-hall. "What an awful position for a chaste young girl! Of course—she is generously paid to do it." That is exactly my prostituted case.

The outlook here, as far as literature is concerned, is dismal to a degree. The *Times* Book Club War has played the very devil with everything. I don't know what further horrors are in store for us.

I am shortly to print your sonnet, but I have not yet been able to do so, having laid up a sort of beaver's store of poems. By the way, I am going to take the liberty of omitting the dedicatory initials. They seem a little compromising, attached to such burning words. In doing this, I am acting on the advice of the Divine Being.

We are all of us upset at A. C. B.'s latest (but oh! not last) autobiography. There are things in it to make an angel weep. I was especially struck with the candour with which he admits that he found, on later knowledge, that there was "more in" his Mother and Sister than he supposed. I met Miss Tait the other night—a wounded tigress. One point which amused me, and will (privately) amuse you, is that Arthur told me the other day, sadly, that he was disappointed, on coming into closer relations, with Donaldson. "He is narrow, poor fellow," he sighed. I had too much curiosity to ask the reason of this at once, but much later Arthur mentioned that poor Donaldson had said that he thought it was time this flow of books should stop. I am being very tender with *Beside Still Waters* in "Books," but poor Arthur is having a bad Press. "Waters still running," one review is entitled.

It will be very delightful to see you. "Come soon," as the poet Shelley remarks. You are much talked of where Evan and I are gathered together. I see much, but much less than I wish to see, of that heart of gold. His Jacobite book is finished, and will presently appear. I must at all events cling long enough to the *Daily Mail* to see it properly praised.

Now that I have really written you a sort of letter, you must write to me again. I should be greatly alarmed at the ravage to your nose, if your description of the effect were less picturesque. But I note, with hope, that you are not sure whether it was a cat or a dog that mauled you. I feel that the most acutely mutilated would know as much as that.

I am mournfully and affectionately yrs,

EDMUND GOSSE.

"Le Banni de Lierse."

In 1907 he published *Father and Son*. Up till now he had been writing biography in accordance with accepted methods. It is true that in his life of his father he had discarded the customary style of promiscuous panegyric, and in his lives of Gray, Donne, Jeremy Taylor, and Sir Thomas Browne, he had written as a keen and penetrating critic. But these works were academic in flavour. *Father and Son* was a different proposition. It was biography and autobiography in one hand. There was no model and no predecessor in literature—the nearest approach to it was probably *Mark Rutherford*, but this differed from it in essentials. Yet it was a subject singularly well suited to his gifts. To begin with, there was no need for detachment, here he had to write the record of an individuality, seen through his own eyes and assessed by his own sensibilities, while tracing the reactions of that individuality on his own childhood.

He approached the theme with poetic imagination, and a profound desire to do justice to the nobility of his father's character. In the situation there was much that was tragic and not a little that was comic, there was much also of "the perilous stuff that weighs upon the heart," the undertaking was beset with difficulties—and nothing but a fastidious taste and a faultless literary judgment could suffice for the task.

The most ardent of his admirers were hardly prepared for the qualities apparent in *Father and Son*. There was something here so new, and so different in its nature and the scope of its achievement from any previous work of the writer that it called for a fresh estimate of his place in English Literature. He was no longer assembling facts and valuing the ideas of others, but calling into existence a work of art deep in its humanity, humour, and emotion. At a bound by the publication of the book he placed himself on another plane of literary accomplishment.

In his essay on Lytton Strachey's *Eminent Victorians*, Gosse declares that "in this country the majority have always enjoyed seeing noses knocked off statues." It was certain that many would imagine that in *Father and Son* the process of defacement was being carried out, with the added piquancy that in this case it was the features of a father which were in question. And sure enough when the book appeared the critics, while recognising its literary excellences, did not fail to moralise on the spectacle of a son "anatomosing" his parent in print.

In the *Times Literary Supplement* the Reviewer in his opening sentence said: "The author of this book has no doubt settled it with his conscience how far in the interests of popular edification and amusement it is legitimate to expose the weaknesses and inconsistencies of a good man who is also one's father." To a later generation the criticism seems whimsical and irrelevant. It reads like the last sputter of the old guard still standing for panegyric rather than truth as the staple of biography. At any rate, it is unlikely that anyone reading the book to-day would detect offence in its pages. The last thing Gosse had in mind was to expose the weaknesses of a good man. He has defined his purpose. His purpose was to give to the world "a record of educational and religious conditions which, having passed away, will never return," and to throw "light on the unique and noble figure of his father." In doing so he shirked nothing which could contribute to the truth of the picture. His father in the result emerges as a figure of rugged force and iron-strong faith, with great human tenderness and single-minded integrity, devoting his life to the passionate pursuit of religion and science in their most irreconcilable forms. Gosse does not pretend that the inconsistencies were susceptible of any intellectual reconciliation. On the contrary he makes it clear that the more science threatened to encroach on his father's peculiar religious beliefs, the more fiercely were those beliefs proclaimed and their exercise observed. But this is shown in *Father and Son* to have done nothing to check the ceaseless solicitude of Philip Gosse for the narrow family circle in which his life was spent, or to diminish his passionate interest and pride in his son's career.

Quite a common criticism on the book was, "How much better the father comes out of it than the Son"—this, said by way of disparagement, happened to be the criticism Gosse most desired to hear, since it implied a recognition that he had succeeded in one of the purposes he had in mind in writing the book. In a letter to Mr. David Lloyd written many years later, he still further defined what those purposes were, and probably no one who has freed himself from the stultifying prejudices which found voice at the time, would deny for a moment that Gosse had achieved his object.

Polurrian Hotel,
Mullion,
To Mr. David Lloyd. *S. Cornwall.*
May 29, 1924.

My dear Sir,—

I regret that my being for a week or two at this remote place has delayed my acknowledging your very kind letter which only reached me five minutes ago.

It gives me great pleasure to know that fifteen of your friends are reading and discussing my little book. I feel sure that whatever any of them may think of the workmanship, all will acknowledge the sincerity of my aim. I desired, before my memory in old age played tricks with me, to set down a perfectly faithful and unadorned picture of a succession of moral and religious incidents which can, in all probability, never recur. Already the position seems a hundred years away, and I do not think that quite young persons are able or willing to comprehend what it was.

One thing I venture to hope that some of your friends may realize, namely, that the book is a monument to the memory of my father, an extraordinary man. It is not of the same order as the lying epitaphs in churchyards, but I hope it is something better, the exact portrait of a good and even great man, whose character was too powerful not to have its disconcerting sides.

With many thanks for your kind letter,

Pray believe me to be,
Yours very faithfully,
Edmund Gosse.

General consent would at the same time probably concede that he added a "classic" to English literature, a much more important matter than the question of purpose. It was fortunate that his circumstances had changed, enabling him to write with a freedom which he had never before experienced. His librarianship had put him in a position of security. He was perched above the literary struggle. This sense of safety may well have encouraged him also to greater freedom when he sat down to write, in that he would feel that no extraneous considerations need now stand between him and any subject. In regard to unconsciousness of any considerations beyond those inherent in a subject, his old friend, Mr. George Moore, had always been an object of envious dismay. Gosse now knew himself what it was to enjoy a free hand, and it is interesting to record that some years before *Father and Son* was begun, the two friends discussed the possibilities of that theme. It had long been cellared and maturing in Gosse's mind. And one morning early in the 'nineties Mr. Moore was reading Gosse's *Life* of his father which had recently appeared. It flashed on him that at the back of what he was reading lay a subject of greater interest. Mr. Moore's own account of the sequel was given to me as follows: "Excited by the prospect of a great literary subject that I had already caught a glimpse of in Gosse's *Life* of his father, I began to consider when and how I should confide my idea to Gosse. Should I wait till the end of the week, and at one of those suppers I was accustomed to attend at Gosse's house, tell him how impressed I had been with his book? That would be as good a way as another. But I could not wait so long, so great was my literary excitement in the project I had of a new book on such a subject. And unable to bear the mental tension, I caught up my hat and hailing a cab told the driver to take me to the National Club. My fear was that Gosse would be sitting with friends and that it would be necessary to wait through long conversations, missing in the end the five minutes which I so ardently desired alone with him. But Gosse was by himself at a table in a room full of people and as I took a chair by my friend Gosse said, 'Have you come to lunch?' 'No, but I've come to tell you that all the morning I've been reading your *Life* of your father and I could not wait before letting you know how much I liked your book.' Gosse in his demure way was capable of much literary excitement, his face flushed and he trembled at hearing his book praised. Seeing this I continued to praise the book, finding qualities—imaginary qualities perhaps—with a view to preparing Gosse's mind for the reception of the new subject. 'I admire your book, Gosse,' I continued, 'for itself and still more for the book it has revealed to me, but I missed the child, I missed your father's life and your life as you lived it together—a great psychological work waits to be written—your father's influence on you and your influence on him, if any—these are matters for you to decide—and as a background for this great story you will have the Plymouth Brethren—the people who came to confide in him—and who received spiritual treatment from him. Your misunderstandings, if there were any, all that, I say again, you can tell as no one else can because you have lived through it.' 'All you say,' said Gosse, 'is of extraordinary interest to me, my dear friend, but a great many of the people of whom I could tell are alive.' 'Oh, Gosse, your record will be full of sympathy—there will be no reproach.' Gosse seemed to lose consciousness of my presence, he entered into memories of the time, and then suddenly speaking out of his memory of that time he said, 'I could tell many stories of that period.' 'Go on, Gosse, speak to me of what is in your mind.' 'At the time I am thinking of we were very poor and I slept in a little cot in my parents' bedroom and one night I woke suddenly and remember seeing my father sitting on a sofa at the foot of the bed reading. I fell asleep again but could not have been asleep for long when I awoke and this time I remember it was the rustle of the door passing over the carpet which awoke me, and I saw my mother standing in the doorway and as she saw my father she said, "Oh Philip, it is cancer." My father folded her in his arms and together they sank down by the bed and prayed. Next day I remembered suddenly the word cancer as from a dream and I said, "Father, what is cancer?"'

"Time passed on. I never lost an opportunity of asking Gosse about the psychological work. Gosse's answer was 'Oh, Moore, you are asking me in the sunset of my days to write a book no one will

EDMUND GOSSE IN A CAVALRY MESS

FROM A CARICATURE BY MAX BEERBOHM

read.' 'It may be,' I replied, 'I am not a judge—but I will not admit it—it is a great subject and cannot fail to find thousands of readers.'

"I continued my persecution, and some months afterwards there occurred to me as a subject for a novel for myself the story of a young man brought up in a Wesleyan family with a taste for music-halls and light theatrical entertainments. When I next met Gosse I said, 'You'll help me with this opening, Gosse.' 'I can do something more than tell you about my father's house,' he answered. 'We were very poor as I have already told you and to save writing-paper my father used to cut off the margins of the newspapers and on these he wrote down accounts of the Plymouth Brethren and of those afflicted people to whom he gave spiritual advice—I have got them and will bring them to you.'

"Gosse went upstairs and soon after returned with yards of spiritual confidences written on margins which he confided to me. I took them home, read, and was more than ever amazed at the dark religious atmosphere in which our brilliant essayist had begun his life. Gosse was fearful I should lose these relics of bygone times and asked for their return. In giving them back to him my words were, 'Here are your father's notes, but you are not going to tell me that you are going to let all this pass unchronicled.' 'You think of it so highly,' he said musingly, 'but how is it to be told?'

" 'Not as a biography,' I said. 'Tell it in the first person.'

" 'You are right,' he said, 'that gets over the difficulty that lingered in my mind.' "

The success of the book was instantaneous. The first edition was sold out immediately and was followed by four impressions within twelve months. These were succeeded by various other editions, the sale of which regularly continues. It was translated into other languages and in 1913 was crowned by the French Academy. Appreciation has steadily grown. No one would now be found self-righteous enough to criticise the book on the score of its unfilial revelations. It occupies a recognised and it is reasonable to believe a permanent place in literature as a classic of the twentieth century.*

* See letter of Mr. Bernard Shaw, post p. 500.

CHAPTER TWENTY-ONE

17, Hanover Terrace,
Regent's Park, N.W.

To Viscount Knutsford. *15.1.'08.*

Dear Mr. Sydney Holland,—

Your letter would have surprised me more—tho' it could not have pleased me more—if Lady Dorothy Nevill had not been repeating to me yesterday afternoon the extremely kind things she had been hearing you say about *Father and Son*! I am particularly gratified by your remarks, because, among the almost innumerable letters from friends and strangers which this book has brought me, yours is the only one which emphasizes the real central point which was in my own mind as I wrote it, namely an exposure of the modern sentimentality which thinks it can parade all the prettiness of religion without really resigning its will and its thought to faith. You have most excellently said it is either my father's creed "or nothing."

To tell you the truth, what I should like to think my book might be—if the idea is not one of too great temerity—is a call to people to face the fact that the old faith is now impossible to sincere and intelligent minds, and that we must courageously face the difficulty of following entirely different ideals in moving towards the higher life. But what ideals, or (what is more important) what discipline can we substitute for the splendid metallic rigour of an earlier age?

If I may venture to say so, I think you, with your devotion to the well-being of the sufferers in society, do much to show us the way. But we cannot all be philanthropists, or even altruists. There must be found some guiding power, influencing artists, financiers, the meditative and imaginative, the self-centred and the speculative, alike. The strength of Christianity was that it did not influence unselfish and lofty natures only, but the publican and the prostitute also.

You must forgive me for boring you with these scattered sparks. Your own ardent and generous appreciation has lighted them. I am glad you were pleased with the fun of the book, and that it did not leave upon your mind, as upon that of my reviewer in the *Revue des Deux Mondes*, the impression of a bitter cry from a world without tenderness and without gaiety, "a lamentable world of darkness!" The perfectly consistent Christian is not dark, and he is not lugubrious.

Believe me, with many thanks for your most generous and stimulating letter,

Yours very sincerely,

EDMUND GOSSE.

17, Hanover Terrace,

To Thomas Hardy.

4.3.'08.

MY DEAR HARDY,—

I have now finished the third volume of *The Dynasts*. I do not know whether your hand grew hotter as you proceeded, or whether the extreme newness of the thing you were producing puzzled me at first, but I have enjoyed vol. III as much more than vol. II as I enjoyed II more than I. I have now, I believe, thoroughly got into step with the poem; and I felt a lingering disappointment, as I closed the volume, because there was no more of it. This, however, no reader should say to a poet, because the poet knows best when to leave off.

I am quite sure that *The Dynasts* will live as one of the most original and beautiful productions of the present age. You have invented, in this outworn world, something quite new. It will be imitated, but no imitator will repeat the bigness and brevity of your touch, nor your panoramic breadth, nor the delicious homeliness and picturesqueness of your episodes.

Surely you must have been giving a great deal of attention to the technique of prosody? The ingenious turns of versification in this latest volume were not lost on me. Even a rondeau, as correct as one of Benserade. The two songs, one so gay, both so sad, are among your best.

Yours always,

EDMUND GOSSE.

When I read over the above, it seems so chilly! I cannot give you an impression of the fervour of joy with which I greet this great, massive, cosmic poem of yours.

17, Hanover Terrace,

To Robert Ross. *13.3.'08.*

MY DEAR ROBBIE,—

I am very much obliged to you for the kind gift of the new edition of *De Profundis*. Your dedication is in the highest degree generous and courageous, but that is what one expects from you. It is also very wise and discreet, and this I am glad to see.

The new portions of *D. P.* I read through with great curiosity. I think you were perfectly well advised in omitting them when it was still quite uncertain how the Pharisees, and still more the Sadducees, would take the whole adventure of publication. But now that the existence of the book is accepted, you have done most rightly to add them. They give certain touches of sincerity to the narrative. They are in themselves picturesque, and they aid us in estimating the character of Wilde. To that character, I am afraid I shall always feel instinctively hostile. But the interest of it, and even the fascination of it, I feel more and more, and most after reading these additions.

Moreover, the older I get the more individualistic I get. I detest nothing so much as the *cliché* in mankind. And more and more personal liberty becomes a passion, almost a fanaticism, with me. Less and less can I endure the idea of punishing a man—who is not cruel—because he is unlike other men. Probably, if the hideous new religions of Science do not smother all liberty, we are in the darkness before the dawn of a humane and intelligent recognition of the right to differences. Perhaps poor Wilde (who alas! was in life so distasteful to me) may come to be honoured as a proto-martyr to freedom, now he is in his grave.

The letters to the *Chronicle*, at the end, are astonishing. You did right, and you did wisely and cleverly, to publish them, for they put Wilde in a better, more human, less ridiculous light than anything else that he wrote. Here is, for once, a man speaking, with real pity, real indignation, real pain. What I principally hated about him, poor creature, was not at all his vices, but his unreality. He was like Punch on a stick, squeaking, and I don't like the squeak. But none in these sad, noble letters to the *Chronicle*.

Forgive this long screed, and forgive me that I am too old and too stiff to bow down more than this to your idol. I was glad to see you to-day, but looking pale. I fear you had got up too soon. Do take care of yourself, and *smoke fewer cigarettes*.

Ever yours,

EDMUND GOSSE.

None of his correspondence is more charming or bears such cogent witness to his interest in young writers, than his letters to Mr. Siegfried Sassoon, of which the following is the first.

17, Hanover Terrace,

To Siegfried Sassoon. *28.3.'08.*

DEAR MR. SASSOON,—

It was very kind of you to send me your delicate and accomplished little masque, *Orpheus in Dilœryum*, which I have read with pleasure and amusement. It reminds me of some of the strange entertainments of the early Renaissance, and of Italian humanism generally. And I observe, with great satisfaction, your own richness of fancy and command of melodious verse. I hope you will make a prolonged study of the art of poetry, and advance in it from height to height.

With all best wishes,

Believe me to be

Very sincerely yours,

EDMUND GOSSE.

Hôtel Continental,
Siena.

To Henry James. *June 11, '09.*

My dear James,—

You have given us immense pleasure by two most welcome letters. What you say about the little Swinburne portrait gratifies me very much indeed.

You are in some sense the source of the success of our present visit, for, after becoming conscious of the isolation from all other scenes of this exquisite remote Siena, we bethought us of your suggestion, and said "Motor!" to one another, with a guilty flush and rising pulse, as of those who really, this time, were going, in the most abandoned manner, to the Devil. On inquiry, it appeared that Siena possesses a motor, and that an "arrangement" was possible, an arrangement meaning that a vivid demon, like a handsome wicked gargoyle, proposed (as such a sacrifice!) terms so preposterous that we broke violently from him, and sat down contemptuously (with our backs to him) to drink *tre vermouth con selz*, so that the demon had, with twitching hands spread wide, and appealing to high heaven, to invite *us* to name a sum, which, with heads still averted, we did, the result being that he fled, or feigned to fly, from the hotel-lounge, as one who was offered bankruptcy to his very face by scorners; and then, we hardly knew how, a medium price—horribly exorbitant still, but no longer insane—has been agreed between us. The demon possesses a splendid car, and he drives with the skill and daring of the Father of all demons. We have been to Cortona, and to Montepulciano, and all round the Lake of Trasimene, and to Perugia and Assisi, and as far as [*illegible*], and have run in the demoniac car right up to the very tip-top of perfectly impossible mountain-towns, and have rioted like the levin into depths beneath. Now we are "lying up" to rest, and let a little money accumulate, and then we are going, *non obstante diabolo*, to do it again on the other side. There is unbridled licence for you, and how after it are we to face the decent world of London? But it was thou who willed it, George Dandin.

The weather has been absolutely exquisite, except for rather too frequent thunderstorms. I have said nothing of Siena itself, which is a paradise. This hotel—it must be *your* hotel—is a delightful place. The people all so kind, our rooms high up and vast, commanding the whole trough of the city between the Duomo and S. Domenico, and an endless campagna. We stay here (d. n. o.) until Thursday the 24th. So glad you are better: but if you were only *here*, you would be quite well.

Love from us all three,

Your devoted

E. G.

17, Hanover Terrace,

To André Gide. *July 5, '09.*

Dear Monsieur André Gide,—

Your beautiful story of *La Porte Etroite* has caused me a real emotion. I do not know how long it is since I have read a book which has so profoundly moved me. I can witness to the penetration, the truth, the bitter sweetness of your searching analysis of Calvinistic pietism, so far more tragic, so far more hopeless and desolating, than any of the ecstasies of the Catholic Church. What are the sufferings of S. Catherine of Siena, of S. Fina of San Gimignano, by the side of the slow and cruel suicide of Alissa? Pages 191 to 203 are among the most poignant in literature, and the most true: I did not read them without the sense of an almost personal agitation and despair.

For many years past—dear Monsieur Gide—I have felt that between you and me there exist some very close spiritual and intellectual ties. Am I presumptuous in saying so? I wish that we might meet. Do you ever come to England? There is no one whom I should more eagerly welcome, or from whose conversation I should anticipate a keener pleasure.

I wonder if you ever saw a book of mine called *Father and Son*? If not, will you let me have the pleasure of sending it to you? When you read it, you will see why I particularly desire that you should read it.

Pray believe me to be, with deep gratitude for the pain and pleasure which *La Porte Etroite* has given me,

Yours very sincerely,

EDMUND GOSSE.

17, Hanover Terrace,
Sunday, 4.30.

To Lady Gosse. *20.9.1909.*

MY DEAREST,—

Here is a day of heavenly brightness at last. I do so rejoice in it for you. I should think that Beaulieu must look quite lovely. Yesterday, at 8 in the morning, before I was out of bed, Evan telegraphed to know whether I would go to the Theatre. I did not like to leave Tessa alone, but she insisted I should go, and I wanted to see Evan, who was only passing through London. We started for Russia by the Moscow express this morning. We dined at the Ritz —such a nice little dinner, cold soup, a trout, a grouse and some raspberries, nothing more—but we could not get any theatre tickets we cared about. So at 9.45 we went to the Empire music-hall, and saw a very clever and amusing ballet, *Une Visite à Paris* (with the famous Apache dance), and afterwards, on the bioscope, the aviation week at Rheims. You cannot think how extraordinarily interesting this last was. To see the strange aeroplanes run along, and then soar up into the sky, and wheel gracefully about like great sleepy insects—most curious! It gave me my first idea of what it is all really like.

Tessa insisted, dear thing! that I must have my usual Sunday walk, so we sallied out from 12 to 1.20, *our* ordinary round, except that Tessa took me in to the garden of South Lodge, which we explored in every corner. You and I must go there, it is charming, and at the back there is a deserted walk, most romantic, like a beautiful lane somewhere deep in the country. When we came back, the nursery-maids and Sunday walkers had all disappeared, so we sat quite alone on the bench in the further enclosure where you and I sit, close to the water, and opposite the sparrows, new [*illegible*]. There we had the delight of seeing a kingfisher! He was fishing further up the water, where the foliage is so thick, and we saw him dive down on the water from the over-hanging boughs at least thirty times. He was in brilliant plumage, and seemed perfectly at home. Where can he have come from?

We have no guests to-day yet. We asked Mrs. Pollock to come in to supper, but she is so "Yes, I will, no I'm afraid I can't, well, perhaps I will, oh! no I can't" that we don't in the least know whether she is coming or not.

Fondest love from your

E.

17, Hanover Terrace,

To Siegfried Sassoon. *Dec. 5, '09.*

My dear Mr. Siegfried Sassoon,—

I was in the depths of public business when your kind gift of your sonnets arrived three weeks ago and it was impossible for me to do any justice to them then. I was anxious not to put you off with a mere perfunctory word of thanks, and therefore waited for leisure. I hope you will pardon the delay when you learn the cause of it.

I have now read your thin quarto with a great deal of care and no little pleasure. You show in it firm advance beyond all verse of yours which I had previously read. You have the sonnet-spirit and something of the sonnet-touch. The picturesqueness of *Autumn* and the tender melancholy of *Evening in the Mountains* leave nothing to be desired. They achieve a rare beauty.

You must, however, be careful to resist a mere misty or foggy allusiveness. The danger which lies before the poet who endeavours in a sonnet to capture one of those volatile and capricious moods of emotion which are peculiarly fitted for the sonnet—is to resign himself to its haziness. However frail and fantastic the thought you embody may be, if it is worth embodying at all, it must have its essence precisely visible, as a painter must draw a melting cloud on the horizon correctly, or at least [*illegible*], if he draws it at all. Your sonnets are not firmly enough drawn.

Your versification is good, but liable to strange aberrations. I have noted four lines in these few poems which are absolutely impossible to scan without an offence against language. They are these:—

p. 10, ll. 8 and 13. p. 4. l. 8. p. 15. l. 6.

It is a great mistake to suppose that irregularity without relation is allowable in verse. The deviations from the norm must be *apparent* deviations only, that is to say their irregularity must be only decorative, not essential, because essential irregularity means, not harmony, but discord. I think a young poet should have learned the technique of his art very thoroughly before he dares to take liberties with his prosody.

To show you how carefully I have read you, may I say that "from thence"* is not English. "Thence" = "from there," and contains the idea of "from." The word "passional" is rare and of doubtful meaning: it is a pity to use it twice in one small set of poems. I hope in these days of outrage, you will defend the purity of the English language.

I look for great things from you, and I shall always be particularly happy to hear how you and your art are getting on.

Very sincerely yours,

Edmund Gosse.

Private and confidential.

17, Hanover Terrace,

To Thomas Hardy. *Feb. 13, '10.*

My dear Hardy,—

I am asked by certain gentlemen to approach you on a matter of some importance.

The oft-repeated experiment of founding an English Academy of Letters has been attempted again, and this time with far more presumption of success than ever before. The new Academy has a small endowment and a *pied-à-terre*. It does not need State protec-

* Gosse is unduly hard on this expression, though for some reason it seems to be much less common than the equally exceptionable "from whence," which everybody uses from Milton downwards: the Oxford Dictionary quotes "from thence" from Wyclif, Pope and George Eliot.

tion or a grant. The question of membership is now the burning one.

There are to be only 30 original members, who will co-opt colleagues, leisurely, up to 40, at which number the Academy will be complete. The system follows closely upon that of the *Académie française*. History, philosophy, poetry, literary history, the novel and the drama are to be represented as proportionately as possible. The only objects paramount are to be the preservation of the purity of the language and a high standard of style. The commercial element, the consideration of what is called *success*, absolutely eliminated.

You will understand that few definite adhesions have yet been asked for. But we have the names of Lord Morley, Haldane and Henry James on our roll. We advance slowly, because we wish for none but the best. And my object in writing to you to-day is that the Committee (which includes some people, like Lord Halsbury and Lord Collins, who will *not* be asked to be Academicians) in its meeting on Friday last unanimously desired me to ask you to do us the favour of letting your name be added to the list of Academicians. It was universally expressed that your name is so essential to us that we can hardly proceed without it.

There will be no financial responsibilities, no charges of any kind. The presence of Academicians at meetings will be welcomed but not essential, as a process of voting, etc., by post will be worked out.

Now, all I have to say to you is, Come over into Macedonia and help us!

Ever yours,
EDMUND GOSSE.

Continental Hôtel des Bains,
St. Raphael (Var),
Sept. 27, 1910.

To Maurice Baring.

MY DEAR MAURICE,—

Here we are perched at last, and shall continue squatting for about three weeks. Do you know this place? Quite delicious. Down on the shore, large windows, looking out to sea, cactuses, oleanders, *pins parasols,* dust, blue everywhere, immense meridional families with bushy beards and great heads of hair, all-day-long bathing and bobbing and screaming, and coming back ravenous to eat enormous meals. It is heavenly here, after our long cold wet English summer. We made ourselves thoroughly tired—and at our age too!—with rampaging over Provence to see sights. At Marseilles we suddenly found ourselves—it was the mistral that finished us—at the end of our forces. We crept here to die, and revived at once, but no more raging and tearing about in trains for the present.

I have, of course, no news. Arthur Benson and I spent ten days together motoring in Wiltshire, where I was rendered jealous by his receiving a long letter from you. I am no longer jealous, because the letter I got at Arles was three times as good a letter as yours to A. Arthur is now in towering spirits and health. I wonder what he will take up to do. He is intellectually a little like those very tight and active terriers one sees rattling about Hotels, immensely alert and occupied, and with nothing to do. Arthur pities me for my idleness, and indeed I have fallen into a dreadful state of laziness and *laissez-faire*. I have slipped into the very ebb of mental energy: it is very shocking. Is it merely old age, or disease, do you think? Or—*reculer pour mieux sauter*? I am afraid I shall not *sauter* any more. I have just received the usual insulting letter about *Father and Son*, from a man who presumes "a mercenary motive" must be the only one which could induce me to write "so useless and destructive a work." He adds, plaintively, "It teaches no moral," so I am so far consoled. The practice of literature is not very rewarding: this is the sort of thing it brings, or else entire neglect.

I brought very little here to read, not enough indeed: the last (viii) volume of *Jean Christophe*. I must go over to Cannes to buy some more books, and some more cigars. There are plenty of sea-urchins at St. Raphael, but no edible literature or potable tobacco. I wish I could have a long talk with you about *Jean Christophe*. It is a wonderful book, but oddly *décousu*. The first four volumes make a most adorable study of strenuous childhood. The second four a vivid and rather priggish analysis of existing French society. The first a splendid work of art, the last a valuable satirical mono-

AT MARISH FARM, DENHAM

FROM LEFT TO RIGHT: WILLIAM DE MORGAN, EDMUND GOSSE, CHALMERS ROBERTS, SARAH GRAND, MISS TOBIN, MRS. GOSSE, WILLIAM HEINEMANN

graph. But Jean Christophe disappears, or is transformed into a sort of mixture of Jesus Christ and Tristram Shandy. But the man Rolland has something of the real Balzac touch—the Balzac of *Les Secrets de la Princesse de Cadignan*, etc. How I should like to discuss it with you!

Life is rather aggravating. You are one of the very few people whom I am always refreshed, strengthened, heartened by talking to: I always leave you feeling that you have given more zest to things, that you understand. You are, oh! so wonderfully, one of the Sunetoi (I am not sure of the spelling): and yet we practically never meet. I am like the gardener of Fontenelle. "I am old, so old, and I soon must die"—it seems such waste. Your account of your happy life at Sosnowka gives me joy. How good for you, and how I rejoice at it. I wish you would give my affectionate respects to Countess Benckendorff, of whom I often think though I seem never to meet. And please remember me (if she has not forgotten me) to the Countess Nathalie.* Tell her I have often and often recalled that long conversation we had at the Ridleys'. There are conversations which are like events, don't you think? Nellie sends you her love. She is not very well: she grows rather fragile, I think. Old, old—we both grow old.

Love me, my dear Maurice, for the little time that is left.

Ever your affect.

EDMUND.

* Honble. Mrs. Jasper Ridley.

CHAPTER TWENTY-TWO

In giving permission for the following letter to be used, Mr. E. M. Forster took the opportunity to reproach Mr. Marsh for neglecting the injunction "to use his influence" on the author of *Howard's End.*

17, Hanover Terrace,
27.12.10.

To Edward Marsh.

My dear Eddie,—

It was truly kind of you to take the trouble, just as you were going away, to get and send me *Howard's End*, which I was very curious to read.

I am afraid, however, that it has been a great disappointment to me. It begins so admirably that at first I congratulated myself on its being an advance on the two earlier books, which (you know) I admired very much. But then there began to enter it a sense of strain and a cloudiness which grew until the book's last hundred pages is nothing but a storm in a fog.

I hardly remember such another disappointment, and I try to analyze why, when *Where Angels Fear to Tread* was so very promising, and when *A Room with a View* seemed to advance that promise, *Howard's End* makes one fear that no good thing will come of these anticipations. I think it is due to the author's having listened to the people who (may have) said that he should give more "story," and that he should be coarse in morals, and that he should coruscate in style. But these three things are not native to him, and so the man who gave us before such delicate and faithful studies of character, and who wrote so simply, now produces a book (which has many details of merit, but) which, taken as a whole, is sensational and dirty and affected.

I should like to know what you think of the new craze for introducing into fiction the high-bred maiden who has a baby? It is the craze of the moment; it is beginning to attract the wonder of the Continent. I have read *three* new English novels this autumn of which it is the *motif*. The French, who allow themselves every other aberration, have at least preserved their horror of this one, which never occurs in their novels. I think it is a mark of feminisation; the only French instance I recollect occurs in a novel of Marcelle Tinayre, which was very severely condemned by French opinion. I do not know how an Englishman can calmly write of such a disgusting thing, with such *sang-froid*. If you will look at Chapter 40 of *Howard's End*, and will put it side by side with an incident in real life, *forcibly, without literature or cant,* you will feel the gooseflesh rise upon you.

I hope you will not be vexed with me for speaking so plainly, because I know that you have influence with the author of this unhappy book, and are genuinely interested in him. I cannot help hoping that you may be induced to say something which will redeem him from the slough of affectation and false sentiment into which he has fallen.

If I were asked to point to a passage which combined all that prose fiction should not be—lurid sentimentality, preposterous morals, turgid and sickly style—I do not think I could point to anything worse than the closing chapters of *Howard's End*.

I meant to say how good, in the earlier part of the book, is much of the character-painting. The real talent of the author is for delicate, ironic painting of straightforward natures. How excellent is Aunt Juley! The quiet lives of people of that type, to whom nothing happens, who do not meet with manslaughterers and bastards and Jane-Eyre-borrowed lunatics in their walks abroad—that is what your author was born to depict. And I am now going to read a few chapters of Mrs. Gaskell to take the taste of *Howard's End* out of my mouth.

Our warmest wishes for your happiness and prosperity throughout 1911, and long afterwards.

I am ever your affectionate,

EDMUND GOSSE.

17, Hanover Terrace,

To Professor Grierson. *April 23, 1911.*

My dear Grierson,—

I am very much obliged to you for sending me your paper in *The World*. Your reasoning is clear and full, and carries conviction with it. It is amusing, is is not, that while one set of lunatics is trying to attach to Bacon everybody else's poems, an effort should be made to deprive him of his one genuine ode?

With regard to your note on p. 154, I do not feel quite sure that the man wounded in Ireland in 1599 (for the 1600 notice seems but a repetition of the former one) was not the poet. You remember that young Thomas Egerton was killed in Ireland in 1599. May not Donne's original service with the Lord Keeper have included the accompaniment of the young man to Ireland? If Donne was looking after him, and was with him when he died, this might be an additional tie binding him to the father.

There was such a name as Done. *The Ancient History of the Septuagint,* 1633, which I daresay you know, was newly done into English by J. Done, who was then alive. This has not prevented Jessopp and others from attributing the wretched treatise to John Donne.

Yours very sincerely,

Edmund Gosse.

17, Hanover Terrace,

To Maarten Maartens. *25.6.11.*

My dear M. M.,—

Your letter was very delightful to receive, except that we cannot bear to think of you ill in bed, taking that horrid aspinal—or whatever it is called. I am sure it must do you harm. What you say about visits quickening the pace of correspondence is certainly true. We are not one whit more fond of you and Ada than we were a month ago, but everything about you has become vivid, and we have a dozen amusing trifles to laugh over in concert. Ach—ja!

How I should like to hear again the motor that has learned to say Odo. But I hope it will never learn to say Bacbac!

On the whole the great Coronation week has gone off very propitiously, and everybody sighs with relief to know that it is over. The weather meant to be horrible, but relented at times. Thursday was hideous, with a wild black wind, but it did not rain. Friday was sunshine, until the procession was over, and then rained for fifteen hours. Saturday was one of the most exquisite days you ever saw, hectic and azure, with a hysterical limpidity. Now, when it no longer matters, the cold rain never ceases.

Our expedition to the Abbey was wholly successful. We drove across to the steamer at Chelsea, dreadfully hampered and almost prevented by the streams of troops in Hyde Park. The steamer was full of peers and peeresses, but few of the former in their robes, and the latter looking pitiful, huddled up in their cloaks from the wind, and holding their coronets on their shivering knees. We called at Lambeth to take on board some bishops and canons in wonderful raiment. When we reached Westminster at 8.20, our troubles were over, for we were inside the cordon, and strolled up into the House of Lords, which was full of scurrying peers robing and calmer peeresses breakfasting. Nellie had nearly an hour's rest in my room, and as late as 9.15 we were able to float along in the privileged tide of peers and peeresses and take our places nearly an hour later than other people. Our places were high up in the East Transept, looking down the nave, and upon each transept and half the Theatre, so that we saw all the approaching processions beautifully, but of course none of the actual ceremony, which indeed comparatively few people saw. The affair went off with the most complete and mechanical exactitude, there was not a hitch, nor a blunder, nor an "incident" of any kind, but it was long, oh! so long; we sat in our narrow seats for 6 mortal hours, and less fortunate people sat for 7, or even 8. Some of the things that struck us most were the acts of homage (the Archbishop of Canterbury in cloth of gold challenging the company north and east and south and west), the shouts of "Vivat Regina" and "Vivat Rex," sharp and loud, like artillery, from the Westminster boys; the Peeresses, an immense cage of identical white birds, putting on their hundreds of coronets with double hundreds of slim white arms at the same instant (the Peers were much less unanimous and graceful), the force of 500 choral voices in that old roof, the splendour of the golden and crimson and white figures stalking over the dark-blue ocean of carpet, the bays high up full of brilliant-coloured figures so pressed together that they looked like gigantic painted windows, the Prince of Wales like a sweet little Galeazzo Malatesta, the Queen with her huge purple train carried by seven peeresses, the last of whom had her own train carried. These are fragments I recall—but you will find the whole thing described with Byzantine exaggeration in the daily Press. We were sorry not to see the actual Crowning, but very thankful to have seen so much.

Yesterday Sylvia* and I were in the Solent for the Naval Review. We were on the *Rohilla*, the House of Lords steamer, and nearest to the Royal Ship. We saw it all to perfection. The one thing that struck me most was the tiny figure of the King, quite alone on the forepart of his vessel, as it steamed slowly between the lines of grey, hideous Dreadnoughts—the white sides and golden-yellow funnels looking fairy-like in the sternness, and the sky melting blue with loose illuminated white clouds high up in it; and the saluting guns pouring out steam that gathered in low clouds, and made the distant ironclads look colossal. But we left home at 7 a.m. and got back at midnight, so tired that the bitterness of weariness seemed past, and we could scarcely eat or speak. Ach-ja!

Much love to you all from us all.

Yours ever,

E. G.

The letter which follows is a good example of the care with which Gosse followed the fortunes of his friends who happened to be engaged on any literary undertaking. He would take pains without end to encourage and assist them, and seemed always to bear them in mind in his reading, not only beating the bush for them, but starting the hare, and catching it for transmission to his correspondent.

* Miss Sylvia Gosse, the artist; Gosse's second daughter.

17, Hanover Terrace,
To Evan Charteris. *July 31, 1911.*

My dear Evan,—

If you will look at Smollett's *Adventures of an Atom* (I have the original edition before me), Vol. I, 56-63, you will not doubt that the Fatzman Quamba-cun-dono is meant for Cumberland. If so, the picture is elaborate, and very interesting. Ximo, of course, is Scotland. Unless the whole thing is irony, Cumberland appears here as the soul of elegance and benignity, and it seems to me most important that you should, at least, examine these pages, which (so far as I know) no one yet has referred to Cumberland. *The Adventures of an Atom* was published in 1769, but was supposed (even to the length of a forged date on some copies of the title-page) to be written and issued in 1749.

In Vol. II, p. 177, I find a reference to the death of Quamba-cun-dono the Fatzman, "whose authority had kept several puppets in awe."

See also a very curious passage (Vol. II, p. 126) about the Fatzman (Cumberland) becoming "estranged from the councils of his kinsman Gio-gio (George III)." In fact you should look through the whole book for the mention of "The Fatzman."

These, my Evan, are the crumbs with which I endeavour to stuff you, as if you were a Strasburg GOOSE.

Yours,
E. G.

Abbaye de Pontigny
(Yonne),
To Evan Charteris. *August 27, 1911.*

My dear Evan,—

The counsel given in your kind letter is in complete agreement with the judgment to which I had myself come, and upon which I acted before I left England.* The letters have been returned to their owner, and I have received a pledge that they shall be sealed

* This refers to certain letters of Swinburne as to which Gosse's advice was asked.

up and locked up, and that no one shall be allowed to look at them unless I give my consent. It may seem a little grotesque that I, who have no legal rights whatever, should adopt this responsibility: but I am very desirous to guard the poet's memory.

Since I have been in France, I have—most curiously—been supplied by word of mouth with other and still more extraordinary stories about S., stories recounted by Maupassant to Heredia, Gautier and E. de Goncourt, and repeated so as to form a sort of Legend—horrible, ingenious and ridiculous! I am glad to have heard all this stuff—some of which (I am now told) Goncourt repeated in his novel *La Faustine*, which I must read, because one deals promptly with such folly if one is ready for it.

Our ten-days here draws to its close. It has been an experience charming and delicate beyond almost anything of the rest of my experience. This is a vast Cistercian abbey of the 12th century—*pons exuedis, hortus, asylum*—close to the noble church where so many great English prelates, St. Thomas à Becket among others, took refuge in the Middle Ages. It has seen Lord Halifax on his knees at the shrine of St. Edmé! It now belongs to that unsurpassed Hellenist, Paul Desjardins, who gathers a group of some 30 people round him. Here are André Gide, the poet Fr. Viélé-Griffin, Jean Bédier who is the first authority in the world on the Chansons de Geste, several professors of the Collège of France, several ladies, in particular four young girls, erudite, enthusiastic, two of them very pretty, all ardent students of the Collège de France. One of them—of whom my wife says that she should have bought one more breadth when she made her dress, so very tight is it—runs down the meadow in front of my window in the morning, in a thin white robe that scarcely conceals a contour. She is like a Botticelli.

Well! We sit out of the burning sun, in a circle, under the elm-trees, and we discuss in *libres conversations* the Tragic—"le Tragique, vous savez, non pas la Tragédie." Paul Desjardins takes the lead, firmly, modestly, slowly, with beneficence and gaiety. It is not at all pedantic or scholastic—bursts of laughter intervene, *calembours, je ne sais quoi!* It is like Boccaccio, in his more harmless pages. How you would enjoy it! It would be a revelation to you, as it has been to me, a revelation of suavity, enthusiasm and beauty.

Alas! we are to part tomorrow: *we* go to Aix-les-Bains. What bathos!

If you write to me to 17 H.T., letters will be promptly forwarded. The new ideas I have got here, the new impressions! I could sob with chagrin to think that I am 62, not 22. To feel so saturated with the love of things, and to know that one must almost at once die or become stupid! Enjoy life while you can—suck it as a wasp drains a peach.

Yours affectionately,
EDMUND GOSSE.

17, Hanover Terrace,
To B. M. Barrett H. Clark. *Oct. 19, 1911.*

DEAR SIR,—

It is difficult for me after thirty years to give a trustworthy answer to your question; but I will do my best.

Stevenson's voice was remarkable and characteristic. I still sometimes recover it in my dreams. It was resonant and penetrating—in moments of excitement tending to be shrill. There was always a marked tone of the Scotsman. In the autumn of 1880 (I think it was) I heard him night after night read aloud the successive chapters of *Treasure Island*, which he was composing. He was then particularly ill, and the vivacity and sustained power of his voice were very surprising. He read the Bible aloud with great propriety and feeling, dwelling carefully on the cadence of sentences. Perhaps, as I try for your behalf to listen back, what I hear most distinctly is his enchanting delivery, one Sunday afternoon in my house—probably in 1879—of the invective of Rabshakeh to Hezekiah in Kings II ("where are the Kings of Hamath," etc.).* He loved all these proper names, and gave them slow euphonic emphasis.

I always considered that there was a relation between Stevenson's careful and sonorous reading and the extreme pains he took in the form and balance of his writing.

* "Where are the gods of Hamath and of Arpad? Where are the gods of Sepharvaim, Hena, and Ivah?" II Kings xviii, 34.

I am afraid these meagre notes will be of little use to you, but such as they are I send them.

Believe me to be,
Dear Sir,
Faithfully yours,
EDMUND GOSSE.

17, Hanover Terrace,
To William Edward Barber. *9.12.'11.*

MY DEAR BARBER,—

A generous reviewer in the *M.P.* said of me that I came forward so quietly that one of these days I should come forward and not be observed at all! The prediction has come true. Seven or eight weeks ago I published for the first time my *Collected Poems* (Heinemann) and not a single critic has noticed it.

I have no friends in the press except the *Morning Post*, which is the kindest of friends. I blush to do so but I venture to indicate how encouraging a criticism (however severe—that doesn't matter —) would be to me at this moment, when I appear to be about to expire still-born.

Yours very sincerely,
EDMUND GOSSE.

17, Hanover Terrace,
To Sir Arthur Pinero. *3.3.12.*

MY DEAR PINERO,—

You must, I think, be coming back from Paris, not a little refreshed I hope after your late exertions at the Pandora. It was exceedingly kind of you to send me the *The Mind the Paint Girl*, which is so vivid and so admirably constructed that I feel as if I had already seen it. I am more than ever struck by your astonishingly firm hold on the essentials of the theatre; nothing wobbles, nothing requires excuse. Each scene marches steadily to its inevitable end. Your satire is severe and just, without passing into caricature. And I conceive that when it has the patina of a generation on it, it will be seen by successive crowds with constantly increasing emotion and interest. You will be to the reign of Edward VII what Farquhar is to Queen Anne, and more too.

Your stage directions are a delight to me. But it was Ibsen who started that, wasn't it? What should we not give for a play of Molière or Congreve to which the poet had appended directions as elaborate as Ibsen's or yours?

I congratulate you on a very fine piece; and I am always

Yours sincerely,

Edmund Gosse.

17, Hanover Terrace,

To Sir Arthur Pinero. *19.3.12.*

My dear Pinero,—

It was in the Spring of 1881, and some little play of Tennyson's in blank verse (perhaps *The Cup*?) was running at the Lyceum. I dropped in on Browning, as I often did on my way down in the morning; and he said, "What do you think? Irving wrote me a letter yesterday in which he asked me to write him a play in verse, like Tennyson's." I replied, "Well, and I hope you will agree to do it. What have you said to him?" "I have just answered his letter, and I have said that it is very kind of him, very civil and all that, but that if he wants to act a play of mine there is *The Return of the Druses* ready waiting for him!"

To this letter, as you may well suppose, Irving returned no reply.

Yours always,

Edmund Gosse.

Au Lion d'Or,

[address illegible] *France.*

To Maarten Maartens. *11.6.12.*

My dear M. M.,—

As we have wandered from town to town in this agreeable Normandy, your *Eva* has been my companion, and I have just finished the careful reading of it. Let me at once congratulate you on a very skilful and distinguished performance, extremely well planned and conducted. The book has amused me enormously, and I think it will rank among your best performances. The mise-en-scène is admirable—the preposterous felicity of Sans-Souci, the two remote Frisian or [*illegible?*] villages, the alternative of Protestant and Catholic—all very original, and to our English way of thinking strange and picturesque. But of course, what interested you most in writing and me most in reading, was the play of character. You are always, for my sentiment, a little Puritanic: I feel it in this book. You hate the Melissants for their sans-souci, you hate them more than I do; you would like to punish them, but you are too excellent an artist to swamp them in a regular descent, as that other Puritan, Zola, would have done. I recognise in Fritz a concession to the probable. But I am not happy about Eva. Unless you had harassed her with long-drawn anguish, where would have been your story? Hence you slip from the atmosphere of observation into that of symbolism and discipline. The public and the reviewers are on your side. But I cannot quite accept the report which you novelists give of the bitterness of the fruits of adultery. I see the dear things, in real life, flourish like the green bay-trees. And I will venture to press you hard with one criticism, which affects you and all writers of this species of romance. You neglect, you wilfully ignore, the effects of time. The act of sex, which, from its violence, one would expect to leave a perpetual impress on the memory, is, as a matter of fact, one of the most volatile of human experiences. In real life Eva, with every reason for forgetting, would simply have ceased to recollect her swift and fugitive sensation after the flight (admirably done the flight, both the flights! my compliments).

Towards the end of the book, I feel here and there a slackening of imagination, you exchange melodrama for the patient record of experience. But I thank you for not forcing too much out of that green-eyed dog: at one moment I trembled. The subsidiary characters, Baroness Bigi, the grand-aunt, etc., excellent. The Pastor good farce; his wife good but overdone. I must close abruptly, and this crude letter is only to show you how attentively and admiringly I have read your book.

Your E. G.

17, Hanover Terrace,

To Siegfried Sassoon. *30.6.12*

My dear Siegfried Sassoon,—

Yes, I am quite pleased. I see progress. But take a longer flight. Try your hand at some objective theme. You must not spend all your life among moonbeams and half-tones. Better than all listening to advice—go on writing hard and reading the old masters.

Yours, with very true wishes for your success.

Edmund Gosse.

The review referred to in the letter to Monsieur Delattre appeared in *La Revue Germanique* for July, 1912, and presented a French estimate of Gosse as a poet. Monsieur Delattre in his review did not claim for Gosse that he was endowed with the inspiration to throw open the heavens, or greatly enlarge the vision of the earth, but of his poetry he wrote: "Elle a l'aisance délicate d'un gentilhomme d'autrefois avec, en outre, les simples et fraîches clartés des pastellistes anglais d'aujourd'hui. Elle est continuellement attentive, discrète, d'une correction parfois méticuleuse et qui, comme s'en plaint le poète lui-même, ne laisse pas de nuire à l'inspiration. . . . Mr. Gosse, qui a beaucoup goûté l'art si allègre et gracieux de Théodore de Banville, 'le dernier des joyeux poètes' comme il l'appelle, qui a écrit une ode somptueuse 'à la terre de France,' vraiment superbe, plaira particulièrement au lecteur français, qui retrouvera dans ce livre, rayon de miel pur, qui a formé le rêve et le labeur de tant d'années, quelques-unes des qualités que notre goût national estime au plus haut prix."

In the following year Gosse was given the Légion d'Honneur. He was not one to despise or profess superiority to any such emblem. Such things caused him the liveliest pleasure, he did not measure them *sub specie æternitatis*, his philosophy was far otherwise and not only for himself but for his friends. He regarded it as a matter for genuine congratulation when worldly honours fell on those he cared for, and would always make a point of writing at once to express the pleasure he felt on such occasions. He never failed to scan honours lists for the names of friends, and congratulatory telegrams would flutter from his hand at the New Year or on the King's birthday at precociously early hours of the day; and in these matters he looked for reciprocity. Of his Légion d'Honneur he wrote to Austin Dobson: "I do not feel at all worthy of so rare a distinction, but if we only got what we are worthy of, where would luck be?"

The House of Lords.

To M. Floris Delattre. *July 22, 1912.*

My dear Sir,—

I owe you very warm thanks for your kindness in sending me the review of my *Poems*. Your knowledge of the English language and literature, your sympathy, your insight, your absence of prejudice, are all admirable. It is an honour as well as a privilege to be judged by a critic of your weight and delicacy. I thank you cordially for what you have so kindly said.

To-day I am mourning, with a sense of shock and loss, for Andrew Lang, my old companion and friend of 35 years. You are acquainted, of course, with some part at least of his abundant and multicoloured work. There dies, with him, what was (no doubt) the most elegant mind that the English-speaking race has brought forth in our time.

I very much hope that I may some day have the privilege of making your personal acquaintance. It would give me the greatest pleasure to receive a visit from you.

Believe me,

Very truly yours,

Edmund Gosse.

Abbaye de Pontigny
(Yonne)

To Robert Ross. *August 23, 1912.*

My dear Robbie,—

I really am in luck's way, for by the same post that I got your most welcome news, I learn that another friend has got something

I wanted him to get. I grow quite conceited. I declare I possess the Art of the Testimonial; one should be firm, modest and yet unctuous: one should seem unwilling to praise, yet forced to do so by an innate sense of justice: dragged, as it were, under threat of torture, to testify. And now, your troubles are not over, for you have to sit down there and now, and tell me particulars.

1. What do you get? I always like to know what they get.
2. What have you to do?
3. Can you hold your Johannesburg post as well?
4. What are you called?

(When the children were small, we knew a family of biggish girls, whose Christians names were Margaret, Irene, and Jane. Philip took a great fancy to the second, but hated to call her "Miss." One day he said, amorously, "Oh what may I call you?" She replied, "You may call me just—Irene." "Then hand over the racket, will you, Just Irene?" And she retained the solemn and beautiful appellation of "Just Irene.")

I am here doing my annual *retraite*. Nellie is not here, and I am the only Englishman. Twenty people of varied sex and charm all reading *Father and Son*, in French at once, is rather an intoxicating phenomenon. Do you know that your poor friend has made quite what they call *un succès considérable*? Two copies of my book have been sold at Tarbes: and three (but one was returned to the publisher) at Brienon-sur-Armançon. God keep us humble.

Your letter, which made me happy, was coincident with a noble bursting forth of the sun. I think the winter is over at last. The voice of the bull-frog is heard in the land.

One of the readers of *Père et Fils* has sent me this story, which is worth sending on. A Protestant pasteur went to déjeuner with another pasteur at his manse. The meal, begun by prayer, was evangelical. Towards the close the visitor said to his host, glancing out at the orchard. "Et, mon Frère, êtes-vous *béni en abricots* cette année?"

But I hear you excellently say: "Cease, old babbler, cease."

Yours ever,

Edmund Gosse.

In a later letter to another correspondent he wrote as a mock corrective to his spirit of growing self-satisfaction, "In Paris at this moment I am the celebrated author of the day. Resist the temptation to laugh and make a long nose. *Father and Son* has appeared in a very excellent translation as *Père et Fils* and has taken the Town. The French Press reeks with it. But I must remember what Mrs. Kenwigs said to her daughter Morleena. 'If when you are playing with the neighbours' children in the court, you tell them that you are having French lessons, be sure you say "But I am not proud, for Mother says, that's wrong."'"

CHAPTER TWENTY-THREE

17, Hanover Terrace,
To Henry James. *9.10.12.*

My dear James,—

It is a great satisfaction to me to receive your letter, for I have felt no little anxiety about you, and yet did not like to trouble you with fatuous enquiries. I do mourn over your painful summer, and have no inclination to think otherwise than gravely of "shingles," which—thank God—I have never yet suffered in myself but have seen most painfully in others. For many reasons, for health's above all, I rejoice that you have definitely taken the step of removing for the clammy months from your garden to Carlyle Mansions, a delightful neighbourhood. And now let me say how flattered I am that you should have pointed me out to your blundering landlords as the very beacon of respectability. A sort of Gig-man, as Carlyle would say. But what kind of asses they must be who ask *you* for any proof of quality? They shall go down to posterity with the bailiff who asked Miss Wordsworth whether it was true that her aged father wrote verses? And with the young lady who exclaimed, "What are *Keats*?" They must be men of evil lives; and irresistibly the question surges up "Can they be themselves respectable?"

You do not suggest that I should write to the creatures. I presume I wait for evidence of their unbelief, which of course will never come. If they do write, I shall blaze back overwhelmingly.

So kind what you say about my Swinburne in the *D.N.B.* I have had a few copies privately printed for the curious: these are not at present distributed, but I send you yours to-day in case it may amuse you for a minute or two. Have you seen G. Meredith's *Letters*? I hope that there are many to you in it. I have ordered the book, but not yet received it. It is amusing to read in the *D.N.B.* vol. II.* the life, and see that all the old shadows of *Evan Harring-*

* Of the *Supplement.*

ton were cast by substances, and that there really was a great sartorial Melchisedek and four advancing aunts.

We have had a very quiet summer, no long holiday. Nellie has been deeply anxious about her favourite brother, Washington Epps, who has been dangerously, and no doubt fatally, ill ever since March. He grows weaker and weaker in a pitiful decline. In consequence she has not consented to leave London at all; and I have only flitted about, twice for a few days to France, to Dorsetshire for a week with Arthur Benson (spending a day at Max Gate with Hardy) and to Buxton for a week, where Norris was. Norris seemed remarkably well, much less deaf. We talked much of you.

Do dictate me another letter when the spirit moves you. It must be less physical fatigue to you than spade-work with the pen.

I heard that Mrs. Cadwallader Jones passed thro' London. I hope she was able to glance at Rye in the passage. But where is Mrs. Wharton, who promised to come? I much desire to see her.

Have you read *Marriage*? Too hard, metallic, rhetorical. I plucked up courage in both hands, and wrote and told him* so—warned him against the growing *hardness* of his books. He replied with the greatest good-nature, not the least offended, saying that he believed it to be true, and that he should make a strong effort to throw it off. I thought it charming of him to take it in this simple and kindly way.

Well! Do not let us be so long again without a word, even if it be only a moan.

Always yours,

Edmund Gosse.

House of Lords.

To Henry James. *10.10.12.*

My dearest James,—

And the foolish creatures *have* applied to me!! I have answered them according to their folly, expressing in one breath reverence for you and contempt for them.

Meredith's *Letters* have come. I am greatly disappointed to find

* Mr. H. G. Wells.

none to you, and very few indeed to Cotter Morison, Leslie Stephen or Hardy. On the whole, the collection seems to me to raise the reputation of his heart a little at the expense of his head. There is lots of fine stuff, but when you have said that he was extremely affectionate and tenacious, highly amative (he comes out towards the end as quite an epistolary Anacreon), and amazingly full of verbal fancy, you begin (or I irreverently begin) to ask where is the commanding brain-power his new votaries extol. (I cannot see my paper: I am writing with my long-sight spectacles, so will shut up.)

But I wanted you to know that they did, in so many words, ask me if you were "in every way respectable and eligible." I swore, looking (or writing) very much down the bridge of my nose, that no other man quite so eligible and respectable exists. But haunting fear comes over me. Was I telling the Truth? *Are* you respectable? The Puritan Conscience working, you see; but I will leave it there, and you with your Gig.

Ever yours,
E. G.

17, Hanover Terrace,

To Henry James. *11.10.12.*

My dear James,—

I am highly delighted at having brought the silly landlords fluttering, like pheasants, to your feet.

Your delightful analysis of your impression of Meredith's *Letters* is of the highest interest to me: especially as I had written, before your earlier letter, a longish review (which the *Morning Post* inscrutably reserves for next Monday), in which, as I rejoice to perceive, I come not much into conflict (if at all) with your view. In distinction from the ordinary reviews—which have been just foolish faces of praise—I am glad to know myself at least on your side.

You crush me by the wit of your comparing my little Swinburne thing to a pincushion! But remember, that a pincushion was all I was asked, or allowed, to make. And I modestly venture to think you would not be so sarcastic if you realized that the work had absolutely to be done from the egg, that no memoirs of Swinburne exist, and that this had to be built up with an infinitude of labour out of all sorts of material. There was the cushion, but it had not a pin in it. But if you will be patient, I may yet give you a portrait of the creature less entirely inadequate.

By the way, how strange it is that Meredith professed himself such a lover of France and student of its language, and that yet there is not a reference to French literature in his letters that is not almost abjectly futile. He is very difficult to comprehend.

Ever most warmly yours,

Edmund Gosse.

To Henry James. *Oct. 13, 1912.*

My dear James,—

You take so fraternal an interest in us all that I do not apologize for letting you know at once what afflicts us. My brother-in-law, Washington Epps, died last night in his sleep, a blessed termination of his long weary illness. Poor Nellie has thus lost, within six months, three of those nearest to her, Emily, Tadema and now this dearly loved brother. She is very brave. We went up to see them this morning. However old one gets, or however one reflects, the form of death is very terrible. One can't resist the *hysterica passio.* The arrogance of a handsome corpse is very humbling. As we get on in life these shocks become more and more frequent, and one ought to feel them less. But three in half a year! The ground seems to shake under our feet. And I see, with more than common sympathy, that dear old Lady Ritchie is a widow. Take care of yourself: the living grow more tenderly precious as they grow more few.

Yours always,

Edmund Gosse.

To Henry James. *14.10.12.*

My dear James,—

Your letter received to-day is a most precious document. I cannot express to you how I value it, nor how extremely I agree with it.

What you note about the absence of perception of the existence of Balzac is of the greatest importance. (It had escaped me.) It is really the key-note to the comprehension of G.M.* On Saturday afternoon I had a long talk alone with Haldane: I told him of your views: he is perfectly in unison with us both; but he frankly admitted that the general effect of the *Letters* on him was to lower a little his sense of the intellectual value of G.M. Haldane, too, is slightly scandalized at the revelation of Meredith as a philanderer. Really, some of those last letters to ladies are a little excessive, are they not? Anacreon, with vine-leaves askew in his grey curls, astride a cask of sherry.

I am ashamed that you should look at my inadequate, hustled, pinched thing in the *M.P.* If I could only have had space, and have written it *after* instead of before consultation with you!

You got, I presume, a *Cornhill* for October I sent you, with a sketch of Swinburne at Etretat, which I hoped calculated to divert you a moment?

We are both so sorry to hear of your relapse. But I am assured that recovery from shingles is invariably retarded by slippings backward: so be patient and good. Obey your doctor; be lazy.

Your letters are a great excitement to me.

Ever yours,

EDMUND GOSSE.

House of Lords.

To Henry James. *Oct. 16, 1912.*

MY DEAR JAMES,—

Your letter of this morning is most exciting. I feel like one who has scoured the habitable world for a jewel that all the while was buried in his own front-garden. The time I have spent in trying to run the Monkey story to earth, and you had it all the time!

Now do pull your priceless memory together, and recall, as exactly as possible, what it was that you heard Maupassant say about the Monkey. It has hitherto been impossible to get nearer than third or fourth hand to it (it circulates only in France) and here

* George Meredith.

are you with it at first hand. Now, let me explain, that from its inception the Monkey story seems to have branched in two directions. The first and most monstrous branch was told to Viélé-Griffin by Heredia as coming from Maupassant, and has reached me, distantly, from two or three other vague sources, as once from the Goncourts, otherwise from Heredia. A man I met in Burgundy told me that it was in the Goncourt Diary, but it isn't, so far as I can find, and could not indeed be printed even in a Goncourt Diary.

The Monkey story in this form relates to a Page whom Swinburne or Powell (they are not distinguished in the story) brought to Etretat, and who became jealous of a Monkey, which was also a member of the household, and how, after a scene (oh! what a scene!) the Page hanged the Monkey outside the master's bedroom door, and then rushed out and drowned himself. Whereupon the master raised a marble monument, not to the Page, but to the Monkey.

Is this the little horror which you heard Maupassant relate?

Or was it the completely anodyne absurdity of Swinburne's having killed and roasted his own pet monkey as a feast for Maupassant, in the spirit of the familiar tale of the Fakir in Boccaccio? This latter I can well believe that Swinburne might sillily pretend to do. But there is a peculiar psychological importance to me in the former story. If Maupassant really did tell that particular version, it is curious in more ways than one.

So I do entreat you, though the typewriter machine should flush rosy-red in the process, to tell me as exactly as you can what you heard Maupassant say. I believe you to be the only person left who can give a first-hand report.

Yours on tenterhooks,

Edmund Gosse.

17, Hanover Terrace,

To Henry James. *27th Nov., 1912.*

My dear James,—

Your letter of the 19th was of the greatest possible interest and value to me, and I should have answered it at once had it not been for a quite unusual pressure of duties, personal and public. The House of Lords, that dying body, has been galvanized into so many violent contortions these last ten days that no one who knows it less well than I do could guess how lifeless it really is. But it has kept me on the run.

Your pages on my new book* give me a lasting flush of pleasure. How good you are! Every word you say about Andrew Lang is most valuable and penetrating. Somehow his memory *irritates* me! He possessed the truth and answered to the heavenly calling, and yet always without joy and almost always without grace. His puerility, as you say, was heartrending. It was very difficult for me to write anything about him at all, in the midst of a flux of newspaper eulogy, all unthinking, ignorant and adulatory. It was necessary to pitch the note low: as it was I have been abused for my frankness. I wish I could have borrowed, and dared to use, your absolutely illuminating phrases about him; but it would, of course, have been wrong to do more than indicate the doors or windows through which, at some future date, criticism would certainly have to enter. The Widow is very fierce and highly dominating: one of the most commanding specimens of the species I have met with. Her lash cracks over the bowed shoulders of Fleet Street.

I cannot tell you how grieved we are at the slowness with which your miserable malady consents to take leave of you. As soon as there is any real mitigation, let us be the first to rejoice with you. My ladies send their love and their best wishes.

I am ever yours indeed,

Edmund Gosse.

To-morrow, at the A. C.,† we crown Masefield, and celebrate Lang and Verrall: Barrie in the chair.

17, Hanover Terrace,

To Sir George Douglas. *27.11.12.*

My dear Douglas,—

Your very kind letter gave me great pleasure. Your remarks about Balestier show high clairvoyance; you would have detested

* *Portraits and Sketches.*

† The Academic Committee.

him. *I* should have detested him, but that he happened to like me very much. He was a queer, strained, tight little type of strenuous Yankee: not important, not (perhaps) worthy of a place in the gallery, but curious and original in his common and imitative way! So also, are you quite right about Lang. He had the heavenly calling, but it brought him no happiness. He could not rest, nor be human, nor look about in radiant idleness. Strenuousness is very unattractive in others, don't you think? though we all want to be strenuous ourselves. Lord, teach me to be lazy! is my prayer: and it is often graciously answered. Not to be too lazy, of course. The old Bishop of Oxford and his sin of—what was it he called it? *Accidia?* How wicked it is of you never to come to see us in London! At Buxton this September a pleasant middle-aged gentleman and lady came up to me and introduced themselves as friends of yours. We had a very pleasant chat, but I did not catch their names. I am sending you a little private book; it is a supplement to the *Swinburne* in *P. & S** merely for reference. It is a bottled antidote to the lies of Watts-Dunton!

My ladies all unite in very kindest remembrances.

I am, my dear Douglas,

Ever sincerely yours,

EDMUND GOSSE.

House of Lords.

To Siegfried Sassoon. *13.2.13.*

MY DEAR SIEGFRIED,—

The Daffodil Murderer is a composition which interests me very much, and about which I feel a difficulty in defining my opinion. It is a very clever, brilliant thing, and displays powers which I had not expected from you. But, apart from the "Preface," which is a very amusing (and well-deserved) bit of satire, what puzzles me about the poem is that it is not really a parody at all. It is a pastiche. It treats a Masefield subject exactly in Masefield's own manner, as if you had actually got into Masefield's own skin, and spoke with his voice. There is nothing comic about it. A tale of rustic tragedy

* *Portraits and Sketches.*

is told with real pathos and power, only—exactly as Masefield would tell it. The end is extremely beautiful.

I have given a copy of the *D. M.* to Mr. Edward Marsh, who is the choragus of the new poets, and has published the interesting anthology of *Georgian Poetry* which I daresay you have seen. Mr. Marsh is most curious to see what else you have written, and I should like you to make up a parcel of your pamphlets, and send them to him.

I should like you to get into friendly relations with Mr. Marsh, who is a most charming man, extremely interested in poetry, and the personal friend of all the new poets. It would be useful to you, I think, as you live so isolated a life, to get into relations with these people, who are of all schools, but represent what is most vivid in the latest poetical writing.

Let me know what you think of this suggestion. It is time, I think, for you to begin to tilt up the bushel under which your light has hitherto been burning.

Yours very sincerely,
EDMUND GOSSE.

17, Hanover Terrace,

To Filson Young. *23.12.12.*

MY DEAR FILSON YOUNG,—

Thanks to the relaxed state of affairs, I have been able to give myself entirely to *When the Tide Turns*, which I have read very slowly and carefully. I seldom read an English novel, which makes me a bad judge. But I have greatly enjoyed some parts of this book. You will be very angry with me for saying "some parts," but I am like the Infant Washington, I cannot tell a lie—about literature. So I hope you will let me speak more at length; and then, in the pride of youth, you will see that I am really a harmless old fogey.

The Prelude and most of Book I. are very beautiful. The description of the Lough, the islands, the water, the sentiments of the boy, are quite marvellously true, and recorded with delicacy and modesty of style. Just as a piece of writing, the sail up the river to Downpatrick, and the scene in the town, and the return (up to the accident) form a passage of quite admirable writing—effective, fresh, never forced.

Then, the end of the book—that is to say, the return to Ireland, and the funeral—is worthy of substantial serious praise.

But, between these comes the long London episode, of which I cannot speak so highly. You seem here and there to get away from reality, that is, to me, from interest.

There are certain things which, while not impossible, are so far removed from experience as to be unfitted for fiction. You *might* find a giraffe, with a lace bonnet on its head, browsing in Kensington Gardens. You *might* find a young artist, quite untrained, without education, living, at the age of 27, in the position and at the expense and in the surroundings in which you reveal Rupert at the beginning of Book II. You *might* find one: but as a matter of fact you never do and you never have. I have known something of most of the artists and men of letters of the last forty years, and there never was one of them who at the age of 27 could give the dinner-party of p. 93 *et seqq.*

In Rupert I see some reflection of two men whom I knew well in their early youth, Rudyard Kipling and Aubrey Beardsley, and a stern vivid study of either of these artists, or of both together, done as Balzac would have done it, would be probable. But this career of "red roses and red wine," oh! dear, it is just books about the wealthy written for the wealthy. The Lord says to an artist, "Come out of all this and be separate."

The women in your book are admirably drawn whenever, and as long as, they are not exhibited as something exasperating sexual desire. And when they are, they suddenly become horrible and false. Mrs. Graeme—it renders me unwell to speak of Mrs. Graeme: she is a Madame Tartuffe made prioress of a nunnery of prostitutes.

I think you were very youthful when you wrote all the middle part of this book. You had heard about the Yellow Book scandal, and thought it would make a good tale. So it would: but it didn't happen like that, with all that money and scent and roses. I ought to know, for I was in the middle of it—I was even part of it. Some day I may tell the real truth, when some sleek withers will wince.

Don't be angry with me. You write beautifully. When you are

looking back at the Lough you are inspired. But do leave the silly lustful wealthy alone. They are not worthy of your least attention.

Yours most sincerely,

EDMUND GOSSE.

17, Hanover Terrace,

To Thomas Hardy. *June 17, 1913.*

MY DEAR HARDY,—

It was very bold of me to broach once more the great theme of manuscripts. But I put all prudery and shame away: I want some of your writing with a greedy and o'ermastering desire: and if I remain modest, I shall never get any. Fortune belongs to the brazen, to the impudent. My claim is so poor, and yet so pathetic! It reminds me of a story of Jusserand's: he was coming to see us once in Delamere Terrace in a hansom cab. At our door he paid the just fare. The cabman asked for another shilling. "Why?" asked Jusserand. "Because I should like it," answered the cabman, and got it, too, for the simplicity of his petition. Apply this anecdote to my own shameless request.

Henry James was here yesterday, and was much pleased to have news of you. He is looking much better, but the *angina pectoris* is there, unrelenting, and he goes nowhere without the strange exploding specific they now give at the moment of paroxysm. Sargent's portrait of Henry James is nearly finished, and I hear is a masterpiece. There is a plaid waistcoat in it, heaving like a sea in storm, which is said to be prodigious. Do not forget ever yours in the faith.

EDMUND GOSSE.

House of Lords.

To Thomas Hardy. *30.7.13.*

MY DEAR HARDY,—

What do you think of the C. Brontë "revelations" in the *Times*? They are not really revelations, because every one knew the contents of them, although the actual text seemed to be lost. But can you understand the humbug of the *Times* and of Spielmann, and above all of Sir Robertson Nicoll, in assuring us over and over again that she was not in love with Héger? Of course she was in love with him, as passionately, blindly and hopelessly as woman ever was. There is a poem, of which I have a copy, not published, in which she tells her heart that love is not for her, that she is plain and unattractive and cannot awaken desire—a dreadful poem, of this same period, and inspired by her longing for Héger. But we are not to say so, and if we say so we are "pitiful and silly" (vide *Times*), because Héger was a married man, and Charlotte Brontë is a national heroine. I see no reason for telling the story at all, and still less for telling psychological and physiological lies about it.

Ever yours,
EDMUND GOSSE.

17, Hanover Terrace,
To Edward Marsh. *31.10.13.*

DEAR EDDIE,—

I am much disappointed that I cannot see you to-day. The doctor still keeps me rigorously in bed. I wanted to ask you about the *New Numbers*, which struck me as a most interesting venture. I immediately subscribed for 2 copies, and wrote them a cordial letter. I should think there can be no doubt of their getting enough subscribers. This is no doubt a better plan than public publishing, which often means very little, and must be costly.

It is a dreadful bore to stay in bed. I read till my eyes wheel round, and as I am allowed no food of any kind, except a very little milk, my head aches with inanition. I have read the new *Life of Borrow* by Clement Shorter, and have written a review of it (unsigned) for the *Morning Post*. Of course Borrow is interesting, but I cannot share the loud Borrovian rapture. Do you? Also I have read *Pickwick* and *M. Bergeret à Paris* and Greville's *Memoirs*, of which, however, I have only one volume. Blessed books! What in the world do sick people do who do not read books? I had a longish letter from Austin Dobson, who is still at Matlock, and seems to be stay-

THOMAS HARDY WITH EDMUND GOSSE
MAX GATE, DORCHESTER, JUNE 27, 1927

ing on there till Christmas. He gives no very good account of himself; he believes his stiffness to be growing into permanent arthritis.

Oh! and how could I forget it, I have read Thomas Hardy's magnificent new volume of stories. What a genius is there, what a glorious painter of life!

Yours affectionately,
E. G.

17, Hanover Terrace,
To Max Beerbohm. *Christmas Night, 1913.*

My dear Max,—

Henry James has been eating his Christmas dinner here with us, and I am anxious to let you know that he started the subject of your *Christmas Garland*, and discussed it with the most extraordinary vivacity and appreciation. He was full of admiration. I told him that you had a certain nervousness about his acceptance of your parody of him, and he desired me to let you know at once that no one can have read it with more wonder and delight than he. He expressed himself in superlatives. He called the book "the most intelligent that has been produced in England for many a long day." But he says you have destroyed the trade of writing. No one, now, can write without incurring the reproach of somewhat ineffectively imitating—*you!* What could be more handsome? And alas! my dear Max, what can be more true? I, for instance, shall never be able to draw another portrait without calling down upon me the sneer, "Not half so amusing as your dinner with Ibsen and Browning!" You are our Conqueror.

And I am your affectionate and ever-amused admirer,
Edmund Gosse.

17, Hanover Terrace,
To Filson Young. *Dec. 31, 1913.*

Dear Filson Young,—

No present this Christmas gave me so much pleasure as your *Letters from Solitude*. We were in domestic solitude ourselves, for it so happened that all projected convivialities fell through, and we were quite alone. Your book was my sympathetic companion by the fireside, and I enjoyed it very much. You have all the qualities required by an essayist, and these qualities have never come to the point with more lustre than in this charming book. I particularly enjoyed the last six or seven essays, so very human and tender in their humour and sweetness.

Reading you carefully, I was caught up sharp on page 221. You call the ticket a "perdurable" thing, as though you thought "perdurable" to mean "easily lost." But surely it has only one meaning, namely that of lasting for ever. "A monument of perdurable brass"—"Cables of perdurable thickness." I know of no other sense in which "perdurable" is used in English, and the notion of a perdurable ticket on the G. E. Railway fills me with distress!

With all warmest wishes for success and happiness in 1914, I am, my dear Filson Young,

Yours very sincerely,

EDMUND GOSSE.

17, Hanover Terrace,

To John Drinkwater. *4.6.13.*

MY DEAR MR. DRINKWATER,—

I am very glad that you have written to me. I sympathize with you greatly in the sore feeling that injustice, a baseless charge, gives one. It seems as though one could not put up with it. I may say, perhaps, without lack of truth, that I myself have in the course of my life suffered from this. More frequently, I believe, than most other writers. But I have always gone on the plan of taking no notice, partly because everybody reads very superficially nowadays, and to rebut a charge is often to concentrate attention on what was not before observed; and partly because the attitude of the young man fighting for his honour in these chimerical tourneys of literature is undignified.

I hope you will preserve silence this time. Your critic is a man approaching 70 years of age, very arrogant and unsympathetic and, to me, as a human being, exceedingly tiresome; but quite honest, absorbed in the love of literature, and always, at his worst, acting in good faith. You will not get the best of such an antagonist in a wordy warfare, for he is practised and hardened in all sorts of controversy. Moreover, my impression is that he has really liked your book and wished to recommend it.

There is something extremely unwholesome in the way reviews are conducted now. Every new author expects, for everything he writes, unmitigated praise. It would be amusing to take one single day's issue of all the English newspapers, and see how many books on that particular day were buttered and soaked in praise which would be preposterous if given to Keats for his odes or Miss Austen for *Emma.* I would not have you seem, by a petulant insistence on your rights, to countenance this vanity. You were born for much better things. Believe in my constant sympathy and interest.

I am very sincerely yours,

EDMUND GOSSE.

CHAPTER TWENTY-FOUR

In 1914 Gosse reached the prescribed age for retirement from his post as Librarian at the House of Lords. Feeling that he had acquired a certain ascendancy which would not easily be displaced, he was confident that his tenure of the office would be extended. He was mistaken. Sir Henry Graham, then Clerk of the Parliaments, insisted on the enforcement of the Superannuation Rule.

During his term of office Gosse had kept a diary. If it is ever to be published it can only be after the lapse of years. On the last page he wrote, "Thomas Hardy says somewhere, 'It is only those who half know a thing who can write about it.' I now begin to know the House of Lords entirely, and I can write no more. I leave my impressions as I wrote them. Some of them I see to have been false—I am surprised to find so many of them by mere force of instinct essentially true. They may have some interest to historians, or gossip-mongers, half a century later. I can add no more to them." He had kept a shrewd watch on passing events and on the personalities who entered his orbit. Peers frequenting the Library can hardly have failed to notice that their Librarian was interested in something more than the books confided to his custody. Their going and coming was closely observed by a pair of piercing eyes which gleamed through gold-rimmed spectacles from a far corner of the Library, where the Librarian sat at his desk. Nothing escaped the observation of those eyes—they were alert to give a welcome to a friend, they were even more alert to condemn a fault. The mishandling of a volume or an aimless interference with the shelves would bring Gosse at a rapid springy trot across the floor of the Library to the side of the offender with a bitingly civil request to know if he could be of any assistance. By degrees, and by rather rapid degrees, he grew to dominate the scene: the Library became his personal domain, with its code of conduct and etiquette as the subject-matter of his autocracy.

Peers who did not know Gosse were inclined to be alienated by his apparent encroachments, and a little intimidated by the air of aplomb with which he exercised some of his disputable privileges as though they were accepted rights. For instance, as his position in the Library became more secure, the hospitality he dispensed became more extended and jaunty. Lively luncheon-parties invaded the sedate dining-room, a fleet of fashionable ladies would sail into the Library at his invitation, and literary friends would usurp seats in the smoking-room to which peers might be pardoned for thinking they had a prior claim. Nor was the contact of his friends with members of the House always felicitous, as the following entry in his diary dated May 16th, 1905, will serve to show: "Andrew Lang's manners are always amusing, if a little exasperating. He has now cut quite short the picturesque 'silken parcels' of his hair, and is covered with a stubble like a new white tooth-brush. He came here with me to-day, to talk over Jacobite history with Evan. By the way, I asked him if he was going to dine to-night with the St. Andrew's University Club, of which he is a Vice-President. He said 'No! I hate dinners and I hate clubs and I hate universities!' I answered rather tartly, 'I believe you hate every thing in the world!' 'No,' he replied, 'I don't hate Mary Queen of Scots.' Evan left us alone in the smoking-room, and in came well-groomed, smiling Lord Monk Bretton. As he looked very curiously at Lang, I introduced them, whereupon Lang violently, after bowing, turned his back on poor Monk Bretton and buried his face in some old newspapers. Presently the Duke of Northumberland came in, and recognizing Lang, bowed and smiled. Lang glared at him like a basilisk through his eyeglass, and the Duke, abashed, presently went out. I said, 'The Duke bowed to you.' 'What Duke?' said Lang. 'Northumberland.' 'Oh, was that he? I never recognize anybody, he belongs to the Roxburghe Club.' That was all he vouchsafed; he behaved like a bear, like a white ant-bear or coati-mundi, but he can be charming company if he chooses." Such varieties of social experience were disconcerting to some of the Peers, and tended to off-set the large number of supporters and friends whom Gosse recruited from their ranks. Moreover, there had been personal encounters not always to Gosse's advantage. For instance, on one occasion he had been seated writing at one of the square tables in the

Library when Lord Camperdown entered and took a chair at the same table. After writing in silence for some time, Lord Camperdown lifted one of the brass network cages protecting the little lamps always kept burning for the heating of sealing-wax, and blew with some violence on the flame to extinguish it. As the fumes from the wick reached the nostrils of the Librarian, he raised his head from his writing and said, "Did you do that on purpose?" "I did," was the answer. "Then," said Gosse, "I must ask you to apologise." "I shall do nothing of the kind," Lord Camperdown replied, seeing cause neither for offence nor penitence. Gosse got up and tripping hastily away repaired to Sir Henry Graham saying that he had been insulted and must receive an apology. But no redress was forthcoming, and the quarrel was never patched up. It is more agreeable to turn to sketches in his diary of two Peers who had won his admiration and friendship:

"March 14. Lord Wemyss, who will soon be 86, went through an incomparable performance this afternoon. He rose from the cross-benches to propose a fiscal Royal Commission, a scheme not supported by either side of the House. An unusually large company had collected to hear him, and was visibly moved when he rose to his full height, with his crests of white hair waving on end, and plunged into an anecdote. His voice was ringing, his gestures, as he chaffed the Tories, and then turned to chaff the Liberals, were full of youth and vigour. He dropped his notes, and stooped to pick them up with the agility of a boy. His spirit and dash were really superb, and when he sat down, after half an hour's oration, both sides of the House applauded, and laughed, and applauded again, and the magnificent old man bowed to right and to left. It was a very extraordinary physical performance, perhaps almost unparalleled in the parliaments of our time."

. . . .

"Yesterday was Lord Wemyss' 86th birthday. He was in splendid form. He came into the House and passing me in front of the Throne, slapped me on the shoulder. I turned, and said to him, as a joke, 'I hope you are going to vote for the Archbishop of Canterbury's amendment?' *'Nolo episcopari,'* he answered, as sharp as possible."

"July 20. After a fortnight's illness, and in consequence of an operation, Lord Cowper died at Panshanger last night. The operation seemed slight, and he was getting over it well, but his constitution was lowered by gout, by which he had for years been absolutely crippled. His hands, ever since I knew him first, which is about six years ago, have been like soft birds' claws. He was a very gentle, dignified, cultivated, rather cold man. From the combined action of his wealth, his dignity, his constant ill-health (which prevented him from taking any species of exercise), he had, to a greater degree than I have ever known in another case, a sort of aloofness. He was very kind and very courteous, but he had long ceased to take any responsibility about his guests, and their fortunes were left entirely to the most competent hands of Lady Cowper. She devoted herself like a slave to him, moulding her whole life on his requirements. I often stayed with them at Panshanger, and once at Wrest, of which Palmerston said, 'There is no more welcome relaxation for a weary statesman, than Wrest in Beds,' and Disraeli, 'Now the weary (that is Gladstone) is at Wrest, I suppose that the wicked (that's me) may cease from troubling.' At Wrest I walked a good deal by the side of Lord Cowper's bath-chair, and enjoyed his conversation. He was exceedingly well read in the literature of the 18th century, and had some knowledge of later writers. His opinions were delicate, cultivated and rather timid. He had no taste for violent and unusual things. He greatly loved French poetry, and knew his Racine well. It was characteristic that he was delighted with Rostand's verse, and actually took the trouble to translate the greater part, if not the whole, of *Cyrano de Bergerac* into blank verse. He was not witty, but graceful, calculated and just in conversation, speaking rather slowly, in a low voice, to which a hanging under-lip gave a slight lisp. He had a passion for the fine arts, and loved, until quite the end of his life, to add to the pictures on the walls of Panshanger. Lady Cowper told me once that she had never seen him so animated as he was in Rome and Florence, visiting old palazzi, watching his opportunity to add to his collection. He was the very type, and probably the last example, of the old class of sheltered, refined, exquisitely proud Whig nobleman, exalted by wealth and station above the faintest fear of a rebuff, and happy to be a Liberal because he saw human nature through rose-coloured glasses, from a great distance. Early portraits display Lord Cowper as extremely handsome, of a Byronic kind, but blond or reddish, with long curled hair framing his delicate, slightly feminine face.* He struck me as a man to whom not only no rough word had ever been spoken, but who had never been in a position to hear anyone say a rude word to anyone else. The only case in which Lord Cowper is known to have come in contact with the rough side of life was once when, as Colonel of Volunteers, a man was brought before him to be reprimanded. With great agility the volunteer divested himself of every stitch of clothing. Lord Cowper looked at the naked being with mild surprise, and said, 'Take him away!' and added, gently, 'And his clothes, too.' "

In the Diary Gosse has noted not only what he observed himself, but much that he was told; for instance:—

"Lord Dunedin, who is an admirable mimic and raconteur, told me two stories of old J. B. Balfour, afterwards Lord Kinross of Glascune. He was celebrated for his extreme politeness. About 1885, when F—— was making a great local reputation for himself, Balfour was expatiating on his cleverness and charm and brilliant qualities. Old Sir Robert Moncrieff, who was present and who hated Radicals, grew red in the face and then burst out with, 'F——, why, he is a thundering cad!' To which Balfour in dulcet tones immediately replied, 'Oh! if he has a fault, I admit that it is in that direction.' At a later time, when he was at his country seat, where he saw much company and regaled them with admirable claret, Lord Kinross happened to entertain Captain C——, who imbibed so much of the wine that he lay on the floor. He was to have re-

* Lord Wemyss tells me that in early days he used to think Lord Cowper the very ideal of a Greek god, "of rather a late period."

turned to Edinburgh by the last train, but this was impossible, so Lord Kinross rang the bell and said to the butler, 'Make up a bed in the blue room: Capt. C—— has kindly consented to spend the night here.' "

The years Gosse had spent as Librarian had been more than usually happy. He had revelled in the security and prestige; he liked playing a part in so exalted an institution, and the fun of dispensing hospitality in the penetralia of the House of Lords had possessed for him a charm of its own.

In summer there was the long cool Library where he could receive his guests, with its windows opening on the river, its air of learning and distinction, its suggestion of study and affairs of state, and with not least the occasional apparition of a Minister or a Lord of Appeal, seeking the society of the Librarian or in need of his official assistance. It was a situation holding some of the implications of the far-off day of baptism at Marychurch: there was about it a sense of heightened importance, of pictorial value, and an interest appealing to his vital pleasure in the emblems of worldly success. He had never been more gay and entertaining than in these surroundings, so exactly suited to his temperament and ambitions. He had served faithfully and he had made many friends. A printed catalogue remains as a token of his industry, and a broader and more literary character in the composition of the Library as evidence of his culture.

17, Hanover Terrace,

To André Gide. *Jan. 2, 1914.*

My dear Gide,—

Conceive the impatience with which, yesterday morning, I tore open the *Nouvelle Revue Française* and read the opening chapters of *Les Caves du Vatican.*

I have awaited this book with unspeakable impatience, with hope and fear mingled. Now all is hope, and joy! Your novel opens with a magnificent originality. I believe this is—perhaps *by far*—

the greatest thing you have written. All is your own; no other writer could have written one of these pages; your sign-manual is on them all.

The conversion of Anthime is superb. Nothing could be led up to better, nothing could be more surprising, more brilliant, vivid with a more sparkling irony. The characters of the women—so finely contrasted—the soft, passive Véronique, the more acid, active and absurd Marguérite. The child Julie promises an admirable character; I see in her a continuation of the force of her grandfather Juste-Agénor. Lafcadio is at present a box of puzzles, anything may come out of him.

There is a singular air of mystery or mystification about these early chapters. I hold my breath in expectation of what that is paradoxical, that is *saugrenu*, will come out of it all, and I can hardly endure the strain of waiting till February for a continuation.

Bravo! and bravo! This, I am sure, my dear friend, is a book which will be enormously attacked, widely discussed, finally immortal.

Have you forgotten me entirely? Months have passed and you have not given me a sign of your existence. I thought you would have written to me in November, but not a word. You do not realise how much your friendship is to me. I am miserable if I think that you have ceased to think of me with indulgence.

We are well, at last. But both my wife and I have had long illnesses since the summer. We were in Paris in August, and then in Wiesbaden for four weeks, ill and unhappy. Since then I have been extremely busy, and much has happened to me. I had the great surprise of a most unexpected and brilliant recognition from the French Government.* You did not write. Perhaps you disapproved?

My wife begs to be remembered to Madame Gide and to you. How is everybody? Has the new theatre been a success? I hear nothing from any of my French friends—a conspiracy of silence! I wish you would come to London.

Ever sincerely yrs.,

EDMUND GOSSE.

* The Légion d'Honneur.

17, Hanover Terrace,

To Thomas J. Wise. *28.1.14.*

My dear Wise,—

I am working away at the Crewe MSS., and have not much left. The letters generally possess some little matter of interest, which I copy, but only one or two out of the mass of nearly 70 could be printed in its entirety. When I have finished copying, I shall ask you to come and look the whole through with me. I have to conquer a feeling that Swinburne was rather sickening: there is a very ugly side to him, and it so deeply permeates his whole existence that I scarcely know how a life of him is to be written. What humbug has been printed about his purity and high-mindedness! And yet, such is the paradox, he was pure and he was highminded—on certain defined sides.

When I have the MSS. by heart, you must dine here, if you will, and I will show you everything.

Ever yours,

Edmund Gosse.

Private.

17, Hanover Terrace,

To Coulson Kernahan. *Feb. 14, 1914.*

My dear Mr. Coulson Kernahan,—

Your article is a marvellously exact picture—the most exact which I have yet met with—of what Swinburne became in his last years. Perhaps the most difficult task his biographer has, is to distinguish this latest form of him (1879–1909) from what he was before the former date. It was unquestionably from 1860 to 1878 that he was most interesting, because most independent.

You describe him—and with marvellous skill and fidelity—as he was in the parasitical stages of his old age, when he had ceased to be *himself*; when his opinions, his attitudes, his very sensations, were founded on and reflected from those of a much poorer intellect but far stronger character than his own. I do not know a harder task than to give a perfectly just representation of this unparalleled phenomenon.

Believe me,

Sincerely yrs.,

EDMUND GOSSE.

17, Hanover Terrace,

To Lewis Chase. *Feb. 22, 1914.*

DEAR MR. CHASE,—

Thank you first of all for your kind congratulations on my *macaron rouge*, which was a delightful surprise to me.

Then, thank you for sending me your remarkable little book on Poe which I have read with great interest. There is a good deal about the early life of E. A. P. which is quite new to me, and you have woven the poetry into the web of biography very skilfully.

It interests me very much to learn that you are making serious investigations into Poe's early associations with England. I do not know how you will set about the task. After 90 years it is scarcely possible to trace the schoolfellows of a little American boy who had none but purely accidental contact with English life.

What I should be even more glad that you should do would be to investigate the dates of composition of his earliest poems. You deal very justly with the mystifications of the preface of 1831. But what data have we earlier than this? I want to know how old he was when he wrote *Helen, thy beauty is to me*, because, when he composed that, his style was completely formed. He went no further.

Your criticism of *Ulalume* (p. 109) is particularly good. But I am sorry that you print the last stanza as part of the poem. He certainly cancelled it; it spoils the balance and charm of the piece; and, if it is preserved at all, it ought to be relegated to a note.

I am surprised at your praise of *Israfel,* which hardly deserves what you say (or quote) on p. 43. It is not wholly characteristic of Poe, and it has disagreeable technical imperfections. From whom are you quoting?

I should like to know what evidence is forthcoming of the

authorship of the verses called *Gratitude*, which you print on pp. 122, 123. I should require the strongest proof to persuade me that they are Poe's. Not a single quality of his writing is to be found in them, and the awkward grammar, the poverty of language, and also all the feeble conventionality of the thought are as unlike Poe's *bad* poetry as possible. I have too much experience of the vagaries of genius to assert that a copy of verses cannot possibly be by a certain writer, if they are fairly contemporaneous in manner, but if *Gratitude* is Edgar Poe's, it is a very strange thing that it should contain not one single cadence that suggests him. I fancy (and with some confidence) that you will find this is a forgery. Pray let me know.

Again: why do you note *Lenore* on pp. 118–120 as "Copyright, 1911"? Except for some obviously false readings in the final stanza, I find nothing that could be "copyright." The lines have been clumsily transposed, by someone who did not know enough of the manner of Poe to be aware that he could not end on a feeble note like "a pæan of old days," but that it was the essence of his mannerism to end on a full pedal sound, like that crescendo in the three last lines of *Lenore* from "To friends above" down to "the King of Heaven." This is a most characteristic trait of his poetic manner. The next text is a mere dislocation of both sound and sense.

If Poe had written a first draft, ending with "a pæan of old days," he *must* have altered it to the recognised form. This is no matter of conjecture: it is absolutely certain that the text you now give on p. 120 is wrong. Again: what is your authority?

It seems to me very unlikely that E. A. P. kept up any communications with friends at Stoke Newington. Odd little exotic boys of eleven do not "keep up relations" for any length of time.

I believe that all Orion Horne's papers came into the possession of Mr.

H. Buxton Forman, C.B.,
46, Marlborough Hill,
N.W.

who would be as likely as anyone I know to aid you in your investigations.

If anything occurs to me, I will let you know. I should be very glad indeed to help you in your investigations. Unhappily, it has been part of E. A. P.'s congenital want of luck that his successive editors and biographers have been people of no literary insight. What a set they are! But I think you will do better.

Very sincerely yours,

Edmund Gosse.

17, Hanover Terrace,

To Thomas J. Wise. *26.3.14.*

My dear Wise,—

I don't know where Swinburne found this Cossu whom he mentions so frequently in these articles. I find him also mentioned in the letters of that year. His works seem to be entirely forgotten, and if we may judge by the passages Swinburne quotes, he must have been one of the worst writers of French who ever lived. However, *demeurera* (without accents) is the word here.

With regard to a possible series of the best of Borrow's Ballads, I am greatly touched by your kindness. I shall be delighted, if it comes off, to help you with an introduction. But—once for all—there must be no talk of payment. Anything I can do to indicate my personal friendship for you and my admiring sympathy with your work for English literature will still leave me hopelessly in debt to you for the generosities and kindnesses of twenty years. So never another word about "a fee."

The last few days have been truly exciting. I have lived in a turmoil of political mystery! And it is doubtless only the beginning.

Your affectionate friend,

Edmund Gosse.

17, Hanover Terrace,

To Thomas J. Wise. *4.4.14.*

My dear Wise,—

My attention has just been called to the current no. of *The Sphere*, where Mr. Clement Shorter, in terms of unexampled insolence, speaks of me as "the so-called critic," and attacks me on the score of an article which he has not seen.

Will you explain to me why I have suddenly received over my head and shoulders this bucket-full of Mr. Clement Shorter's bedroom-slops? Can it be that he supposes me to be the author of some attack on him?

If so, pray reassure him. I never attack him, for I never mention him.

Yours,

EDMUND GOSSE.

Confidential.

House of Lords.

To Thomas J. Wise. *6.4.14.*

MY DEAR WISE,—

Your advice about the irresponsible little journalist* is excellent. When I wrote to you on Saturday, I was for the moment infuriated by having just had his attack on me pointed out. But such feelings evaporate like salvolatile. I think no more of it—or of him.

What do you think of our sending a copy of *Les Misérables*† to Lord Crewe? It is owing to his kindness that we were able to discover and reprint it, and I think he would very much appreciate it.

I was very greatly interested in what you told me of your last visit to Putney. What do you think now of your asking him, on my behalf, for permission to make such short extracts‡ as are needful to illustrate the text of my Memoir? If he would do this—and I can hardly see that he could refuse—it would marvellously simplify my task.

* Clement Shorter, who attacked Gosse in his *Literary Letter* in *The Sphere.*

† *A Study of Victor Hugo's Les Misérables by A. C. Swinburne. With an Introduction by Edmund Gosse.* Privately printed by T. J. Wise in an edition of thirty copies.

‡ Extracts from the full notes made by Mr. Wise of his talks with Watts-Dunton about Swinburne.

Watts-Dunton and Gosse were very hostile at this period, and Watts-Dunton would not meet him. The situation had a certain piquancy. Watts-Dunton wished to be well spoken of in Gosse's *Life of Swinburne*, while Gosse was anxious to obtain information which only Watts-Dunton possessed. The olive-branch was received with expressions of good-will and harmony, but the proposed meeting never took place.

The enclosed letter is my olive-branch, if you will be my dove. I think that the time has come for a reconciliation with the Old Man on these lines. (But, as ever, I leave it, without reserve, to your judgment, far better equipped than mine in the matter.)

Ever sincerely yours,

EDMUND GOSSE.

Monserrate, Cintra,
Portugal.

To Maarten Maartens. *May 26, 1914.*

MY DEAR M. M.,—

The great pleasure your last amusing letter gave us was much tempered by the bad account of yourself. These accounts, altho' you are very patient, continue, and grieve us by their continuance. We long to see you, and we insist on seeing you in good health.

We left Southampton on Friday last, and had a luxurious voyage to Lisbon. The immense ship was like Britannia, and ruled the waves; we were not in the least inconvenienced. We put in at Vigo and had two hours on shore; reached Lisbon early the next morning, saw Belem, and took an afternoon train to Cintra, whence mules brought us hither at a breakneck trot. It is very amusing to think that you know this miraculous place. The house, although so grotesque in appearance, is comfort itself inside. At first, the profusion of the garden, all lianed with scarlet passion-flowers and dripping with magnolias and roped with roses, a little oppressed us, but we found early this morning that we could escape from its lemon-scented grottoes to a delicate arid forest above, with snake-paths, through the scrub-oak, where the air is quite cold over the crimson wild gladioli and the little gentians and the incomparable rock-cisti, of five luminous varieties. We struggled up the ridge of rocks, like the broken vertebræ of some antediluvian rhinoceros, and gazed down the abrupt grove-lands, to the saffron plain dotted with red and white Portuguese cottages far, far down below us, and on to the Atlantic that was breaking in great white walls of foam infinitely far off. Nellie likes this contrast: you will be glad to hear that she bore the journey very well indeed. We have been talking much of you. Both of us long to be again with you and Ada. What a merry quartet we were, and what a merry quartet we will be again. *Pazienza!* Life lasts much longer than its incommodities, if one only waits for things to come round. I write this looking over the magic garden to the plain northwards, everything twinkling in the last sunlight. What strange things thoughts are! We look towards Holland, and the Pyrenees are insufficient to intercept our thoughts of you both. Our love to you both.

Your affectionate Friend,

EDMUND GOSSE.

Gosse was experiencing a good deal of secret dismay at his severance from the House of Lords—but in no outward degree did he appear less cheerful during this summer. Then with the coming of August 1914 and the effacement of personal matters, the Library for the moment was forgotten, though the thought of it was time and again to return.

17, Hanover Terrace,

To Earl Spencer. *August 3, 1914.*

CHER AMI,—

You have been much in my mind, for I fancied you caught in Contrexéville, and subjected to great inconveniences. I am thankful to think that you are safe. What you say about my retirement is very dear, and like yourself. But I feel that there is a certain appropriateness in my going at this precise hour when the old order changeth so suddenly. One realizes that Europe, that England, that life in all its forms and with all its interests, is never going to be the same again. It is all to be broken up and swept away, and I am an old man and cannot hope to see the new world settled. A few friendships—how precious!—are now what one has to live for.

What days these have been! Yesterday Haldane telephoned for me to come and cheer him up in the interval between the Cabinet meetings. At the door Grey was showing Cambon out—such an aged, and drawn, and flushed Cambon! Grey was perfectly calm, but grave to solemnity, and it was he who told me that the Germans had seized Luxembourg. I found Haldane very depressed, but resolute, and all the finer part of his theoretical intellect exposed. He is at his very best at moments when it is not detail, but a wide and even imaginative grasp of situations that is required. I urged him to lie down and rest, but he refused altogether, saying that to talk was the only rest possible. I stayed an hour and a half. Meanwhile Grey took the motor, and went off to the Zoo, to spend an hour among the birds. Was that not characteristic? At 6 Lichnowsky called, for a few words with Haldane before the Cabinet at 6.30, so I vanished down the back staircase. If the whole thing were not too serious, the behaviour of Lichnowsky would make me smile. He is so absurdly infatuated with England and so unwilling to fight us. So, at least, they all pretend. But H. thinks Germany has been playing a very long game, and has very subtly chosen this moment as the least unfavourable to her scheme of domination. The poor French are in despair at what they take to be our irresolution, but perhaps they will find that we are not so irresolute as they think. Will the Germans manage to break out of haven with their ships? That is the predominant question, and that may at any moment precipitate the ruin of the world. Last night we did not know exactly where the German fleet was. This was causing anxiety. Happily the newspapers seem to ignore the point. Winston (whom I have not seen) is, Haldane says, almost too splendid in eagerness and resource and an ardent half-boyish determination. We may see Winston develop great powers.

About ourselves, we had made all arrangements for going abroad almost at once. Nellie and I were to stay first with some delightful friends in an island off the mouth of the Loire, and then to go south. My daughters talked of Normandy, Paris and Rome. What happiness that we had not started! I smile a grim smile at your supposition that I am *répandu*! Not one single engagement of any sort or kind looms before me. As to your hospitable suggestion for next Saturday, don't you feel that one must make no engagements at this rapidly revolving and detonating hour? One can only sit still, with a cold wind in one's hair, trying not to frighten other people. But a little later, when the war has taken its horrible channel, if we still can move about, shall I come to you for a day or two? I would not disturb you: I would read and write in some corner of your great house, and you should not know of my existence.

If you like to be written to, I will write again and tell you what I see and hear. If I can push my way into the gallery this afternoon, I shall hear Asquith's statement: and we have our own debate at 6. Meanwhile, where are the German ships? I believe that Winston has a shrewd guess. God bless England in this hour of our adversity. Write me a line—just one line.

Yours always,

Edmund Gosse.

17, Hanover Terrace,

To Earl Spencer. *Aug. 22, 1914.*

Cher Ami,—

It is just three weeks since I wrote you. It has been impossible for me to write again—the passage of events (for the waiting for events is an event, and one of the most cruel) has immobilized my mind. One seems to be listening, half in a dream, with one's hand to one's heart, for something loud and sudden, which does not come. How often have my thoughts been with you, in your silent park, in your great beautiful house, among all the pictures of your ancestors. I wonder what you have been feeling. What overpowers me most is the completeness, the inevitably of the change. Suddenly the whole world has taken a *salto mortale*, everything everywhere has changed, new heavens and a new earth, and what a blood-boltered earth, what iron heavens! I have seen very few people, except, almost daily, Haldane. He has been here often, walking with me in our leafy enclosure, sharing our Spartan meals. He has come out very splendidly, with a new and revived sense of intellectual command, totally disinterested, accepting without a murmur the fact that his plans and schemes have been swallowed up and completed, without a complaint of the ingratitude of a vain population. I was able to be of slight use at the psychological moment, in telling him exactly the hour when it was needful that he should have a frank understanding with Kitchener. It was a wonderful chance—I overheard a conversation not intended for my ears. Someday I will tell you how wonderfully it turned out. Kitchener is rather splendid; he moves about like a thundercloud, alarming, reposeful too; he has tremendous shortcomings, but he is the national mascotte, and Haldane is there to mollify his severities and to urge the humanities. Kitchener is perfect with Haldane, and seems to appreciate his worth, the more no doubt because Haldane, with delicate tact, avoids all self-prominence, gives K. all the credit. Edward Grey, at last, shows some signs of physical weariness, is anxious, in conversation, to demontsrate that he acted rightly, troubled most needlessly by the dictates of delicate conscience. He has no need to defend himself, he has made not one mistake. Asquith is not heard of, but he directs the storm. The unity of the Government seems to be above all reproach. I have not seen Lloyd George, but I am told that he is behaving admirably, quite changed in manner, without levity, not anxious for advertisement, but soberly patriotic. The man who has behaved quite disgracefully is ——. Wounded in his senile vanity, he has been chattering like a chimpanzee, and doing his best to encourage the Americans to take the German side. Haldane said to me the other day, "The worst enemy of the Government, almost the only one, is ——." John Burns has thrown himself with ardour into Red Cross work; poor old Morley is not doing anything to embarrass the country, but his nerves gave way. He could not stand the racket of war, the sudden passage of bills, the rapid development of events; he has withdrawn to Putney, a very old, old man in despair. There seems to be no despair elsewhere. Haldane says, and so does Grey, that there will be disasters, horrible carnage, great distress and alarm, but England must come out right in the end. God grant it! To-day, by the War Office's advices, the great battle begins. It is unlucky that France seems to have suffered a serious reverse in Lorraine. Can they, can we, can anyone support the crash and storm of the metallic charge of Germany? I am afraid that the nation has been buoyed into a vain optimism by the supposed "successes" of the Allies in Belgium. These were nothing, mere skirmishes, all has now to begin.

The Germans are at Ostend. Why? They will have the amusement of sending a Zeppelin or two over to Kent to frighten us, but we must not be frightened. They can do nothing definite to us at present. France is the real field of action, and all must depend on France. We have had letters from French friends, and the delightful Jusserand has been over for a day or two on his way to Washington. Our friend M. Edward de Billy, sent over by the French War Office to buy certain implements of war at Birmingham, dined with us one night. They all tell the same tale, of the gravity, the fortitude, the *silence* of France. Will the loathsome tyrants, who trample children to death, and strip and then stab innocent women, be allowed to run a sword through the heart and brain of France? I cannot believe it, and yet—I fear it. The danger of our country, and perhaps its happiness, is ignorance of Germany.

But how I have chattered on! You will have other things to do than to read all this idleness. So good-bye. Write to me. Tell me how you are. I dread lest all this anxiety and tension should impair your health.

Cher ami, bien à toi,

Ton,

EDMUND GOSSE.

Ireland is now the terrible danger in front of us. Up to yesterday no *modus vivendi* had been found. Ulster is most threatening, sullen, provincial, egotistical. Suppose that, after all, Ireland should be the reef upon which the Empire is to founder!

House of Lords,

To Thomas Hardy. *Sept. 11,1914.*

MY DEAR HARDY,—

Your poem touched me more than I can say. It is really the only effusion of the British Muse, worthy of the occasion, which has yet been put forth. Your old novels, too, take on a fresh bloom in the light of this new war, which reproduces so many of the psychological features of the Napoleonic time.

Like you, I have felt incapable of any exercise but poring over newspapers and meditating, now hopefully and now dejectedly, upon the situation. But I rejoice that I was still alive when so great an event rose upon the world—it is like a huge, terrible and beautiful aurora. We must, all of us, be at last the better for it.

I wish we could see you. The little fact you give about the Austrians is weighty. They may yet pull down the Germans by hanging on their necks.

Our kindest remembrances to Mrs. Hardy.

Yours ever sincerely,

Edmund Gosse.

House of Lords,

To Viscount Haldane. *Sept. 15, '14.*

My dear H. of C.,—

I never heard you make a more beautiful speech. It made my heart beat and filled my eyes with tears. It ought to be printed as a leaflet and circulated in thousands. But nothing would reproduce the grace and persuasion of the utterance. I feel very proud of you.

Yrs.,

E. G.

17, Hanover Terrace,

To Earl Spencer. *23.11.14.*

Cher Ami,—

I have been very unwell—I got a severe gastric chill at the beginning of this cold weather—or I should have acknowledged sooner your most kind and rather sad little letter. Haldane tells me—but it is done to smooth down my sorrowing feathers—that he thinks I am lucky to be out of the House of Lords, which he says has become a most doleful place. However, as you know, I loved it, although my love ever seemed to you absurd, as though one should love a mangy old poodle or a decayed charwoman. Only there are cases in which, irrational as it is, the charwoman and the poodle get loved, and so I loved the House of Lords. When it drove me forth without a word of regret, I felt hurt, and I still feel hurt. I deserved better treatment from the mangy old poodle. But there it is.

I hope your boy is progressing well. You do not say, so I hope the best. My son is in the Army now, very active and happy. His mother and I are completely pleased, and if we had ten sons, we would give them all. Perhaps it is easier to give ten than the one? I don't know! Do look at a letter I print in the *Times* to-day, from our friend Mme. Bulteau. The spirit of it seems to me adorable.

Cher et fidèle ami, farewell. Write to me again. Your letters give me such immense pleasure.

EDMUND GOSSE.

CHAPTER TWENTY-FIVE

In 1915 Gosse was elected to the Marlborough Club. The election of an eminent man of letters as a member was something of a novelty. The experiment was justified. Gosse became a regular user of the amenities of the Club, lunching there every Monday and frequently giving eclectic dinner-parties. He was thoroughly content at occupying so exceptional a position, devoid as it was of all trace of professional rivalry; indeed, it may be said to have softened the breach with the House of Lords, providing him with a *pied-à-terre* in Pall Mall whence he could conveniently date his correspondence, and bringing him into contact with a society in which he could meet old friends and establish new social relations while indulging his predilection for the gossip of Mayfair—about which he was always immensely interested and seldom correctly informed.

His identity as a man of letters was not at first universally recognised, and more than once led to some embarrassment. Soon after his election, when mounting the stairs with a guest to an early luncheon, he was hailed by a well-meaning fellow-member who associated him vaguely with books, with the greeting, "Well, Gosse, off to the meeting of the Booksellers' Union, I suppose." Gosse, rather out of countenance, testily answered, "No, certainly not," while pursuing his way to the dining-room. Again, when he had already been some time a member, his son Dr. Philip Gosse published a highly successful volume, *The Pirate's Who's Who*. A distinguished naval officer meeting Gosse in the Club said, "Hullo, Gosse, I've just read a capital book of yours about Pirates. I'd no idea you were a writer." Here the compliment to his son from so eminent an authority completely outweighed the reflection on his own comparative obscurity. He was amused and pleased. In later years, when he was compelled to wear a patch over one eye, it was said of him, as he sat in his favourite corner, that he had the appearance of a retired and somewhat delicate pirate himself; this was especially the case when from the unencumbered eye was shot a glint of disapproval at some too jaunty member of the Club indulging in remarks which were uncongenial to him. He was essentially "a clubable man"; he delighted in the to-and-fro of varying personalities, with whom he could exercise his friendliness; his wit was always ready to hand; and he had an extraordinary faculty of giving life to sedate and passing occasions by his humour. He enjoyed getting into another atmosphere away from literature, and building up a niche of his own with a distinctive prestige; and there is no question that the Club added very greatly to his pleasure in London life. In the same way his election to Grillion's to which for some years he acted as Secretary with Sir George Murray brought him an incalculable amount of entertainment. He would genuinely look forward to the Wednesday dinners, and nothing but illness would stand between him and the occasion. Here with Archbishops and soldiers, Prime Ministers and men of letters, lawyers and philosophers, he was at his best, shedding a dancing lustre over conversation conducted on a level worthy of his best wit. Totally without embarrassment, a warmth of friendliness in his attitude, and beaming through his spectacles on the company, he would unobtrusively exercise a dominating influence. The *mot juste* would fall like a shaft of light to show a new channel for a discussion growing turbid, or a witty parallel would be forthcoming to vary and illuminate a topic. He was the sworn enemy of *longueurs* in conversation, and with a dexterity which was consummate and a skill that was devoid of offence he would manage to unseat the most prolix and yet leave him satisfied with his contribution.

He talked to enjoy and never to show off. His spontaneity and alacrity of mind had the power of fusing his company into a concord of gaiety. And it is a mistake to suppose he was acid or malicious without being provoked. He could pink an adversary as neatly as the most accomplished duellist and find pleasure in the act, but this was only when a real or fancied attack had caused him to draw a sword. No one could on occasion take a carping reference to himself more good-humouredly.

When Arthur Benson sent him a recent volume of his diary, "as it had already amused Lady Ponsonby and Henry James," Gosse eagerly reading it came on an account of a visit to Hanover Terrace in the following words.

"Breakfast with Gosse. I dislike people who are bright at breakfast."

"Dinner with Gosse—champagne; and yet he complains of poverty."

These entries after the first shock gave Gosse unalloyed pleasure.

In another sphere, as Trustee of the National Portrait Gallery, the same gifts were brought to the service of the Board—and there was seldom a discussion in which either his knowledge or his personal reminiscence did not contribute to the conclusion which was reached.

17, Hanover Terrace,

To Compton Mackenzie,— *Jan. 5, 1915.*

My dear Compton Mackenzie,—

If I put off much longer the pleasant duty of thanking you for your letter, you will think me churlish. For that letter was one of the most agreeable that I ever received, and I should be ungrateful indeed if I did not let you know how much I value it. But I was anxious so far to reciprocate your generosity as to discuss with you your own latest work. In doing that, I have been confronted with many delays. It was some time before my bookseller sent me the second *Sinister Street*, and then I was delayed again by the *Edinburgh Review* wanting an article in sharp time for its January number. Finally and not least, the book itself is one of the most voluminous that I know in the history of fiction. Are you aware that *S. S.* contains a great many more words than *Tom Jones*, and is more than twice as long as *Humphry Clinker*? Nor is it a book that can be read quickly. It demands careful study of every page, and from me it has had that.

But first I must thank you for your Poems. I value the book, and shall bind it and preserve it among the poets. Yet you will let me be quite frank. Your verses are highly accomplished and full of delicate grace, but they are lacking in temperament. There

I miss a vocation. These are Guy Hazlewood's poems, written at Plasher's Mead, because he was determined to write poetry. It is quite different with *Sinister Street*, because you have the temperament of prose. You are a most interesting and advancing prose-writer—far and away the best of your generation. Therefore, it is worth while to apply the most powerful lens to your performance. Certainly, you have written hitherto nothing so good as this second volume of *Sinister Street*. Your verbal felicities are more numerous and more sparkling than ever. Don't let them be too deliberate. You are so precise that you should be always exact. Sometimes you miss the right word. I notice rather prominently "serge" when the proper word would be "rep." One observes these little things because the phrase is so violently illuminated. In a shoddy writer one notices nothing, for the general atmosphere is fog. You blaze almost too unintermittently.

Still I notice what I ventured to suggest to you before, a sacrifice of structure to ornament. You hardly give yourself time to build a sentence, you puff out little flotillas of brilliant phrases. I wish I could induce you to submit to the charm of the periodic manner, not to be constantly used, but trotted out for purposes of reflection and the building of an argument. Just do me the honour of regarding pp. 742, 743, from "Nevertheless." This is a very good passage, interesting and original; but in its texture, is it not a little staccato? Read it aloud, and tell me, hand on heart, if the succession of tiny sentences does not get upon your nerves? It wants to be fused into greatness.

The Oxford part, from a more general point of view, is delightful. Far and away the best account of University life that ever was written. Though I had the ignominy—as Michael and his friends would think it—of being Cambridge, I was deeply moved.

Now what shall I say to you about "Book Four"? I should like to discuss it with you orally for hours. The separate pictures in it are incomparable. I put the fight on the stairs at Neptune Terrace quite at the top. It is really worthy of comparison with the very first descriptive things in literature. Everywhere there is abounding vision, the sharp hard light thrown on colour and form. A little *too* hard, sometimes? I don't know, but I might read you a sermon on "Rudyard Kipling: or, the Shocking Results of an Early Intemperance in Style." But in your case, only just a little *hard* sometimes. What puzzles me most, however, in this Fourth Book is the return to the picaresque manner. There had not been a picaresque romance in English for generations. Here we are again, Gil Blas in full blast! You use Fane and his not very interesting physical infatuation to introduce us to scene after scene into which without his fatuous intervention we could never penetrate. Quite right, but frankly picaresque; and please hesitate before you do it again. I have a million more things I want to say. Do write and tell me that you are not offended with my frankness—yourself and your work interest me so deeply that I must be sincere with you.

Ever truly yrs.,

EDMUND GOSSE.

17, Hanover Terrace,

To Miss Haldane. *14.1.15.*

MY DEAR MISS HALDANE,—

I delayed to answer your extremely kind and welcome letter till I had seen our Great Man again, which I did last night, when he dined with us here. I think he is very cheerful and placid now, in much better spirits since the recent *éclaircissements*. I am very glad indeed to have your approval of what has been done. So long as no notice was taken, the libels simply grew and grew, and the libellers considered it safe to prolong and exaggerate their charges. The disgraceful tone of the *National Review*, *Blackwood's* and the *Daily Express*—in which I cannot help seeing something gravely like a conspiracy—made me feel that some counter-action must be taken. The L. C.'s best defender has been himself in his really stirring and noble speech last Friday in the H. of Lords. This moved even Unionist opinion very favourably, but there are some enemies who are implacable, and who do not shrink from subterranean methods.

I was very angry indeed with the L. C. for putting his resignation in Asquith's hands ten days ago, when the attacks were at their worst. (If you did not know this, please do not mention it to him.) I have made him give me a promise that he will not do this again, under any circumstances, without discussing it. It is absolutely out of the question that he should play in this mode into the hands of his enemies, who would insist that they had scored a victory.

Very sincerely yrs.,
EDMUND GOSSE.

The following letter refers to a volume of typewritten copies of letters from Burne-Jones, with notes of his conversation.

17, Hanover Terrace,
To Lady Horner. *Feb. 12, 1915.*

DEAR LADY HORNER,—

This Book of Beauty I have kept too long. But you do not know what a temptation it has been to keep it longer. I found I had got into the habit of constantly dipping into it to remind myself of some lovely saying or fragment. So this morning I took myself very roughly by the shoulders (it is so difficult to do) and shook myself and said quite loud to myself, "This is not your Book, it is Lady Horner's book, and if you keep it much longer you will be Run In, and your family will be spat upon and your children be branded as the children of a Thief." So I have hurried (or am hurrying) it into an envelope, that I may be out of temptation, and I am going this very blessed morning to leave it at your door.

I cannot, really, thank you enough for your great kindness in lending it to me.

Some day I must tell you of my success in attracting E. B. J.'s* attention on the earliest occasion on which I met him. It is very pleasing.

Yours very sincerely,
EDMUND GOSSE.

17, Hanover Terrace,
To Thomas J. Wise, *20.2.15.*

MY DEAR WISE,—

I am very glad you were quite frank about the Marston incident, and I trust to your always being so. I am grateful to you.

* Sir E. Burne-Jones.

The story, which I am glad to know, is pure invention. I was very slightly acquainted with P. B. Marston, and I was not at any time a great admirer of his poems. I cannot recall that I ever discussed them with Swinburne, and I *never* reviewed a volume of them. The only work of Marston's which could be referred to is *All in All*, which was published in 1875. A glance at Swinburne's letters to me will show that so far from Swinburne's having "dropped" me, he was never more intimate and affectionate than he was during this and the next four or five years.

I think my memory is correct when I say that I have never mentioned the name of P. B. Marston in print. I was very sorry for his affliction, and I once paid him a visit, when he was very gentle and kind. To tell you the truth he was not very sympathetic to me, and if I had praised him with fervour, I should have felt that I was insincere. But his forlorn and afflicted state, and the patience with which he bore it, would have made it absolutely impossible to "run down the book and its author."

You were not at all indiscreet to tell me of this calumny. That Swinburne was successfully prejudiced against me after he went to Putney, I knew of course. But I should be grieved that you should think me guilty of mean and cruel treachery to a poor blind man.

Yours most sincerely,

EDMUND GOSSE.

17, Hanover Terrace,

To John Drinkwater. *24.4.15.*

MY DEAR DRINKWATER,—

No doubt you have received the dreadful news, which has just been telegraphed from Turkey, that our beloved and admired Rupert* died yesterday in the French hospital-ship. I know how much you will feel this blow, which falls not only upon us who loved him, but upon English literature. He was our Marcellus—and I see no one, all round, from whom more could have been reasonably expected than from him. I am very much agitated to-day, because

* Rupert Brooke.

I dreamed about him over and over again last night (of course because of yesterday's bad news). He appeared to me in his usual guise, but with an expression insufferably sad. He seemed in an agony to say something, but no sound whatever came from him, and I woke—not once, but twice—in the agony of trying vainly to help him to speak. I rarely dream, and the vividness of this vision has quite unmanned me. Let me turn to other things.

We very much enjoyed your visit, which I hope was not a disappointment to you. At last, indeed, with Lord Haldane's remarkable speech, it became, I think, memorable. I was feeling so ill, that I am afraid I was poor company for you. I send you the little book you asked to see: I shall be very happy if you will read it carefully, if you read it at all. It appeals to older readers: it is possible that you are too young to care about it: but perhaps you will.

Yours very sincerely,

EDMUND GOSSE.

Excuse rather an old edition: there have been six or seven since this, each with some little change, but I have no copy later than this, and they are all essentially the same.

17, Hanover Terrace,

To John Drinkwater. *May 1, 1915.*

MY DEAR DRINKWATER,—

The Swords and Ploughshares have clattered in at last, and have had a very warm welcome. I have just finished reading the book right through—of course there are a good many pieces I knew already. I think this is the best book of lyrics you have written—you have now got a definite personal manner, a firm stride. "Of Greatham"—very beautiful. "The Poet to the Heroes"—delicate and affecting to a high degree. I think you want to study the value of *words* a little more: am I forgiven for saying so? Sometimes you are content with the second-best, or even the third-best. But poetry lives on the best, and nothing less. And some words you use (and all the other young poets too) as mere counters. For instance, if I had my way none of you should be allowed to use "gold" again for ten years: it has ceased to have a meaning.

Yours most truly,
EDMUND GOSSE.

17, *Hanover Terrace,*
To André Gide. *May 30, '15.*

MY DEAR GIDE,—

Miss Stephens has sent me your graceful and touching article, *Les Réfugiés,* which I have enjoyed putting into my best colloquial English and sending back to her. How delightful it is, dear and noble friend, for me to be allowed to collaborate with you in your admirable piety! My thoughts go out to you often and often. When shall we meet again? Surely this horror will some day, or some year, be overpast?

Every English heart goes out in warmest union of heart with you in France. But how terrible it is! We have lost, and are daily losing, our most gallant and splendid young men, the very brain and nerve of England, dying on the fields of Flanders.

God bless you and keep you. Mrs. Gosse sends her warmest regards to you and to Madame Gide.

Yours affectionately,
EDMUND GOSSE.

Do you know that the Marcellus of our age, the most promising of all the young English poets, has fallen in the Dardanelles? This was Rupert Brooke, who lies buried in Tenedos.*

EDMUND GOSSE.

17, *Hanover Terrace,*
To Henry James. *25.6.15.*

MY DEAR JAMES,—

I read your letter† with the liveliest emotion. It is splendid of you, and beautifully like yourself, to make this sacrifice for us.

* Rupert Brooke's grave is in Scyros.

† Announcing his intention to be naturalised.

You give us the most intimate thing you possess. It is most moving, and most cheering, a *grand geste* indeed.

Now as regards Asquith, I am as sure as I can be about anything, that he will rejoice to be your sponsor. I cannot conceive an objection, and I can think of no occasion on which he would more certainly desire to express his own natal citizenship. Don't hesitate to ask him.

How I rejoice to think of you as about to be *of* us in this anxious time, as you have been *with* us without fail ever since the trouble began! I think it even an augury of good news which, Heaven knows! we have waited long for, and I suppose must wait long yet.

I shall keep your secret religiously, even though it is possible that I shall see Asquith to-morrow evening. But you must produce to him your own delightful tale.

Always most sincerely
and "patriotically"
Yours,
EDMUND GOSSE.

R. Y. S. Castle,
Cowes.

To Thomas J. Wise. *7.8.15.*

MY DEAR WISE,—

Lord Redesdale went over and saw Mrs. Leith* on Thursday, but we are not going there to-day. She is not willing yet to see me. But she advances in friendliness and all will be well. She told Lord Redesdale that Watts-Dunton had assured her that I was "such a very dreadful character," that she could have nothing to do with me, but that she had discovered, before he died, that all he told her was "a tissue of lies." She does not wish to hear Watts-Dunton's name mentioned.

Lord Redesdale says that she is the most charming old lady possible. She is just 80, but bathes every morning (*swims,* like Algernon!) in the sea, and gallops over the country on horseback.

* Swinburne's sister.

Mrs. Leith explained to Lord R. clearly that her objections to me were founded, now, on three points:

1. The attribution of the *Fraser's* verses to Algernon.
2. The "caricature" of his appearance.
3. The exposure of his habitual drunkenness.

But 1 has been removed, 2 has been modified, and 3 is a matter about which she and I can come to a complete understanding in five minutes.

Ever sincerely yours,
EDMUND GOSSE.

17, Hanover Terrace,
To Thomas J. Wise. *20.8.15.*

MY DEAR WISE,—

There is much to tell you. Mrs. Leith consented to read my first chapter, and wrote to Lord Redesdale her comments. She corrected some family points, added practically nothing, and found most fault with statements made by A. C. S. himself, who indeed was a sad romancer. Lord Redesdale very clearly told her that if she read the chapter, and corrected it, I should express my debt to her, and that afterwards she must not repudiate it. (This was with reference to Isabel's having denied that she helped me.) Mrs. Leith acquiesced in this.

She remains, however, very disagreeable. She will not mention me by name, even to Lord R., and her comments, which covered five or six pages, do not contain a single word of approval or civility. As you point out, this does not really matter, but it is painful to me, for I like to live at peace with all men, and I know of no sort of reason why these old ladies should be so fierce.

However, having got back my MS. from Lord R. (Mrs. Leith refused to communicate directly with me) I made all the corrections she desired, and I took the whole book yesterday to the Macmillans. After a long conversation with Sir Frederick Macmillan, it is decided that the book shall originally appear in a demy octavo library form, and not be put into the English Men of Letters series till later. I think this a very great improvement, because people cannot get into their heads that a book in a series is a work of original importance.

We talked much over the scheme of your and my ultimate publications, and Sir F. M. is evidently inclined to make us an offer. But for the period of the war, nothing can be done. My *Life* is to be *printed* at once, but not to be published till after the peace. This may delay it till I am dead, but you will continue my work. We have, I think, snatched the memory of Swinburne out of the paws of the Philistines, and I do not think that now things can go very wrong. I wrote my Preface yesterday morning, and when I came to mention your share in the undertaking, I felt how cold and poor any acknowledgment is of your extreme goodness. But the way to look at it is that we are really *one* in this interest. There never was a collaboration more complete, and if I do not live to see it finished, it will be a great consolation to me to know that it will go on in your hands.

Ever sincerely yours,

Edmund Gosse.

Mrs. Disney Leith told Lord Redesdale that when Isabel is stronger, the two intend to combine in writing a book about Algernon's early life!

17, Hanover Terrace,

To Earl Spencer. *28.9.15.*

Cher Ami,—

It was very good to get news of you again. We only came back from Scotland on Saturday last. Our month was highly rewarding. We started by a visit to old Lady Airlie at Airlie, then we went to the Lyells at Kinnordy and to the Strathmores at Glamis, and then we went to Dunkeld, where the Dunedins and Lady Tullibardine were most hospitable. We were in the hotel at Birnam. Then we finished up with a few days with the Haldanes at Cloan. It was quite a new experience for us, who always go off alone to distant places on the Continent. We had never paid a round of country visits before, but it was extremely pleasant, and everybody so marvellously kind.

To get back to London is to get back to the tension and grief of the War. We have brief letters frequently from my son, but he has been silent the last few days, doubtless because his hands are full with the wounded. He is, or was, five miles west of Armentières, in the trenches, whither he had brought up his ambulance. It seems to be all splendidly organised now, and this coming winter should be less painful than the last.

I have seen few people since I came back. The Speaker, who is less anxious about his wounded son, now in hospital at Calais, but still doleful about the War. I had a long talk with Lord George Hamilton last night, who has a good deal of information. He told me that two of our Generals were killed in Saturday's battle—Capper and another. How little information the War Office gives us! I dread the casualty lists so much.

You will be astonished to hear that I am going to France at the beginning of November. A fortnight ago I received a wholly unexpected invitation from M. Delcassé, through the Embassy, to go to France as the guest of the French Government and describe the state of things behind the front. I telegraphed back I must refuse so great an honour on account of my health. But Delcassé would not take my refusal, and an emissary of his—a very interesting M. Leyret, who was Waldeck-Rousseau's private secretary—called here on Monday and would not go until I consented. I cannot see the utility of it to them, and I told him so. They declare they want a statement from me, "sentimental and intellectual"! I feel dreadfully unfitted for the task, and ready to weep with apprehension, but I could not continue to refuse. It is a tremendous compliment, but like being slain with gold pieces. What do you think?

Sir George Murray, whom I have just seen, thinks our financial position very bad in comparison with that of the Germans! I see the *Economist* (a paper to me much suspect!) thinks so too. These financiers are too subtle, I hope.

I spare you more, though I could chatter on to you for sheets.

Always sincerely yrs.,

EDMUND GOSSE.

To Our Dead.

The flame of summer droops and fades and closes,
  While autumn thins the embers of the copse,
And ever more the violent life of roses
  Grows keener as the roseate foliage drops;
O strong young hearts within whose veins was leaping
  Love like a fount, hate like a dart shot high,
My heart o'er yours, its dolorous vigil keeping,
  Is pierced with sorrow, while in joy you die!

Your ashes o'er the flats of France are scattered,
  But hold a fire more hot than flesh of ours;
The stainless flag that flutters, frayed and tattered,
  Shall wave and wave, like spring's immortal flowers.
You die, but in your death life glows intenser;
  You shall not know the shame of growing old;
In endless joy you swing the holy censer,
  And blow the trumpet tho' your lips are cold.

Life was to us a mist of intimations;
  Death is a flash that shows us where we trod;
You, falling nobly for the righteous nations,
  Reveal the unknown, the unhoped-for face of God.
After long toil, your labours shall not perish;
  Through grateful generations yet to come
Your ardent gesture, dying, Love shall cherish,
  And like a beacon you shall guide us home.

Edmund Gosse.

CHAPTER TWENTY-SIX

The reference to Caruso in the letter which follows requires explanation. The reflection made is not on the famous singer but on the moral qualities of a cat who bore his name. Every visitor to Hanover Terrace will remember Caruso; he figured at meals on a chair beside Gosse, and was always to be found in his vicinity when he was reading or at work in his library. Like Bayle's friend, Mlle. Dupuy, who attributed her skill in playing the harp to "the critical taste" of her favourite cat, Gosse seemed to draw some opiate quality for his nerves from the very proximity of Caruso, and his predecessors and successors. The serenity and majestic indifference, the padded paws and noiseless step, the green eyes set in jet black fur with their grave regard, seemed to communicate calm and subdue agitation. Even Gosse's conversation would assume a more intimate and serene quality if it was accompanied by the purring of Caruso or, in later years, of his successor Buchanan. In his essay on cats Gosse, quoting Paradis de Moncrif, relates the story of "Mahomet who, being consulted one day on a point of piety, preferred to cut off his sleeve on which his favourite pussy was asleep, rather than wake her violently by rising." Modern sartorial conditions would frustrate any such operation, but it was a gesture with which Gosse would have sympathised. He would deprecate interruptions which involved readjustments in his cat's scheme of inertia. In his household there was none of the outrageous tyranny exercised by favourite dogs, but the rights of a constitutional sovereignty were assigned to the cat, and his sway accepted within legitimate limits. Occasionally there was protest, as is evident from a letter written in 1915 to John Drinkwater, who was ill at the time and who owned a cat named Punch. "I hope you will take the greatest possible care of yourself, and obey Dr. Punch, whose expressed view I know to be that you should stay in bed and make warm corners in the coverlid for him to fold his paws into. There I envy you, for instead of seeing that pansy face smile and purr up at me, I have to endure the fierce contempt and sneering malice of Caruso, without any question the most ungenerous cat in Christendom. There is no doubt that he is a German at heart, and he rules us on the system of 'frightfulness.' There is a theory that the atrocious soul of Nietzsche has entered into him." But Caruso was only one in a line of succession, which was never suffered to lapse or to know a vacant throne. Théophile Gautier divided his affection between cats and the singular choice of white rats; Gosse favoured no other species of domestic animal, but like Chateaubriand and Victor Hugo, like Baudelaire and Sainte-Beuve, gave his undivided preference to cats.

Marlborough Club,

To Siegfried Sassoon. *20.3.16.*

My dear Siegfried,—

I was very glad to get your jolly letter and the poems. I sent Hamo the one addressed to him, and I have given the rest to Eddie Marsh. I suppose you know that three of your things are coming out in the *Westminster*. I am much struck by the increased firmness of handling and the sincerity of your work. I hope you will not overdo the irregularity of versification. Now and then a prosodical irregularity may be a beauty, but the ear hates to be caught up by an incessant jolt. The laws of verse which were good enough for Keats and Wordsworth are good enough for you. I fancy Bridges, with his arrogant disregard of the tunable instinct in the human ear, is responsible for a good deal. I am very glad that there is some prospect of your collecting your things in a volume. I very much approve of that. You are in the best of hands while Eddie looks after your interests, and he and I often discuss you.

If you find time, I hope you will write to me often. Your letters give me the greatest pleasure. Take care of yourself—how tedious this immense octopus of a war is! It seems impossible to see a vista opening (or shutting) in any direction. Two excruciating old gentlemen are talking at the top of their voices and they say, "I hope we shall give these damned Germans such a thrashing that the infernal scoundrels will be ashamed of themselves!" It seems a lame conclusion. I have long outlived any wish that anybody should receive any moral impression. The Germans are like Caruso, impervious to moral impression: or like a chimney-pot that falls in a high wind upon a baby's perambulator. Well, good-bye. My ladies all join me (I mean they would join me) in sending you their love. And I am ever most truly yours,

EDMUND GOSSE.

Max Beerbohm had started a game which he played with Gosse, by the terms of which a sonnet was sent to and fro by post till each writer had contributed his quota of alternate lines. A reproduction of the sonnet referred to in the following letter appears opposite.

Rigg's Crown Hotel,
Bowness-on-Windermere.

To Max Beerbohm. *30.6.16.*

MY DEAR MAX,—

You are a perfect Pelican in the Wilderness. Your letter has cheered and delighted me beyond measure. You have the art of giving satisfaction. Your finger, with a fairy touch, lays boric ointment on the sores of life. (Beautifully said, I think, *Hein?*)

As to our sonnet, I can no longer recapture my own share in it. Our two mighty brains melted into one over it, like the vast clouds on the brow of Helvellyn. (I like to be local.) By all means communicate to Mr. Hunter and the World this great sonnet; in which the twin strands of our geniuses are so inextricably woven. Let there be no concealment. In this sonnet we stand forth to Posterity as the Great Siamese Twins of Sentiment, "with careless ostentation shouldering" one another, as Wordsworth so beautifully said. (Wordsworth is like the Book of Common Prayer, there is something in him for everybody.)

We are enjoying our visit—our *first* visit—to the Lakes very much, though tormented with an excessive vicissitude in weather, icy cold and burning hot, dazzling light and sheets of rain. I have been unable to take any exercise, for I fell down a hole in Hawshead Church (Wordsworth again!) and inflicted a horrid wound on my leg. But this is a very jolly hostel to stay in, although there is a certain pardonable exaggeration in Wordsworth's description of it:

> "It is a splendid place, the door beset
> With chaises, grooms and liveries, and within
> Decanters, glasses and the blood-red wine."
> (*The Prelude*, Bk. II, ll. 142–144.)

We are just starting on a very long excursion to visit the poet Gordon Bottomley at Silverdale, but, as Wordsworth says:

> "Now that we're dressed and all ready to go,
> Oh! see, dear Mamma, how it rains!"

We expect to stay here, unless rained upon beyond all endurance, till the end of next week.

I meant to do a great deal of reading and writing here, but not much has come of it. One has got into the habit of talking so much, that the severer inlets of knowledge are clogged. I was struck the other day by an expression of some Frenchman that Mme. de Staël remained *une ignorante* owing to her wasting so much of her time *en des conversations*. But, on the other hand, how about Johnson? At all events, I cannot read stodgy books steadily as I used to do.

"Just God of Christianized humanity," how one does waste one's time!

Thus I go on prattling to you, my Max, in the evident aura of senility.

There is very little evidence of war here, except the curious absence of young men, which gradually forces itself upon the most languid observation. But the throng of wind-reddened and white-skirted females is immense and garrulous, motor-cars whizz in all directions, food is heaped on every table, and there is a total and very unaccountable absence of khaki. We have motored over 200 miles, threading this district hither and thither, and have scarcely seen one soldier!

"St. George of England! keep a watchful eye
On conscienceless objectors!"

as a poet says to whom I hesitate to refer again.

This is a most silly letter to send you in return for "those breathing tokens of your kind regard," the sheets of your enchanting letter. Take it, take it, "Angelic Boy," (W. W.) as the tribute of an aged Friend, who is determined to die an Englishman.

"Roll on, ye spouting Whales, who die or keep
Your independence in the fathomless Deep:"
(*Wordsworth.*)

Give our affectionate regards to dear Mrs. Max. I began a sonnet in the local manner, addressed to her, beginning

"Lady, a Pen ——"

but I could not get any further. Let her accept this single leaf in lieu of a laurel garland.

Take great care of your own precious self—

"So haply shall thy days
Be many, and a blessing to thyself."

(in the beautiful words of—oh! I simply can't write that fatidic name again).

The Pilgrim of Winandermere,
EDMUND GOSSE.

Rigg's Crown Hotel,
Bowness-on-Windermere.

To John Drinkwater. *1.7.16.*

MY DEAR JOHN,—

I got your kind card and the gracious Ludlow sonnet a few days ago, but I waited to acknowledge them till we had been to visit Gordon Bottomley, which we did yesterday.

He lives very remotely, out of sight of a house, in a kind of labyrinth of overgrown foliage, barbed wired with huge wild-rose bushes, like a sleeping Beauty. When you arrive at the very summit of the maze, a neat and ingenious little house, as smart as a new pin, is suddenly discovered, and the Bearded Bard with his charming little wife—all great antelope eyes and snow-white hair—are smiling at you from the porch.

I have only very lately come to know Bottomley, but he attracts me greatly. His wonderful courage in the face of so mysterious and crushing a malady, his wistful cheeriness, his intense and unfeigned love of letters, are most winning. He is unlike any other human being I have ever known, and I think he is of the type of the Lakists of a hundred years ago. Just thus could I imagine a brother of Coleridge or a cousin of De Quincey living.

We (my Wife and I) have been here for nearly a fortnight. It is our first experience of the Lakes, which have pleased us immensely. I was quite prepared for Wordsworth's exaggerations, and on the whole I think he kept more within bounds than I expected. We were charmed with Ullswater, deeply moved by Derwentwater, excited by Coniston, and stirred to faint and not unkindly derision by Rydal Water. I believe you know all these and the other lakes?

G. B. spoke of you with great affection. He has a golden heart, simple, large and loving. Nellie sends most affectionate messages to both of you.

We are here till Thursday next.

Ever your friend,

EDMUND GOSSE.

I have more and more serious bulletins of Lord Redesdale. I fear his life is ebbing out.

E. G.

Wynyard Park,
Stockton-on-Tees,

To Lady Newton. *18.8.16.*

MY DEAR FRIEND,—

I have just received a telegram to say that Lord Redesdale died quite peacefully last night. It makes a great difference to me. Although I only met him eleven years ago, our friendship had become a very close one. No one ever had a kinder or more loyal or more gallant friend. His sympathy was incessant, his interests as wide and keen and rapid as those of a man of five-and-twenty. We lived in an incessant intellectual interchange, and I don't know how I shall fill the void he leaves. In fact, of course, I never shall fill it. He has had a very distressing illness of thirteen weeks, during which his mental power and his longing for life have never flagged, and I got his last brief and almost illegible letter only a few days ago. He took to his bed the day after my lecture, at which he so graciously presided, and has not left it.

I stay here till Monday. It is melancholy to see this great and familiar house shrunken to a few rooms, and inhabited solely by the splendid being we have always seen surrounded by a court of admirers. She strains my heart with pity, for she has no notion of beginning Chapter II now Chapter I has closed upon her.

I am afraid to write, even to you, so conscious am I of my being, as I say, such poor company. But the more we lose, the more precious seems what remains. Your kind friendship is one of my treasures. I am afraid I am rather incoherent. But I am ever your affectionate Friend,

EDMUND GOSSE.

17, Hanover Terrace,

To André Gide. *Sept. 16, 1916.*

MY DEAR GIDE,—

I am coming to Paris, next Tuesday (the 19th). I have been invited by M. Briand as the guest of the French Government. Of course I have accepted, but with great apprehension for I am getting old (I shall be sixty-seven next week), and I am not in good health. However, I must obey. M. Briand's invitation was the most flattering that anyone could receive. I am to be taken to Reims. If only I shall be inspired to write something ever so infinitesimally useful to France—my adored and adorable France!

Every day I pray that I may live to see the final and glorious victory of France. How slow history is, and how rapidly life ebbs away!

I suppose I shall not see you, alas! I have written for René Doumic's *Revue des Deux Mondes* an article on the literary entente. Very stupid—and I don't like my own style in a different language. But—I had to accede to Doumic's wish. I took pleasure in hauling in *your* name, my dear! *à propos de bottes!*

Ghéon's poems were sent to me by the publishers. I read them with great emotion, and wrote him at once a long letter. Ask him whether he received it: I should like a post-card from him.

Our son, after nearly 14 months at the front, is still unwounded: but we live in the constant anguish of anxiety.

In Paris, I believe I am to be put up by the Government at the Hôtel Crillon.

Ever your affectionate Friend,

EDMUND GOSSE.

My Wife joins me in all best messages.

Gosse's letters during the War are the utterances of a highly sensitive nature responding to every change and fluctuation of fortune. Posterity, we may be sure, will be curious about the attitude of those who lived through the Great War as civilians in England. In an essay, *War and Literature*, Gosse attempted to reconstruct the relation of the war of 1870 to the intellectual life of France. He could find in the course of his researches no single memoir which dealt expressly with "the disturbance in literature and the fine arts." A hundred years hence, unless Providence shall in the meanwhile have interposed another and greater cataclysm, the question will arise as it arises to-day in connection with the Napoleonic wars, What was the outlook, what the mental commitment of the onlooker? Did he pursue his ordinary avocations or were his energies deflected into stagnation or alternative activities? And the man of letters—did he sink into silence and apathy, or did he flower into new forms of literary productivity? To these questions Gosse's correspondence supplies a notable answer. He was not like the "elderly authors" in the Franco-Prussian war, "struck dumb with consternation." He did not like Guizot take to his bed, nor "fall into a sort of stupor" like Dumas *père*, nor like Jules Janin retire with his pet parrot to a cottage in the country to come forth no more. On the contrary he was stimulated by the notion that "he also is a patriot who dedicates his imagination to the glory of his country"; he was determined that so far at any rate as he was concerned literature should suffer no eclipse. On the other hand, in his letters he is revealed as mercurial in temper—doubting all things, believing all things—one day in the abyss, the next floating gaily on the crest—credulous of every report, and agitated by every gossip; gleaning rumour in the market-place, and hearsay in the club: profoundly bewildered and at times groping like a blind man for his familiar landmarks. In October 1914 he wrote in despair of the effect which he anticipated the War would have on literature: in April 1915 he wrote exulting at the falsification of his prophecy: literature had pursued her way, literary ambition had not been disturbed. The Pamphlet had taken a new lease of life, there had been a whirlwind of verse, there had merely been a "winnowing away of those interests which have never been very firmly rooted in our habits"—and then in a lighter vein he continued: "*The Journal of Egyptian Archæology* continues to enlighten us, although bombs may any morning be dropped on Beersheba: Mr. Russell calmly goes on distinguishing Sensation from Imagination in the pages of the *Monist* . . . While gentlemen of the highest erudition continue to discuss *Newton's Hypotheses of Ether and Gravitation* I feel that I should bemean myself if I despaired of the Republic. The recent publication of a work on *Homogeneous Lineal Substitutions* cheered me more than any amount of attacks on the horrors of Prussianism . . ."

Through the violent outward oscillations of his temperament he maintained at heart and within himself a cardinal steadfastness of purpose and simplicity of resolution, those twin associates of courage. Literature seemed to acquire a new value—it became more than ever a refuge to which he could withdraw—there to refit, to restore his sanity of judgment, and repair the ravages of the spirit.

In 1916, he published *Inter Arma*: in 1917, *Life of Algernon Charles Swinburne*, and in 1918, *Three French Moralists*. In 1916 he organised the Red Cross Sale of literary rarities at Christie's—

and throughout the war years he did not slacken in his output of criticism and magazine articles. In 1916, at the invitation of the French Government, he visited Reims and the French front—with what object is now not very apparent, unless it were to enlarge his understanding of the attitude of France—an end hardly to be achieved by the sight of a trench and a glance at a damaged Cathedral. But in those days, in the search for means to an end, even the visit of a man of letters, it was hoped, would produce some moral effect. However that may be, the invitation came at least as a tribute to Gosse and a recognition of the part he had played towards the literature of France. After his visit, during which he was under the guidance of Maurice Barrès, he wrote an account of his experience *Reims Revisited* in the *Fortnightly*.

During these years of the War, Gosse's own anxieties and special perturbations seemed to quicken his power of suffering, always very great, for and with his friends. When occasion arose he gave out a sympathy delicate in its expression and understanding, and glowing with the sincerity of the impulse from which it sprang.

The Letter which follows refers to a privately printed volume, *Pages from a Family Journal*, which elsewhere in *Soldier Poets of the War* he describes as "a document of extraordinary candour, tact and fidelity, and it is difficult to say whether humour or courage is the quality which illuminates it most. It will be referred to by future historians of our race as the most vivid record which has been preserved of the red-blooded activity of a spirited patrician family at the opening of the twentieth century."

17, Hanover Terrace,
To Lady Desborough. *3rd September, 1916.*

My dear Friend,—

I find a difficulty in expressing to you what impression the reading of your marvellous volume has left upon my mind. The purpose or basis of it is so poignant, so (to speak foolishly) disappointing and irritating in the waste of glorious material, that one surprises one's self, as one reads on—as one reads the darkest pages, to find that the dominant effect upon the mind is—positively—one of *triumph*. This is aided, I think, developed to the full, by the very leisurely and copious method which you have wisely chosen. This was no occasion for flash-lights or brief record. If these typical lives were to be appreciated, it must be in the amplest realization of their rich setting, their *place*.

One thing you have done, unconsciously but splendidly. You have given the only picture that has ever been given of a highly sensitive, wholly extended, and (if I may say so) sumptuously executed family life at the end of the 19th century. It is quite extraordinary, and the extreme simplicity of your method, and the most felicitous introduction of the other three children, helps the development of this theme. Probably no other "family" in Great Britain expanded in those years on quite the same scale. But that is just what happy visitors to Taplow saw, the rounded family life, burnished and radiant—pursued on the same lines as hundreds of other family lives, but with a magnificence all its own.

This, of course, has added to what I call the disappointment and the irritation. (I use these weak words, because I will not cheaply say "tragedy.") But much more they added, by the light so steadily kept glowing behind the figures of Julian and Billy, to the *triumph*. It was all, as I feel it, of a piece; as everything was in the lives of those Dioscuri, "frates Helenae, lucida sidera." I like to think of them as "shining stars," the supreme effort of their race under its most favourable conditions.

And this brings me, dear Friend, to venture to say to you what I did not dare to say until I found that you had the courage to compile this book, that your attitude now really should be one of *joy*, of a grave and serene ecstasy, for you have borne and bred two sons who will be a part of what is noblest in English history, and will be prominent in that part, as long as England exists. I wish I could express it better. I feel that this is a very clumsy letter, but it is sincere in its poor attempt.

Believe me ever,

Dear Lady Desborough,

Yours most truly and affectionately,

EDMUND GOSSE.

VILLINO CHIARO, RAPALLO

Note for Evan, in case he wishes to use the inclosed Sonnet

I am not sure whether it was Walter Raleigh or I that invented the Sonnet game. I often played it — sometimes in a room, sometimes by post.

In the Spring of 1908 Gosse offered to play a round with me. We played it by post — by return of post, every time.

I wrote the first line, Gosse the second. The even-numbered lines are his, and the odd-numbered mine.

Max

MAX BEERBOHM'S NOTE ON THE "SONNET GAME"

To Henry James.

Say, indefatigable alchemist,
Melts not the very moral of your scene,
Curls it not off in vapour from between
Those lips that labour with conspicuous twist?
Your fine eyes, blurred like arc-lamps in a mist,
Immensely glare, yet glimmerings intervene,
So that your May-Be and your Might-Have-Been
Leave us still plunging for your genuine gist.
How different from Sir Arthur Conan Doyle,—
As clear as water and as smooth as oil,
And no jot knowing of what Maisie knew!
Flushed with the sunset air of roseate Rye
You stand, marmoreal darling of the Few,
Lord of the troubled Speech and single Eye.

SONNET "TO HENRY JAMES." ALTERNATE LINES IN THE HAND-WRITING OF MAX BEERBOHM AND EDMUND GOSSE

17, Hanover Terrace,

To Lady Desborough. *11th August, 1917.*

My dear Lady Desborough,—

If I did not answer your last very precious letter it was that your suggestion was working in my brain. I have hitherto written not a word about the English poetry of the War, for a variety of reasons. However, your letter carried almost a command with it, and I write now to tell you that I am obeying it. My next (October) article in the *Edinburg Review* will be on "Some poets of the War," and I am already putting my notes together. It is difficult to keep Julian within bounds of fairness to the rest, for I feel more and more strongly that "The naked earth"* is the only great lyric of the War, and the only one in which the spirit of British arms is adequately transcribed. But I hope to write without prejudice of them all—I mean of the six or eight who are worth mention at all.

I shall ask you to look at a proof, when the paper is set up, as you are, in Shakespearian phrase, "the onlie Begetter" of it. Will you? I shall so much value your help.

Most sincerely yours,

Edmund Gosse.

Hôtel de Crillon,
Paris.

To Earl Spencer. *Sept. 25 '16.*

Your last kind letter, cher Ami, reached me just as I was leaving England, and I have not had a minute till now to reply to it in. And even now I wait for the tootling of M. Briand's motor, which is in a few minutes to take me—a long day's adventure—over the whole battle-field of the Marne. It is hopeless to give you an impression of my wonderful week—doubtless the most wonderful of my life. I have seen Reims, I have been taken along the Champagne front, where at Cernay I was suddenly and unexpectedly under fire for a few minutes (an enchanting experience in dram-drinking!). I have been (what I believe no other Englishman has

* *Into Battle.* Julian Grenfell, 1915.

ever been) entertained at dinner by the *Académie Française*. Perhaps most interesting of all, I have seen M. Briand in the intimacy of his house, and have had several hours of his conversation.

The French are the most glorious people in the world. I always suspected, and now I know it.

But adieu! I shall be back in England almost before this reaches you.

Ever yours affectionately,
EDMUND GOSSE.

The Hotel,
Church Stretton,
Shropshire.

To Lady Charnwood. *Oct. 14, 1916.*

MY DEAR LADY CHARNWOOD,—

We (Nellie and I) flew down here rather suddenly, for we realized that "the summer is done and the autumn is over, and we have not" had our usual holiday, in the pathetic words of the prophet Zephaniah. This is a beautiful wild place, among bare hills that play the mountain very decently, and bracing enough to raise the hair off our heads. We shall be (D.N.) here all next week. Do you know what D.N. means? D.N. means *diabolo non obstante*, which I think is much more modest than D.V.

EDMUND GOSSE.

The Hotel,
Church Stretton,
Shropshire.

To Viscount Haldane. *Oct. 15, 1916.*

MY DEAR RICHARD,—

I have now read Begbie's* book with extraordinary emotion. It is a very remarkable *action*. I use this word advisedly, because

* *A Vindication of Great Britain*. Harold Begbie. In another letter Gosse said the book should be called *A Vindication of Lord Haldane*.

it is not a mere contribution to controversy, or a set of argumentative statements, but it is a positive *act* of high courage. It will surely be effective? I find singularly little in it which is to be challenged as a matter of taste. It seems to be thoroughly impeccable. A very indignant man, exposing a shameful conspiracy, could scarcely be more moderate, and I am amazed that his just anger does not betray him into exaggeration. I find not a page in his book which does not command respect, and I do not know who will answer him, or in what terms. I have the conviction that no answer will be attempted. The wicked newspapers will simply boycott the book. They will try to destroy it by ignoring it. I am extremely curious to see what will be said, but I am convinced that the enemy will say nothing. It will be the cleverest, although the most ignominious thing that they can do. I only see the *Times* here: it says nothing. Has the *Morning Post* taken the same line? Do tell me.

We are enjoying this wild, bare place, with its mountain atmosphere, exceedingly, and the improvement in Nellie's health is manifest. I do not intend to come back to London until Monday week, the 23rd.

I have written a very cordial letter to Begbie, but I do not suppose that he will acknowledge it. What one feels to be his weak point is his excessive and exclusive interest in journalists and professional politicians. I notice one or two amusing little evidences that the artist does not exist for him. This is of no importance: his attitude is all the more courageous, and he has helped us to the very utmost of his power.

Affectionately yours,

EDMUND GOSSE.

To John Drinkwater. *Nov. 14, 1916.*

MY DEAR DRINKWATER,—

I was delighted with every part of your letter this morning. At the same time I heard from Mr. Humphry Ward, who is very much pleased at having secured you.

The little criticisms which you have to write will be very useful practice. They are on so small a scale that you will feel the necessity of cutting down every redundancy. You will have to withdraw into the quintessential. This is very salutary for us.

You must do justice to Lord de Tabley. I find myself more and more impressed by his genius. He had a brocaded splendour all his own—with, of course, great inequalities. I hope you will observe that, as a trained naturalist, he writes more accurately about animals and plants than any other poet of his time. He is as far as possible from the poets for whom every flower is a rose, and every bird a nightingale. He had odd scientific sides. Do you know that, as a botanist, he was the greatest living authority on *brambles*?

I look forward with much curiosity to see what you will say about Henley. My own conviction is that his violence, his assumption of the brutal, was a pose—adopted no doubt in consequence of his appreciation of his physical disabilities. I think you will find that as a poet his successes were really of two kinds—the thrillingly sentimental, in which he was much influenced by R. L. Stevenson, and the elaborately elegant, where he is the most successful of all the disciples of Austin Dobson.

Let me give you a tip. You should look up in the *Cornhill Magazine* of about 1876 the originals of Henley's Hospital Sonnets. Unless I am much mistaken, though he used these sonnets twenty years later in lyric forms, he never reprinted the sonnets themselves. I don't think this fact has ever been noticed, and it might make a good point for you.

That you should spend your money on a portrait of me, shocks me! At the same time, if you will have a Rothenstein, I shall be proud that this particular one should be in your possession. I think it is considered an excellent likeness.

My wife is much gratified that you like the queer little panel. She is going to send it to you.

The doddering octogenarian to whom your new volume of poems is so indulgently dedicated is looking forward very eagerly to its arrival. But all books now are so delayed that the marvel is that they ever appear at all.

Give our warmest regards to dear Mrs. Drinkwater. Tell the new puss that I hope he is trying to be worthy of Punch.

I am affectionately yours,

EDMUND GOSSE.

17, Hanover Terrace,

To John Drinkwater. *Dec. 27, 1916.*

MY DEAR DRINKWATER,—

I am wondering how you are getting on through this dark and bewildering Christmas, so unlike any previous one in my life. We exist in a kind of suspense, very trying to the nerves. I have been looking out for some reviews of *Olton Pools*, but I have not seen any. No doubt there have been many (for I see nothing) and I trust all good. The fall of Phaethon-Asquith, dragging Maecenas-like Eddie down with him, is disastrous for literature. Never was there, in all our Island story, a Prime Minister who cared a third part as much about letters and the sorrows of scribbling men, as Asquith did. Apollo bless him for it. Our new Dictator is without one scrap of the humanities: I suppose we must not even whisper a complaint, the fate of the country being—so they say—in his hands.

I hope Punch's successor continues to be a success? The War has so affected Caruso that he now spends the whole day in a hay-lined box; he has trained the servants to bring all his meals to his bed-side. What an ideal life! The fog has given me a tame chronic bronchitis, very vexing in the hollows of the night. Such is life. We all send you both our love.

Ever yours,

EDMUND GOSSE.

17, Hanover Terrace,

To Siegfried Sassoon. *17.2.'17.*

MY DEAR SIEGFRIED,—

I have just been reading with admiration your striking verses called *Conscripts* in the *Spectator*. But there is a phrase in them which I sincerely hope you will modify before you republish them. You say, "Many a sickly, slender lord . . . went home." This is a cruel and unworthy libel. No section of the whole community has shown more courage or devotion than the class you have so gratuitously sneered at. The House of Lords has sacrificed, in proportion, more of its members and connections than any other in the country. I am unable to guess who the "many slender, sickly lords" are whom you have met on their way skulking home. I have heard of none, and I think your attack on the class, in order to butter up the "common ones," is a very unworthy one. Do not let it deform your book, from which I have been expecting great pleasure.

Yours affectionately,

EDMUND GOSSE.

I have been very busy with Red Cross work.

17, Hanover Terrace,

To Gordon Bottomley. *29.3.'17.*

MY DEAR BOTTOMLEY,—

The *Annual*, with your truly delightful letter, has just arrived, or arrived about an hour ago, which hour has been joyfully spent in reading its contents. I had heard of the *Annual*, but I had not seen a copy. I was lazily wondering whether I should buy it. Now, instead of buying it, I shall send you next week a copy of my *Life of Swinburne*, which is to be published next Tuesday—at last! after having been talked about so long that I fear everybody must be tired of hearing it announced. I shall not be able to write your name in it because I am going down to Parkstone in Dorsetshire for a week or ten days next Saturday, but I will send you a piece of paper to fix into the fly-leaf—if you will.

My wife and I had been talking only two days ago about you both, so that it is plain that brain-waves still continue in spite of all the artillery-disturbances over in France.

Now about your poems. Whoever edited the *Annual* did right to put you first, for on this occasion, at all events, your contributions are manifestly the most important. You have never written such excellent lyrics before. *New Year's Eve*, which I had just been reading in *The Times* when your parcel was brought in, is a masterpiece of delicacy and charm both in melody and thought. I have already read it, silently and aloud, many times, and it is going to be a source of permanent pleasure. *A Surrey Night* continues the same order of reflection, and is very lovely. *All Souls, 1914* is so poignant that it brought tears to my eyes.

Your position as a poet is remarkable. You combine the new with the old. You have adopted the freshness of observation, the reminting of language, of the very young, but you have kept to the ancient landmarks. I feel more at home with you than with, shall I say Gibson, who is so metallic and exterior, or with Davies, who seems to me like the person in the *Rejected Addresses* who was "lax in his gaiters, laxer in his gait." I cannot consent to rhyme "starve" and "move" (see p. 21): if one takes the trouble to write at all, why not learn the pattern? And yet Davies, with his socks down over his ankles and no stud holding his collar, is yet an authentic poet, which Eastaway* seems to me authentically *not.* Sturge Moore is a curious writer, to me always a little uncomfortable and unapproachable: but *Micah* is really rather splendid in its way. Well! there is nothing else in the volume so good as *Cartmel Bells.*

My wife and I cannot hope to get North this year. The act of railway-travelling is made more and more difficult. I was in France as the guest of the French Government last September, and in October we were in Shropshire for a fortnight. Since then I have not been out of town. I am so glad you have the Fuller-Maitlands for neighbours. They are most charming people. Will you tell him I am so very sorry we did not know last summer that they were so near, or we should have ventured to call on them?

This is too long a letter—you will be tired of reading it. Please give our love to the Pride of Westmorland, and both of you accept from both of us our warmest wishes.

Ever sincerely yours,

EDMUND GOSSE.

* Pseudonym of Edward Thomas.

Haven Hotel,
Sandbanks, Parkstone,
Dorset.

To Viscount Haldane. *April 2, 1917.*

My dear H.,—

I have not had time till to-day to thank you for the gift of Seth's book on *God*, for which I am very grateful to you. I read the opening chapters before I left town, and saw how fascinating it is. The style is charming. It calls for careful study, which I shall give it when I go back. But I feel my ignorance of philosophical phraseology.

This is a curious and charming place, built on the sea at the extreme end of a very narrow peninsula running south into and almost closing Poole harbour. The hotel is delightful, kept by French people—exquisite food, excellent wines and—with the sand and pines and blue sea—reminding me much more of the Bay of Biscay (an amalgam, one might say, of Arcachon and the Ile de Rhé) than of the coast of England.

My *Swinburne* comes out to-morrow. I have no pleasure in the thought, nor hope of success. In these dreadful times—growing more dreadful every day—who is going to give a thought to Swinburne? I am dreadfully upset at the destruction of St. Quentin, such a beautiful old heroic town, with its great cathedral and its matchless gallery of La Tour's pastels. Those monsters are making a desert of Europe, and I see no evidence of our getting any advantage or making any impression on them. Do you? I am told that our airmen who have pushed on to the Line of Hindenburg find a vast glacis 3 miles broad of smooth and solid masonry descending. What are we to do against that?

Well, one has just to be patient, and to think of the long, happy years that will never return. And your great and splendid schemes of education, what future can they have in a starved and ruined Empire? And the workmen at Barrow and on the Clyde? Your hope and your intelligence have often lifted me over my depression, and I daresay they will again. But I like the trend of things less and less. Except that Russia seems all right.

I hope you are resting? My only disapproval of you in any capacity is that you are so like a steam-engine. I should always like to act upon you as a brake. If I were at Cloan, where I suppose you are smothered in snow, I would pull you away from your papers; we would put on mufflers and snowboots, and we would climb that endless succession of rising braes where we spent such a divine afternoon. Do you remember the spring where we lay on our stomachs and lapped the crystal water like dogs? Please give my love to your dear ladies.

Yours affectionately,

E. G.

CHAPTER TWENTY-SEVEN

MUCH had been expected of Gosse's *Life of Swinburne.* He had known the poet with some degree of intimacy before the long captivity of Putney had begun. He had heard of his earlier years from many who had known him in childhood and youth; he had contributed the article on Swinburne to the *Dictionary of National Biography* and had already written a monograph on him which had been translated into several languages. But the subject was full of difficulties—he had to deal with a complex character and with a personality which in many ways was an enigma. In going behind the scenes he had to consider the susceptibilities of the living, yet he was expected to lift or at any rate reduce the opaqueness of many veils. Moreover it might be questioned whether the moment for a critical estimate was not exceptionally unpropitious. It was not the least menacing period of the War, and public preoccupation was at its most intense: the glamour attaching to Swinburne's poetry was rapidly losing its brilliance, and it was too soon to attempt a stabilisation of his fame by a final judgment. The book was well received, but there was a sense of disappointment; and just as in 1907 the critics had taken him to task for revealing too much in *Father and Son*, so now they were inclined to call him over the coals for revealing too little. It was thought that the book had the taint of a bygone biographical orthodoxy. At a moment when an extreme candour in portraiture and a lively indiscretion in personal disclosures were coming into fashion, Gosse seemed to have fallen from grace and reverted to caution and circumspection. The *Life* is mainly a work of narrative—criticism is subordinated to biography—facts and incidents are marshalled in scrupulous chronology—and it is only in the final chapter, "Personal Characteristics," that Gosse writes with enjoyment. It is one thing, and a good thing, for an author to know more than he tells, it is another and less good thing that he should be obliged to suppress what he knows and wishes to tell. That was Gosse's case. In his letter to

Mr. Baring on p. 407 he sets out the disabilities from which he suffered. As a result the portrait is incomplete; often where Gosse could have painted with lively colours he has been forced into a certain insipidity of treatment: even the motionless existence led by the poet at Putney, which Gosse could have discussed with no less wit and irony than had Beerbohm, has to be dealt with in a tone of enforced amiability. He is obliged to be merciful, Watts-Dunton escapes with a few pen-pricks; and it is necessary to read almost invisible ink between the lines to get any idea of what Gosse really felt. But the work is lightened by a multitude of characteristic passages, as for instance his comparison of the emotional conditions in *Idylls of the King* with those in *Chastelard*. Of the former he says, "His (Tennyson's) Elaines and Enids were conventional women of the reign of Victoria, travestied against a romantic background of semi-barbarous romance, but preserving all their latter-day prejudices," and then contrasting these with the ladies in the time of Chastelard he goes on: "In *Chastelard* a little group of delicate exotic women, rustling in their bright emptiness like so many dragonflies, are presented to us caged in a world of savages and scarcely less acrid ascetics." But Gosse wanted a clear field, more perhaps than most writers; warning notices of "Private" and "Trespassers will be prosecuted," clipped the wings of his wit and cribbed him in an elegant formality. But it is by other contributions to literature than pure biography that we may suppose Gosse will be judged hereafter.

17, Hanover Terrace,

To Maurice Baring. *April 13, 1917.*

My dear Maurice,—

It was good of you to send me your noble and passionate Elegy,* which I have just read to myself and then read aloud to my thrilled ladies with an emotion to which I can give no expression. You have never approached this height of melody and ardour before, but who has? I look in vain among the poems of the present age for another so uplifted. It places you at a leap in the forefront of

* *In Memoriam A. H.*

living poets. No sculptor could raise a more lovely or more enduring monument to your heroic friend, who will live to all time in your magnificent verses.

It is absurd to confine so splendid a work of art to 35 copies. I want that you should—at all events before long—admit a wider circle to the enjoyment of it.

I will mix no other subject with this. Write to me soon.

I am your ever affectionate and admiring friend,

EDMUND GOSSE.

Nellie and the girls send their love, and their deep appreciation.

"Whether some brave young man's untimely fate
In words worth dying for he celebrate."

Cowley wrote that for you.

17, Hanover Terrace,

To Maurice Baring. *16.4.17.*

Swinburne.

MY DEAR MAURICE,—

Your letter has arrived. Thank you very much indeed for it. It is the most useful I have had. I take your points:—

1. The story about Jowett and the "bad songs" is new to me and priceless. It comes just in time for me to use in the preface to the *Posthumous Poems.*

2. I cannot make up my mind whether it was *Rosamond* or *Chastelard* which he read to Stubbs. Some day, probably, a letter will turn up and settle the point.

3. You are perfectly right about *Super flumina Babylonis.* I sheer forgot it.

4. The influence of S. on d'Annunzio is very important. I am taking a note of it.

5. Clutton-Brock (did you see his review in the *Times Lit. Supp.*?) takes your view about the later poems. I think you are both right.

So are you in your other critical remarks. The book would have been better if I could have consulted you.

I suffered from a number of severe disadvantages. 1. The extraordinary hostility of the family. 2. The embargo laid on any mention of drunkenness. 3. A still heavier sexual embargo. 4. The weight of the Watts-Dunton legend, which I had to break down without seeming to do so. 5. The fact that I was obliged to keep the Correspondence for another publication. I think no biographer ever had more to contend against. If I could, I would withdraw the whole book, and re-write it from beginning to end. I ought to have been more daring, less reserved; but if you knew the difficulties you would see how cramped I was—particularly until the deaths of Watts-Dunton and of Isabel Swinburne.

But I think the numerous other publications—the *Posthumous Poems*, the *Letters*, the *Triameron*, etc.—will give me opportunities to complete the picture.

I am most cordially yrs.,

EDMUND GOSSE.

17, Hanover Terrace,

To Theodore Wratislaw. *22.4.17.*

MY DEAR MR. WRATISLAW,—

It gave me a great deal of pleasure to see your signature again after so many years, and to read your generous letter. You have always been one of those who most instinctively (and therefore accurately) perceived the central qualities of Swinburne's nature. I was very glad to have your pictures of your own visits to him to put up in my gallery of first-hand impressions of his talk and appearance. The extreme deference to his keeper was founded on *fear*, expressed, in the case of so fine a gentleman, in terms of elaborate courtesy. But there are few who know how harshly he was treated.

Like yourself, I have no love of the "literary world" as such, and my life, which is a busy one, is spent almost entirely outside it. I have never thought its atmosphere healthy for a spirit of any independence.

It was a most kind impulse which made you write to me. I trust we shall meet again: it would give me great pleasure to see you.

Yours sincerely,

EDMUND GOSSE.

Gisburne.

To Evan Charteris. *Whit Tuesday, 1917.*

MY DEAR EVAN,—

It is impossible to be here without thinking of you so much as to be obliged to write to you. I have been here since Friday. No one else, except Miss Adelaide Lister. Just at first, the empty house seemed full of ghosts, but now we are all very gay, and giggle through the live-long hours. I have been given the little book-room out of the hall, with my books and papers. I have begun my Royal Institution Lectures here,* and get through some pages of Vauvenargues with great diligence every morning. Ribblesdale is thinking about his *Reminiscences*, and I sit with him outside the hall-door, in the sweltering heat, and help him to plan a scenario, which is just what I like doing, and we talk of old times and swap stories. He is in splendid form. We eat the produce of the estate, lamb that we have seen skipping by its mamma, and venison that we go out with our little gun and treacherously shoot. All the books seem to have belonged to other people. I just took down a volume inscribed "To Violet from Evan," and indeed that is what induced me to throw off my post-prandial lethargy and write to you. We read Wordsworth aloud in the evening, and Miss Adelaide plays her own compositions on the piano. It is all deliciously quiet and easy, and the solemn elderly butler, who looks like a Lord of Appeal, and whom Miss Adelaide calls "Couttsey-boy," looks after me cynically, as one for whom the toilet has ceased to offer any mysteries. R. is his best as a host: he could not be more charming. I have been asked to stay on till Tuesday of next week, as if I were a character in *Sense and Sensibility*—so mind you answer this letter. I claim a reply. When I am not writing about Vauvenargues,

* *Three French Moralists.* 1918.

I am reading La Bruyère—you see the connexion? La B. was a stunner: I came across a passage in the *Quelques Usages* just now which made me squeak with pleasure. I thought I would copy it out for you, but it (the weather) is too hot, and besides you are such a cynical devil that you'd very likely sniff at it. Miss Adelaide and I are now going off to call on a neighbouring squire who was such a sad dog that ladies used not to be able to call on him, "but now he's paralysed, of course they can!" Bless you.

EDMUND GOSSE.

17, Hanover Terrace,

To Mrs. Joseph Pennell. *17.6.17.*

MY DEAR ELIZABETH,—

I have just finished reading your little book called *The Lovers* and I feel constrained to tell you how it has moved me and filled me with sad and sweet emotions. I have met with none of the innumerable records of the War which has seemed to me so tender as this. The last pages I could scarcely get through because my eyes were misted with tears. I think you have told the whole story—so delicate and so edged about with pitfalls—with the most beautiful discretion, and I am particularly glad that you did not hide the harsh and ugly facts, they are so essential to the exquisite truth of the narrative.

I wish your book might be read by thousands and thousands of readers in America. All that seems to me to be wanted now is that the great mass of your people should *understand*—it is only want of knowledge that can keep them aloof from sympathy. It is such a deep and true joy to me to know that you are now openly with us at last. It makes such a tremendous difference. I had a splendid letter the other day from Nicholas Murray Butler, full of firm hope and grit.

Thank you again for writing your little lovely book. It is like a primrose from one of those dreadful Flemish battle-fields.

Ever your affectionate old friend,

EDMUND GOSSE.

17, Hanover Terrace,

To Robert Ross. *20.7.17.*

Dear Robbie,—

Thank you for letting me see Mr. Tonks' letter,* which is very interesting and gratifying. It (his interest) is one of the many things I owe to your untiring friendship.

I am grieved that Mr. Tonks invariably mis-spells my name! It somehow always depresses me—it saps one's sense of individuality. But Goose is worse. And the other day when an institution for promoting the Disfranchisement of Women appealed to me twice as "Mr. Edward Jesse" I felt as the nautilus must feel when it is dashed against the reef.

I am very thankful that you expect better news about our poor Siegfried. Do let me know when you get it.

Prothero has sent me the *Q.R.* and I find Bailey excellent about Swinburne.

Your visit yesterday did me a great deal of good.

Always yours,

Edmund Gosse.

17, Hanover Terrace,

To Viscount Haldane. *August 21, '17.*

My dear Richard,—

You have written me two precious letters, so that I am much in your debt. Your last was quite a Saturday night's epistle. I have read it several times, and shall often refer to it. It breathes a high philosophy, but the worst of me is I am so poor a philosopher. You speak of giving up ambition, but I am as ambitious as ever I was for myself and still more for those whom I love, only more and more exasperated by my lack of influence and my declining force. You speak of "the peace which the years bring," but they bring no peace to me. I want to refashion all things nearer to the heart's desire, and I hate to see stupidity and ignorance crowned in the market-place.

(There appears to be an air-raid going on at this moment, but

* A letter from Professor H. V. Tonks dealing with *Father and Son*.

unless I am sure I shall not go indoors: I am writing on my wind-swept balcony. The guns may be our practice: but I think not.)

This parenthesis has disturbed my reflections on your beautiful letter, which closes with words which even I can take to myself—"let us be thankful for great mercies." Yes, our mercies have been great, and we must leave it there.

Your invitation is most tempting in all its details. Of course it is the champagne which tempts me most, but also I am not insensible to long walks on the brae, and the prolonged joys of conversation. But it would be a very long journey to take for so few days, and I should not have got over the fatigue of coming till I was faced with the anxiety of going. I must make up as well as I can with letters, which you are so kind in encouraging.

Tommy Colebrooke told me of a *mot* of Morley's which ought not to be forgotten. It was at the very outset of the War, at luncheon: Morley announced he was leaving the Government; Beauchamp declared that he should do so also, but not in terms which brought much conviction. Beauchamp said, "I wonder who will be your successor?" To which Morley, with a *sourire malicieux*, replied, "I shall not be at all surprised if it turns out to be—my predecessor." Which, of course, it was!

Write to me soon.

Yours affectionately,

EDMUND GOSSE.

17, Hanover Terrace,

To Evan Charteris. *Aug. 27, '17.*

MY DEAR EVAN,—

I have had one glimpse of you since you left, in a letter from Maurice, who said that he had seen you far away at a mess-dinner, and that you looked "like Hermes among the Olympians." I have meditated much on this sentence, which piques (but does not satisfy) my fancy. I have been living the most monotonous life imaginable, working every day for a couple of hours, and then walking a great deal, which I find good for me. I think you will admit that the *dies non sine linea* does tell, for I have written two of my three lectures for the Royal Institution (La Rochefoucauld and La Bruyère) and begun Vauvenargues. I have also finished a thing for the Jubilee of Baudelaire and—what will interest you most—done my *Edinburgh Review* article on the Soldier Poets. This was a very tough job indeed. You will find I have quoted you, very discreetly.

Now, how are you? I should very much like to know every detail about your life. I can't imagine what it is. The Tanks and Hermes, how do they combine? But in this amazing age, everything is liable to coalesce. Do you like your work? What *is* your work? I entreat you to stick your caduceus in the shell of your tortoise, and cross your golden sandals, and write me a minute personal letter, full of information. Or else I shall raise a small ugly statue to you as Mercurius Malevolus, and shy oystershells at it.

We are living here in a state of suspended animation. Everyone else is gone away. The gossips are very pessimistic. The C. Beresfords heard from Lord Northcliffe yesterday that he relies *exclusively* on American support, without which Germany *must* win, hands down. Russia seems as rotten as nuts. What does Hermes think of the general situation?

I went a fearful mucker the other day, the 1st edition of Perrault's *Hommes Illustres*, 1696, a huge folio, with the most beautiful impression of the one hundred portraits that has ever been seen, in the original vellum, untouched. The owner's book-plate, a dark green lozenge with an elephant in the middle and a star at each corner. Whose can that be? I am longing to show it you: the letterpress is as fascinating as the engravings.

Now by Zeus, and by holy Maia your mother, if you don't write me a really cheering, vivid, copious, egotistical, dishonest and ptenopedilic* letter, I shall spit into your favorite tank, and that would make you look foolish.

Ever yours as you treat me,

EDMUND GOSSE.

* It would be interesting to know how Gosse got hold of this word, which does not appear in the Oxford Dictionary. Liddell and Scott quote πτηνοπέδιλος, "with winged sandals," only from an Orphic Hymn, which would have been outside the range of Gosse's Greek reading.

17, H. T.

To Earl Spencer. *Sept. 1, 1917.*

Cher Ami,—

How nice of you to take an interest in my Uncle Johnnie.* The book-ticket is apparently in the thinnest possible dark green leather gilt. I send you a rough tracing of it, but I am such a horrible draughtsman that I don't know whether you will make anything out. The binding is contemporary (1700 or 1701), and the book comes from a *French* collection. If any one can throw light upon the mystery, it is yourself. I should like to know who the lady was who owned my beautiful book. It is so spotless and has been preserved with so much care that I should like to think it had belonged to Mme. la Princesse de Conti, who was "la plus propre personne du monde et la plus recherchée dans sa propreté."

I am absorbed in the *Memoirs of Saint-Simon*, which I never read consecutively before. Surely this book is more thrilling than any other in the world. Everything pales beside it. I have just been reading of the disgrace of Mme. de Torcy, who sat in the wrong place at dinner, and I feel that I have just been a spectator of the amazing occurrence. Do tell me if you do not adore Saint-Simon? Why in all these years have we never discussed him? He wrote precisely for you and for me: and here is a curious reflection. This remote French hermit, under lock and key, more than two hundred years ago, wrote an account of the ingratitude of Louis XIV to Vauban which has so excited me in this far-away time and place as to cause me (absurdly but truly) a slight bilious attack from anger. Is not this a remarkable instance of the vital power hidden in really good literature?

I have been wretchedly low from the weather and missing my usual companionship. Everybody is away. But Colebrooke comes back on Monday, and he will cheer me up. I was not born for solitude.

Nellie sends you her all-kindest remembrances. I close abruptly for the post.

Toujours,

Edmund Gosse.

* The phrase signifies an act of extravagance, and is borrowed from the Baring vocabulary.

17, Hanover Terrace,

To Dr. Sim. *Oct. 22, '17.*

My dear Sir,—

Your letter has pierced me with the most exquisite memories. The word Aultnagalagach! I have not heard it for two generations. It was in the marvellous autumn of 1879. I had been staying at Braemar with Robert Louis Stevenson; and leaving him, at Aberdeen I met Hamo Thornycroft, and we went wandering. The solitude, the rough freshness, the great bath of air, at Aultnagalagach, and we two, climbing Snilven and Canisp, swimming in the black lakes, whence we believed that the sword Excalibur might at any moment be brandished, dreaming all our dreams of poetry and art! I remember Thornycroft had the grandiose, the Michelangelesque conception of a colossal "Echo" to be carved in the face of the cliff behind the little inn. The spirit of youth was dancing in our veins—nearly forty years ago, alas! and the difference between then and now. I am not sure that I do not owe you a grudge for starting all these sad ecstatic recollections ringing in my brain.

Yours very faithfully,

Edmund Gosse.

17, Hanover Terrace,

To Robert Nichols. *31.10.17.*

Dear Mr. Nichols,—

I am very glad to get your letter. Why wait for Eddie Marsh? When the troubles you speak of have passed away (and all cloud shadows do pass in time), write and tell me, and I will propose a meeting. I want to see you. Your state of mind interests me immensely, and I believe I am really able to comprehend. I believe in you thoroughly: and I am a world-worn old cynic not easily pleased at all: I have seen too many shoals of poets glitter and vanish in my long life. But you will not vanish, if you are true to yourself.

Your stanzas in *The Times* were noble in sentiment and imagination. But not good enough for you in execution. Are you angry with me for saying that? Study technique, that is the shoal on which most of the glittering bubble-poets break. And don't blaspheme Keats. Fix firmly in your mind that all the great craftsmen of the past, whatever we ridiculously call their "school," are worthy of our high loyalty and wonder. It is the mark of mediocrity to speak ill of the great dead.

It seems as if I were scolding you already! Forgive me! There are so few, so few, that are worth the trouble of scolding. I have not many years to live, but I want to see you up, high up, where no one climbs without "ardour" and "endurance."*

Most sincerely yrs.,
EDMUND GOSSE.

17, Hanover Terrace,

To Max Beerbohm. *14.11.17.*

DEAR WONDERFUL MAX,—

You have never done anything more irradiated with genius than this new Rossetti series. I hung enamoured along the line from end to end, and back again. The Madox Brown and Holman Hunt is perhaps my favourite. But Swinburne reading *Anactoria* to a shocked William and a relaxed Gabriel—quite splendid. And the Watts-Shields-Caine! And the incomparable Jowett with his nasty little question about the Grail! But I might go on to the end. *My* picture was a startling surprise. I was quite unprepared for it: I had not reached it; when I heard a gentleman say to a lady, "The Gosse is very funny!" They were absolute strangers to me. I think the little red fairy Swinburne tugging my impassiveness along, stamping and savaging with impatience, is beyond praise. Genius, simply, and divination—which is the flower and summit of your genius. It was very kind of you—and so like you—to drag me into the scheme, and believe that I do gratefully appreciate the singular sweetness you have shown me these years past—always so indulgent.

* A reference to Mr. Nichols' volume *Ardours and Endurances.*

It made me very angry to find I had missed you both on Sunday. I was at Oxford: I never pass under Magdalen Tower without glancing up to see if there are any signs of the beautiful little ceremony which you alone among European antiquaries have been fortunate enough to witness.

When am I to see you? We must somehow meet; it is so very long since we did. I have written a strictly confidential paper describing Swinburne's moral eccentricities and failings. It can never be published, but there are so many legends about, that I thought it right to leave the truth on record. I should like you to read it.

Your affectionate old Friend,

Edmund Gosse.

17, Hanover Terrace,

To Thomas Hardy. *16.12.17.*

My dear Hardy,—

You are very kind to send me that inscription. But I deny with indignation that the "lyre is worn-out"! In certain directions, I think you have advanced as a poet further in this volume than ever before. Your command of stubborn material was never more remarkable. The greater part of the collection I have read aloud to my wife and daughters in the evenings of last week. The poems are sometimes so poignant in their revelation of character and the sad fatefulness of life as to be almost too painful for the voice, but the sincerity, penetration and lyric beauty are wonderful.

I suppose you wrote a great many of these poems long years ago? Often I seem to hear the voice of plaintive and distracted youth, sorrowing with the bitterness that we forget when we are confident and old. How I should like to talk the whole wonderful budget over with you in your study.

"Digging in the garden," indeed! At your age! What does Mrs. Hardy say of such juvenile energy? I should guess that what you have been suffering from is not rheumatism, but strain of muscles unaccustomed to such labour. I also am in bed, but I have not been digging in the garden. I have, like Falstaff, "a great whoreson cold." I think it is rather amusing to be obliged sometimes to spend a day in bed, and regard life horizontally. More than one day of it is a bore. Do you remember my coming to visit you in bed when you had the jaundice? Wasn't it at Tooting or somewhere there; you were dictating the *Laodicean*, I think. I see you now in my mind's eye.

Please our kindest remembrances to Mrs. Hardy, and believe me ever,

Your affectionate old Friend,
EDMUND GOSSE.

17, Hanover Terrace,
To Thomas Hardy. *21.2.18.*

MY DEAR HARDY,—

Your last letter has given me great satisfaction, for I had spotted of my own accord the influence on you of Wordsworth's first preface.

You ought not to regard what the ignorant say about "lack of form." Your form is abundant, excellent, and deserving of careful analysis. It is one of your strong points. Without "form" poetry is void, and it is part of your genius as a poet that you are always so interesting linguistically and prosodically. I am dwelling on this matter with some elaboration in my *Edinburgh* review.

It is quite true that the Press still irritatingly treats your poetry as a by-product. But be patient: time will set that straight.

I bought the *Life of Keats*, but I find it to be dull, overloaded with triviality and conscientiousness. It is a Blue Book about Keats.

Who made the selection from your poems? It excludes a number of my greatest favourites, and I don't understand its principle of selection.

I have not been able to get hold of the Wessex edition of your works. I found I did not possess it, and I asked Mr. Bain to get it for me, but he says that it is out of print, and *introuvable*. Never mind, I am perfectly soaked in the text of the poems themselves.

Behold the shamelessness with which my blushing pen whispers. Do write me another of your precious and illuminating letters!

Always yours,
EDMUND GOSSE.

17, Hanover Terrace,

To Harold Cox. *16.3.18.*

My dear Harold,—

I want to say a word or two about your health. Very few people seem to notice that a crisis takes place in the life of every man of sedentary habits. I have noticed it over and over again, and most of all in myself. When I was just your age, I had a sudden break-down, not like yours, but a break-down, with much pain and languor and powerlessness. It depressed me very much, lasted some months, and then passed away like a cloud and has been no more repeated.

Now, I feel convinced that you are going through this critical change, and it is very important (1) that you should not take a tragical view of it, and think your active life is at an end, and (2) that you should not evade a clear and common-sense conception of what it means. It means that we have, more or less suddenly, reached the Second Age of Man, and that it is of no use, it is even of great danger, to attempt to resuscitate the First Age. It means that we must be content to be less violent, less on the strain. It means going to bed earlier, resting more often, holding what we have but not adding to it, making others do the little tiresome things and keeping ourselves for the really important things. If you face the crisis deliberately and sagely, there are before you twenty years more of activity, health and pleasure. Only you *must* plan it all on a more selective system—you must have the courage to be lazy and even selfish. It is extraordinary how much is left of activity when one has cut away the unessential, the secondary business.

I venture to write this because you have been very much in my thoughts, and because I want to strengthen your patience. Be *patient*, and you will swim up again into health and vigour on the restricted but highly efficient plane of old age.

Affectionately yours,

Edmund Gosse.

(419)

17, Hanover Terrace,
March 20, '18.

To Dr. Sim.

My dear Sir,—

Your letter of the 16th reached me with fair punctuality, and I should have answered it sooner had I not been extremely busy. When I retired from the House of Lords, I thought that I was entering a cold cellar of abandonment, but as a matter of fact I have never in my life been more continually occupied than since that withdrawal.

Everything in your letter interested me, and I lift my hands in astonishment at the extent of your acquaintance with the literary history of our time, and at your sympathy with the poetical portion of it.

You conjecture quite rightly that Robert Nichols is the son of Bowyer Nichols of Oxford. Robert Nichols is a very remarkable young man, with a face that in profile has a striking resemblance to that of Keats as Severn recalled it some years after Keats' death. He is distractingly violent, mercurial and excessive, but most attractive in his flaming zeal and pale vehemence. I hope his brain will not be overstrained: there the danger lies.

If you see Compton Mackenzie, pray remember me warmly to him. What you tell me of the youngest son of W. S. Landor interests me very much. How curious that the temperament should have survived without, I suppose, a grain of the talent.

To-day, if the weather here could be transported to Aultnagalagach, what an enchantment it would be, for here in London the air is crystal, the sky like the palest blue china, and the sticky buds of the trees, rashly bursting, glitter like bits of glass in the sunshine. Florence, London, Aultnagalagach—what a trio—and I suppose that I shall never see the first or the third again save with the inner eye which is the bliss of solitude.

My two volumes of Swinburne's *Correspondence* are in the press, but all the delays of trade augment. I hope you will write to me again: I enjoy your letters much.

Yours very faithfully,

Edmund Gosse.

The bantering protest addressed to Mr. Moore, which follows, had reference to Mr. Moore's volume *Avowals*. The *locus in quo* finally selected was Regent's Park, beside the lake; a concession to Gosse's attachment to that scene, in which from his window in Hanover Terrace he watched the seasons come and go with something approaching a sense of proprietorship and a sentiment of affection which every year increased. Gosse's own comment on this *mise en scène* is to be found in *The Carpet and the Clock*. "In Dialogue XVI," he writes, "I am astounded at my own audacity in leading Mr. Moore to a pleasant seat by a lake at the other end of some garden. But the triumph is a physical, not a spiritual one. In the discussion which ensues (if discussion it can be called, when one party incessantly agrees with Mr. Moore), the atmosphere is exactly that of 121, Ebury Street. The turf at our feet is the Aubusson Carpet, and the handsome beech tree above our heads is no other than the lyre shapen clock."

17, Hanover Terrace,

To George Moore. *21.3.18.*

My dear Moore,—

There is one point which I must emphasize without delay. You say that I am to be "announced by the servant," and to be introduced into your study, and immediately to ask you "to give some account of the work" you are "engaged upon." In other words, you present me to your readers as a *journalist* come to interview you for some newspaper! This I absolutely refuse to allow you to do.

You must not start by giving yourself *le beau rôle* and making me venal and ridiculous. You must treat me as well as yourself, and I insist on the place chosen being a neutral one. We can be walking together somewhere out of doors, wherever you like. And you can represent me as mainly desirous to hear your views, not anxious to put forward my own. But I cannot allow you to put me into the degrading and subaltern position which you propose in your letter to-day.

The thing will be great fun if you will only do it properly: but

GEORGE MOORE　　EDMUND GOSSE　　HADDON CHAMBERS

IN WILLIAM HEINEMANN'S GARDEN AT OCKHAM, 1919

you start with the idea of humiliating your interlocutor, and I won't allow it. Come out in the open and be a hero.

Ever sincerely yours,

EDMUND GOSSE.

We might be walking together in Regent's Park, in the garden opposite this house.

How DARE you propose that I should "apologize for interrupting you at your work"? Damn your infernal cheek.

E. G.

Don't think I am opposed to the scheme: it will be very amusing, but you *must* behave like a little gentleman, or else I won't play with you.

E. G. bis.

17, Hanover Terrace,

To George Moore. *22.3.18.*

MY DEAR MOORE,—

In my last letter I "chaffed" you with too heavy a hand—I am apt to do so. It is a sin that doth easily beset me. But you will not take it too seriously, for you know how much I admire you, and how vivid an interest I take in all the movements of your unique imagination.

Your idea of finding me on the balcony reading Lamb is *perfect.* These dialogues are always greatly heightened by a slight bright landscape-setting. I ever admire the opening of Berkeley's *Alciphron*, where the philosophers, before they begin their metaphysical debate, see from their window the fox-hunters sweep across the lawn below them. In a few words you will paint the park below and in front of us, perhaps with the pink hawthorns in full bloom against the lake and the blue smoky distance. This will be a charming setting; and you will pour out, as you have so often delighted me by doing, your paradoxes and your discoveries.

Of course, my letter was a joke. But too heavy a hand—that is always my fault!

Ever your affectionate friend,

EDMUND GOSSE.

17, Hanover Terrace,

To George Moore. *11.4.18.*

MY DEAR MOORE,—

There can be no doubt that Sterne started the *Sentimental Journey* in 1765—after launching the ninth and last volume of *Tristam Shandy*—because he felt that the public was getting a little tired of the mode of that book. I do not think he had any idea, either in T. S. or the S. J. of writing a story, as we consider a story. He wished to express himself more fully than he had done before, and he wrote to a friend that in writing the S. J. "I have torn my whole frame into pieces by my feelings." He thought that the S. J. was more refined and spiritual than *Tristam*, and did more justice to his own fine feelings.

I am disappointed to learn that I have been ejected from your dialogue, and replaced by a supposititious Mr. Arthur Mellowes! Why have you done that? The whole point of a *dialogue* is gone if you argue with a non-existent adversary. I should have thought you would have considered me more amusing than "Mr. Arthur Mellowes."

Your remark that to apprehend the genius of Landor it is necessary to try to write a dialogue is most sound.

Very truly yrs.,

EDMUND GOSSE.

17, Hanover Terrace,

To Lady Charnwood. *22.5.18.*

MY DEAR FRIEND,—

Many things and nothing have happened since we met at the R.A., an agitated emptiness has been my lot. The day I saw you I went down into Berkshire, as a paying guest of some ladies I had never seen in my life. It was a great success; they fed me not wisely but too well, and I wandered all day long over commons and through woods. I came back much refreshed, and the change of air and diet brought out a mild attack of gout as gently as the pin draws forth the periwinkle. I am now quite well again, and sitting at the moment in the capacious balcony of this house, flooded with the perfume from the great burning bushes of red hawthorn which line the Park. But above all are the horse-chestnuts, vast candelabra crowded with creamy candles—and the grace of the leaves, and the flash of the waters, and the soft blue sky, and the pink blouses of the far-away young ladies disporting on the lake! Talk not to me of your rural scenes. Regent's Park beats the lot of them.

Everybody seems to have gone away. I lunched with Haldane on Thursday, and he left for Scotland; I dined the same night with A. J. Balfour and he left for Gloucestershire.

I seem to have this effect on statesmen: I point them to my bleeding breast, and they shriek and flee away. We had the Struthers here on Sunday: Lady S. spoke of you with an honourable discrimination. Lord Newton is on the point of resigning: he attributes the attacks on him about the prisoners in Germany to Lord Northcliffe's desire to get his place for a pal. It is therefore, as I point out to Lord Newton, illogical to resign so as to make things easy for the intruder. *Extrudez l'Intrus*—or *l'Intruse*—should be everybody's domestic motto.

I hope you are being good, and a nice influence among the local Clergy? Is his Lordship coming up to help to dine the Italian professor on Thursday? It is his duty and he should.

We all send our love to you all and,

I am ever

Yours,

EDMUND GOSSE.

17, Hanover Terrace,

To Evan Charteris. *Whit-Tuesday, '18.*

MY DEAR EVAN,—

It is about a year ago that you recommended me to read *South Wind*. Some trifle prevented my doing so, and I have only just carried out your command. I must not delay in thanking you. I would not have missed so singular a book for the world. It is extraordinarily whimsical, refined and witty, and it bears about with it a perfume of the Mediterranean which is really amazing. The fault of it is a certain monotony—Mr. Keith's tirades are rather boring. But how delicious are all the appearances of Miss Wilberforce, and how splendid the Little White Cows! The humours of St. Dodekanus too are splendid; and I must not forget the arrival of Don Giustino "the assassin," and the trial which ensues—a masterpiece. The author must be a curious person, so completely "a-moral" and detached. It is refreshing to read him after the nausea of letters to *The Times* by the Bishops of London and Willesden. I get to be more and more a Frondeur in morals as I get older and older.

Where are you? If at Stanway you have A. J. B. with you. I spent an evening in his company last week, he scintillated and glowed by turns.

Yours affectionately,

EDMUND GOSSE.

17, Hanover Terrace,

To Viscount Haldane. *June 2nd, 1918.*

MY DEAR H.,—

I have not much to say to you, and yet I must write. I did not sleep well last night, and you much occupied my thoughts. I felt you, although you were so calm yesterday, to be discouraged and a little sad. I do not wonder at it, for there is nothing in public or in private matters to make you cheerful. But I want to remind you of certain things which came to me in the watches of the dark. An innocent and noble poet, whose whole life was persecution, wrote just before his death:

"Abandonné ne m'a jamais la Muse:
Aucun n'a su avoir puissance là."

I often think of that when I think of you. The Muse, that is to say the fount of intellectual liberty, the spirit that holds the indomitable fortress—neither the dangers of our country, nor the coarse ingratitude of man, nor the cowardice of friends, nor the turns of fortune, can touch that. You have that strength, and the security of your soul rests in it. I daresay you might have been happier if you had been obscure and irresponsible, but your genius made that impossible. And you have nothing to regret, nothing in all your past to wish undone. Your present troubles—if we can call them troubles—are all the direct result of your patriotism, of your energy, of your unceasing and unflinching response to the call of duty. Just now, in this black hour, all this seems to be forgotten, and in spite of your wonderful courage, you cannot help feeling it. But I want you to remember that *"abandonné ne t'a jamais la Muse,"* and also that no one is ever in the long run the victim of his persecutors, but only of *himself*. You must hold the record of yourself at arm's length and look steadily at it. It is beautiful, it is almost unique, and posterity, when all the rest of us are forgotten, will look at it and say, "he was a faithful servant of England." The insects that buzz and try to sting will be forgotten —their very names; and the false friends will have slipped into obscurity.

It seems rather silly and almost impertinent, to write all this to you. But I owe so much to you, to your unfailing goodness and serenity, in short I love you so much, that I venture to send you this word of comfort, unimportant as I am and unworthy to hold up one of your hands in the battle. At least I know you, and know what you are, and that must be my excuse.

Your affectionate,

EDMUND GOSSE.

17, Hanover Terrace,

To Siegfried Sassoon. *June 25, '18.*

MY DEAR SIEGFRIED,—

I have two letters from you, for which I thank you heartily. The first of these had been fished out of the deep, and was scarcely legible, but I finally made it out. You do not say whether you received the letter I wrote you in the first week of May, about your new poems, of which I had just read the proofs. My sense of their power and originality has only increased since then, on a further study. You have certainly been writing admirably.

Your mother is coming up to Town this week, and we hope to see her. Hamo and Agatha dined with us a few nights ago, and were very calm and optimistic. What a pity they can't lend some of their aplomb to our agitated friend! A third Thornycroft has been made a Sir—yours is the most beknighted family in England. You will be certainly Sir Siegfried before I pass away in my obscurity.

The family all sends love to you, even Caruso, who is in some ways a changed character. He now consents to eat rice, bread and pancakes, explaining that he does not like these comestibles, but that every cat must "do his bit" in war time.

Affectionately yours,
EDMUND GOSSE.

17, Hanover Terrace,
To Lady Charnwood. *26.7.18.*

MY DEAR LADY CHARNWOOD,—

"*Re* the pig," as the Maori chieftain said to the English Governor's lady: I come to you, do I, on Wednesday the 7th? You must give me full directions, for I shake like a blanc-mange to contemplate the journey. "*Re* the pig's clothes"—will it do if I bring a dress-jacket and not a long-tailed evening coat? Shall you forgive it? Will your BUTLER forgive it? The luggage-question is so appalling. You are never sure of more than the hand (or two hands) can carry.

Yours affectionately,
EDMUND GOSSE.

To J. C. Squire. *Aug. 3rd, 1918.*

MY DEAR MR. SQUIRE,—

You make me proud. I am immensely pleased to see my named pinned to the cover of your noble and original poem of *Birds*.

This I have read already twice, once aloud. This is the only final criterion.

If somebody—say Goldsmith or Falconer—could have risen to this mode of heroics, the classic age need never have come to an end at all. I am enormously interested in the technique of this poem of yours, which treats the couplet more sensitively than has been done elsewhere since Swinburne. And Swinburne, though he introduced a buoyancy and an elasticity into it, had not your courage in modifying it. I am delighted at your self-restraint; you don't boil and bubble into anapæsts at every moment, but you keep them for effective occasions. A most effective occasion is presented by the quatrain about the gulls, "A dizzying tangle," which is superb, not merely as a picture, but as a bold and shining example of what a sure hand can do in extending the heroic measure—stretching it without breaking it. And when this is over, this ecstasy of gulls, your metre does not sink at once, but sways down through the cormorants to a sober admirable octet, without license of any kind, that might be pure 1760. A very beautiful and complete poem, for which I take off my hat to you.

But the quatrain about the gulls, that puts you "where all our great forefathers are, from Homer down to Ben."

Now for one nasty question, Line 12. Why "Amid"? Is this not being rugged for ruggedness sake? Why not "Mid"?

I sent on your inquiry to E. Marsh. I quite agree with you. Had you any reason for not mentioning once Marsh's name in the review of Rupert Brooke? I fear he will be a little disappointed. I like your review, and your parallel with the young Goethe is most ingenious. It would never have occurred to me, but I accept it at once. I will give you another example. The early "knowing man-of-the-world" pieces of Rupert are just like the Annette lyrics of Goethe's Leipzig period. Also did you happen to see acted the little playing called *Lithuania*? It was very bad, but bad in the regular *Sturm und Drang* manner, just what Goethe might have sketched after seeing *The Robbers* acted.

You are very kind and just to poor Siegfried Sassoon. It is profoundly true that he writes these horrors about sodden buttocks and mats of hair, simply because fortune won't let him alone to write about the things he loves.

Yours most truly,
EDMUND GOSSE.

I have just read the *Birds* over a third time. After this you should be capable of anything.

Not able to bite your elbow? Shame! Try again.

To J. C. Squire. *August 18, 1918*

MY DEAR SQUIRE,—

(Pray let us over-master one another no longer!) I found your poems awaiting me here. You did well to arrange them in chronological order, and I have fantastically begun to read the book from the wrong end, because I want to put myself in instant sympathy with you as I know you. You are a poet of a high order and a mind in curiously close sympathy with me. I feel myself singularly in tune with you. I understand exactly what you say. It is so rare.

Perhaps I am rash to speak so plainly. But I have lost so much time, it seems foolish to delay. I have a strong feeling that if you will let me say so I have found a friend. It is rare to do this at my years, but I feel we may talk together of the things that matter to us both, for the remaining period of my life, which must be short. You have all before you, and I all behind me. But for a little time I can give you sympathy and comprehension, if you will have them. You will make a great name, and last when the ephemerides have died down. I want to watch you growing as long as I can.

We must meet again soon. I will propose something.

Yours very sincerely,
EDMUND GOSSE.

17, Hanover Terrace,
To Robert Nichols. *August 19, '18.*

My dear Robert,—

You have made me a splendid gift, and one which no one would appreciate more than I. I recollect Sarah Bernhardt (in some play of Racine) magnificently flinging down her papers—"*Je dépose en vos mains mes titres de noblesse!*"—before an elderly person, who replies: "*Soit! Je conserverai vos parchemins, Altesse!*" I will preserve these your *titres de noblesse* with affectionate care, and I am already thinking what shall be their most appropriate shrine.

Ever sincerely yours,
Edmund Gosse.

On Saturday I dined in the sullen magnificence of St. James's Palace with Osbert Sitwell, who is Captain of the Guard. He is writing poems zealously. What a poetical animation there is everywhere. Pieria seethes like an ant-hill!

The White Lion Hotel,
Bala, N. Wales.
To George Moore. *Sept. 14, 1918.*

My dear Moore,—

So glad to get your letter. We arrived here yesterday in great comfort, but were rather startled to find the hotel—instead of being lapped by the celebrated Lake—¼ of a mile away in the street of the town. However, it is a very comfortable, old-fashioned hostelry, with good food and wine, and the few guests are all well-bred people, mostly clergy of the fisherman type, gentlemanly and claret-drinking. So here we shall settle down for a fortnight or so. The Lake, when you do at last reach it, is mild and broad, like a very fat woman with a perpetual smile.

I wish you were here. What talks we would have! I think I agree with you in essence about Anatole. That is to say I have always perceived in him an element of what you define as insipidity. It is difficult to be precise, because most people would say that you and I must be insane to call Anatole France "insipid." And, of course, his essential genius is one of sparkling purity, but—if I may be so bold—it always seems to me as though his dazzling lumps of purity floated about in a sort of *purée* of very mediocre character. We ought to work this out with the books before us. But don't let us forget how splendid his wit is when it does shine.

You also, as I was thinking, are a *pure* writer; so was Stevenson and so was Sterne. So much writing, even good writing, is more or less turbid. Even Landor's prose is rarely quite pure: there is a grittiness. I will not deserve the reproof with which you threaten me by pretending to depreciate *Father and Son.* I read it again, after a very long interval, the other day, and I conceived that if some other fellow had written certain parts of it I should have been unable to refrain from praising him. But I think it is already almost forgotten. But happily, not by you.

The weather is deplorable to a degree. I look up and down the cheerless slaty street of little Welsh houses, through a dark and sodden atmosphere, and wonder why we came. But hope will return with the morning. My wife sends you all kindest greetings. Let me have a line from you soon.

Ever yours,
EDMUND GOSSE.

The White Lion Hotel,
Bala, N. Wales.

To Robert Ross. *17.9.18.*

MY DEAR ROBBIE,—

We are very happy here. How to be happy, tho' wet. For the weather is past a joke; it rains for hours and hours and hours, and then hot hectic sunshine bursts forth and we rush out, only to be caught in torrents of rain. You would laugh to see us crouching behind hedges, like two purple mushrooms, with our storm-cloaks draping us to the ground. The inn—a real old provincial inn, all twisty stairs and dark cut-throat passages, is as jolly as possible. The food good and the wine remarkable: we have a charming sitting-room, and I am writing a tri-centenary Panegyrick on Sir

Walter Raleigh, which has to be delivered at the Mansion House next month. (Damn this pen, it has got bubble in the nose.)

Wise has found a new Swinburne *Song before Sunrise* of 1867. But you are a wicked atheist about my favourite poet, and you poison the minds of the younger generation, which reverberates upon poor me. Oh! I hear of your innuendoes. We are very happy here; the air is beautiful—oh! the beautiful wet air from the wet morasses round the wet, wet lake. But we drink too much sherry at lunch. Nellie sends her love to you. She is very fond of you, quite a culpable weakness.

Affectionately yours,
EDMUND GOSSE.

17, Hanover Terrace,
To J. C. Squire. *26.11.18.*

MY DEAR SQUIRE,—

You must think me very ungrateful, but indeed it is not so. I have been thoroughly enjoying *Solomon Eagle*, and tho' I read most of it when it came out, I have now read again, with fresh enjoyment, every word from cover to cover. When you reprint—this time I hope on decent paper—you must make one or two small corrections. On p. 146, the real reading is "the Rev. John Gray," doubling the newspaper blunder. You are on the edge of giving me severe physical pain in what you say of Wordsworth, but you always just save yourself. P. 158, *The Maiden's Blush,* was translated from the Latin of Fracastorio (who wrote the celebrated epic about the Pox) and I wonder you could resist quoting Sylvester's final couplet:

"Here, death preventing Fracastorius,
This late-begun he left un-ended thus."

I would give you a better example of misprints than any on your pp. 245, 246. About thirty years ago, Walter Besant gave me a proof to read for him. He had written: "Monographs on obscure points," which the gifted printers had translated as "monograms on obscene prints," you see, a triple error. When Browning died I wrote that to the end he was "faint, yet pursuing." The printer's reader queried this, and being angry about many things, I scribbled "Rats!" at the side. They printed that the venerable poet died "faint, yet pursuing rats."

Ever sincerely yours,

EDMUND GOSSE.

CHAPTER TWENTY-EIGHT

SAINTE-BEUVE, after accepting Véron's invitation to write his *Causeries* in the *Constitutionnel*, explained to his readers the reasons which had led him to undertake the work. *"Au fond,"* he wrote, *"c'était mon désir. Il y avait longtemps que je demandais qu'une occasion se présentât à moi d'être critique, comme je l'entends, avec ce que l'âge et l'expérience m'avait donné de plus mûr et aussi peut-être de plus hardi. Je me mis donc à faire pour la première fois de la critique nette et franche, à la faire en plein jour, en rase campagne."* When in 1919 Gosse was invited to begin in the *Sunday Times* the series of criticisms which he continued till his death, he might have explained his position in much the same way. The journal provided him with a "pulpit," to borrow his own description, from which he was able to give his views every week on past and present writers and literary problems.

He quickly caught the ear of the public, and week by week was listened to with delighted attention. And it is perhaps necessary to go back to those same *Causeries* or the pages of the *Examiner* to find a corresponding level of sustained excellence. In an essay published in 1922, *The Hôtel de Rambouillet*,* Gosse writing of Malherbe said, "No man of letters has lived in any country, who was more possessed than he by the necessity of watching over the purity of language, of cultivating in prose and verse a simple, lucid, and logical style, of removing from the surface of literature, by an arrogant discipline, all traces of obscurity, pomposity and looseness. He held the honour of the French language above all other obligations." The changes of fashion may enhance or diminish the reputation of Gosse, but at least what he here says of Malherbe will remain true of himself. In the preceding pages his letters must have made it abundantly clear that the art of writing was the passion of his life. His aim in criticism was to communicate that passion to

* *Aspects and Impressions.*

others. He was gifted with the means for bringing this about, perhaps beyond all men of his time.

In an essay on George Eliot he quoted a pronouncement of Lord Acton's to the effect that "no writer had ever lived who had anything like her power of manifold but disinterested and impartial sympathy. If Sophocles or Cervantes had lived in the light of our culture, if Dante had prospered like Manzoni, George Eliot might have had a rival." On this Gosse's comment is, "It is very dangerous to write like that." It was one of his merits that he never did write like that, he never dogmatised, he never claimed finality even for his most cherished convictions. He revealed the strength of his preferences, but he banged no doors and brandished no sledge-hammers. Literature was a house with many mansions, and turning a key of exquisite workmanship, and with a tread that never resounded, he threw open doors, to illuminate without pedantry or affectation the mansions that he entered. "I ask that literature should give me pleasure; I do not dictate to writers by what route they shall approach me," he wrote in a review of Miss Sitwell's poems,* a sentence which gives a clue to much of his charm as a critic. He certainly neglected no means by which that pleasure could be transmitted to his readers. That was one of the functions of the critic, to excite curiosity and interest, to rouse the reader by delectable visions, and persuade him of the enjoyment to be derived from a cultivated understanding of literature. "To dress her charms, and make her more beloved." But this was not to be done by superlatives or emphasis, nor by assuming the rôle of a teacher seeking to instruct. "Moral reflections," he wrote in his criticism on *The Essays of Mr. Lucas*,† "especially if introduced with a certain polite air of solemnity, are to the British public what carrots are to a donkey: they cannot be resisted, the audience runs to read. But the appetite is satiated as quickly as it was aroused, and no form of literature fades out of sight more suddenly or more completely than do volumes inculcating Magnanimity in Humble Life or the Combating of Error by Argument." Gosse is a showman not a lecturer, he eschews moral reflections, and as he passes to and fro

* *Leaves and Fruit. Miss Sitwell's Poems, p.* 260.

† *Books on the Table, p.* 107.

among the company with which he has crowded his stage, he delights us with the banter and wit by which he draws attention to the individual figures, and the lightness with which he adorns a weighty judgment or a pronouncement of discriminating insight. What could better this from his "sermon" on Clough?* "Is it not probable that the strenuousness of Dr. Arnold blew through his docile pupil as through a flute, and that in Clough's 'sermons and admonitions,' and in all the extraordinary zeal with which he proselytized at Rugby, he was really more passive than active?

"At all events, when he went to Oxford, where he stayed for ten years, as there was no one to lead him, he entirely ceased to be a leader. It has been alleged that he took part in the Tractarian Movement, but, as Mr. Osborne shows, he sat completely aloof from it in his garret at Balliol, subduing the flesh by ascetic practices which had no ecclesiastical meaning, plunging into the frozen Cherwell, sitting through the winter without a fire, and eating coarse and scanty food. Why did he do this? Not, as Newman or Keble might have done it, because the extremity of spiritual ecstasy burned up all bodily desires, but 'with an eye to self-discipline.' 'A mental struggle was going on in him all his life,' and he regarded it 'as a guarantee of the rightness of a course of conduct that it should lead away from, rather than toward, the attainment of any concrete good.' So he wrestled with himself under the cold roof, singing, 'O let me love my love unto myself alone,' until large bunches of his brown hair came out. He was gentle and inoffensive; he was pious and irritatingly meek; and he sat counting the pulse of his own conscience until he heard no other sound.

"Then he burst away from Oxford, and rushed off to Chelsea to sit at the feet of Carlyle, who welcomed so susceptible a victim, and dropped the vitriol of Teufelsdröck on Clough's quivering spirit.

"In later years Clough was accustomed to say that Carlyle 'took him into the wilderness and left him there.' In that solitude the conscience of Clough ate him out like a white ant; it completely hollowed him, so that if any one leaned against him for spiritual support, Clough sank in dust under the pressure."

* *Books on the Table*, p. 130.

Here in the vehicle of his humour he carries judgment and enlightenment, with a delicate levity he introduces and attracts the reader to his theme; and in accordance with the rule he laid down in his criticism of O'Shaughnessy's poetry, the first approach to his subject is through sympathy and admiration. The same characteristics are seen in his article *The Agony of the Victorians*, of which Mr. Moore writes: "many days and years may pass, generations will go by before the English language produces an article so full of sagacity and beauty," and in his essay *On Reading the Bible*, of which the same writer says, "how exemplary, how worthy and how wise." Indeed few of the pieces in his many volumes of criticism are wanting in the sagacity to which Mr. Moore refers; none, it may be said, fails to give that quality of pleasure which he himself looked for from literature. Whether he is writing of Montaigne or Mr. Sassoon's *Satires*, Mallarmé or *The Fathers of the Church*, Queen Victoria or the Novels of Bourget, Ibsen or Théodore de Banville, we find the same vivacity, the same faultless construction of paragraph and sentence, the same clearness of expression.

"We cease to be savage and caustic when we are acquainted with the inner existence of a man, for the relentlessness of satire is only possible to those who neither sympathize nor comprehend," he wrote in the preface to his volume of *Kit-Kats*. In his writing he was never savage and rarely caustic. He could disparage, he could ridicule, he could demolish, but it was done with a turn of the wrist, a mere lowering of an eyelid, and so deftly, and with such an air of geniality and good spirits, that the sting of the blow is at first hardly perceived. Take his review of Mrs. Watts-Dunton's *Home Life of Swinburne*. "Let it not be imagined for a moment that I am reproving these revelations. I delight in them as I delight in the snapshots of the newspapers"—and in a later passage, "On the other hand I am free to admit that in my desire to insist on the ineffable gusto and blaze of the unfettered Swinburne of the earlier period, I may have undervalued the gentle records of the long captivity. The bird in the wood seemed to me so far more inspiriting than the same bird pecking hempseed in its Putney cage, that I may have undervalued the latter. If so, no harm is done. For now the reader possesses the record of Mrs. Watts-Dunton. He becomes aware that 'Swinburne had his boots made of calf leather, while Walter* preferred a soft kid.' I am properly reproved: it appears that Swinburne was allowed a complete freedom of choice in at least one direction."

As another illustration of his method, take his review of Mrs. Humphry Ward in *Silhouettes*; in which when writing of *Marcella* he says "It was a triumphant piece of carpentry, well designed, carefully proportioned, and defiantly executed. A very large number of persons, especially in America, thought it interesting."

Unlike Sainte-Beuve, whom he regarded as a writer more than any other to be imitated, he seldom used his critical gifts to injure an enemy, often as he used them to benefit a friend. A rare instance of the misuse of his powers was his review of George Wyndham's letters. In an earlier publication of those letters privately printed there had been a disparaging and rather wounding reference to Gosse—which, coming from one of Henley's disciples, seemed to him to be charged with a deeper significance. It was the kind of thing which he did not forgive easily and, nothing occurring to remove the impression he had formed, he took the opportunity when the public edition of the letters appeared to pronounce from his "pulpit" a commination which there and then killed the book. It must not be assumed that he did not feel the disapproval he expressed, or that he called attention to defects which he saw no reason to condemn; but it was patent to the eye that he wrote with malice, and moreover that mixed with the malice was a good deal of enjoyment. But—and here again he was unlike Sainte-Beuve—his personal prejudices did not make him unsafe as a guide among the living. With his *"nature vive, mobile, toujours à la fenêtre,"* he was interested in every movement of literature, old or new. He brought to bear on a new writer his critical faculty as impartially as though he were considering a classic. It was said with more unkindness than truth, that in the case of a "modern," however much he might have held back yet he would be found on the platform when the day of public recognition came—that he would

* Watts-Dunton.

only come on board when the sails were up and the vessel under way. His correspondence will have shown how little truth the indictment holds. He was generous to the young, he was on the look-out for talent from whatever quarter it might appear. Whether it was the Sitwells, that "delightful but deleterious three" as he called them, or Mr. Siegfried Sassoon, or the author of *South Wind*, or the poets of the War, he was equally ready with his appreciation. In one of his most charming reviews, that of Mr. Marsh's *Georgian Poetry*, he confesses that "Criticism of contemporaries must always be limited and superficial, since growing organisms cannot be definitely measured." Having entered the *caveat*, he proceeds to assess—he mildly complains of the similarity among the Georgians, and reminds Mr. Marsh that "although the shepherd knows his individual sheep by their faces, a whole flock is apt to look very much the same to a candid public." Nevertheless he picks out from the flock those he approves, and contrasting them with the Victorians reflects that the Georgian poets may be regarded as jewellers and the Victorian poets as sculptors, but that equally with sculptors jewellers have much to be said in their favour. But if the width of his appreciation is to be understood, it should be studied in his essay on Miss Sitwell's poems; there he defines the liberties which he considers permissible in poetry, and while recognizing that the poems under review rarely abuse those liberties, goes so far as to say that "Nothing is forbidden to the experimenter except failure." He did not take exception to the "proud young spirits" throwing the furniture out of the window or assuring the world that they were perfectly comfortable on the bare boards—what he did object to was their proclaiming that no one had ever been comfortable before. He was even ready to look back dispassionately on the era of which he had been a part, and smile at his own adulations and awestruck idolatries. He was ready to laugh with those who laughed at the excesses of reverence into which the Victorians had fallen. And in pruning the ivy from the façade he could be as drastic as the most exacting iconoclast.

But he was not a fearless critic. It is probable that he would have hesitated to express in print a good many of the opinions that are to be found in his letters. He would never have been *contra mundum* from his "pulpit"; there were cases in which it was better before or after the sermon to whisper in the vestry. He cannot therefore be credited with the disclosure of any alarming discoveries, or with backing a dark horse or an outside chance in print. Such temerity was in truth outside the scope of his talent as a critic. His business was to call attention to the idols, and much more rarely to idols in the making. After all, no more than his master Sainte-Beuve had he occasion to hunt in the byways and hedges for buds that might never flower, or fruit that might never ripen. But in criticism he was a safe and illuminating guide, an incomparable master of the *mot juste* whether in speech or writing; and in later years he spoke with an authority in all matters of literary judgment, unequalled among the critics of his day.

It is impossible to take up any one of his volumes of critical reviews without being aware of the high spirits and genial vision with which he approached his task. "On peut les lire à peu de frais." He is never dull, he is always good to read. He threads his way through the landscape like a silver stream, even and clear, reflecting few shadows but a great deal of light—the reader must not look for deep still pools. It was said of Queen Caroline by Leibnitz that her curiosity was such that she sought to know the "why of a why." Gosse's curiosity was of a different kind. He embarks on no metaphysical enquiries—we do not find him "seeking out of sight the ends of being," or involving himself in moral, political or religious speculations. He is content to read and point the way without analyzing too closely the materials of which the way is made. He is an artist rather than a thinker. The "reason of the thing" is a subordinate matter. If we wish to scale the mountains we must seek another guide; with Gosse we must be satisfied to amble through the meadows, and enjoy the colour of the fields and the serenity of the noonday sun.

I have already suggested that in the 'seventies he was a member, or perhaps at one moment leader of a sect of criticism which rebelled against the *ex cathedra* pronouncements of an older school. His brother critics had all the sense of a high calling common to the Victorians, but lacked the Victorian solidity. If the reaction to a literary work was pleasure, they had an adequate basis for criticism without any sizing-up of moral values. And however high Gosse may rank as a critic, it must be in a different category and under another tradition than that of Hutton, Matthew Arnold and Leslie Stephen. We are often told that Gosse is seldom profound. But if the extent of the territory through which he ranges is visualized; if we consider the charm and interest he has added to the study of literature and the shrewd animation with which he has infused so great a variety of topics; the temptation to place him in company with the foremost English critics is not easily to be resisted. In one branch of literature at any rate he has few rivals. As far back as 1879 he had written to Stevenson: "I think I should make a good biographer, of any man, that is, whom I loved. For all the little fireside ways that distinguish men from one another are easily observed by my temperament, and go far to help me in building up a memory." It was just this gift, of which he was so early aware, that enabled him to give brilliant portraits of the men he knew. He worked in pastel; his visual impressions have not exactly the bite and crispness of Carlyle's; but they equal them in vividness and intimacy. It can perhaps be safely surmised that future students who seek "the fireside ways" of Cromer, Tennyson, Coventry Patmore and a host of others, will turn not to the official biographies but to Gosse's gallery of portraits. He was hero-worshipper and observer in one—he approached the temple with awe, but once the threshold was passed, he suffered no clouds from the incense to obscure his vision. He noted everything with the detachment of a scientist and recorded it with the skill of an artist.

In 1920 he received a tribute from more than two hundred of his friends, including many of the leading men of the day, and was presented with a bust of himself in bronze by Sir William Goscombe John. The presentation took place at Lord Balfour's house, 4, Carlton Gardens. Towards the end of his address on the occasion Lord Balfour said: "Higher praise cannot be given to the literary critic than to say that he interprets lovingly and wisely the literature of the past; that he judges those of his own age with an under-

PRESENTATION OF THE BUST. FROM A CARICATURE BY MAX BEERBOHM

1. Lord Beauchamp
2. Mr. Pearsall Smith
3. Mr. G. K. Chesterton
4. Lord Harcourt
5. Mr. George Moore
6. Mr. Kipling
7. Lord Curzon
8. Mr. Maurice Baring
9. Mr. Arnold Bennett
10. Lord Howard de Walden
11. Lord Crewe
12. Archbishop of Canterbury
13. Mr. Gosse
14. Lord Londonderry
15. Mr. Conrad
16. Mr. Hardy
17. Lord Morley
18. Mr. Gosse
19. Lord Spencer
20. Mr. Ryman
21. Lord Haldane
22. Sir Frank Swettenham
23. Sir A. W. Pinero
24. Mr. Archer
25. Mr. Hewlett
26. Mr. Austin Dobson
27. Mr. Evan Charteris
28. Sir. E. Ray Lankester
29. Lord Balfour

standing sympathy and greets the younger generation in a spirit of hopeful expectation. All this can be said of Mr. Gosse* . . ."

Court Royal,
Bournemouth.

To J. C. Squire. *Feb. 7th, 1919.*
At the end of the pier 9.50 A.M.

MY DEAR JACK,—

I have indited several letters to you in my mind, but I have been too lazy to write them down. Now I expect you will be too busy to read this. I see you thoroughly enjoying the Revolution, like the lady in Erasmus Darwin, you "roll your red eye and languish for the storm." I, poor agoraphobist that I am, am so intensely glad to be out of your shouting, struggling, striking London. Oh! the calm here: I survey miles of early morning emptiness, and see no sign of life, except, far, far away, what seems to be one melancholy prostitute vainly endeavouring to attract the attention of one wounded soldier. It was very good of you to send me *Land and Water*, but as I always mingle blame with praise, I will not conceal from you that I thought the puff on the cover in bad taste. If Conrad is the greatest living novelist, it is needless to brag: if he is not, it is an insult to your readers. Moreover in the lifetime of Thomas Hardy, no other man dares to be called our "greatest living novelist." The result on me was that I did not read and shall not read a line of the new Conrad. I don't expect yellow journalism from you, my dear.

Your two articles on George Meredith are absolutely admirable. You have judged him better than anyone did before you, and indeed you have dug the foundation for a new and solid criticism of his work. The effect on me is desolating, for I had fixed on G. M. for my next *Daily Chronicle* article, and when I began to think of it, I was obliged to abandon it, for I could do nothing but

* During an illness in 1925 Lord Balfour read straight through a number of Gosse's volumes of criticism—and told me that he had seldom enjoyed the pleasures of reading so much.

cry ditto to Mr. Eagle. You will be the ruin of my old age, for you are forever saying what I was just going to say. It is odd how sharply our two minds sound in unison.

I was coming back to town to-morrow, but your railway Bolsheviks forbid. Some timid souls here fancied that they saw last night to the north-east the dim red light of London blazing. Spare the innocent females of my family in Regent's Park! Spare, O Emathian conqueror, the humble 17th-century 4tos of our [*illegible*]! When is George to be executed? And is the other George (Lloyd) already accepted as the President of the Republic? We know nothing of all this in Bournemouth, which preserves so sweet a quietness that you can hear old Triton blow his wreathed horn.

I miss not having seen you for a fortnight. Evasive creature, how can I chase you over your barricades? God knows when, if ever, I shall see my dear friend, and my cat and the faces of my poor family.

But as the servant-girls say, when this you see, remember me. At this hour, one hundred years ago, Mrs. Ruskin, wife of an entirely honest merchant, was in labour with the immortal John.

Ever yours,

E. G.

Confidential.

17, Hanover Terrace,

To John Drinkwater. *13.3.19.*

My dear Drinkwater,—

I am mortified at having to tell you that I cannot review your poems. I have been dismissed by the *Daily Chronicle* without a day's warning. One day they were discussing the subject of my next article—the next day they bluntly informed me that no more articles would be required. I hear from a roundabout source that they have sacked me in favour of Arnold Bennett, who, no doubt, will suit their public ten times better than I do. But the abruptness, the callousness of it. I leave you to think how pleasant it is, at my age, to be treated like this!

Keep this to yourself. We are heartily glad to know that you are better.

Yours always,
EDMUND GOSSE.

17, Hanover Terrace,
To Earl Spencer. *19.5.19.*

CHER AMI,—

I go sometimes to exchange gossip with Lord Reay, who, save for his broken leg, is brighter than ever he was. When it is fine and sunny, he likes to be driven up and down Farm Street in his bath-chair, and I walk beside. As we passed Rosebery's *back* door, there was a closed motor there. Ld. Reay said, "R. must be coming out: I want to say something to him." Next moment there emerged a little withered figure in a railway-cap of cloth, who stood blinking in the sun. Snow-white hair, closely-shaven drawn parchment cheeks, dull eyes that gazed out blankly. I should, positively, not have known who it was. Lord Reay spoke cheerfully to him, and he shook hands with us both, but said not a word; stood there, without a smile, then turned, still not speaking, and was pushed by two servants into the motor, which had the blinds drawn down. Lord Reay, ten years his senior, very much animated by excitement and distress, looked quite young, and turning to me said, "We have seen a dying man! What a rapid and fatal change! We ought not to have stopped, nor have spoken! Who could guess that he had suddenly become like that?" It really was terrible, and we were quite under the shadow of it till Lord Reay remembered a story to tell me about Clemenceau and President Wilson.

This is the story:—

Wilson (speaking bad French very slowly), *"Je suis un Convaincu."*

Clem., "Calmez-vous, M. le Président, vous aurez votre revanche."

I sat at dinner the other night by Alfred Carpenter, the hero of Zeebrugge, such a striking personality. How are you? Are you never coming up to town? It is not my turn to write, so I will say no more.

But Oh! that sad yellow phantom of a shrunken Rosebery—I can't tell you what it was!

Toujours ton E. G.

Gisburne,

To Evan Charteris. *April 3, '19.*

My dear Evan,—

What a shame it is that you did not come down here with us yesterday. The Peer* is in great form, and we should have been a diverting trio. We stay till next Wednesday, so you have still a chance. I was very sorry not to lunch with you on Tuesday, but I was simply driven all day.

My arrangement with the *Daily Chronicle*, of which I told you, came to an untimely close, but I was instantly snapped up by the *Sunday Times*, in whose columns I make my bow next Sunday. If you choose to do so, you may commune with me in your dressing-gown, between your bloater and your sausage, at the cost—I believe—of twopence.

I attended the Peer (who has a stomach-ache and so have I, a sympathetic one) to a horse-show this morning. He was superb, and the animals, ridiculous in emerald chains and rose-coloured rosettes, seemed to perceive a master. He has fished this afternoon. George Eliot, in a so-called sonnet, has the beautiful line,—

"They said:—Our little sister hath fished well,"

and so hath our tall brother, for in a twinkling he had landed five trout and a couple of dace. I was offered the dace for my dinner, but I modestly declined, having no lust for river-fish.

I may tell you, as a matter of the law, that I learned a lesson in not making a contract with the *D.C.* and have bound over the *Sunday Times* to put up with me for a year, at the end of which time I may probably be as tired of them as they can be of me.

We are quite alone here, only conversing with the agent Mr.

* Lord Ribblesdale.

Starkie, a shrewd little man with a Jacobean beard, who breeds horses, and is a treasure, the Peer reports.

You do not deserve a letter, having failed us so cruelly, but I am all sweetness and pardon, so here goes,

Ever yrs.

EDMUND GOSSE.

17, Hanover Terrace,

To J. C. Squire. *16.6.19.*

MY DEAR JACK,—

What a splendid letter you have written me. It seems to me so like you to be extending (as the poet says) over all the provinces of Scotland as if you were John the Scholastick or John o'Dreams. I love Scotland, and I wholly agree with you about the generosity of the Scotch. Their literary atmosphere is not quite the same as ours; there are English reputations which expire as they cross the Tweed. You must not be one, and you will not be. I am glad you have been reading R. L. S.'s letters. I had the loveliest time with him in Scotland in, I suppose, 1880. I wish I could scour Perthshire with you now.

The *Times* came out on Saturday very loud and prominent with the Hawthornden prize. I hope you will let me know very clearly for how long a time you want me to speak. It will not do to pronounce a long hour's lecture on such an occasion, and yet the public must be given something not too brief. You propose, I imagine, a variety entertainment. I have been reading Shanks with very high approval. If your choice fell on him, I could be eloquent. I hope, for goodness mercy sake, you won't choose a novel, or prose at all. The young prose of to-day is uniformly bad, except yours.

How capital the *Owl* is; hardly one poor thing in it. Your song moved me more than ever. Max is inimitable. I am going to chatter about the *Owl* in my next causerie—Sunday week. How shocking that you should have paid 9d to a whoreson Scots gossoon for your *Sunday Times*!

I have been reading, for pure private pleasure, some of the remoter writings of Dr. Samuel Johnson. They are full of priceless things. This was quite new to me: "Let no man suffer his felicity to depend on the death of his aunt." Is that gem familiar to you? And here is a cryptic sentiment on which I have meditated long: "Wigs and boots and snuff-boxes are vain without a perpetual resolution to be merry."

Well, try to be merry whatever the state of your wig and boots. I don't know when this unnecessary scrawl will reach you: I send it to Chiswick to be forwarded.

Our kindest remembrances to Mrs. Squire.

Yours

Edmund Gosse.

17, Hanover Terrace,

To Siegfried Sassoon. *5.7.19*

My dear Siegfried,—

I have read and re-read *Picture Show* with much emotion. It is full of the peculiar force—sometimes a little tinged with violence—in which you are alone in your generation. And there is rare beauty, too, a beauty which is all the more poignant because it comes in the pauses of the violence. Out of the strong there comes forth sweetness! I am greatly delighted at the progress you are making and have made. I only now ask for a little more self-restraint and a little more technical discipline. You have it in your own hands to decide whether you will go right up among the notable English poets.

Let me come to grips with you about discipline. Your opening copy of Alexandrines (on page 1) is very beautiful, till we reach line 9, when the effect, which ought to be now culminating for the climax in l. 10, drops away, like water in sand, in the feeble "and have been." Your ear ought to be too sensitive to permit this.

Then, rhymes. On p. 11 what rhymes to "lords"? It is not *necessary* to be exactly full in your rhymes, but the ear should never miss them. The song called *Middle Ages* (which is technically a new departure for you, and is hauntingly admirable—an anthology-piece!) does not need more rhymes, for the speed of it is rich enough.

You are remarkably untrammelled by memories of your predecessors, therefore the echo of R. Bridges in *Wraiths* is a little tiresome. A phial-ful of Bridges is an excellent ingredient, but you must not overdo it.

I seem to say nothing but curses when I want to bless. But the fact is your *Picture Show* is very hard to pick holes in. It is full of things which it would be impossible to praise too highly. *Concert Party* and most of the war-pieces in your peculiar sardonic vein are masterly. On the opposite side of you, *Memory* (10) and *Idyll* (25) are exquisite, perfect. And there are more—and more!

Your advance and your sureness of touch give me intense pleasure. You justify, and more than justify, all my hopes for you ten years ago. Now work away like a nigger, and don't be distracted by anybody or anything from the direct call of your own spirit and heart.

When shall I see you?

Your affectionate old Friend
EDMUND GOSSE.

17, Hanover Terrace,
To Gordon Bottomley. *8.7.19.*

MY DEAR BOTTOMLEY,—

I return you your two plays with many thanks for your kindness in letting me be among the first to read them. They are very fine and very characteristic of you: no other living writer could have written them. You have, in the second one, treated *Macbeth* as you treated *Lear* before. It is a feat of reconstructive criticism, very bold, but I think justified in its audacity by success. Your Gruach is an incarnation of fantastic and aristocratic ambition, fed in solitude; and you have cunningly indicated her possibilities of virtue and even of tenderness if her birth and education, and perhaps a touch of hereditary madness, had not from the first warped her nature. She dominates Macbeth, as in Shakespeare, but you present—I think very cleverly—a fresher, younger and therefore more manly Macbeth, not yet wholly corrupted. The touch about the horses is admirable.

Both of these plays would be attractive on the stage, but in particular I should like to see *Gruach* acted. Only you need to call Mrs. Siddons back to earth to do it rightly.

I congratulate you on these evidences of your ripe poetic power, and I am ever your sincere old Friend

EDMUND GOSSE.

17, Hanover Terrace,

To Dr. Sim. *July 10, '19.*

DEAR DR. SIM,—

The blushes mantle my cheek to receive another kind and interesting letter from you and to realise that I never acknowledged your last, although I received it with the greatest pleasure. I have been extremely busy this winter and spring past, and have been tempted to neglect correspondents who were not near enough to reproach me face to face.

I marvel at the extent of your knowledge of what goes on in the literary world. What you say about the *Letters* of Swinburne is very pleasant to me. Especially as the public, which bought the *Life* with great avidity, has not responded to the *Letters*, I suppose because of the absence of what is called "human interest." But I think all real students like yourself must feel the charm of his untiring literary enthusiasm.

Mr. Wise and I have in the press—delayed by Labour troubles, like everything else—a new volume of *Selections*, intended completely to supersede the old one, which was made by Watts-Dunton for the gratification of his own vanity. We are also at work on the great *Complete Works*, which we hope to finish in some 12 volumes. I do not know that I am likely to live to see this enterprise concluded, but I hope to see it begun. A very large, indeed even an intimidating, quantity of unpublished stuff, principally from the years 1858 to 1861 (all of it interesting, and some of it good, but none of it first-rate), has turned up, and we are puzzled what to do with it.

I am thinking of printing privately, in a few copies, a catalogue of the Swinburniana in my own library. When I do so, I shall send you a copy, for it may have some interest for you?

You ought to get Vol. 5 of Ward's *English Poets*, though with your almost miraculous knowledge of the 19th-century verse you will perceive many [*illegible*]. But I advise you to wait for the second edition—because it will contain an additional essay on and selection from Flecker. There was an almost unanimous shout from the reviewers at the omission of Flecker from the first edition. I myself thought the absence of Oscar Wilde almost as deplorable, because, if Wilde was no great poet, he marked a period. I argued in vain with T. H. Ward in favour of a brief selection from Wilde: Philistia triumphed.

I am now writing a great deal for the *Sunday Times*, where, since March, I have had a long signed article every fortnight, and generally an unsigned one in the weeks between. It is quite a new experience for me, but I enjoy having a platform from which I may address a (supposititious) crowd exactly as I please.

Trench has sent me his *Napoleon*, but I have not read it yet. There is so much to read! I suppose people will soon begin to write *Hindenburg*: *an Earth-Epic,* and *The Hierarchie of The Hohenzollerns*: *a tragedy in a hundred acts.*

Olivero sends me his books, and I read his *Nuovi Saggi* lately. He has great ardour, but he seems to me to have need of a guide. You might be useful to him in helping him to distinguish what is really important from what is temporary and journalistic. Moreover, a general outline of recent English belles-lettres would be, I should think, of more service to Italian readers than mere superficial essays on [*illegible*] figures.

I suppose this letter will be forwarded to you at Siena. But no! I see you give me your Sienese address. How I wish I could mount on the wings of the morning and descend by the cold brink of Fonte Branda! How I love Siena, but I shall never see it again: I am too old for the adventure of Italian travel. Do write to me again, and believe me

Sincerely yours

EDMUND GOSSE.

17, Hanover Terrace,

To Robert Nichols. *17.7.19.*

Dear Robert Nichols,—

You say that the sentiments of the poem you have sent me "will probably pain" me. I am entirely indifferent to these sentiments, which I probably share to a great extent.

But what does "pain" me exceedingly is that you should write so badly. These verses are execrable, and I am shocked that you seem unable to perceive it. Such lines as

"Replace rapine by thieving pure"

(which is one of the worst ever put on paper),

such bathos as

"Bears war but not war's *mitigation*."

such rhymes as

"walk"—"mock"—"talk"*

are disgraceful in "the eminent poet" (as I see you are now styled).

I am afraid that flattery and excitement and the silly criticism of an adoring circle of admirers have completely turned you, for the time being, out of the true path.

You want a period of quietude and silence, with deep and modest study of the technique of the great masters. I have seen several pieces of yours which you have published lately, which have filled me with distress by their intolerable faults of workmanship, and I feel that, although you will probably scorn the advice, I should not be honest not to give it you. It is this: be very careful, for you are on the brink of poetical bankruptcy.

Yours most sincerely

Edmund Gosse.

* This is a good little instance of the hasty judgments into which Gosse was sometimes led by the alacrity of his mind. Perceiving that "walk" and "mock" do not rhyme to the eye, he forgot that to the ear they are only the long and the short of the same vowel-sound, and on exactly the same footing as Shelley's "thought" and "spot," Rossetti's "abroad" and "God," and a host of other rhymes to which no one has ever demurred.

17, *Hanover Terrace,*
To Robert Nichols. *19.7.19.*

My dear Nichols,—

The last thing in the world that I want to do is to depress you. I want to stimulate you, to stir your literary conscience.

If I had not the greatest possible interest in you, if I had not a deep and affectionate hope, and even confidence, about your future, do you think I should take the trouble to be "rough" with you, as you call it? It is because, since almost your very earliest appearance, I have taken the most sanguine view of your talents, and have judged them to be of a very rare and delicate order, that I am jealous of any disturbing and retarding influences. I want to see you develop steadily and healthily.

The new ballad you send me to-day has great beauty and force, but even here the language is not winnowed as it might be—and should be. A lyric ought to be perfect, a chain of golden grains without a flaw. I want to see you *flawless*, and this you can only be by taking pains—infinite pains.

It grieves me much that I should disturb you, and such is the frailty of human judgment that it might happen that I am quite wrong and you quite right. But one has to work by one's lights, and it seems to me that having given you so much of my sympathy and even of my anxiety, I am bound to be honest.

The matter is not tragic, and you have but to be calm about it. To go over what you have written without complaisance—that is all I ask you to do.

I am most truly and most anxiously yours

Edmund Gosse.

17, Hanover Terrace,
To Lady Newton. *July 19, '19.*

My dear Friend,—

Nothing has given me so much pleasure for a long time as your victory.* It is splendid in form and bulk and dignity: it is complete.

* In a libel action brought by Lord Newton against the *Daily Mail* who accused him of jeering in Parliament at prisoners' sufferings. The jury awarded £5,000 damages.

Early yesterday morning I tried to telephone to you. But you and his Lordship had already gone forth, no doubt to the procession. We sent you a long message, but it is unlikely that it reached you. However, it reaches you now. Maurice de Bunsen rushed in, to share the good news.

I am thinking all the time of the load of anxiety, of wearing vexatious doubt, that has been harassing you; and now this horrid load lifted and gone! It is too delightful. You will perhaps say that Newton's position was too obviously just and firm to justify anxiety. But I know too well the risks of advocate and judge and jury, and the rarity of real justice in our vastly over-praised law-courts, to be ever sure that right will prevail. At all events, it has prevailed, magnificently, in this case. I am just as pleased as though I had won a suit myself.

Now, I take the liberty of an old friend to urge that you will now not fling the whole of this £5000 away with a *beau geste*, but will first of all, before anything else is done, recoup yourselves for every penny of expense (for of course the "costs" will not cover nearly your payments). Reflect that your victory is not complete so long as the spiteful action of the newspaper has impoverished you by a single penny. Of all the mental cost and nervous expense nothing can be said.

Forgive this long and tiresome letter. I am overflowing with the subject. But you must be buried in letters.

Yours ever,

Your affectionate Friend

EDMUND GOSSE.

17, Hanover Terrace,

To J. C. Squire. *July 25, 1919.*

MY DEAR JACK,—

Your slender book thrills me. I am greatly touched at the honour you do me by inscribing it to me. *The Birds* is now, to my mind, already a classic: I read it for the tenth time with more admiration than ever. The solidity of the beginning, the way in which it opens out, and then the incomparable passage about the gulls! That will be read as long as anyone reads English. The other pieces are mainly new to me. *Processes of Thought, I,* admirable—a very subtle and almost unseizable condition of mind is fixed—as though liquid glass had been poured over it—in a fascinating melody. But *Harlequin* I cannot praise enough: it is delicious in every way, as a picture, as a symbol, as a melody. Wonderful. The two songs are among the best that our time has produced. *A Far Place* is pre-eminently pictorial, a riot of colour.

In *Processes of Thought, II,* I note what a potent spell Walt Whitman still contrives to exercise. In *Processes of Thought, III,* I see my J.C.S. in a new aspect, as the writer of exquisitely balanced prose which possesses (as it should) no slightest trace of melodic or prosodic character. You are good alike at prose and verse. But I regret that *Processes of Thought, III,* should be divided into paragraphs with capital letters, because the ignorant will conceive that is meant for verse, which of course it does not wish to be. Prose is prose and poetry is poetry.

On the whole, I doubt if any pamphlet of new verse and prose, so slender as this, ever contained more genius, or more enchanting variety.

I want very much to see you. But you are sunken in affairs. I suppose it is vain to ask you here this next Sunday.

Always yours
EDMUND GOSSE.

The Black Lion,
Llangurig,
Llanidloes.

To Viscount Haldane. *Sept. 18, 1919.*

MY DEAR H.,—

I am greatly touched at your finding time, amidst all your avocations, for writing me such charming letters. They are my greatest pleasure. I think of you addressing your great audience, and wish I was among your listeners.

To-day I received from Squire a rhymed epistle, immensely

clever, all on one rhyme. I must copy for your amusement a fragment of it:—

"The noble Viscount, I repeat,
Is really annoyingly discreet.
If he weren't so damnably discreet,
He'd find himself in another street
With all the public at his feet;
And even the scribes who with horrible heat
For five long years have steadily beat
His pate for plotting our utter defeat
And a victory final and complete
Of the Hunnish Tirp and his beastly fleet,
Would be bound perforce their words to eat
(I admit a most rancid and nauseous meat)
And stand in a row in a pure white sheet,"

and so on, and so on. Monstrously clever, Squire is.

Your affectionate
EDMUND GOSSE.

Black Lion Hotel,
Llangurig,
Llanidloes, Mont.

To Max Beerbohm. *Sept. 22, 1919.*

MY DEAR MAX,—

I WILL have those MSS.; I WILL have that caricature! I am unblushingly greedy. I *must* have them. What a lovely caricature you will make. Do bring in the two Archbishops, with their mitres and their croziers. What fun it all is! I can't take it seriously; I shake with hysterical laughter. What has possessed you all to make such a painted pagan idol of poor old third-rate me? But I am very grateful, deeply touched and horribly ashamed.

Don't you think Crewe's covering letter a masterpiece of lapidary prose? He says in it such a tremendous lot for the space.

We have been nearly 3 weeks in this exquisite lonely place on the spurs of Plinlimmon. The infant Wye is a thread of wasted silver a few yards off. The weather has been enchanting until to-day, when—the neighbouring town of Aberystwyth (25 miles west of us) having laid out thousands to entertain the Fleet—a gale has risen out of the uttermost West and no Fleet can come. So, at least, the postman reports. We have buzzards here and ravens, but no shops; and otters, but a defective postal system, so that while letters tell us that England's Independent and Majestic Press rings with Me to-day, not a newspaper has arrived.

When is your new book to be out? I am very anxious to know. Do say on a postcard (if you can afford no more).

Nellie joins me in all kindliest messages and thanks, and I am ever, dear Max, your devoted old friend,

EDMUND GOSSE.

"The Notorious Septuagenarian."

How ridiculous to be 70!!!

17, Hanover Terrace,

To J. C. Squire. *Oct. 7, '19.*

MY DEAR SQUIRE,—

At last the embargo is taken off us, and the pent-up accumulations of nine days' post pour down. I hasten to return *The Moon*: it has not been my fault that I have kept it so long. I read it all carefully aloud to my wife, and we both enjoyed the splendour, the ingenuity and the refinement of an extraordinarily sustained and noble piece of work.

I have only one small piece of technical criticism to make. In this poem and in other writings of yours, I notice you careless with regard to the ambiguity in using words which are identical as past participles and as transitive verbs. It is a very awkward thing. For example, in stanza 1. v. 3. "Her boughs spread"—what did they spread? The attention is tripped up at once. You have perhaps never thought of this before, but I think you should attend to it in every case. It is of so great importance that no disturbance of thought should break the impression.

St. 20. L. 5. bad grammar "but *thee*" is. St. 22. L. 4. I don't think this line comes off. The irregularity is excessive, and therefore more disturbing than pleasing.

St. 26. L. 9. "prayerless" is too weak to bear three stresses. It is really a dissyllable—you can easily add a syllable to this line. St. 28. A magnificent stanza.

St. 20. L. 4. Rather a heavy line. I think you might improve "dropt."

St. 8. L. 1. "Shone upon the ground?" Across or along?

All this is very poor trifling. Your poem is magnificent.

We think of returning to town next Friday.

Always cordially yours

EDMUND GOSSE.

St. 20. Ll. 1 and 3. Identical rhyme. Why not say "cold" in L. 3.?

17, Hanover Terrace,

To Thomas Hardy. *Jan. 18, 1920.*

MY DEAR HARDY,—

It is a whole week since we spent that delightful day with you and Mrs. Hardy at Dorchester. Every day I have meant to write to you, but I have been so busy that I could not manage it.

I want to tell you a little more about my earliest experiences of Weymouth. We went there first in April 1853; where were you then? We lived in lodgings there until December of that year, my Father all the time working away at marine zoology like a nigger. His principal employment, whenever weather would permit, was dredging in Weymouth Bay, sailing with a fisherman called Jonas Fowler. They dredged from Whitrose to Church Hope, and from St. Aldhelm's Head to Portland Bill. My Father was all this time collecting living specimens for the newly-formed aquariums, and sending them to the Zoo in Regent's Park, and the Crystal Palace and elsewhere.

He started, in the Weymouth lodgings, a salt-water tank of his own (Sept. 5, 1853) and this was the first private aquarium ever made. I possessed it, until about 1893, when it fell to pieces.

At Weymouth, at this time, he wrote his very popular book called *The Aquarium*, which is all full of his adventures in the sea off Weymouth.

In March, 1854, he took us down to Weymouth again, and now he wrote his *Manual of Marine Zoology*, which Ray Lankester tells me has never been superseded. He left Weymouth, however, to settle at Ilfracombe before his book was finished.

I feel rather injured that none of the guide-books—which put in their pages so much rubbishy information—take the trouble to mention the connection with Weymouth of the most distinguished marine naturalist of last century. Don't you think they ought to do so? I have not been able to find the address of the lodgings we lived in. The 1854 visit I still very dimly recollect from the circumstance that we were going for a steamer excursion to Swanage which had been long looked forward to, when a coal popped out of the sitting-room fire in our lodgings and slightly burned me, so that my mother and I had to stay behind.

I wonder if I ever brushed up against a big boy called T. H. as my Mother took me in her hand along the streets of Weymouth in 1853? Tell me whether you think it possible.

My wife has had a very kind letter from Mrs. Hardy which she will shortly answer.

To-day is our friend Austin Dobson's 80th birthday. He seems to be very well (except for rheumatism) and still writes verses.

Ever very sincerely yrs.

EDMUND GOSSE.

17, Hanover Terrace,
N.W.1.

To Maurice Baring. *April 22, 1920.*

MY DEAR MAURICE,—

I was delighted, and a little self-reproached, by your charming letter. I only quite lately heard of your serious and painful illness.

I do earnestly hope that you are now steadily recovering. Not only did Henry James write to me from the Tregenna Castle, but I also wrote to I-don't-know-whom from the room there where you are sitting. I cannot remember the year, but I should think it must have been 1896. We went down to St. Ives to be near Leslie Stephen, with whom I took immense walks, of a wholly speechless character. He and I went to the Wrestling at Redruth, I remember. The neighbourhood of St. Ives is full of charming nooks and coves on the coast, and the town of singularly filthy smells.

I am very glad you are reading H. J.'s Letters, although I can quite understand that you are not entirely in sympathy with him. You are more *romantique* than he was or than I am. But you praise the Letters very handsomely.

I hope to see the good, the peerless Squire this evening. What a pearl of man he is! I do not think there could be found a better specimen of the Intellectual Man. *C'est presque le plus bel exemplaire de l'homme de lettres qu'il m'ait été donné d'admirer.* I wish some millionaire guiltless of his country's crimes would endow him with a £1000 a year.

You will not, alas! be able to grace my blushing honours on May 10, when A.J.B. is to present to me your gift of the bust. It will be very embarrassing for me to face so much music, but I hope not to sink in confusion.

Tessa has just come back from the Lizard. I wonder if you were there together? You must promise me to be very careful about the Pirates at Penzance. And Jews are said to be excessively rife in Marazion, which is still closer to you. Ah! what dangers threaten the invalid who travels. And in the purlieus of St. Ives, cats have less than seven lives.

What is a yrsmb?* I have tried it up and down, in vain. Bmsry—that is hardly any better. This w[ld.] be a good word for the new poets of the Dada School to employ. Are you a convinced Dadaist?

Evan is roaming about, radiant and fugacious. He has just bought, for thousands and thousands of pounds, an immense picture of a female inebriate scowling, by Augustus John.

* This is a hieroglyph for "Yours M.B."

Take great care of yourself, and get well quickly. The household of Gossidemus salutes thee in the Lord.

Your affectionate old

EDMUND G.

R. Y. S. Castle,
Cowes.

To Earl Spencer. *May 20, 1920.*

CHER AMI,—

You will wonder at this address. I was carried off by Sir William Portal yesterday, and am staying here as his spoilt guest till Monday. My bronches have been too obstinate for anything—I haven't at 71 the recuperation I used to have. I hope this enchanting change will cure or, at all events, mend me. The beauty of the weather is unspeakable—all blue and silver. Before leaving Town yesterday morning, I sent you my new book. You have read, or had a chance to read, most of the contents, but accept it with my love.

Of course, you know this Castle? I stayed here in 1915 with dear old Redesdale. It is, I think, one of the most delicious places in England. This morning, at 4 a.m. I could not sleep, and I leaned out of my bedroom-window which opens on the foam of perilous seas, and I can't describe the beauty. The sea at my feet all dim mother-of-pearl, and a bar of pale orange on the horizon. The sleeping yachts black in silhouette—the most Japanese effect you ever saw.

Coal, I hear, is pouring into England, but none of it may be sold to factories. However, I suppose it will be available when the strike is over for industrial purposes. I had a letter two days ago from a friend of mine in Copenhagen, who is in a very large way of business. He is a loyal friend of the Allies. He has just returned to Denmark from a prolonged tour through Germany, and he describes the state of that country as stupefying. Everybody hard at work from dawn to dark, all the factories humming, an air of universal prosperity and a firm decision to conquer in a war of revenge in less than ten years! My Danish friend asks me why no one in England seems to be aware of all this. He says the Germans are well aware of all our strikes and unemployment, and that they say, "England is dying of laziness." What is one to think?

EDMUND GOSSE.

17, Hanover Terrace,

To Max Beerbohm. *June 14, 1920.*

MY DEAR MAX,—

Kind Edward Shanks has hastened to bring me your precious gift. I shouted with laughter: it really is one of your masterpieces. The aspect of the Archbishop is perfect: my wife instantly recalled that action of the hands, the large fingers pressed together at the tips. And H. J. himself! The mixture of surprise and horror with insatiable curiosity, "Will Your Grace beautifully indulge me with the *details*? Do not spare me!" expressed in every contortion of face and figure! Thank you a thousand times for a precious treasure.

We are actually starting, in a couple of hours, for Cambridge, where I am to walk a new-plumaged Doctor, in a strange procession of quasi-celebrities, such as Bonar Law, M. Bergson, the Prime Minister and Lord Burnham. Imagine this file of flamingos, in scarlet and rose, flinging down our harps on the jasper floor of the Senate House and singing "Holy! holy! holy! Erudite and mighty Arthur James Balfour, we, thy lost opportunities, salute thee!"

We join in love to you both.

Your affectionate Friend

EDMUND GOSSE.

17, Hanover Terrace.

To George Moore. *June 4, 1921.*

MY DEAR MOORE,—

Your letter of dedication, so beautiful and gracious, is as happily expressed as it could be. Alter nothing. I am profoundly touched and pleased.

I suppose it is because you are an Irishman that you are so fond of saying "myself" instead of "I"? I do not criticize—I only observe. When you say (in your delightful picture of Valoir) "under whose piers Mallarmé and *myself* were nearly drowned,"—I should have written "M. and *I*." But which is best I do not decide. *Myself* seems to indicate emphasis on the person, needless in this connection, but I don't know.

Gratefully and affectionately yrs.,

EDMUND GOSSE.

CHAPTER TWENTY-NINE

Gosse had many friends among French authors. Since the day when as a clerk in the British Museum he had sent forth one of his earliest *ballons d'essai*, in the form of a letter addressed to Théodore de Banville expressing his profound admiration for the poet, he had never ceased to keep in touch with current French literature. He was a daily reader of the *Figaro* and the *Débats*, and no new publication of the least importance escaped him—he would often take as the subject for his "pulpit" address the work of a French author, and in his appreciation was never behind and once at least in advance of the opinion held in France. Such was notably the case with André Gide, whose future he predicted years before he had attained his present celebrity. Nobody would have imagined him to be a French scholar, who had heard him pronounce two words of the language, but his artistic intuitions, a sense of style, an inspired taste, in a word his literary touch made him as trustworthy a guide in French as in English literature. Of more than one French writer he had read every available written word. Such was the case with Pierre Loti, the compelling perfection of whose style made him say, "All I feel is that I am obliged to read any rubbish he chooses to write," and with Zola, of whom he said after seeing him in London, "Such a nice, kind, honest man, but for that unfortunate dash of obscenity like a smudge on his face," and again with André Gide, whose least utterance in print he followed with all his animated interest. In France he was regarded as an authoritative interpreter. *French Profiles* (1904) in a series of delightful essays had shown him to be an acute and suggestive critic of current French literature, and this he had followed by numerous criticisms of past and present writers. He had known Alphonse Daudet, Zola, Verlaine, and Ferdinand Fabre; he could number among his personal friends, Henri Davray, Madame Duclaux, known as an English poetess under the name of

Mary Robinson, André Chevrillon, Paul Bourget, Henri de Régnier, Marcel Prévost, Maurice Barrès and André Gide. Throughout his life he was stirred by a passionate attachment for *la douce France*, for her prose and poetry equally with her cities and forests, her byways and rivers—the sort of attachment felt by many even of the most critical Englishmen, and probably without a counterpart among other nations of the world. It was therefore fitting and no less than his due that in 1921 he should have been invited to the University of Strasbourg to receive an honour and deliver an address. On this expedition he was accompanied by his friend Mr. William Bellows, who organised the journey and did what he could to absorb the shock of preparation and arrangement. The tumult of anticipation in Gosse's mind on such an occasion was quite abnormal—every detail had to be thought out with tremulous care—no loophole must be left for error to creep in—the whole undertaking being visualised from start to finish, and every hour accounted for in imagination. He was incapable of acting at a moment's notice; his mind was in a flutter till the train was caught, and then, as the end of the journey drew near, was in a tremor lest some flaw in the scheme should make itself apparent. The Strasbourg expedition was especially alarming—involving an address in French, a banquet, and a sojourn in the house of strangers, the Comte and Comtesse de Pange. Indeed he would not trust himself to translate into French the address he had prepared in English, and enlisted for the purpose the good offices of his hostess. Having secured the translation he was in acute anxiety about his curiously uncouth pronunciation, and nothing would satisfy him but a full-dress rehearsal at the home of the Panges the evening before his appearance at Strasbourg. Corrections were invited as he declaimed from a reading-desk in the centre of the drawing-room: these were tactfully given by his host and hostess, whose small son also contributed to the evening's entertainment by every now and then interrupting with the exclamation: "Oh, but Monsieur Gosse—we *never* hear that word pronounced like that." The University, however, were well content with the result, and an audience of two thousand persons greeted the English man of letters with enthusiasm. He returned to England elated with his success.

To Lytton-Strachey. *17, Hanover Terrace,*
May 21, 1922.

My dear Mr. Lytton Strachey,—

Your new book being out, I asked for it to review. Alas, it had been snatched by Mr. Stephen McKenna. As I could not exist without it, I had to buy it, which I hated doing, because I am very mean. However, I grudge nothing, for it is enchanting. The two best essays are inimitable, except by yourself. You are the best writer living under fifty—but as everyone tells you so, you will soon be insupportable. I thought I knew all about Dr. Akakia, but that incomparable episode shines with new lustre in your pages.

Of course I read the Browne and the Beddoes with emotion. *Re* the Browne (my dear friend Mrs. R. L. Stevenson told me that the King of Samoa always said "*Re* the Pig" in reference to his favourite food)—*re* the Browne—you make out an admirable case, and I suspect that I was wrong. About 1895 the persistency of the young gentlemen of Fleet Street in believing that dazzling diction excused emptiness of thought got the better of my temper. But you are excellent on Browne, and I believe you are right. And *most* courteous and kind to me.

Re the Beddoes—the most tragic accidents have not failed to dog that poet, your praise of him being almost the only fortunate thing that ever happened to him. All his letters and MSS. have totally disappeared! Quite lately I have retrieved a few slight data about his early life and mysterious death. I will keep them till we meet. Mr. Ramsay Colles (if he exists) owes you a debt, for he added absolutely not one grain of dust to knowledge or appreciation of Beddoes. His hand was deep in my pocket all the time, but I let him have my biblio and biographical ha'pence without protest.

I congratulate you on a very lively and pertinent book, of which I have read every page with pleasure. But, remember, this achieve-

EDMUND GOSSE AT HANOVER TERRACE

ment does not absolve you from still bolder and ampler creations in the future.

Yours very sincerely,

EDMUND GOSSE.

So glad about the 15th. Is not Swinburne more likely than Tennyson to be the Cowley of the future? Let us discuss this one day over a cigar. I put T. higher than you do, in some places. He is such a perplexing Curate's Egg. But conceive what the height of a *very* small selection would be, if courageously conceived.

E. G.

Carnarvon Arms Hotel,
Dulverton.

To Evan Charteris. *Sunday, June 11, 1922.*

MY DEAR EVAN,—

It is vexing that we did not manage to meet before I came away from town. I expect that you have been extremely busy, and so was I. We made a great effort to break away, and came down successfully to this lovely place, which is full of solitude and green light and cold air, most delicious. It was quite a toss-up, but we have all the luck. I never struck a lovelier place; at the foot of the garden runs the river Barle, rushing with pure dark water straight from the moors. It is full of trout, and winds between fresh woods, and meadows positively starred with buttercups and clover and germander speed-well. I have very seldom, since I was a child, seen the face of England at this moment of the spring transfiguration. It is so lovely as to make one faint. Everything is just a fortnight behind London, so that we have the white and the crimson mays and the laburnums at their highest. It seems so disappointing to be old when the whole world is so brilliantly young. But this is morbid.

We arrived by a train which brought your sister, Lady de Vesci. I don't know where she was going. She looked very beautiful, like some symbolic figure. We stood beside her on the platform for some time, but as I saw she did not recognize me, I did not disturb her meditations. I do not know where she was going, perhaps to Pixton which hangs on the hill-side above us.

I have brought with me very little to read. A silly little book of scraps from the girlhood of Jane Austen, a sort of Daisy Ashford futility. Why do not great writers destroy their juvenilia? They do themselves much wrong. We seem very far indeed here from Genoa and Lord Northcliffe and Mr. de Valera. Did you know that Haldane went over to Dublin last week for three days? His impressions were highly interesting, but rather pessimistic. I think his optimism was disappointed with the apathy of the mass of the Irish people—frightened, sick with illusion, but quite incapable (from mere fear of the gun) of the slightest movement of self-assertion. I should not be surprised if we see Petrograd and Moscow repeated in Dublin.

You have been very gay, I suppose? I imagine you taking part in all the social splendours I read of dimly in the papers. I admire your physical endurance: the mere thought of it gives me a head-ache. I wish you would write me one of your charming letters. I enjoy them so much always, and most of all when I am transferred from the scene of action. To be here is like living in a Leyden jar.

Now do write to me, or else I shall think you have forgotten your old

EDMUND GOSSE.

17, Hanover Terrace,

To Siegfried Sassoon. *St. Swithin's Day, 1922.*

Why no name on the title page?

MY DEAR SIEGFRIED,—

I much approve of *Recreations*. You must not dream of excluding *Fragment of Autobiography*, or of altering it in any but a formal way. It is highly original and amusing. All I would suggest is the addition of dates, where I have pencilled them. This would give the reader a notion of what is to come, and would prepare him for it. Also, I would propose keeping the whole thing in the present tense. I see no advantage and some confusion in having a change from *came* to *know*. You will gain a continuity by keeping to the present tense. The poem is a vision, in 1920, of what was in 1910, and a hint of what may be in 1930. Give this your polite consideration.

I am proud of my "graceful" recognition. Indeed, you must alter nothing essential. But I propose putting "Nineteen Ten" in line 3 to balance the "Nineteen Twenty" and "Nineteen Thirty" lower down. A poem of this kind can hardly be too closely knit.

The rest of the poems I have read with enjoyment and approval. Except *The London Museum*. This, I think, is a mistake. If you abandon rhyme and metre, you must retain something, or else it is not verse and should be printed as prose. If, in this piece, you had chosen—and had persisted in using—a beat, a sort of drum-noise, I should ask for nothing else, but you do not do this. For instance, if you had written this sort of thing (mine is pure nonsense, of course, to show you what I mean):

In holographic farthingales of commonwealth & council
Are memories and ghosts out of yellow-candled mortuaries,
Compared with the gruff murmur of some sleepy-headed Secretary,
Or a single scolding word out of great Eliza's lips.

That would have satisfied all requirements, but at present *The London Museum* (appealing only to the ear) gives the ear nothing to feed upon.

I have read all the out door country-pieces with immense pleasure. *Falling Asleep* is still my best favourite.

Always yours,

EDMUND GOSSE.

Hôtel du Havre,
Caudebec-en-Caux.

To Philip Gosse. *Sept. 24, 1922.*

MY DEAREST PHIL,—

This is a line to warn you, if so disposed, to address us after the receipt of this, to Hôtel du Rhin, Dieppe. We are going from here to Fécamp next Thursday (the 28th), and then to St. Valéry-en-Caux, and on to Dieppe, where we shall stay two nights and come back home on Wednesday the 4th of October: that at least is my plan. Our holiday has developed into the greatest success possible. When we woke up on my birthday, it was to find that the weather had completely changed from winter to summer. We took a motor and had an enchanting drive of 70 kil. through the forest to the handsome town of Pont-Audemer and round, crossing the Seine twice in different steam ferries. The life here is excessively amusing, now the warmth has come. It wants sunlight and blue air. There was a torchlight procession late last night, magnificent *sapeurs-pompiers* in white and blue marching four abreast hither and thither all over the town, which is holding its annual fête. This morning, under our bedroom-windows, and between us and the river, an enormous mushroom in the shape of a circus has sprouted in the night. Mother loves this sort of thing, and visits every stall and peep-show. It is very pleasant and amusing to find Sylvia so at home in all the little ways of the townsfolk. I had a very pleasant surprise yesterday in the form of an unexpected extra cheque for my *Aspects and Impressions*, of which it appears that Cassells sold 2800 copies in the first two months. But I must go out. Nothing will check mother, what she loses on the roundabouts, she makes on the swings.

Ever your loving,

EDMUND GOSSE.

Aspects and Impressions referred to in the preceding letter consist for the most part of reprints of articles from *The Edinburgh Review, The London Mercury, The Modern Languages Review* and *The Fortnightly Review*, covering a wide range of subjects from Malherbe to Lord Wolseley, and from Henry James to Clemenceau. Many of the articles show Gosse at his best; this is especially true of the piece on George Eliot, which among many illuminating sentences says, "Her prose has many fine qualities of force and wit, it is pictorial and persuasive, but it misses one prime but subtle merit, it never sings. The masters of the finest English are those who have received the admonition *Cantate Domino*! They sing a new song unto the Lord"—and that on Henry James which exhibits the deftness of Gosse's gift for personal observation and sympathetic insight into character, and again the study of the Hôtel de Rambouillet, informed by a scholarly appreciation of the literary implications of the circle of which he writes.

17, Hanover Terrace,

To Filson Young. *14.1.23.*

My dear Filson,—

You were very kind to lend me this book, which I should have been sorry not to read. I have read it all; the beginning is the best. What you said to me on Friday of the man's object in writing it strikes me as certainly just. I would add that *vanity*—bordering on madness—was another cause. But the wish to work up excitement by fighting his battles o'er again is the dominant note. How melancholy, how appallingly wretched must be the old man capable of writing this book. I should suppose him on the very brink of suicide.

I am sending the volume back to you direct with very sincere thanks for your kindness in lending it to me.

You are doing most brilliant work in editing the *Saturday*. You have made it as good as, if not better than it ever was.

On Friday I enjoyed myself immensely. Your dinner-parties are always delightful. I was none the worse the next day, and have been better ever since.

Yours ever,

Edmund Gosse.

17, Hanover Terrace,

To Siegfried Sassoon. *Jan. 14, '23.*

My dear Siegfried,—

It was most kind of you to send me those two volumes. I was delighted with your young friend*—he looked like a chinchilla, with his grey clothes, sharp nose and wonderful eyes. What eyes!

* Edmund Blunden.

Those of Keats must have had that expression. I thought him perfectly charming, so simple and ardent and responsive.

The excitement of entertaining two fiery bards must have been too much for my aged frame, for while I was dressing next morning, I had a cardiac seizure and fell on my back among the furniture. Accordingly I was put to bed, and am still in the doctor's hands, but mending. In bed I began W. Owen's poems, but they were not suited to my headachy condition, though I thought your preface admirable in its economy. The *Voyage of the Bonaventure* we are keeping to read aloud in the family circle o' nights, when I get well.

I find that the Manchester Liberals who have bought the *Nation* are Sir John Simon and his gang. In the *Observer* of this morning, Garvin gives them avuncular advice in terms I think unparalleled.

Don't be alarmed about my health. I shall be perfectly all right soon.

Yours ever,

EDMUND GOSSE.

Marlborough Club,

To George Moore. *18.7.1923.*

MY DEAR MOORE,—

I have the greatest difficulty in writing to you this morning because I was really too nervously anxious that your play should succeed to know whether it did. And my inexperience of stage matters is boundless. I thought the third act quite brilliant. Miss Seyler is surely wonderful, and I thought Faber's get-up and manner excellent, but he spoke so low that I could not catch half he said. As I must be perfectly frank, I did not think the action in the second act quite clear enough, although I had read it and understood it in the reading. How extraordinary is the difference between the words read and the words listened to across the footlights! It was delightful to hear—when I could hear—pure English on the stage, so eloquent and clear-cut. But what did you think yourself? I long to hear your own account of the matter, and all the side-issues. Of course, the audience was bored, and made a little angry, by the insufferable "waits" between the acts. This put them out of temper: no doubt this afternoon it will be better.

Your affectionate Friend,

EDMUND GOSSE.

17, Hanover Terrace,

To Sir Humphrey Rolleston. *Oct. 14, 1923.*

DEAR SIR HUMPHREY ROLLESTON,—

On returning from a month abroad, I find your very kind gift of *Medical Aspects of Old Age*. I have read it with great admiration of your skill and science, but with acute misery, since I find myself either afflicted or about to be afflicted by every malady which you so coolly describe. It is a dreadful book to give to a poor old creature in his 75th year. I palpitate, after studying it, in every nerve, with what my friend Frederick Treves calls anxiety-neurosis. All you say, however (tho' so terrible!) is intensely interesting, especially what you say about Metchnikoff, whom I knew well.

I am proceeding with my lecture for you on the 20th of November,* but with every anticipation of being an object of ridicule to your learned company. How was I ever tempted to enter your den of lions?

You are very much better, I hope, for your holiday in the West? I am particularly well, except for my endarteritis obliterans, and (of course) for the chronic stenosis of my aorta.

Yours very sincerely,

EDMUND GOSSE.

17, Hanover Terrace,

To Dr. Sim. *Nov. 17, 1923.*

MY DEAR DR. SIM,—

I am very much obliged to you for reminding me of Sydney Dobell's Centenary. I shall hope to write about it in the *Sunday Times* when the date comes.

* Delivered at the Royal College of Physicians and entitled *Literature and the Medical Profession.*

Your knowledge of poetical criticism is so very extensive that I can add little to it. In several places I have touched on the Spasmodists, but never, I think, have expressed a detailed view of S. D. There are mentions of him in my *Life of Swinburne* and in *More Books on the Table*. He had a great deal of imagination, no sense of form or proportion, and a plentiful lack of taste, was (in fact) not a poet, but a sort of poetic fragment: but very interesting to the student.

I wish I could attend your reading of Arnold. He is very much out of favour with our Neo-Georgians, but I remain the faithful slave of his intellectual melody.

It is always a great pleasure to me to see your handwriting, and I thank you for your kindness in bearing me in mind.

Yours very sincerely,

EDMUND GOSSE.

An interesting young professor, Dr. Mario Praz, has been here. He is a great Swinburnian. If you come across him, please be kind to him.

17, Hanover Terrace,

To Monsieur Pierre Legouis. *Dec. 10, 23.*

MY DEAR MONSIEUR LEGOUIS,—

I am exceedingly glad that you applied at once to me.

The fact is that piracies of Swinburne's copyright—which Messrs. Heinemann bought from the poet's widow* at great cost—have been so frequent that they are obliged to ask payment for the use of Swinburne's verse and prose.

But I am very anxious to be of service to you and your review, and therefore I will get over the difficulty by paying the five guineas myself. Please accept this as a small token of my great regard for your personality, and my unfailing wish to promote an understanding between France and England.

Lest you should demur to this arrangement, let me tell you that

* Mr. Gosse was mistaken. The letters were not actually purchased from Mrs. Watts-Dunton, but, from Mr. T. J. Wise.

the thing is done! I have this morning paid a cheque for 5 guineas to Messrs. Heinemann, and you are free to print *Ave atque Vale* as soon as ever you like!

I am reading your *Spenser* with delight. It is the best monograph on that poet yet written.

Believe me, with cordial regard,

Very sincerely yrs.,

EDMUND GOSSE.

NOTE BY MONSIEUR LEGOUIS.

I had written to Sir E. Gosse for the sake of the *Revue Anglo-Américaine*, which desired to publish a verse translation of Swinburne's *Ave and Vale* by M. Lafaircade but demurred to pay to Mr. Heinemann, the publisher, 5 guineas for the copyright. I had simply prayed Sir Edmund to see if he could make Mr. Heinemann come down to a more moderate price, 5 guineas amounting then to 600 or 700 francs.

Note his spontaneous generosity, as a proof of which the letter is worth printing.

17, Hanover Terrace,

To Professor F. C. Roe. *March 19, 1924.*

DEAR SIR,—

I am afraid I can say little or nothing about Taine which will offer you any interest. His work had very slight influence on me in early days. My earliest acquaintance with it was in 1875, when I read the opening volume of the *Origines de la France Contemporaine* when it was published. This gave me great pleasure, but of course had no relation to literary values. Then I read the *Littérature Anglaise*, but with more irritation than enjoyment. I thought it was a very brilliant exercise, but that the judgments were incorrect. It would take too long, and would not interest you, if I were to explain why the *idée* of Taine with regard to literature, has never either attracted or influenced me. I am the disciple of one man, and of one man only—Sainte-Beuve. No one else has been my master. At the time when everybody was gathering under *l'arbre de Taine*, I was much more tempted to take shelter under the branches of Renan, whose infinite intelligence and ravishing style have always strongly attracted me. But Renan, although he has delighted, has never "influenced" me.

Of course I know that Taine was a great thinker, a beautiful writer and a philosophical force in his age, but he is not—dare I confess it?—a very *interesting* figure to me.

Pray believe me to be,

Dear Sir,

Very faithfully yrs.,

EDMUND GOSSE.

Marlborough Club,

To Maurice Baring. *April 24, 1924.*

MY DEAR MAURICE,—

If I were free I sh[ld.] think nothing of coming to Brighton for so delightful and noteworthy and romantic an occasion.* But unhappily I am deeply engaged. Till 6.30 Ethel Smyth is to be at our house, a presence not to be put by. How wonderful to think that you will be 50! I cannot realize it at all. Were you not 16 when I saw you first at Eton? Surely not much more. And all through the years you have been so uniformly kind to me! I often think of it, when I "count my mercies."

Well, blessings crown the almond that crowns your Mount Everest of a pate! Continue to be indulgent to the dull old fogey who is yr. devoted friend,

EDMUND GOSSE.

17, Hanover Terrace,

To Sir Clifford Allbutt. *April 28, 1924.*

DEAR SIR CLIFFORD,—

Your welcome letter is not merely very kind and encouraging, but it is definitely valuable as well. There can be no doubt that you are now the solitary survivor of those who knew the strange Brontë family personally. My dear old friend, Lord Knutsford, used to talk to me about Charlotte, and her visit to him. He remembered the green dress she is wearing in our National Portrait

* A birthday party.

Gallery picture. But he was born eleven years earlier than you were. How curious it is that there should still be so much universal curiosity about that bleak and queer trio of young women at Haworth.

My wife thanks you for your very kind message, and we both hope you are well. I shall keep your charming letter as a historical document.

With best regards, I am,
Yours very sincerely,
EDMUND GOSSE.

The Hotel,
Rumbling Bridge,
Scotland.
Oct. 3, 1924.

To J. C. Squire.

MY DEAR JACK,—

Your kind gift of the *Grub Street Entertainments* has arrived, and has been eagerly welcomed. I had a momentary disappointment in finding that there was not a single one of them that I had not read before! But they all deserve to be read again, and yet again. We have been reading aloud, before our open hearth of logs, *The Castle of Otranto*—what fatuous trash! But to-night we begin to read *Grub Street* aloud, and it will be a welcome change.

You did wisely, I think, to start with *The Man who kept a Diary*, which is perhaps the most polished, but of course a little more obvious than the rest. It is satire and not intellectual romance, but not less welcome on that account.

The purest beauty is in *The Success*, which is a masterpiece of delicacy and pathos. Here are in almost poignant degree, the *lachrymae rerum*. *The Lecture* is the most boisterous, it is like a nightmare, but most amusing. For pure comedy, again sharp with satire, I put *The Man who Wrote Free Verse* first. *The Golden Scilens* is of a bewitching ingenuity, but (as I told you at the time) verging on extravaganza. *Baxteriana* is extraordinarily powerful, but very painful. I wonder if you knew when you wrote it that a correspondence of this kind between Gray and an Italian professor is said to exist. I should need to see it before I admitted the truth of what has been said about it. Very possibly it would prove comparatively anodyne or otherwise explicable. Before I took the melodramatic attitude of Mr. Hawke I should want to know whether Baxter in his acknowledged writings had pretended to adopt a hortatory attitude; in other words whether he was a sexual Tartuffe. The question of hypocrisy, of conscious moral falsity, would have a great deal to do with my censure. I could not bring myself to forget Gray's charms and virtues even though he stood convicted of an instinctive abnormality. The proof that he was cruel or sly would really be more painful to me. I think in this instance you force the note a little, do you not? The things about your stories, thus united, is the fact that there is not one which is no good of its kind. I do not find a single story which seems to be put in for padding. This is very remarkable, so is their variety. They impress the reader more in this composite form than they did when they were published separately. I wish that the publishers had refrained from using that hideous jacket with the disgusting melodramatic picture. It does serious injustice to the solid merit of the book.

In the meantime, and always, I am your affectionate friend,

EDMUND GOSSE.

17, Hanover Terrace,

To André Gide. *August 25, 1924.*

MY DEAR GIDE,—

For a long time past I have been intending to thank you for the gift of your *Incidences*, but I have been prevented by the mass of work which I have had in hand, and by a certain indolence which creeps over my old age. I will delay no longer. In reading *Incidences* I have once more found myself listening to the voice which (almost more than any other) fascinates and allures me. Many of the little essays I had read before in the *N. R. F.*, but they gain a new accent, a fresh significance, in re-reading. Your mind is excessively limpid, I see strange and beautiful things moving in its depths, as in the [*illegible*] of a pacific sea.

ON THE QUAYS, PARIS

I will not specify more particularly what pleases me than to say that no one has written so well (*nearly* so well) on Proust as you have. *"Si désintéressée, si gratuite,"* nothing could be more excellent. Your article on Gautier interests me very much, because, when I was quite young, about 1873, his prose and verse exercised a violent influence over me, which, a little later, the preface to *Les Fleurs du Mal* accentuated. Now I cannot read Gautier any more; Théodore de Banville has faded for me also, but not nearly so much as Gautier. It is like the pleasure one takes in Fragonard's pictures: the thing may not be very well worth doing, but no one does it better than Banville. But all through *Incidences* I enjoy your line of thought: it goes *leaping* along, with great *jumps*, and I joyously jump with it.

You did not send me *Corydon*, so I had to buy it. Perhaps you thought I should be "shocked." But that is not my way. There is nothing in the whole diversity of life which serious men cannot seriously discuss. I think you show great courage in writing this book, although I do not know quite *why* you wrote it. But that is your business, and I read with sympathy and respect everything you choose to write. No doubt, in fifty years, this particular subject will cease to surprise anyone, and how many people in the past might wish to have lived in 1974!

You will have seen that we have lost Conrad—a beautiful figure. But he had said all he had to say, and went on writing in order to make money. He will live in half a dozen of his early books. Here, in England, literature is in a deplorable state, dying of collectivism and emptiness. Well, well! I wish you would write to me, but at least I am glad that you have not forgotten me.

I am always sincerely yours,

EDMUND GOSSE.

17, Hanover Terrace,

To Maurice Baring. *Oct. 12, '24.*

MY DEAR MAURICE,—

When I acknowledged your *Punch and Judy* yesterday, I was preparing to read the volume through. Quite unsuspecting, I read on to the chapter on Ibsen. I really cannot express with what a variety of emotions I entered upon it. Will you believe that I never saw or heard of this article before? Where did it appear? How can I have lived seventeen years without having been aware of the most beautiful and the most generous sentences that anyone of authority ever dedicated to my work? I write—it is verbally true—with tears in my eyes. I never was so moved, and I lack language to tell you how much I am touched. And to think that I have reached extreme old age—nearer 80 than 70!—without knowing what so dear a friend and so wise a judge had honoured me by writing.

Dearest Maurice,—I press your hand, and I thank you from my heart for your goodness to your affectionate old friend,

EDMUND GOSSE.

17, Hanover Terrace,

To Max Beerbohm. *4.8.25.*

MY DEAR MAX,—

Your kindness and your indulgence overwhelm me. On this dark and chilly day, I am walking about like a radiator in full action. I could love the world, so excited am I at being thus (undeservedly) loved by you. I can't bear having to keep my pride to myself. I want to jubel *"Seid umschlungen, Millionen, diesen Kuss der höchsten Max!"*

Your preface is the most lovely thing. But won't you be blamed for it by the masses who don't take your indulgent view of me? Well, that's your look-out. I can only thank you—and with a glow and a delighted wonder.

The extra pages of extended "Mote" (There's a subject for your pencil—A Mote expanding under the breath of Henry James!) are quite delicious. I have gummed or glued them in my precious first edition, exactly as you direct.

I have never told you how delighted I was with your caricature of me and my infant self. The evangelical ardour of the child—most unbecomingly robed in white, and belted in the service of Jesus—is delicious. I thought it one of the very best, where all were good. It was bought by Philip Guedalla, that intelligent historical epigrammatist, who has quite an important gallery of your gallant inventions. One walks up his staircase grotesquely attended by them.

Please give Mrs. Max our united warmest greetings, and believe me ever, my dear friend, your affectionate and grateful

EDMUND GOSSE.

Cloan,
Auchterarder,
Perthshire.

To Lady Newton. 5.9.'25.

MY VERY DEAR FRIEND,—

What a curious coincidence! I was sitting down to write to you, when your letter was handed to me. I wanted greatly to have your news.

And now, first, about your book. I entirely approve of the dates 1660–1760. Ought not the words "New Impression" or "Second Edition" to appear in the advert. of *The House of Lyme*? I am not sure: you might consult Evans. In all other respects, the prefatory matter seems all right.

I must tell that just before we left town, Evans* came to lunch with me. I asked him what important books they were publishing this season. He mentioned yours first of all, and he said that they were very proud of it, so "highly creditable to the firm," and that they thought it would be a financial success, but that even if it was not, it was a great advantage to have a work of such solid merit in their list. He also volunteered the statement that you have been so kind and responsive throughout, listening to every suggestion, and so prompt and businesslike. He added, "I only wish that we had more writers like her in that." All this was without any suggestion on my part.

(This letter is really written by my own hand, though you never would guess it from the calligraphy (?) which is due to a local

* Mr. C. S. Evans of Messrs. Heinemann.

pen, evidently used centuries ago by a witch in correspondence with the Devil.)

We came down here on Wednesday night (Thursday morning) and stay here till next Thursday the 10th. I won't tell you where we go after that, because I want first to have another letter from you here. The only other guests are the Bishop of Durham and the Dean of St. Paul's. We make a capital mourneval (I have told you before what a mourneval is) because:

Lord Haldane is a confirmed optimist; the Bishop is a confirmed pessimist; the Dean is a sham pessimist; and I am a sham optimist; so we have gloriously prolonged and incoherent conversation.

Tell Newton that he has guessed wrong about the review of the new Memoirs. I have hitherto not read the book, which I opened on a rude remark about myself and shut at once. Haldane tells me to tell your husband that he was greatly interested in N.'s article on Russia in the *Sunday Times*, but wanted more. I wish you would make him write Rees another article on his impressions of Esthonia.

This is a provisional letter. Haldane is still suffering much from sciatica, but I think improving a little. The weather is gorgeous. My love to you all.

E. G.

Fortingall Hotel,
Perthshire.

To J. C. Squire. *Sept. 16, 1925.*

My dear Jack,—

Your charming and amusing letter gave me very great pleasure. I expect that the sudden change in your life will prove of much service in turning your mind into a fresh channel and providing wholesome interests. My own life has been extraordinarily static —I have only lived in two houses in more than fifty years—largely from timidity and that dread of change which makes me such a timorous conservative. But I think it is a mistake not to live more "dangerously," and most likely I might with advantage have been more boldly nomadic. You, I think, have much more of the strayed reveller in your constitution than I have. Your poem amused me very much, especially the lines about Hudson, with which I seriously agree. Even in these days of spurious enthusiasm, no one has had so much clotted nonsense written about him as Hudson. Why is it? I find his works essentially second-rate, his mind poor and wandering, and his attitude to life mean. Occasionally there is an agreeable piece of observation, but never anything to excuse the raptures of our wild delicious friend, Cunninghame-Graham, who simply proves that a *beau sabreur* can be a detestable critic.

This is the most lovely place, so silent that silence is a sort of noise, great mountains peeping over one another's shoulders at us, and a broad salmon-river fussing beyond the stubble fields. I think we shall stick it out here till the end of September.

With our love to Mrs. Squire, I am ever your

Affectionate friend,

EDMUND GOSSE.

Fortingall Hotel.

To Philip Guedalla. *Sept. 21, 1925.*

MY DEAR GUEDALLA,—

Are you quite sure you have not received my acknowledgment of the Bonaparte opuscule?* I do not doubt that you are right, and I will tell you what happened. It arrived the very day we left for Scotland, and as soon as I had read it, I wrote off to you my thanks and my appreciation. But in the hurry of departure it can never have been posted, and now I make no doubt still languishes on my table under other papers. Pray forgive me. I thought it most interesting, and the impression left upon my mind after weighing your evidence was that some *verbal* direction of the sort must have been made by B. but never confirmed in writing. But the matter is a very curious one, and the point well worth making, especially at the present juncture.

You must unquestionably do L'Aiglon, who I think suits your particular and individual method.

I must read Wells' new novel. Here in the shadow of the stainless

* A lecture entitled *Napoleon and Palestine.*

mountains we have been reading, for a change, Arnold Bennett. I took up poor Conrad's fragment, but I could not get on with it. I am afraid he had said his say: he ought never to have been *popular*. Popularity rubbed all the gold powder off his wings. I brought a Molière with me. How the *Précieuses Ridicules* explains the Blanks! But I must not let my idleness distract your busy-ness.

The above is our address until the 29th, when we return home.

Sincerely yours,

EDMUND GOSSE.

17, Hanover Terrace,

To the Rt. Honble. Stanley Baldwin. *Jan. 9, 1926.*

MY DEAR PRIME MINISTER,—

You will not, I hope, think I take an unpardonable liberty if I tell you with what extreme pleasure—indeed with a certain *exultation*—I have read your speech yesterday on the Classics. It will have a wonderful effect. It lifts public life into a higher atmosphere, and it will, in a variety of ways, strengthen the hands of those who are trying—often under great discouragement—to fight the hordes of the Philistines. Thank you a thousand times.

This address must not be allowed to disappear with the newspapers. You really must reprint it. Remember, you almost promised me to print your Rectorial Address. But this is a grander *geste*.

You are not to fatigue yourself by acknowledging this letter. We shall meet soon, I hope, at Grillion's, and then you may spare me a nod!

Yours always sincerely,

EDMUND GOSSE.

17, Hanover Terrace,

To J. C. Squire. *14.2.26.*

MY DEAR JACK,—

Thank you for the very delightful gift of your poems. I spent a couple of hours last night reading over again my old favourites and liking them better than ever. But you are the latest poet I shall ever admire. I have come to the end of my tether, and the younger bards bore me to extinction. It is purely age, the cataract on the appreciative eye; but there it is! I can take no pleasure in any of the young Immortals. In vain am I addressed by what a French girl at an English school recited, "The swettest and the beast." But you I can still enjoy: you are the last—Chaucer to Squire, that's my ritual. But I am a very dreary old man, the waste-paper-basket of Parnassus.

You are ahead of me again, as usual, this Sunday with Raleigh. But I deal with him next week, and I have one advantage over you—you did not see him day after day in 1884! What a homuncule you must have been in 1884!

Affectionately yours,

EDMUND THE EMPTY.

Flattered by your dust-cover, but why, oh why, make me write bad grammar?

17, Hanover Terrace,

To Siegfried Sassoon.

7.4.26.

MY DEAR SIEGFRIED,—

It is perfectly charming of you to send me your Poems, very sensibly selected, I think, though I have favourites which are not there. You have made a bibelot of the book, for which I shall order a case, so as to keep it unspotted from the world. We are all pleased with your portrait, and the exquisite calligraphy of my particular cosset, the Eighteenth Century Poet. I feel very proud of you as I read and cogitate.

Have you seen two new Cambridge memoirs, those of Henry Jackson and of F. Jenkinson, heavenly twins born at the same hour of the labouring Pitt Press? They have been pleasing and exasperating me—they are so haughtily and exclusively Cambridge. Did you know much of Henry Jackson? I was always ashamed of myself for not being able to like him. Isn't there some tribe of the heathen that worships a great brown bear in a cave? I always felt H. J. to be that bear, and the more he growled, the more the College (and the University) grovelled before him on its belly. He was a great man in his way, and that a valuable way, but not *my* way.

Affectionately yrs,
In Phœbus Apollo
EDMUND GOSSE.

17, Hanover Terrace,
July 29, 1926.

To Viscount Haldane.

MY DEAR H.,—

Let me greet this morning of your 70th birthday, as you greeted mine, by a heart-felt wish for your happiness and increasing power for usefulness. I bless the lengthening years which preserve for me the inestimable treasure of your friendship. Among many good and wonderful things which I have enjoyed, I place this among the highest.

The Lord bless you and keep you. The Lord make his face to shine upon you, and give you peace. That is to-day the prayer of your affectionate old friend,

EDMUND GOSSE.

The following is addressed to Bruce, Lord Haldane's dog:

17, Hanover Terrace,
Aug. 11, '26.

DEAR BRUCE,—

I hope you are very well and catching rats. But it is not about Rats that I am writing to you. This letter is very confidential, and you must be careful not to let your Papa see it, or even your Aunt Elizabeth. Well—perhaps Aunt Elizabeth? But you must be very careful.

You know that your Papa is very, *very* clever, and wide-awake about all sorts of things. But I daresay you have noticed that he is very weak about one thing. He can't resist the ladies, especially youngish handsome ladies from a great distance, who talk to him about Relativity and Humanism and all that sort of thing. Now I must tell you that a most dangerous specimen of this class is coming to Cloan this week, and I want you to be very clever and watch her. Don't get excited and bark, but keep quite close to your dear Papa, and *watch*. If you see the American lady sit very close to him, you might growl a little, but not much or else they will turn you out of the room. But if you see her edge her chair close to your dear Papa, and say something about what a wonderful light he has thrown on the Pathway to Reality, and take his hand in hers, don't hesitate a moment (for a black dog that hesitates is lost), but go right in and bite her ankle. When you have done that (but perhaps not before) you can go quietly out and tell your Aunt Elizabeth, and she will come suddenly in, with you at her heels, and she will say in a loud voice to the American lady, "Unhand his Lordship!" and then we must hope that the motor will come round to the door.

I shall be very anxious till I hear from you that this is done. You know who I am, so I will only sign myself,

A Well-Wisher.

CHAPTER THIRTY

As years went on, the shadow of the Churton Collins episode became less intrusive; at the same time the recognition given to *Father and Son* had revealed to Gosse the authority he exercised in the world of letters. The growing confidence which resulted brought him immunity from many nagging fears and hesitations, and that potential ambiguity in the significance of social contacts, so apt to haunt the sensitive, grew much less insistent. He mellowed, his high spirits broadened, and his letters show him splendidly at ease. France and Scandinavia, by the honours they bestowed, were showing their appreciation of the service he had rendered to the cause of literature, while in England his tale of success had culminated in his being acclaimed on his seventieth birthday as one of the leading men of letters. Certainly the dream of the clerk poring over catalogues half a century back in the British Museum had been more than realised. But in spite of this tonic encouragement criticism never lost its terrors; it remained a bogy. At the mere sound of battle the old wound would open, and Gosse would be on the *qui vive* in a state of prickly agitation, starting at shadows, and suspecting ambushes. The bogy would even invade and darken his friendships. Storms would blow up, mostly, it is true, of short duration, but rocking the house itself while they lasted. For instance, on the appearance of *The Brook Kerith*, Gosse wrote to Mr. Moore deprecating his use of the phrase "More than you think for," alleging it was bad English. Mr. Moore wrote back, "Shakespeare uses it and my parlourmaid uses it, and an idiom which Shakespeare and my parlourmaid use is good enough for me—Idiom is sacred, you can't criticise it any more than you can criticise trees or rivers or hills," adding by way of a good-humoured riposte, "Your own writing, my dear Gosse, would be improved by idiom." Gosse, at once scenting battle, was deeply offended, and many explanations were necessary to avert the danger which menaced a friendship of forty years. Indeed, it would be an error to suppose that friendship with Gosse was always plain-sailing, or that explanations were always successful. The break in his long friendship with Arthur Benson was a more serious matter, incurable for many years and then only partially healed. With his friend Sir Thomas Elliott again, a slight cause brought about a result only possible with someone at times morbidly touchy. A banquet was due to take place at which both men were to be present. Gosse telephoned to ask if decorations were to be worn, and was answered in the negative. Later Sir Thomas ascertained that he had made a mistake—but there was no time to let Gosse know—Gosse arrived late—the first thing he noticed was that decorations were being worn, they danced before his eyes, mocking him from every quarter, and sparkling derisively from every breast—he tripped up to Sir Thomas and in a voice of concentrated anger said, "You have insulted me," refusing thereafter to be comforted or to listen to any explanation. Such things were the outcome of raw nerves and of a side of his character which had never grown up. It was difficult for him to assess any set-back with the eye of a philosopher, he might know there had been one ice age, but it did not seem to strike him that there might be another. For him every moment of life and friendship was charged with impetuous obligations, which for his part he was eager to meet, and had the right to expect others equally to fulfil. He was incapable of letting things slide, or of chancing the probability that they would right themselves. Giving so lavishly himself and importing into friendship such vehement activity of spirit, he was easily checked and far too ready to fancy slights, "cut up rusty" and mobilise his forces of resentment. No account of Gosse can afford to ignore this aspect. On the other hand, it was the rarest thing for him to miss a chance of reconciliation. No man desired peace more, but neither experience nor reason seemed able to give him security. Many illustrations could be given, but let one suffice. At the time Mr. Desmond MacCarthy was literary editor of the *New Statesman*, an article on Swinburne, signed by Mr. F. L. Lucas, appeared in that periodical, the opening passage of which referred to the ordeal of hostile criticism through which all poets had to pass, and the reviewer compared it to crossing a wilderness inhabited by malicious monkeys. Further on he quoted from the *Encyclopædia Britannica* article by Gosse on Swinburne in which the moral tone of some of Swinburne's poems was deplored.

The inference was possible that Gosse was a "malicious monkey." He wrote to the *New Statesman* protesting that after all he had done for letters and for Swinburne's poetry in particular, such a comparison was monstrous. But on hearing from the Editor that the implication had been an oversight in proof-reading, he instantly wrote a charming letter accepting apology and withdrawing his protest from publication. MacCarthy, who was acquainted with Gosse and responsible for the proof-reading, omitted to write personally. He felt rather guilty, but two months later he was astonished to find himself "cut," and nearly a year afterwards to hear Gosse say in a loud voice to his neighbour at a luncheon-party, "You see that man opposite; he called me a vicious ape." The fact was that when anything hurt Gosse he could not help attributing it to malice prepense on somebody's part. In this case he had brooded over his pain till he had convinced himself that Mr. MacCarthy had deliberately inserted an insult over another contributor's name.

The strained relation lasted three years, at the end of which time Gosse's *Life of Congreve* was republished, and Mr. MacCarthy, thinking highly of the book, reviewed it accordingly. Gosse at once wrote gratefully acknowledging the terms of the review, and the quarrel was at an end—reconciliation warm and complete immediately followed. But if Gosse resented things on slight provocation to himself, he was even more hasty to draw a sword for the defence of a friend. He would jump into a combat of this kind impulsively and as if he welcomed an opportunity, and no second in a duel could show more solicitude for his principal than would Gosse for the subject of his intervention. Sir Walter Raleigh told me that he once received a letter from Gosse, in which he called his attention to a gross inaccuracy in a recently published book, the letter concluding with the enigmatical sentence "Now is your chance!" On his writing to enquire what was meant, Gosse replied, "Don't you remember the author was the man who wrote a vicious review of your book *The Novel*?" It was an amiable and generous trait, rooted in "the secret places of his nature" and in that love of friendship which to him was a philosophy of life and a religion from which he never departed. The vulnerability which brought such agitations in its train was the penalty he paid for being preternaturally alive to the personal element in human relations. Sudden humours used to descend on him, disapproval crystallise on his countenance, and a gleam of anger flash through his spectacles—something had gone amiss—there was someone in the company he did not wish to meet—he was being ignored—or if it was a meal, he was in a wrong place, or not getting enough of his neighbour's attention. As for instance when seated at dinner next to Lady Griffin on whose other side was Mr. George Alexander, with whom she was obviously anxious to talk—observing signs of inattention as he spoke to her Gosse said, "If you would rather listen to Mr. George Alexander, pray do"—"Oh may I?" said Lady Griffin, and at once did so. Such social misadventures used to make him very huffy. But it was easy to bring him round, and extricate him from his discontent, and if Lady Gosse was there such a mood was dispersed in a moment under the influence of her beneficent tact, which at all times was ready to intervene between her husband and social troubles.

17, Hanover Terrace,
To André Gide. *August 22, '26.*

My dear Gide,—

It gave me great pleasure to receive your letter from Cuverville. I did get your earlier letter from Central Africa but did not know how to respond to it, as you seemed moving across incalculable deserts over pathless sands! But I welcome you back to France, and I hope you will give us impressions of your strange adventures such as you, alone, are capable of doing.

You must write them soon, if you please, for if you delay too long, I shall not be here to welcome them. In a few days I shall complete my 77 years, and although I am not conscious as yet of any mental infirmity, my body gets more and more "cranky" (as we say). I shall certainly never come to France again, but I hope to see you in London.

I read everything you publish, and always with admiration of your sincerity and your courage. I do not always agree with you, but that is another thing. I admire extremely your *rectitude*, and it is all the more marked because most of contemporary literature seems to me to be cowardly and conventional. It all tends to be standardized, and the only salvation for us is to specialize—to say clearly and boldly what we, individually, believe and feel. I should like you to know that I sympathize deeply with your determination to see things as they are to you.

May I venture to wish, however, that you would try to release yourself from your bondage to the Russians, and particularly to Dostoieffsky? We have all in turn been subjected to the magic of this epileptic monster. But his genius has only led us astray, and I should say to any young writer of merit who appealed to me, Read what you like, only don't waste your time reading D. He is the cocaine and morphia of modern literature.

Do not be long before writing to me again. Tell me what works you are projecting, and what use you are going to make of your African travels. Will you not come over to London, say towards the end of October? I should like to organise a public déjeuner in your honour. Will not that tempt you?

Your affectionate Friend,

EDMUND GOSSE.

17, Hanover Terrace,

To John Drinkwater. *Oct. 21, '26.*

MY DEAR JOHN,—

Your publishers have sent me your *Book for Bookmen*. I am a Bookman if ever there was one, and I have been reading it with infinite profit and delight. These are just the disquisitions I enjoy, so different from the cloudy metaphysics called Criticism by Mr. —— and Mr. ——! What you so kindly and indulgently say of me touches me to the quick. It is nobly said, even if you are blamed for your good-nature, but I will hope that this will not happen.

But there is one statement that fills me with amazement, and (unless there is some mistake) would seem to be one of the strangest

EDMUND GOSSE AND ANDRE GIDE
HÔTEL DE BOURGOGNE, PARIS, MAY 2, 1928

coincidences possible. Look at page 175 of your book. On the 16th of August 1875, my Wife and I, being on our wedding-journey, drove from Clovelly to Bude. It was a wild morning of storm. We turned a little aside at Hartland, intending to call and pay our respects to Mr. Hawker, but on approaching the confines of Morwenstow heard the passing-bell and, stopping to enquire, were told that the news of the Vicar's death on the preceding day had just reached the village.

Now, is it possible that T. Hardy made the same vain attempt at the very same time? It seems barely credible. Or did I tell you of our experience, and have you transferred it to T.H.? I have just shown the account I give above to my Wife, who confirms it in all particulars. It made a great impression upon us. I should like to know what you conclude about it.

Affectionately yours,
EDMUND GOSSE.

17, Hanover Terrace,

To Philip Guedalla. *Dec. 3, 1926.*

DEAR GUEDALLA,—

The enclosed is from Lord Palmerston's great-grand-step-daughter, Lady M. Levett. I think you will like to read it. The hide-and-seek among the guns and the anecdote of the toad are very pleasing.*

Your note last Monday made me very angry. I cannot think how you could allow yourself to say that you would be proud if you could believe that I "meant half that I wrote." I always mean exactly the whole of what I write. I believe that you expressed yourself in haste and not with a wish to wound me. But you should not be so anxious to be "smart" at all risks.

Please return me Lady Margaret Levett's letter.

Yours truly,
EDMUND GOSSE.

* The letter of Lady Margaret Levett refers to the fact that Lord Palmerston every day fed a toad which had for many years lived in a fractured cannon-ball in the grounds of Broadlands. On this eleemosynary errand he was always accompanied by one of the children of the house.

17, Hanover Terrace,
Regent's Park, N.W.1.

To Siegfried Sassoon. *28.12.26.*

MY DEAR SIEGFRIED,—

It was very kind of you to send us this pleasant little edition of *Calico Pie,* that poignant and exquisite poem. I place Lear high among the poets of his time. His verse is an excellent example of the *poésie pure* of which the Abbé Brémond has been writing (with such amazing reverberations in the Parisian Press!). In everything except actual direct meaning, the best of it is at a high level, and Lear has a strange plangent melody all his own. What a cry of unsatisfied adolescence is *The Duck and the Kangaroo*, and your *Calico Pie* seems to be a perfect expression of finite passion. I am quite serious—I think it, and many of Lear's other things, near to the source of tears.

I think that our noble Edith enjoyed her visit. She wrote to say that she did, in a letter as kind as it was sensible, without a touch of oddity. We both like her very much, and I admire her sincerely. I feel that she is a sort of chrysalis, in a silken web of imperfect expression, with great talents to display if only she can break out into a clear music of her own. There is no one I watch with more interest, and her personal beauty and dignity, which are even pathetic, attract me very much.

You will be amused to hear that on Christmas Day I got a long letter (entirely unexpected and unfished-for) from the Poet Laureate, very affectionately expressed, and dwelling on the length of our friendship, which indeed has lasted nearly 53 years (we met in 1874). I was very much touched, for he rarely expatiates, and I don't know what made him write. He speaks of having lately, after a very long silence, done a quantity of "work." I wonder what it is?

Nellie and I went last night to the first performance of Noyes' romantic play in verse of *Robin Hood in Sherwood Forest.* It was enthusiastically received by a crowded audience and is indeed a very pretty thing, but the verse—it is all lyrical—could not be very easily distinguished, though the actors did their best. I shudder to think what the Georgians (the children of Eddie Marsh) would say to such unashamed romance, but none of them were there.

Well, goodbye in 1926, and thank you for all your kindness to me in the past year. I value your friendship very highly indeed, and as long as I am not too decayed to appreciate it, I beg you will continue it. Come soon again to see

Your affectionate old friend

EDMUND GOSSE.

17, Hanover Terrace,

To E. S. P. Haynes. *Dec. 31, 1926.*

DEAR MR. HAYNES,—

I should be delighted if I could help you, but I was not acquainted with Mr. Herbert Spencer. I never spoke to him nor received a letter from him.

That I may not be completely irresponsive, I will write down a trifling impression, which is at your service if you think it at all amusing.

Herbert Spencer was a member of the Committee of the London Library, on which I also was elected to serve in 1883. I sat in Committee with him only once, in that year. He sat just opposite to me at the table, and took no part in the business, until suddenly he interrupted it by saying that he had a proposition to make. He then proceeded to say that the tone of the books purchased by the L.L. had greatly deteriorated, and that he attributed it to the intrusion of "works of fiction." He pronounced these words with haughty scorn, as if he smelt a bad smell. Then he made the definite suggestion that in future no novels, "except of course those of George Eliot," should be purchased for the Library. The Committee was very respectful to him, but this was really too much, and his proposition was rejected, I think unanimously. He then rose, in dreamy dignity, and left the room, without saying Goodbye to anyone, and I never saw him at a Committee meeting again, although I do not think that he resigned until ten years later, 1893.

But this is not worth your acceptance, I am afraid, unless you make a corner for it in some note!

Yours very sincerely,
EDMUND GOSSE.

17, Hanover Terrace,
To André Gide. *Jan. 7, 1927.*

MY DEAR GIDE,—

I have now read *Si le Grain ne Meurt* very carefully, to the end. I have already read much of it twice. Up to page 44, tome III, I have nothing but admiration of your art, your originality, your exquisite manner of writing. There are passages here which will bear comparison with the best modern literature.

But when I read the *Deuxième Partie*, I am confronted by an immense difficulty. What can I say? Yet I must not leave what I feel unsaid. I pray you to bear with me.

The *facts* here related offer me no surprise, since I divined the truth when I read *L'Immoraliste* more than twenty years ago, while later publications have confirmed my knowledge. This has not affected my feeling, personal or literary, since I have never allowed the idiosyncrasies of my friends to blind me to their qualities. I am not a critic of temperaments, nor so ignorant as to believe myself fitted to be a judge.

But now you have gone much further, and I cannot help asking myself, in the face of this narrative—Was it wise? Was it necessary? Is it useful? I am incapable of answering these questions, which leave me in a very painful perplexity.

Heaven forbid that I should be such a prig as to put my instinct in the matter before yours. You have acted not without reflection, certainly not without a marvellous courage. You possess so unusual a genius that perhaps it may claim to be a law to itself. But *why* have you done it, and what advantage to anyone can accrue from it?

If you think that my old (and undiminished) affection gives me a right to ask you this question, I beg you to send me a full and clear reply. I do not ask it from curiosity, or in a priggish or dictatorial spirit; I ask it in deep sympathy and in an earnest wish to comprehend your position.

I am, my dear Gide, now as ever

Your attached friend,

EDMUND GOSSE.

17, Hanover Terrace,

To Siegfried Sassoon. *27.1.27.*

MY DEAR SIEGFRIED,—

I have had a very crowded week, and only been able very occasionally to give ½ an hour to your MS., of which I have read Parts I and II. But I think you will be anxious for a word from me, and so I write provisionally to say that I am *delighted* with it so far. There is no question at all that you must go on steadily. It will be an extraordinarily original book. I am particularly glad to find you resisting the temptation to be what is called "fantastic"—the usual cheap trick of the age.

The hunting-scene in Part I, is one of the best things of the kind in the language. Give us more hunting-scenes, and beat all the surteeses and Beckfords.

When I have finished I shall write again, and you must come and talk.

Yours always,

EDMUND GOSSE.

Your handwriting is as clear as mine. Can I say more?

17, Hanover Terrace,

To Siegfried Sassoon. *3.2.27.*

DEAR SIEGFRIED,—

I have been so extremely busy this last week—and not very well—that I have not been able to write to you, but I have not neglected your MS., and still less your letter. I feel that in the last part of your book, as I have it here, you have gone off the rails. The beginning, up to your hero's going to Cambridge, was so very delightful, and so *right* in tone, that I cannot help being disappointed by the continuation. You are not called upon to draw a sarcastic picture of a slack and idle young man. That is off the rails altogether, and would interest nobody. If you can do no better with your hero than this you should leave his character alone.

Suppress all this second part, which is in a false key. You can use the episodes, which are good, although the second cricket-match is dangerously near being a copy of the first. But you must entirely revise the character of your hero. At Cambridge, although he had no aptitude for college-work, he played games, and above all he hunted. You seem to have forgotten the vacations. You seem to forget that the whole purpose of your book is to portray a hunting man. You may give him mental refinement, even (if you like) æsthetic tastes, but *hunting* must be the centre of the picture.

I suspect you of having made no preliminary sketch of what you mean to write. Such a book—and indeed any book—can be brought to perfection only if a complete skeleton of its purpose and plan exists beforehand in the writer's mind. I suspect you of aimlessly scribbling episodes without having set down a firm plan of the whole book. This will never do.

I am afraid that you are giving way to indolence and irresolution. You must pull yourself together, and make this, as you well can make it, a really good book.

Remember, no satire and no sneering! *Hunting* has to be the subject and Dixon has to be the central figure.

Ever yours,
EDMUND GOSSE.

17, Hanover Terrace,

To E. F. Benson. 2.5.27.

MY DEAR FRED,—

Your publishers obliged me with a copy of your *Francis Drake*, with, as I flatter myself, your approval. I have read it with great care, and I want to congratulate you, and to thank you for the pleasure it has given me. It is composed with unflagging vivacity, and I recognize in it an incessant attentiveness—as though you were never content to be merely floating on the tide of accepted opinion. The result is that tho' you deal with familiar matter you never fail to give an impression of novelty. Your long practice of the art of fiction gives you facility in making history amusing. Indeed, I always think that the novel should help the historian, if only—as you do—he realises the distinction of the genres.

But I must not tire you. I write only to express to you the very genuine enjoyment which your eloquent and witty monograph has given me.

Always cordially yours,
EDMUND GOSSE.

You are illuminating—to me—about Q. Elizabeth!

Savoy Hotel,
Bournemouth.

To Professor Grierson. *Sept. 26, 1927.*

MY DEAR GRIERSON,—

Thank you for your delightful and amusing letter. I have been thinking much about you, and wishing to have your news. A long illness drives one's memories back upon one's friends, and one cultivates reveries. I have been isolated for nearly nine weeks by the most serious illness I ever had. It was typhoid (Heaven knows how I caught it), and for the first day it seemed that in the preface to *Donne's Minor Works* (which I eagerly look forward to) you would have to make faint reference to "the late E.G." But they pulled me through, and here I am, feeling more myself every day, and able to work, as you will see from next Sunday's *Sunday Times* onwards.

I hate to correct you, but G. Saintsbury is 82 (not 81), and going strong. I constantly have cheery postcards from him, which take hours to decipher but are worth it. He suffers, he says, from giddiness, which confines him entirely to the house, but his brain and pen are as efficient as ever. Earlier in the summer, we paid several visits to T. Hardy at Max Gate. He is a wonder, if you like! At 87½ without a deficiency of sight, hearing, mind or conversation.

Very tiny and fragile, but full of spirit and a gaiety not quite consistent in the most pessimistic of poets. He and I collogued merrily of past generations, like two antediluvian animals sporting in the primeval slime.

I am astonished at your activity. You are like the man that

"hunts the lion
Through France and Portugal and Spain
And back to old Albion."

I should like to know what you thought of Lisbon. It struck me as a little sinister, when I was there early in 1914. But how I approve of your determination to settle in the Shetlands! Is there not a delectable island called Foula, all cinctured with cliffs and cormorants? I imagine you there, like a sort of sublime Casabianca. Like you, I am driven mad by the noises of civilisation. In this hotel (which is the most comfortable we ever struck) there is no noise at all. A broad garden runs down to a cliff road overlooking the sea, where no motors or the like are allowed to pass. All we hear is the wind and the sea at rough times, but normally nothing.

. . . .

I look forward to your edition of the minor prose of Donne. Especially to your treatment of *Biathanatos*.

My dear Grierson, your attached friend,

EDMUND GOSSE.

17, Hanover Terrace,

To the Rt. Honble. H. A. L. Fisher. *4.11.27.*

MY DEAR FISHER,—

I have read the Lecture you have just sent me with breathless excitement! This is not an exaggeration, for I happen to have been full of Valéry lately, without becoming *quite* a convinced Valérian. I saw him the other day, took the Chair for him at his *conférence*, and had a long talk with him about Letters. He is a real charmer, in person as well as in work. But I am very glad that you have not strained the chord of eulogy as his French idolators do. The bathos of "entre deux chemises" is typical of a fault that worries me a little.

The metal is not molten, but has to be hammered. It is true that the workmanship is usually superb. What lovely bits you have chosen! They sing like rivulets in the hills:—

Et la lune perfide élève son miroir
Jusque dans les secrets de la fontaine éteinte,
Jusque dans les secrets que je crains de savoir,—

the beauty of it brings tears to one's eyes. I don't think anyone has analysed Valéry's peculiar merit so judiciously as you have. Your lecture is a very precious fragment of criticism.

I have just sent to press a few words about him, *à propos* P. Souday's little book, but I had no space to turn round: nor could I compete with your broad treatment of the theme.

Have you seen the Abbé Brémond's lucubrations about *la poésie pure*? He sent them to me, with a very civil note, but I can make nothing of them. He seemed to me to have caught the right sow, but by the wrong ear, or rather it is all ear and no sow.

Don't you find in Valéry a curious echo of Théodore de Banville? I suppose the true Valérian would rend one in pieces if one suggested it! It would be like venturing to point out that T. S. Eliot had been reading Tennyson.

Now, I am going to turn back to your admirable Lecture and read it carefully again.

Ever sincerely yours,
EDMUND GOSSE.

17, Hanover Terrace,
To G. K. Chesterton. *27.11.27.*

DEAR CHESTERTON,—

You will not, I hope, think me intrusive if I cannot resist the impulse to write to you? I have just finished reading the book in which you smite the detractors of R.L.S. hip and thigh. I cannot express without a sort of hyperbole the sentiments which you have awakened—of joy, of satisfaction, of relief, of malicious and vindictive pleasure. We are avenged at last. Seriously, you have said, in your own inimitable way, exactly what wanted saying, and I can only, page after page, repeat "Excellent!"

It is, and always since his death has been, impossible for me to write anything which went below the surface of R.L.S. I loved him, and still love him, too tenderly to analyse him. But you, who have the privilege of not being dazzled by having known him, have taken the task into your strong competent hands. You could not have done it better.

The latest survivor, the only survivor, of his little early circle of intimate friends, thanks you from the bottom of his heart.

Yours sincerely,

EDMUND GOSSE.

In January 1928 Gosse acted as pall bearer to his friend Thomas Hardy in Westminster Abbey, together with the Prime Minister (Mr. Stanley Baldwin), Mr. Ramsay MacDonald, Sir James Barrie, Mr. John Galsworthy, Professor A. E. Housman, Mr. Rudyard Kipling, Mr. Bernard Shaw, Mr. A. S. Ramsay, Master of Magdalene College, Cambridge, and Dr. E. M. Walker as Pro-Provost of Queen's College, Oxford. The following letter with its reference to the occasion and its generous appreciation of Gosse as a writer, will be read with interest.

To Philip Gosse. *18th January, 1929.*

DEAR MR. GOSSE,—

I have no letters. My intercourse with your father was always viva voce. Until very late in our careers we used to meet only at committees; and as he was a most combative man and had a sense of humour which he could never control we sparred and chaffed rather than communed on these occasions. Four or five years ago, when I was in Scotland at Gleneagles, I met him at Cloan, where he was staying with the Haldanes. As I had never had any opportunity of talking to him about his work and shewing him that I knew it and valued it, I took the opportunity to discuss the condition which the history and criticism of the literature of the Restoration had been in when I started (silly tales about Etheredge and the like) and

IN THE GARDENS OF MALMAISON, MAY 3, 1928

what a difference his studies made. This appreciation was perhaps rather unexpected: at all events he sent me a copy of his *Life of Congreve* with a friendly inscription.

The last time we met was at Hardy's funeral, where he introduced me to Kipling, whom I had never met. We left the Abbey together; and I told him I had just been staying at Cliveden with the Astors, and, finding in my bedroom there a copy of *Father and Son*, had read it straight through. He said, "Had you not read it before?" I said, "Yes, of course: I read it when it first appeared; but this second time was the test; for I could not lay it down until I had been right through it again; and though I had always sworn by it I found it even better—more important—than I thought." "It is," I said, "one of the immortal pages of English literature." He stopped in the roadway and said, "Oh, my dear Shaw, you are the *only* one who ever encourages me."

I was greatly pleased by this. It was one of those occasions on which men of our age wonder which of them will be the next to go; and I am very glad that we parted affectionately and that he finally classed me among his friends. In my opinion he, too, should have been buried in the Abbey; for the little room that is left there should not be reserved for Best Sellers whose work has been fully recognized and rewarded during their lifetime, but allotted for preference to those workers who have loved literature for its own sake and done the things for it that only scholars appreciate, leaving big-drum celebrity to people like myself, for whom literature is only a means of self-expression.

Faithfully
G. Bernard Shaw.

Hôtel de Bourgogne & Montana,
7, Rue de Bourgogne,
Paris.

To Dr. Sim.

May 4, 1928.

Dear Dr. Sim,—

It amuses me that you have attended Dr. Baker's lectures on George Meredith. I presided at the opening of the series, at King's College, but did not know that he was travelling round Europe with them. The interest in Meredith has grown *very* faint, and will scarcely I think revive. He had brilliant gifts, but no cultural discipline, and he was essentially *unreal*, in speech and character. I am afraid my remarks at Dr. Baker's lecture, although I was as polite as I could be, gave some scandal to the admirers. Meredith will live in literary history as an oddity—something like Marino or Gongora. I remember having tea in the House of Lords, on the day of G. Meredith's funeral, with John Morley. Morley said, "A dear fellow, and very bright, but alas! not founded on the humanities!"

D. G. Rossetti is in a very different category. You are kind enough to ask whether I am writing on the Centenary. Yes, as you will see in next Sunday's issue. How extraordinary that you should recollect the sonnet on the Voice! I had entirely forgotten it. There was a sonnet of juvenile enthusiasm written in Norway about 1871. I wonder if that is the piece you mention? D.G.R. was greatly touched by it, but I remember said, "I am afraid it will bring the hornets down upon you." He was already beginning to be affected by that mania of persecution which tormented him later on.

You ask for my portrait. I had not sat to a photographer for many years, but it happens that only a few days ago I yielded to the persistence of Elliot and Fry, and let their "artist" come to my house. I have not seen the results, but if they are decent, I will do myself the pleasure of sending you one. There was a very amusing full-length portrait of me, in colours, last Xmas, in the Xmas no. of what is called (I think) *The Bookman's Journal*. My family liked it.

I am, however, getting much too old for the vanity of portraits. At 79 and with only one eye, the scribbler is no object of beauty. I am over here in Paris for a few days, but have not been very well: the changes of temperature have been trying. Yet even when one is not feeling strong, Paris is exhilarating. I go back to England tomorrow, as I have to give the toast of "Literature" at the Royal Academy next night. A chill no bigger than a man's hand is rising and may cover my sky, but I hope for the best.

With very kind regards and as you would say *"auguri sentiti"* I am very sincerely yours,

EDMUND GOSSE.

In the last years, an infirmity of sight limiting him to the use of one eye, a fall in the street in avoiding a motor-car, and a malady borne with indomitable patience, had brought about changes in his activities. But although neither his "elastic gaiety of spirits" nor his intellectual keenness suffered eclipse, it was apparent to his associates that a greater effort was needed to maintain his high level of energy. The pattern made by the sunshine was altering with the fall of the leaf. The buoyant spirits which had never failed him blew upon the world through a more slender reed, and it was evident that the tide of life was turning.

At the end of April, 1928, accompanied by Mr. William Bellows, he visited Paris. On May 4th, they returned to London. Gosse was in good spirits, and elated to have been once more in France. The next day he was taken to a nursing home, where to the last he continued to write his articles for the *Sunday Times* without abating his practice of being three weeks ahead of his immediate obligation. On the eve of an operation which he knew to be attended with grave risk, and which in the event was to have a fatal result, but maintaining an equanimity of mind which never forsook him, he wrote to Mr. Bellows: "You will think of me in this hour with sympathy and hope. There seems good reason to think I shall survive the shock. In any case I am perfectly calm, and able to enjoy the love which has accompanied me through such long years and surrounds me still."

The calmness did not desert him, and, surrounded by the love of which he spoke in his letter, on the evening of May 16th, 1928, in his eightieth year, Edmund Gosse died.

In the last years, an infirmity of sight limiting him to the use of one eye, a fall in the street in avoiding a motor-car, and a severe [illegible] borne with indomitable patience had brought about changes in his activities. But although neither his "elastic gaiety of spirits" nor his intellectual keenness suffered eclipse, it was apparent to his [illegible] signs that a greater effort was needed to maintain his fresh energy. The pattern made by the sunshine was altering with the fall of the leaf. The buoyant spirits which had never failed him then looked upon the world through a more sombre veil, and it was evident that the tide of life was turning.

At the end of April, 1928, accompanied by Mr. William Bellows, he visited Paris. On May 4th, they returned to London. Gosse was in good spirits, and elated to have been once more in France. The next day he was taken to a nursing home, where to the last he continued to write his articles for the *Sunday Times* without abating his practice of being three weeks ahead of his immediate obligations. On the eve of an operation which he knew to be attended with grave risk and which in the event was to have a fatal result, but maintaining an equanimity of mind which never forsook him, he wrote to Mr. Bellows: "You will think of me in this hour with sympathy and love. There seems good reason to think I shall survive the shock. In any case I am perfectly calm, and able to enjoy the love which has accompanied me through such long years and surrounds me still."

The calmness did not desert him, and, surrounded by the love of which he spoke in his letter, on the evening of May 16th, 1928, in his eightieth year, Edmund Gosse died.

GOSSE, SIR EDMUND, Kt., cr. 1925. C.B. 1912, LL.D., Litt.D.:

Asst. Librarian British Museum, 1867–75.

Translator to Board of Trade, 1875–1904.

Clark Lecturer in English Literature, Trinity Coll., Cambridge, 1884–90.

Librarian, House of Lords, 1904–14.

A Trustee of the National Portrait Gallery.

Hon. M.A. Trinity Coll., Cambridge.

Hon. LL.D. St. Andrews, 1899.

Hon. Litt.D. Cambridge, 1920.

Hon. Dr. Strasbourg, 1920.

Hon. Dr. Gothenburg, 1923.

Hon. Dr. Paris (Sorbonne).

Member of the Academic Committee.

Knight of the Royal Norwegian Order of St. Olaf, First Class, 1901.

Knight of the Royal Swedish Order of the Polar Star, 1908.

Knight of the Royal Danish Order of the Dannebrog, 1912.

Commander of the Legion of Honour, 1925.

Chairman of the Board of Scandinavian Studies, University Coll., London, since 1917.

President of the English Association, 1921.

APPENDIX

BIBLIOGRAPHY

Mr. Norman Gullick has kindly prepared the bibliography which follows of Gosse's more important writings.

A LIST OF WORKS BY SIR EDMUND GOSSE, C.B.

Madrigals, Songs and Sonnets. London: Longmans, Green and Co. 1870.
Of the poems in this volume 32 were written by Edmund Gosse, the remainder by J. A. Blaikie; they were never reprinted.

On Viol and Flute. London: Henry S. King & Co. 1873.

The Ethical Condition of the Early Scandinavian Peoples. Reprinted from the Journal of the Victoria (Philosophical) Institute. London: Robert Hardwicke. 1875.
This essay has never been reprinted.

Een Nieuwe Meteoor aan Engeland's Letterkundigen Hemel: Algernon Charles Swinburne. 1876.
This essay had appeared in the Dutch magazine *Die Banier*, after having been translated into Danish, German and Swedish. A few copies of this rare private issue were printed in Holland. The original English text was not printed until 1925.

King Erik. London: Chatto & Windus. 1876.
This book was actually published at Christmas, 1875. A "remainder" of 250 copies was issued by William Heinemann in 1893, with a new title-page and binding.

The Unknown Lover. A Drama for Private Acting, with an essay on the Chamber Drama in England. London: Chatto & Windus. 1878.
The sheets of this play, originally printed in Reading for private use, were subsequently bound up and published with the essay.

Studies in the Literature of Northern Europe. London: C. Kegan Paul & Co. 1879.
A revised edition, entitled *Northern Studies,* was published by Walter Scott in 1890.

New Poems. London: C. Kegan Paul & Co. 1789.

A Letter to the Editor of the "Athenæum." Privately printed. 1886.
This essay was written as an introduction to the Hunterian Club edition of Rowlands' Works (1880). 6 or 8 copies were issued privately.

Résumé of a Pamphlet on the Industry and Trade of Germany during the first year of the new Protective Policy. London: H.M.S.O. 1881.

This Parliamentary Paper consists of 10 pages. That part of the text occupying pages 3, 4 and the first quarter of 5 is initialled "E.W.G." The author has written of this Paper: "The publication of this *Résumé* led to a curious incident. Copies were sent to Germany, and one fell into the hands of no less a person than Bismarck. He read it and was furious; and he sent a request to the Foreign Office, through the German Embassy, that the author of the *Résumé* should be reprimanded. This was thought a great joke, and so far from being blamed, I was commended."

Memoir of Thomas Lodge. 1882.

This essay was written as an introduction to the Hunterian Club edition of Lodge's Works. 10 copies were printed for private distribution.

Gray. London: Macmillan & Co. 1882.

This volume belongs to the *English Men of Letters* series. A second edition, considerably revised, was published in 1889.

Cecil Lawson: A Memoir. London: The Fine Art Society. 1883.

There was a small-paper edition, bound in light green cloth boards, of 150 copies; and a large-paper edition, in white parchment boards, of 200 copies. It has not been reprinted.

A Critical Essay on the Life and Works of George Tinworth. London: The Fine Art Society. 1883.

Nearly the entire edition of this book is said to have been destroyed by fire soon after publication. It has not been reprinted.

Seventeenth Century Studies: A Contribution to the History of English Poetry. London: Kegan Paul, Trench & Co. 1883.

An Epistle to Dr. Oliver Wendell Holmes on his seventy-fifth Birthday, August 29, 1884.

This poem was issued privately in an edition of only 40 copies, without wrappers and printed on a single sheet folded to 4 pages.

Notes on the Pictures and Drawings of Mr. Alfred W. Hunt. London: The Fine Art Society. 1884.

This essay, published as an introduction to an exhibition catalogue, has not been reprinted.

Six Lectures written to be delivered before the Lowell Institute in December, 1884. Privately printed in an impression of only four copies at the Chiswick Press in London, October, 1884.

This book is the rarest of Edmund Gosse's private issues. Its collation is as follows: Quarto (8½ x 6¾); leaves 1 + 31 + 36 + 32 + 34 + 33 + 33; consisting of title-page and text, the verso of each leaf being blank. The text is divided into 6 essays, each with its own pagination. Originally issued untrimmed and unbound, with a hole punched through the top left-hand corner of each leaf except the title-page.

Perhaps the only existing copy is that recorded in J. R. Lister's *Catalogue of a Portion of the Library of Edmund Gosse*, 1893, and now in the library of the compiler of this list. The copy is bound in red-and-black marbled cloth, with a leather label on the spine. It contains numerous alterations and additions in the author's handwriting, and was used for the composition of *From Shakespeare to Pope*, 1885, of which it is the true *editio princeps*.

From Shakespeare to Pope: an inquiry into the causes and phenomena of the rise of Classical Poetry in England. Cambridge: at the University Press. 1885.

The Masque of Painters: as performed by the Royal Institute of Painters in Water Colours, May 19, 1885. Privately printed. 1885.

Copies of this book were sold as programmes at the performance of the *Masque*. There was also a large-paper edition of 50 copies.

Firdausi in Exile and other Poems. London: Kegan Paul, Trench & Co., 1885.

The title poem of this volume had originally appeared as the introduction to Helen Zimmern's *Epic of the Kings*, 1883. There were an ordinary edition and a large-paper edition of 50 copies.

Raleigh. London: Longmans, Green & Co. 1886.

A Letter to the Editor of the "Athenæum." Privately printed. 1886.

This pamphlet is a reprint of an open letter, replying to an attack by Prof. Churton Collins on *From Shakespeare to Pope*.

Life of William Congreve. London: Walter Scott. 1888.

This book was issued in two forms, foolscap *8vo.* and demy *8vo.*, the same type being used but in the latter case leaded. The second edition, revised and enlarged, was published by William Heinemann Ltd. in 1924.

A History of Eighteenth Century Literature (1660–1780). London: Macmillan. 1889.

On Viol and Flute. London: Kegan Paul, Trench, Trübner and Co., Ltd. 1890.

This volume contains 69 poems, 33 of which had appeared in the original edition, 1873. The remainder represented all that the author wished to preserve from his other volumes of poetry, up to and including *New Poems*, 1879. There was a large-paper edition of 50 copies.

Robert Browning: Personalia. Boston (U.S.A.). 1890.

There were an ordinary edition and a large-paper edition of only 6 copies. The American sheets were used for an English edition, published by T. Fisher Unwin in 1890 and 1891. The book has not been reprinted.

The Life of Philip Henry Gosse, F.R.S., by his Son. London: Kegan Paul, Trench, Trübner & Co., Ltd. 1890.

Gossip in a Library. London: William Heinemann. 1891.
There were an ordinary edition and a large-paper edition of 100 copies.

Shelley in 1892. Centenary Address delivered at Horsham, August 11, 1892.
This *Address* was issued as a pamphlet for private distribution. The number of copies printed was probably very small, and the compiler of this list has never seen one of them.

The Secret of Narcisse: a Romance. London: William Heinemann. 1892.

Wolcott Balestier. A Portrait Sketch. Privately printed for John W. Lovell, 2, Dean's Yard, Westminster. 1892.
This essay had originally appeared in the *Century Magazine.* 100 copies were printed, 90 on hand-made paper and 10 on Japanese vellum paper.

Questions at Issue. London: William Heinemann. 1893.
This book, which has not been reprinted, was issued in an ordinary edition and in a large-paper edition of 60 copies.

Inscription for the Rose-tree brought by Mr. W. Simpson from Omar's Tomb at Naishápúr, and planted to-day on the Grave of Edward FitzGerald, at Boulge. 1893.
40 copies were printed for private distribution.

In Russet and Silver. London: William Heinemann. 1894.

The Jacobean Poets. London: John Murray. 1894.

Critical Kit-Kats. London: William Heinemann. 1896.
Of the essays in this volume two had already been published as introductions to editions of *The Sonnets from the Portuguese* and *The Poetical Works of T. L. Beddoes* respectively, both issued by J. M. Dent. There were an ordinary edition and a large-paper edition.

A Short History of Modern English Literature. London: William Heinemann. 1898.
This book was actually published in 1897. It has been reprinted and brought up to date many times. The latest edition, 1924, had a considerable amount of new matter.

Henry Fielding: an Essay. London: Archibald Constable and Co. New York: Charles Scribner's Sons. 1898.
This essay was written as an introduction to an edition of Fielding's Works (Constable, 1898), and 12 copies were printed separately for private distribution.

The Life and Letters of John Donne, Dean of St. Paul's, now for the first time revised and collected. Two volumes. London: William Heinemann. 1899.

Queen Victoria. New York. 1901. From *The Quarterly Review.*

This was a "pirated" reprint of an essay which had been published in an American periodical, probably the *Century Magazine.* The compiler of this list is unable to give the name of the publisher, as he has never had a copy of this rare book in his hands.

Hypolympia or The Gods in the Island: an Ironic Fantasy. London: William Heinemann. 1901.

Commemoration of the Reign of Queen Elizabeth. Reprinted from the *Geographical Journal* for June, 1903.

This contains 4 essays, the second of which, entitled *Walter Raleigh,* is by Edmund Gosse. It was an edition of very few copies for private distribution.

The Challenge of the Brontës. Printed for private distribution. 1903.

This edition of only 30 copies was issued by T. J. Wise, to whom the manuscript belongs. It was an address delivered before the Brontë Society on March 28, 1903, and subsequently printed in the Society's *Publications,* February, 1904.

English Literature: an Illustrated Record. Four volumes. London: William Heinemann. New York: The Macmillan Company. 1903.

The first volume was written entirely by Richard Garnett; the second by Richard Garnett and Edmund Gosse; the third and fourth entirely by Edmund Gosse. Volumes 3 and 4 were reprinted in 1906.

Banquet à M. Edmund Gosse, Restaurant Durand, Paris, Mardi le 9 Février, 1904.

This is a foolscap quarto of 6 leaves, the title being imposed upon the head of the first page of the text, which is printed upon the recto only of each leaf. It consists of a speech by Edmund Gosse, and is of interest as giving some details of his descent from a Huguenot family of Bordeaux. A few copies were printed for private distribution.

L'Influence de la France sur la Poésie anglaise. Traduite par Henri Davray. Paris: Société du Mercure de France. 1904.

The original English text was published the following year in *French Profiles.*

Jeremy Taylor. London: Macmillan & Co., Ltd. 1904.

This volume belongs to the *English Men of Letters* series.

French Profiles. London: Hodder & Stoughton. 1905.

French Profiles. London: William Heinemann. 1905.

Coventry Patmore. London: Hodder & Stoughton. 1905.

Sir Thomas Browne. London: Macmillan & Co., Ltd. 1905.

This volume belongs to the *English Men of Letters* series.

British Portrait Painters and Engravers of the Eighteenth Century: Kneller to Reynolds. Paris: Goupil & Co. 1906.

There were an ordinary edition and a special edition of 100 copies on Japanese paper, the latter with a duplicate set of illustrations.

Ibsen. London: Hodder & Stoughton. 1907.

Father and Son: a Study of Two Temperaments. London: William Heinemann. 1907.

This book was originally anonymous.

Catalogue of the Library of the House of Lords. London. 1908.

This book, a demy quarto of xx + 729 pages, with a Frontispiece, was issued with trimmed edges and bound in three-quarter red-grained morocco. Not more than 20 were printed. The Introduction, with the Frontispiece, was issued in a separate edition of 40 copies, untrimmed and in buff paper wrappers, for private distribution.

Biographical Notes on the Writings of Robert Louis Stevenson. London: privately printed at the Chiswick Press. 1908.

The text of this book consists of biographical and bibliographical notes which had been distributed through the *Pentland* Edition of Stevenson's Works (Chatto and Windus). There were certain corrections and additions, the most important of which was the printing for the first time of several verses which it had been thought advisable to omit from the published editions of Stevenson's poems. Only 50 copies were printed.

The Autumn Garden. London: William Heinemann. 1909.

The label on the spine of this book is dated 1908.

Swinburne: Personal Recollections. Reprinted from the *Fortnightly Review* for private circulation. 1909.

This is an off-print of which only 25 copies were printed.

A Paradox on Beauty. Reprinted from *Fasciculus Joanni Willis Clark dicatus*. 1909.

This is an off-print from the privately issued *Fasciculus* (Cambridge: at the University Press. 1909). Only a few copies were printed.

The Collected Poems of Edmund Gosse. London: William Heinemann. 1911.

All the poems in this volume, except *The Land of France*, had already appeared in volumes recorded above.

Two Visits to Denmark: 1872, 1874. London: Smith, Elder and Co. 1911.

Browning's Centenary. London: Asher & Co. 1912.

The text consists of three addresses, by Edmund Gosse, Arthur Pinero and Henry James respectively, delivered before the Academic Committee of the Royal Society of Literature, and reprinted from the *Transactions*, R.S.L., Vol. XXXI, Part IV.

The Life of Swinburne. With a Letter on Swinburne at Eton by Lord Redesdale. London: privately printed at the Chiswick Press. 1912.

Only 50 copies of this book were issued. The *Life* was written for, and afterwards appeared in, the third volume of the New Supplement to the *Dictionary of National Biography.*

Portraits and Sketches. London: William Heinemann. 1912.

Lady Dorothy Nevill. An Open Letter. London: privately printed at the Chiswick Press. 1913.

Of this *Letter* 32 copies (not 30 as stated in the certificate of issue) were printed.

The Future of English Poetry. London: The English Association. 1913.

Sir Alfred East. London: Ernest Brown & Phillips. 1914.

This essay was the introduction to the catalogue of the Memorial Exhibition at the Leicester Galleries, February, 1914.

Two Pioneers of Romanticism: Joseph and Thomas Warton. London: Humphrey Milford for the British Academy. 1915.

Catherine Trotter, the Precursor of the Blue-Stockings. London: R.S.L. 1916.

This is an off-print from the *Transactions,* R.S.L. Vol. XXXIV; 25 copies were issued for private distribution.

Inter Arma: being Essays written in Time of War. London: William Heinemann. 1916.

Reims Revisited. Reprinted by permission from the *Fortnightly Review,* November, 1916.

This was a private issue of 20 copies.

The Life of Algernon Charles Swinburne. London: Macmillan and Co., Ltd. 1917.

Both the first and the second impressions appeared in April, 1917; the text of the latter, however, differs from that of the former in a few details.

Lord Cromer as a Man of Letters. Reprinted by permission from the *Fortnightly Review,* March, 1917.

This was a private issue of 20 copies.

The Novels of Benjamin Disraeli. London: R.S.L. 1918.

This is an off-print from the *Transactions,* R.S.L., Vol. XXXVI; 25 copies were issued for private distribution.

France et Angleterre: L'Avenir de leurs Relations intellectuelles. London: Hayman, Christy & Lilly, Ltd. 1918.

This essay was reprinted from the *Revue des Deux Mondes.*

A Visit to the Friends of Ibsen. Cambridge: at the University Press. 1918.
This is an off-print from the *Modern Language Review*, Vol. XIII, No. 3. It is found in two forms: a few copies were issued with an advertisement on the last page of the paper wrapper; 20 copies, for private distribution, were issued with an extra leaf (short-title with blank verso) but without the advertisement on the wrapper.

Three French Moralists, and the Gallantry of France. London: William Heinemann. 1918.

Some Literary Aspects of France in the War. London: R.S.L. 1919.
This is an off-print from the *Transactions*, R.S.L., Vol. XXXVII; 12 copies were issued for private distribution.

The First Draft of Swinburne's "Anactoria." Cambridge: at the University Press. 1919.
This is an off-print from the *Modern Language Review*, Vol. XIV, No. 3. It is found with two varieties of pagination: a very few copies were issued with the pages numbered 271-277; 10 copies, for private distribution were issued with the pages numbered 1-7.

Some Diversions of a Man of Letters. London: William Heinemann. 1919.

A Catalogue of the Works of Algernon Charles Swinburne in the Library of Mr. Edmund Gosse. London: privately printed at the Chiswick Press. 1919.
Only 50 copies were printed.

Malherbe and the Classical Reaction in the Seventeenth Century. Oxford: at the Clarendon Press. 1920.

Books on the Table. London: William Heinemann. 1921.

Aspects and Impressions. London: Cassell & Co., Ltd. 1922.

Byways round Helicon: an Article by Edmund Gosse, C.B. (Reprinted by permission of the *Sunday Times.*) 1922.
This pamphlet was issued by William Heinemann Ltd. as an advertisement of a book by I. A. Williams.

The Continuity of Literature. London: The English Association. 1922.

More Books on the Table. London: William Heinemann Ltd. 1923.

A Review of "The Life of Lord Wolseley." (Reprinted by permission of the *Sunday Times.*) 1924.
This pamphlet was issued by William Heinemann Ltd. as an advertisement.

Silhouettes. London: William Heinemann Ltd. 1925.

Tallemant des Réaux, or the Art of Miniature Biography. Oxford: at the Clarendon Press. 1925.

Cambridge and Charles Lamb. Cambridge: at the University Press. 1925.
This volume contains 4 essays, the third of which, entitled *The Earliest Charles Lamb Dinner*, is by Edmund Gosse.

Swinburne: an Essay written in 1875 and now first printed. 1925.
This volume, issued for private distribution, contains the original English text of the essay on Swinburne, printed in Holland in 1876, together with a preface describing the adventures of the manuscript. 125 copies were printed for Norman Gullick and J. G. Wilson.

Leaves and Fruit. London: William Heinemann Ltd. 1927.

Two Unpublished Poems. 1929.
14 copies of this 4-page pamphlet were printed by E. H. Blakeney at his private press in Winchester.

INDEX